Educational Psychology

A Behavioral Approach

Francis J. Kelly
Southern Illinois University

John J. Cody
Southern Illinois University

Charles E. Merrill Publishing Company
A Bell & Howell Company
Columbus, Ohio

Standard Book Number: 675-09539-5

Library of Congress Catalog Card Number: 69-14631

1 2 3 4 5 6 7 8 9 10/ 73 72 71 70 69

Printed in the United States of America

Dedicated to

J. Carson McGuire

Preface

Educational Psychology: A Behavioral Approach was written for use by instructors who take their commitment to behavioral science seriously. Educational psychology is presented as a science for exploring complex human behavior rather than as a "cookbook" of procedures which a teacher should follow. Research regarding human and animal behavior is cited, and an attempt is made to mold these data into a conceptual model which imposes some order upon the seemingly diverse factors related to behavior. The authors assume that the student has been exposed to an introductory course in psychology; however, students who have *not* been exposed to previous psychology courses should *not* experience great difficulty in following the text.

Since psychologists have conducted only limited research within the school setting, much that is presented must be moderated by conditional expressions such as "might" and "possibly." Such an analysis of education and psychological theory, by necessity, reveals more areas of uncertainty than areas of certainty. Therefore, the reader is not asked to believe notions or recommendations which have *not* been verified empirically. Rather the reader is asked to look at ideas and results of research and to consider educational practices which seem likely to produce intended outcomes. The tenor of the book is that educational psychology is a study of ways of (1) inquiring, (2) evaluating practices, and (3) applying theory to the practical setting of the classroom. For example, imitation learning is presented as a means which a teacher *might* use in the classroom rather than a means she *should* use.

Individual differences have been a central theme of many educational psychology courses; however, seldom has the complexity of individualization been made explicit. The present text is designed to correct this oversight. These complexities are *not* presented to confuse, but rather to emphasize that behavioral scientists are expecting too much when they assume that an exposure to the notion of individual differences is all a teacher needs to become effective. The task of producing positive change in the educational endeavor is viewed as a task which requires the collaboration of administrators, academicians, teachers, technicians, media specialists, systems specialists, and behavorial science researchers. The intent of these authors is to recruit among future teachers a body of willing participants in the scientific study of school related behaviors.

A Note To The Instructor

Harper, Anderson, Christensen and Hunka, in their preface to *The Cognitive Processes: Readings* (Prentice Hall, 1964), suggested that undergraduates at the University of Alberta can comprehend complex conceptual models presented in their book. Indeed, they suggested undergraduate students, after acclimation to the terminology, could apply cognitive theory to classroom problems. However, it must be noted that they also found such teaching placed a strain upon the instructor. The senior author of the present text taught educational psychology at the University of Alberta under the Harper *et al.* program and concurs with their assessment. Because of the diversity of concepts presented in *The Cognitive Processes: Readings,* the students were confused for the first three months or more. It was evident that some consistent conceptual model could lessen the students' confusion.

The present book was written in an attempt to capture the excitement generated by inquiry into complex conceptual models and at the same time reduce confusion and instructional strain. The consistent development of a multi-variate model representing the complexities underlying human behavior is the major vehicle used to meet the stated objectives. The model is a behavioral science model which can incorporate most potentially measurable theories. The model represents a combination of Osgood's "Mediational Hypothesis" (1953), and McGuire's "Adaption Level Model" (1961).

For a two-course educational psychology sequence, the brevity of this text allows a great deal of flexibility. Extensive use of the primary references following each topic is recommended. If library facilities are limited, a number of excellent books of readings are available. One course can cover the topics adequately with some selective reading of the primary references.

Since the text is written in the conditional tense the instructor can adjust the course to focus on any topic he selects. For example, if the instructor favors cognitive views, several weeks can be devoted to the topic without imposing time pressures upon the students. The authors have found such in depth study of favored topics stimulating to the students, and we strongly recommend the practice.

Table of Contents

Introduction 1

Overview

This chapter presents the ground rules used in this book. The central theme presented is that educational psychology is a *behavioral science.* As a *science* of behavior, conclusions must be supported by experimental evidence (data). Although such a definition of educational psychology seems reasonable, it immediately presents problems. For example, before we can experiment to determine what is an effective educational technique, we need to agree upon what consequences we want in student *behavior.* At the present time, our goals of education are not specified. We do not know what a student should be able to do as a result of working through our course of study. Because of this problem, there is little evidence to indicate one technique is "best." On the other hand, educational psychology has some data relating to how humans behave. The discussion in this chapter suggests that these data may help you to select techniques that seem applicable to attaining your *goals* of education.

Also, a discussion is presented in this chapter regarding the nature of knowledge (epistemology). The discussion emphasizes that behavioral sciences have as a foundation a number of acts of *faith* (assumptions).

These acts are specified in order to enable you to examine them and decide whether or not to accept them. If you reject these assumptions, you might wish to read this book pretending the assumptions are "true."

An $S \rightarrow O \rightarrow R$ model is introduced in this chapter. The "S" represents the stimuli, the "O," the organism (person) and the "R," the response of the person. We assume these are the only observables we have as a science.

Noting relationships between these observables (the stimuli and the individual's response) provides the evidence from which we develop theories of human behavior. Further examination of $S \rightarrow O \rightarrow R$ relationships provides a check on the theory and can lead to theory refinement.

A brief overview of the text is provided in this chapter to help you anticipate the direction of model building.

Glossary

Since the reader may be unfamiliar with a number of terms used, a glossary is presented for each chapter. To increase the use of the glossary, it is presented *before* the textual material. The reader is urged to look through the glossary before reading the chapter (such behavior should minimize page turning). Although an attempt is made to define these terms within the textual material, sometimes these attempts do not communicate to all students.

attitudes: a manner of acting, feeling, or thinking that shows one's disposition, opinion, etc.; an aspect of personality inferred to account for persistent and consistent behavior toward a family of related situations or objects.

behavior: any activity of the human organism which can be observed (smiling, walking, talking, vascular constriction, etc.).

concept: an idea one holds regarding some set of experiences which the individual uses for the purpose of acting upon future experiences. A mental image of things and relationships.

concept-formation: the process of forming concepts by abstraction and generalization.

conscious: pertaining to the process of being aware or knowing; as having sensations, feelings, thoughts, strivings, as being aware.

coping: action that enables one to adjust to the environmental circumstances, to get something done.

curriculum: a specific course of study or collectively, all the courses of study in a school or university.

deterministic: any doctrine that acts of the will, social changes, etc., result from determining causes. Essentially a position that assumes lawfulness in the universe.

discrimination: making or perceiving distinctions and differences.

discrimination task: a piece of work assigned to an individual to enable him to perceive distinctions and differences.

dualistic: (dualism) the theory that man has two natures, physical and spiritual; the world is composed of two basic entities, mind and matter.

dyad: two units regarded as one, a pair. As used in this chapter — the term is used to represent a dualistic view as a unit.

empirical: relying or based solely upon experiment or observation.

epistemology: the theory or science of the methods and grounds of knowledge, especially with reference to its limits and validity.

fundamentalist: used in this context to indicate evangelical religious individuals who take the Bible as the fundamental (literal) word of God.

habits: an act done often and usually easily; an act that is acquired and has become automatic; a tendency to perform a certain act or behave in a certain way. An acquired act, usually a relatively simple one, that is regularly or customarily manifested.

linguistics: the study of the structure, development, etc., of a particular language and of its relationship to other languages.

monistic: (monism) the doctrine that there is only one ultimate substance or principle; the one substance may be either material or spiritual.

neo-behavioristic: a general point of view that emphasizes the central position of *response* in the definition of psychology; turns from analysis of the consciousness to investigation of what organisms do and to conditions under which they perform effectively. A position that extends beyond a simple conditioning principle.

response or R: Any organic process resulting from stimulation; any muscular or glandular process that depends upon stimulations; any psychic process, consequent or previous psychic process, the unit of the executing processes of the organism or person.

self-concept: the notion and belief an individual holds regarding himself. This also includes values regarding self (i.e. "I am a good boy.").

semantics: the scientific study of the relations between signs or symbols, and what they mean or denote, and of behavior in its psychological and sociological aspects as it is influenced by signs; the branch of linguistics concerned with the nature, structure and changes of the meanings of speech forms.

set: an adjustment of an organism in preparation for a certain definite kind of activity; a temporary but often recurrent condition of an organism that orients it towards certain environmental stimuli or events rather than others, selectively sensitizing it for apprehending them.

stimulus: three basic concepts appear in various combinations. A stimulus is something that: (a) stirs or prods the organism, (b) is external to the organism or a definitely organized part of an organism, and (c) is associated with sensory processes.

unconscious: (postulated) region of the mind not open to conscious scrutiny.

Why Educational Psychology?

Most teacher-training programs include a required course in educational psychology. Apparently, educators believe that psychological studies aid teachers. Unfortunately, no unequivocal evidence is available to support this belief. The lack of evidence can be attributed, in part, to the difficulty involved in the assessment of effective teaching. The criterion of effective teaching should in all likelihood be the consequence of the teaching upon student performance. The problem, however, is that delimiting relevant performance demands a value judgment. Some educators and parents express preference for student performance on achievement tests as the important criterion in teacher evaluation. Others argue that social skills are the significant consequences of education. Appreciation of the Western culture and of man's knowledge is held by still others to be the sought-for end of education. A few will settle for productive, self-sufficient citizens as the criterion for evaluating education. These latter objectives of education are extremely difficult to assess because "appreciation" and "self-sufficiency" mean many different things to different individuals.*

If we select student achievement as the criterion, assessment of effective teaching would appear to be a rather straightforward task. We determine what is to be achieved, construct tests which will reliably assess the level of achievement, and then see which teachers produce the most high-achievers. Unfortunately, even this straightforward approach raises problems. Some students seem to achieve in spite of the teacher, and others do not achieve to spite the teacher. A number of factors can introduce bias into this matter. For example, bright middle-class students will usually conform to the teacher's expectations and therefore show achievement. Conversely, slow learners from "culturally deprived" homes lack preparation for rapid school achievement. Apparently, fair estimates of teacher effectiveness as measured by achievement test performance must account for these student differences. A number of

*Quotes are used to indicate poorly defined words. They are intended to put the reader on guard.

statistical techniques are available to adjust for these biasing factors. Using such an adjusted measure of effective teaching, we could then give a sample of teachers a course in educational psychology and select a control group which does not receive the course. We can follow these teachers for ten years to determine the long-range effects of educational psychology studies upon effective teaching. Of course, by then the content of educational psychology courses would be markedly changed, and thus the study would be *ad hoc* (for this case only) research and therefore would not yield generalizations to new situations.

With the rapid escalation of knowledge, a number of academicians have suggested that the measure of teacher effectiveness should *not* be performance on achievement tests since such tests tend to stress facts. Learning how to think and study are skills held by these academicians to be the important products of education. Unfortunately, the assessment of such skills is difficult to achieve. Professionals can observe students in the classroom and assess the effectiveness of the teacher and her contribution to the development of thinking students, but the observers seem unable to arrive at a consensus of opinion of what constitutes "good thinking," let alone "good teaching."

In view of the preceding discussion, one might conclude that education is run by incompetents. The determination of "What is good education?" is, however, exceedingly complex. Society must determine what the product of education *should* be, and then the educator must determine how the desired product can best be achieved. The curriculum, the teacher, and the student then interact, and educators purporting to implement the curriculum must assess these interactions. But often the community inhibits such studies. The investigation into children's attitudes, values, etc., at times is seen as an invasion of the privacy of the home and the individual. Applied research is therefore difficult as well as costly.

In lieu of an empirical rationale for a required course in educational psychology, the authors shall assume that theories regarding complex human behavior are sufficiently interesting on their own merits to warrant inclusion in teacher education programs. We do not know whether a study of this text on educational psychology will or will not make you a "better" teacher. The purpose of this text is to bring together a number of theories and data regarding complex human behavior and to indicate possible implications of these theories for teacher behavior. As parents and members of society, the authors *hope* that conceptual manipulation of these data will provide the students with a system of organizing information that will lead to "effective teaching," but as psychologists we must defer judgment until solid evidence is available.

Please *note,* educational psychology is *not* the only required university course which lacks an empirical rationale. Little evidence is available to indicate that a course in government produces "better" citizens. We suggest that *all* required university courses fall into an unsupported classification. Hopefully, future research might reduce this "knowledge" gap.

The Task of Teaching

As a teacher, you will be asked to manipulate the children in your charge in some manner. Because all of us have attended school, we have a number of ideas regarding how a teacher should behave. In order to illustrate the diversity of teaching, two extreme cases of classroom interactions are provided below. Intuitively, you can evaluate the two teachers illustrated; upon completion of this course, we hope you need not rely upon intuition alone.

Illustration 1. You are invited into a first-grade classroom. Upon entering the room you notice the teacher among a circle of ten children; she is apparently teaching reading. Twenty other children are at their tables cutting out pictures. The teacher introduces you to the class and returns to the group while you sit down and look around the room. The children are cutting out animal pictures for a notebook of sorts. Some children are neat workers, being careful not to get cuttings on the floor; others seem to think that the floor is a good place for unwanted scraps.

You listen to and observe the teacher. She has a flannelboard beside her and asks a child to point out the felt circle on the board. He does so and the teacher says, "Fine, Billy. Can anyone show me the square?" Apparently, she is working on some discrimination task. A boy off to your right grabs a girl's picture, and the teacher notices the activity. She says, "*Some* boys are working very nicely without bothering anyone." The boy ceases his diversionary activity and returns to his pictures. A little girl yawns and then proceeds to pick at her face to remove a scrap of egg. A boy gets up for a drink of water and knocks his chair over.

The teacher finishes with the children in the circle, and they return to their tables. Recess is approaching, and the teacher says, "May I have your attention please?" Most of the children look at the teacher although one or two seem intent upon finishing just one last cut. Finally all are looking at the teacher. "Children, we must now get ready for recess. Can anyone tell me what we must do?" she asks.

"We must put our work away and clean up our desks," a serious girl states.

"Good. Anything else?" asks the teacher.

A boy says, "Yes, teacher. We must do it quietly."

"Fine," replies the teacher.

On the playground, the children run games, some with enthusiasm and others with quiet dignity. One child tries to tag another child running around the circle, but try as he may, he cannot catch him. Finally he gives up, and another child volunteers to be "it." A rugged looking boy seems to think all males are sparring partners — who does he think he is?

Illustration 2. Your next visit is during the first period in a fifth-grade classroom. Fortunately, the children have not entered and so your introduction will not be disruptive. The girls enter first and go quietly to their seats. Occasionally, they look in your direction with a quizzical look; one even smiles. Entrance by the boys is a little noisier, but quite acceptable. The bell rings and the teacher enters. The class president calls the class to stand and pledge the flag. Enthusiasm for the task is not overwhelming. A few do not bother to mouth the words. All then sit down. Arithmetic books are taken out of the desks and the teacher asks the children to open their books to page 42 and work on questions 1 through 10. As the children work the division problems you walk around the room to observe. The teacher hands back the previous day's work. One boy receives his paper marked with a zero; he dismisses the paper from his mind and starts work, for about a minute; then he looks out the window. A slight commotion is heard from the other side of the room. The teacher says, "John, leave Pete alone and get to work, or I shall keep you after school." John sneers and pushes his paper about. Time slowly marches on, the bell rings for the next period, and the students put their books away. The teacher says, "Now, keep your hands to yourselves when you leave the room, or I shall give all of you extra homework."

Enough by way of illustration.

Epistemological Considerations

The preceding descriptions present specific instances of student behavior. The task of teaching would be impossible if each behavior were unique; fortunately, there appear to be repeated similarities in the universe of behaviors which enable one to predict the actions of others with some degree of accuracy. In our day-to-day interactions with inanimate objects, we develop theories regarding outcomes of the interactions. For example, we encounter four-legged objects that lead to the formation of informal theories of "chairness." We act on these theories and find them supported. (Occasionally a theory may not hold, and we are let down.) Likewise, we develop theories regarding human behaviors. From close and frequent interaction with family and friends, we have some notion how these *others* will behave under given situations. For example, if you are a child and come from a working class home, you might walk through your living room accidentally kicking over your father's full can of beer. Undoubtedly, some typical behavior on his part can be expected. Prediction in this case might be dependent upon complex variables other than the presence of father when the can was upset. For example, the number of beers he has previously consumed might be an important variable. If your home is middle-class, beer might not be the beverage. It might be cool-aid or a martini; nevertheless, the father will likely exhibit a typical predictable behavior. Many behaving situations are similar, and prediction may be simple. On the other hand seemingly similar behaving situations produce diverse behaviors. Apparently, in some situations complex unknown variables upset the prediction. Closer examination may make the unknown known and therefore lead to more effective predictions.

In a sense, the theories one develops as a consequence of noting repeated similarities in the environment (animate and inanimate) are "codes" which are then used on a probabilistic basis for adapting one's behavior to the expected outcomes of action. One consequence of forming these "codes" or predictable thought systems is that the individual develops assumptions regarding the nature of what is real and what is fantasy. Historically, man has developed "codes" and assumptions regarding the universe which are manifested in diverse forms. For example, many people today believe that evil spirits invade bodies and make man ill. Others believe that microbes *cause* "dis-ease." The first group of people call in the *shaman* to exorcise the spirits; the others introduce antibiotics, on the suggestion of a medical man, to drive out the microbes. Under both treatments some patients live and some die. We in the Western World believe the success of the medical man is superior to the shaman's, and we even call upon statisticians to prove our point and our "truth." Yet, the statistical procedure itself is based upon an assumption regarding the probability of obtaining a certain class of events as outcomes. *Apparently, "truth" rests upon having faith in one's experiences and the "coded" assumptions derived from the experiences.*

Many students and professors who work in psychology assume man to be a dualistic creature — part matter and part "soul stuff." Within this dualistic view of man, some human behavior is the result of impingements from the physical world activating the material human structure (e.g., stick an intact man with a sharp pin, and he will move). Other behavior might be due to the non-material "soul stuff" activating the material human structure.

Another large number of students and professors assume that man is a monistic creature — an energy system (and its correlate — a matter system) interacting with other energy systems. All behavior, in the latter view, is a consequence of a physical confrontation between two energy systems.

A few persons may even believe, along with Bishop Berkeley, that the universe is a monistic system of ideas. That is, man is an idea and the physical universe is an illusion.

Each of these three views regarding the nature of the universe and human behavior attracts adherents who are relatively "intelligent." Many pleasant evenings can be devoted to the exploration of these views with the intent of determining which of them is "really true." Although these matters might be very interesting, a discussion of them falls beyond the scope of this text.

The theories and data presented within this book are based upon the monistic view that behavior is a consequence of the physical interaction of energy systems. We do *not* wish to imply that this monistic assumption is the "real truth." You as the student are *not* expected to accept any such assumption. A dualist may wish to view these theories as relevant codes for the materialistic facet of his dyad. If you do not care to accept even this position, then accept the monistic position on an "as if" basis. Pretend monism is "real," and you then can explore a "coding" system held by a number of psychologists when they attempt to predict behavior.

Assumptions of Determinancy

Underlying the materialistic monism maintained in this text is the further assumption that uniformities exist within the physical universe and predictive relationships imply causality. The implication is that behavior of an organism is determined by its interaction with the environment.

Particle physics during recent years finds the need to postulate an "indeterminancy principle." In the past, predictions in the physical realm were near perfect; however, sub-atomic physics introduced greater errors of prediction. Some physicists, probably because of personal values, saw in this imperfect prediction a degree of capriciousness in the universe (freedom if you will). Other physicists, such as the late J. Robert Oppenheimer, retained a causal position, and assumed that the unpredictable relationships encountered in sub-atomic study were due to a failure to control the relevant variables. Adherents in this latter camp assume that imperfect prediction indicates a need to develop more refined instrumentation and to generate more powerful theories.

Due to the complexity of human behavior, prediction in the behavioral sciences produces errors of greater magnitude than those encountered by physicists. Although errors of prediction are rather large in psychological research, recent progress indicates that a deterministic position and a search for the relevant variables lead to a reduction in the errors of prediction. The deterministic position assumes that behavior is predictable. If this is so then research tenacity should lead to more inclusive "coding" (theories) and even better prediction. We as behavioral scientists might be wrong on at least two points: (1) our minds might be too limited, and therefore our invented "codes" may fail to adequately represent the "real" complexity of the universe, and (2) we might be completely wrong in assuming that prediction is possible— perhaps capriciousness does exist. Nevertheless, behavioral investigation will continue as long as we have scientists who behave like rats on a variable-ratio reinforcement schedule (that is, they work long and hard for a few pellets).

These epistemological considerations may appear to be beyond the realm of educational psychology. They are included, however, because a number of young professors ridicule religious students for accepting on *faith* the teachings of the Bible. Particularly, biblical accounts such as that of Adam and Eve are held up to derisive comment. Yet, apparently the scientist *accepts on faith his own* assumptions regarding the physical universe. Since both positions are "intellectually" defensible, ridicule of religious faith can be countered in an intellectually honest manner.

Let us consider a possible extreme fundamentalist view. If one assumes that God is omnipotent (all powerful), then anything is possible. Following this view, one can rationalize that archeological and evolutionary artifacts might have been placed within the universe in order for the "true believers" to identify the followers of evil (which in this case might be paleontologists, archeologists, psychologists, etc.). Essentially, if one assumes a literal biblical interpretation of Genesis is true, then the All Powerful can account for other deviations. These assumptions are as intellectually defensible as are other acts of faith regarding the nature of the universe. Apparently, as a result of different experiences, individuals develop different theories to account for the unknown. Unfortunately some of us desire to force others to accept our own conclusions. By definition, empiricists must remain open for new evidence; our truths are at best tentative. Some empiricists and non-empiricists believe they have the whole truth, and therefore, active selling of their beliefs is understandable.

Relationship of Control to Epistemic Considerations

In America, teachers are expected to manipulate the classroom stimuli in order to achieve certain educational goals. The principal usually wants a quiet room, parents want their children to come home without wounds (physical or "mental"), and someone else probably expects the children to acquire coping skills of sorts. Such expectancies regarding teacher performance tacitly imply the assumption that student behavior can be manipulated on a physical level. If the teacher can manipulate behavior, then student behavior is at least in part determinate. On the other hand, the matter of choice remains. B. F. Skinner and Carl Rogers (1956) devote some time to debate over the value of the concept of "human choice." Skinner, a psychologist who maintains a strongly operationalist position, holds that "choice" is not a necessary construct for the scientific study of behavior. Rogers, a psychotherapist, suggests that for much of conscious behavior, action demands a choice. The student may wish to read the debate since both men present cogent arguments. The material within this text tacitly assumes that behaviors which Rogers calls "choice" are a function of complex causal interactions (see Chapter 6), and thus our position lies somewhere between that of Skinner and that of Rogers.

Subject Matter of Educational Psychology

For the purposes of this text, the subject matter of educational psychology is defined to be complex human behavior mediated by the conceptual nervous system. Although educational psychology is considered applied psychology, it cannot exist in a vacuum. The investigation of teaching strategies alone seems a restricted approach to studying behavior as it relates to education. As indicated earlier, theories at the present time are inadequate, and therefore our presentation must be basically a study of complex theories as they might apply in the educational setting.

Behavior can be loosely classified into three categories:

1. *Instrumental behavior,* such as speaking, raising one's hand in the classroom, pressing a lever to receive a sugar pellet, walking to the store for milk, etc. (These can be called global locomotor behaviors.)
2. *Affective behavior,* which includes vascular constriction and dilation as a result of central processes, galvanic skin responses, adrenal secretion in "threat" situations, respiration rate, heartbeat, etc.
3. *Expressive behavior,* such as smiling, posture, etc. (essentially non-goal-directed behaviors which indicate some internal "feeling" state).

Although these classifications are somewhat arbitrary, they are valuable handles for thought and discussion.

Further, theory constructed to predict and summarize human behavior has tended to follow three research strategies. One of these strategies has been primarily concerned with the relation between stimulus characteristics and reinforcement of instrumental responses in humans and non-humans. Rigor in relation to design and controlled observation has been the forte of this strategy. Another approach deals primarily with neurophysiological aspects of instrumental behavior. Neurophysiological investigations include neurochemical components of intelligent behavior, effects of proprioceptive stimuli upon instrumental behavior, etc. The third strategy is characterized by its concern with verbal reports regarding values, attitudes, self-concepts, feelings, etc. This last approach has had considerable influence upon recent educational psychology since the approach tends to apply to the "whole child." Unfortunately, many unsupported generalizations have emanated from some followers of this strategy (not due so much to the strategy employed as to the overgeneralizations made from incomplete data).

A new trend, however, seems to be developing in modern psychology. With high-speed digital computers now available to researchers, more rigor can be applied to investigations regarding complex human behavior. To be sure, some educational psychologists still sneer at the work of the "rat psychologists" and the educational psychologist is considered to be prostituted in the views of some "pure research" psychologists. The authors believe that both views will rapidly become outdated. Indeed, evidence arising from one domain of research strategy has often led to more productive theorizing and research in the other domains. The contents of this text should demonstrate this point (see especially Chapter 2).

A Conceptual Model

Regardless of the psychologist's theoretical orientation, he has only three factors from which he can develop his theory. These factors are: (1) the *organism,* (2) the *movement* of the organism (both external and internal), and (3) the *physical universe* impinging upon the organism. Schematically, one can represent these three components as is illustrated in Figure 1.1. Impingement 1 (I_1) through impingement n (I_n) indicate the universe which has contact with the individual organism. Figure 1-1 is limited since the organism and its actions are included in one component. Figure 1-2 schematically separates the action from the organism. The action is indicated by "R" (response) while

FIGURE 1.1

The organism in an environment.

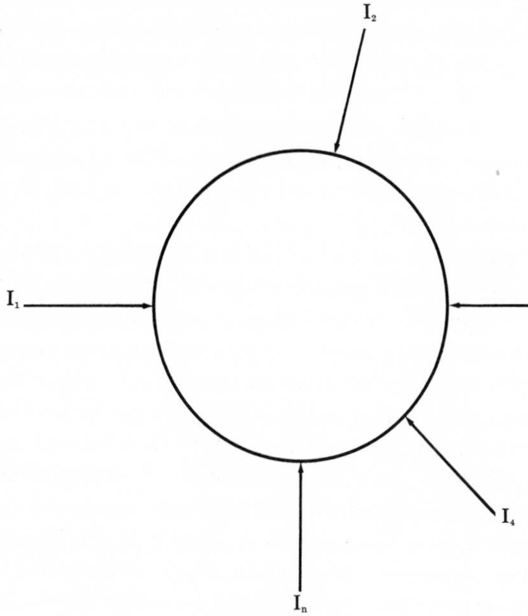

FIGURE 1.2

The organism with stimulus (S) and response (R) specified.

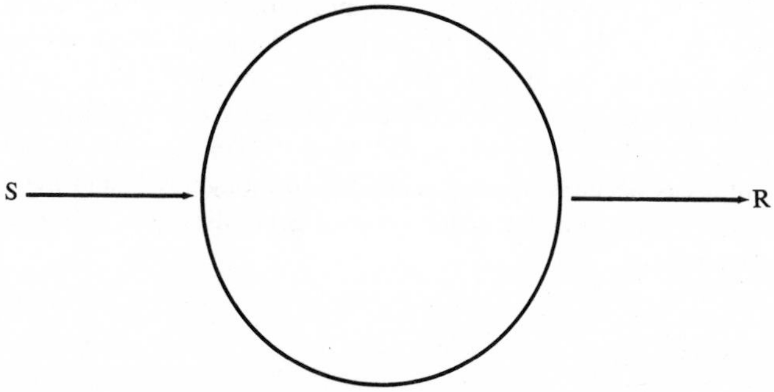

"stimuli" (S) has been substituted for the term "impingements." Students who have had a course in general psychology will recognize the model as the $S \to O \to R$ code. The distinction between "stimuli" and "impingements" might seem trivial; however, for conceptual purposes, the distinction is significant. Not all energy impingements upon the organism lead to central neural activity or to other organismic behavior. As you read this book, slight variations in light waves are impinging upon your retina, but they may be of such low magnitudes that they result in no measurable change in neural firing. Larger variations of light impingements might be sufficient to modify neural firing and affect overt behavior (e.g., cause movement of the book). Impingements which result in such electro-chemical changes in the central structure will be called "stimuli."

From the simple model expressed in Figure 1.2, we shall attempt to account theoretically for human behavior. When this brief model is inadequate, we shall add options in an attempt to account schematically for the inadequacy. When the model becomes too complex, we shall discuss models which depart from the $S \to O \to R$ schema. The $S \to O \to R$ model influences the thinking which underlies the writing in this text, for even though complex behavior is discussed in what is called "cognitive terms," we have only the above-mentioned three factors from which theories are formulated, interpreted, and applied.

Note: A number of favorite terms which are in common use among educators today are quite "fuzzy" in meaning. Examples include "creativity," "appreciation," "happy," etc. According to educators, children *should* be "creative," they *should* be "happy," etc. We must ask, "What specific behaviors (R's) do you mean? To the statement, "Children *should* learn to 'appreciate' art and music," we must reply, "What behaviors express appreciation?" If a person sighs upon conclusion of Beethoven's Fifth Symphony, is he appreciating? Or is he bored? Too often, "fuzzy" terms are used to designate the goals of education, and if you as a teacher are unable to determine what behaviors curriculum writers want (because *they* don't know what they *mean*), then how can you be expected to achieve the goals? An $S \to O \to R$ model should help point out areas which have not "really" been thought out, and the model should serve as an effective check on over-generalization of limited data and poor thinking.

Overview of Text

Each chapter in this book includes a discussion of a few simple concepts. If the student will keep in mind that all elaborations are only extended facets of simple ideas, he should be able to master these concepts. A short glossary, an overview, and a summary are provided for each chapter; reading these devices prior to reading the body of the chapter should facilitate the development of the ability to abstract the simple concepts.

An Important Statement: The presentation within many of these chapters might seem impersonal since people are often referred to as *organisms.* Individuals who look upon teaching as a confrontation with live, lovable children might find such discussions "inhuman." To make objects out of *"real"* humans is indeed a nasty task, and why should the authors intentionally take such a view of humanity? The answer rests upon the belief in careful inquiry. To "really" help lovable children we must apparently understand how the human animal works. Personal involvement in the subject matter of inquiry has many pitfalls. Consider the educator who comes across what appears to be a new effective technique. If he believes this technique is "good," he will want all children to benefit from exposure to the technique. Unfortunately, education is rife with "good" *untested* techniques. In order to moderate the influence of faddism, an inquiry frame of reference is taken. No technique is assumed to be "good" unless evidence is available to support the assertion. Therefore, well controlled studies regarding organismic behavior are sought.

Essentially, the viewpoint held within this text is that harm might be done to lovable children by employing "good" intentions when teachers have nothing more than a hunch to suggest their worthwhileness. To avoid this pitfall, an objective research orientation is adopted for this presentation. Readers should note that an understanding of how children behave is also essential to discussing research intelligently in educational psychology.

Chapter 2 includes a discussion of the characteristics of the developing organism. A point of view is developed which maintains that development is a joint product of the interaction of genetic and environmental factors. Environmental factors are broken into five sections, using Donald Hebb's framework. Data presented to support Hebb's position are used to modify the $S \rightarrow O \rightarrow R$ model (Figure 1.2). The model presented indicates that the authors assume acquisition of new responses (learning) is a result of association of the response with various stimulus complexes. A number of comparative animal research studies are summarized and implications for education are suggested.

Concern with language acquisition and language use provides the content for Chapter 3. Language acquisition is related to the $S \rightarrow O \rightarrow R$ model and draws heavily from Charles Osgood's work. A departure from psychological studies is made regarding language usage in that concepts from the fields of linguistics and semantics are presented to indicate the significance of linguistic systems upon the thought of man.

In one sense, the meaning we derive from experience is limited by the language codes we inherit from our mother tongue. Language devices employed by Korzybski to overcome the limitations of our Indo-European language structure are discussed and the possible educational values of these devices are suggested. Work regarding meaning and the orienting reflex (the "What is it?" response) conducted by Russian psychologists is presented within this chapter. Some time is devoted to the relatively recent work on proprioceptive feedback (stimulation from muscles, tendons, and joints) and the relation of such stimuli to the individual's construction of meaning.

"Measurement of Central Processes" is the title of Chapter 4. The title is purposely vague, since the content of this chapter touches upon areas of human behavior (e.g., "intelligence") which have been loaded with somewhat distorted meanings in education. "Intelligence" is discussed as a conceptual invention designed to summarize behaviors which purport to influence man's adaptation to the complex universe. Alternate concepts regarding the structure of the intellect are presented, especially those of J. P. Guilford, who theorizes that "intelligence" is composed not of one factor, but of many. He has proposed 120 theoretical factors of which more than 80 have been identified. This orientation has a number of implications for educational practice, one of which is that teachers may wish to train the intellect to utilize these factors rather than teach "skills" and "habits" that seem relevant to the concept of a "general intelligence."

Chapter 4 also includes a discussion of measurement of "attitudes" and "values" which are learned and which apparently provide sets toward action probabilities. A modified quasi-mathematical model of McGuire's adaption-level paradigm is presented and the research value of the model is discussed.

Note: Some members of the American culture are very concerned with the activities of the "brain-watchers" (psychologists). The material presented in Chapter 4 touches on some of the tests which attempt to assess how individuals think; according to those who distrust testing, the next step after assessing man's thought processes is to brainwash individuals and to gain control over man's thinking. As measurement and prediction become more refined, the risk of manipulation through motivational research is increased. Researchers attempt to retain confidentiality of data obtained; however, the generalizations regarding behavior which are derived from testing in the public schools are public information. Measurement progress has much "good" to offer by way of job selection as well as for the rational control of society, but measurement concepts can be equally destructive in the hands of exploiters. A number of psychologists conduct what is euphemistically called "motivational research" for advertising agencies. "Motivational research" usually uses measurement procedures to determine which symbols affixed to a product will result in higher sales. Although no censure is intended, it must be pointed out that extensive use of future research might pose a possible threat to society if used for purposes of obtaining power. Recent presidential elections have included image-building campaigns which might have markedly distorted the message of the candidates. Research shall continue and better means of control will undoubtedly be found. In any case, the negative use of scientific investigation might be prevented by an aware, sophisticated citizenry, and by the psychological fraternity.

Chapter 5 departs from the $S \rightarrow O \rightarrow R$ model to include presentation of concepts entertained by what is usually called "cognitive psychology." Included in Chapter 5 are: (1) Berlyne's concepts regarding the motivating effects of "cognitive conflict," (2) Bruner's concept of the "hypothetical mode" in teaching, (3) Piaget's delineations regarding the development of concepts, (4) Maltzman's ideas regarding teaching of creativity, and in addition (5) Skinner's non-cognitive concept of operant conditioning. These five ideas are compared to the $S \rightarrow O \rightarrow R$ model and a degree of reconciliation with the neo-behavioristic view is attempted. Since Chapter 5 deals extensively with concept formation and gross response acquisition, the educational implications are numerous.

A self-theory of behavior (Carl Rogers') is presented in Chapter 6. The theory utilizes a rather broad summary of conscious experiences in order to discuss human behavior. The presentation is systematic and follows Rogers' 19 propositions regarding human action. The central theme is that when the self-concept (what a person thinks he is) is congruent with what the person "really" is, the individual's coping potential is maximized. Conversely, self-concepts which depart greatly from "reality" create potential adaptive problems. Although Rogers' constructions are not explicitly response oriented, the generalizations provide a set toward summarizing the relevant behavioral variables which can be of value both to the teacher and the researcher.

Socialization is discussed from primarily an imitation frame of reference in Chapter 7. Development of "moral" standards and of deviations from social norms are viewed from an orientation presented by Bandura and his associates. Attention is given to the notion that acceptable behavior is a function of what people *call* acceptable, and therefore behaviors which depart from social norms are considered to be character "defects" rather than something "bad" that the person has inherited. "Inner-" and "other-directed" societies are discussed using Riesman's *The Lonely Crowd* as the central orientation.

Chapter 8 centers upon technology in education. This chapter is less theoretical but discusses problems associated with employing technology. Indeed, marked changes in educational practice are possible with the new technology. However, due to public relations efforts to keep up with the times, these changes are not forthcoming. For example, films and video tapes provide an opportunity to break away from the large classroom lecture, but in practice, films are used in mass education to substitute for the lecturer. Programmed learning is discussed, and a 151 frame program is provided to illustrate a linear program. Other technological innovations (e.g., computer assisted instruction) are also discussed in the chapter. The program is inserted for two purposes: (1) to provide the student with an opportunity to "experience" the act of using a program as a learning device, and (2) to familiarize the student with common statistical terms encountered in psychology. No other chapter devoted to statistics is included in this text, although from time to time statistical concepts are introduced as they are needed to help develop the ideas of educational psychology. The student might wish to work through the program early in the course, since learning the language employed might facilitate comprehension of previous statistical considerations.

Chapter 9 is an attempt to examine the classroom child in view of the parts presented in preceding chapters. Problems relating to the teaching role are considered. The "whole child" is revisited and seen as a "whole" set of complex interactions not necessarily impossible to deal with, although not an easy organism to direct.

Questions

The questions are listed at the end of each chapter to stimulate the reader to draw together several of the topics discussed and thus formulate a response. The questions are reasonably broad and perhaps no correct answers could be identified. However, our intent is to provoke the reader to speculate about some notions concerning classroom instruction. Our position is simply that the study of educational psychology should lead to inquiry. Progress seems most probable when educators examine critically what exists, speculate concerning what ought to be, and evaluate the outcomes of attempts to implement their speculations.

1. What assumptions do you make regarding the causal factors influencing behavior? Are you a monist, dualist, or some other "ist"?
2. What do you feel the aims of education should be? Why?

3. Can you conceive of a teaching situation in which the teacher is not attempting to control the learner? (Remember, even inspiration may be a causal factor.)

4. Are you aware of the "motivating" stimuli provided by advertising? Look through some ads, "You tiger, you."

Further Readings of Interest

Herbert Feigl provides a very readable discourse on "The Scientific Outlook" which the authors believe should be read by individuals interested in behaviors (one of *our* evaluative judgments). He also presents a critique of "common misconceptions" regarding the scientific endeavor.

A reading of Skinner's fictional *Walden II* can provide a view of a society theoretically based upon experimental procedures. As an antidote to *Walden II,* read J. W. Krutch's *The Measure of Man.* Krutch, a humanist, abhors Skinner's controlled society. Some think Krutch objects to Skinner's position because such a society makes the task of being virtuous very easy.

References

Feigl, H. The scientific outlook: naturalism and humanism. *Amer. Quart.,* 1, 1949, 135-148. Also reprinted in part in L. Garlow, & W. Katkovsky, *Readings in the psychology of adjustment.* New York: McGraw-Hill, 1959, 5-14.

Krutch, J. W. *The measure of man.* Indianapolis: Bobbs-Merrill, 1953.

Rogers, C. R., & Skinner, B. F. Some issues concerning the control of human behavior: a symposium. *Science,* 1956, 124, 1057-1066. Also reprinted in L. Garlow, & W. Katkovsky, *Readings in the psychology of adjustment.* New York: McGraw-Hill, 1959, 500-522.

Skinner, B. F. *Walden II.* New York: Macmillan, 1948.

Organismic Development

2

Overview

In the preceding chapter the assumption was made that the essential sources of information for education are: the stimulus (ΣS), the organism (person), and the response (R). Within this chapter the $S \rightarrow O \rightarrow R$ model is modified to account for learning. One can ask a child to add 2 and 2 and he gives you an answer, "4." Apparently the "O" (organism-person) is not an empty transmitter of input. Transformations are made. We call the internal processor a *residual* of experience (abbreviated "rs"). See Figure 2.1. Because children apparently do not emit addition responses without special training, we infer that addition transformations are learned.

Early in life, most animals are exposed to diverse stimuli and respond in the presence of these stimuli. The importance of adequate early stimulation was indicated by a number of studies which used sub-human animals raised in restricted environments. These studies suggested that the ability to successfully cope with problem situations is limited for animals who lack many of the early experiences commonly encountered during the first few months of life. Even the response to noxious stimuli,

FIGURE 2.1

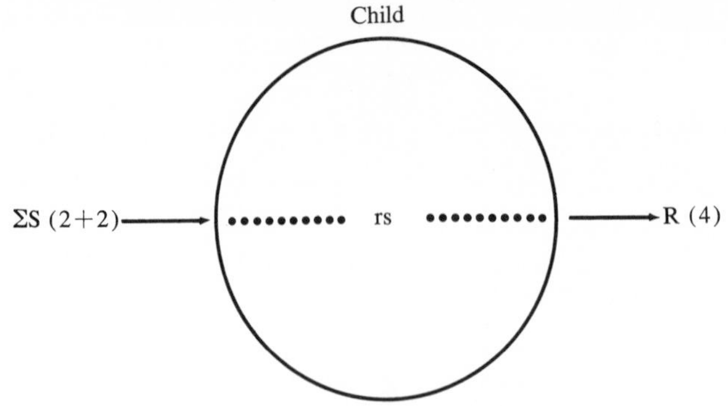

which we would call painful, is markedly different for these animals. In light of these data the proposed S → O → R model should include a host of residuals of early experience which enable the organism to acquire new complex learnings (residuals). Language response inadequacy, often associated with "cultural deprivation," seems to parallel these animal findings.

The definition of a *response* takes many forms depending upon the investigator's interests. For example, a minute electro-chemical change in a cell might be called a response for some biological research purposes. On the other hand, the total number of correct pencil markings on an IBM form might be called a response for an educational researcher. Each of these descriptions of a response apparently requires some push behind the individual responding. Some neurological considerations are introduced in this chapter to account for the source of the push (drive) behind behavior. This discussion relies heavily upon the writings of Donald Hebb, a Canadian psychologist. When sense receptors are stimulated, the energy released travels via neural pathways to specific areas of the cortex. Stimulation of the rods and cones in the eye results in some activation of the cells in the posterior occipital lobe. This transmission system is called by Hebb, the Specific Projection System (SPS). As the neural excitation passes through the brain stem, some of the electro-chemical impulse is tapped-off through collateral pathways to the Recticular Formation which is composed of a complex of neurones. The neural transmission from the recticular formation to the cortex apparently does *not* follow specific pathways to specific cortex areas but leads to diffused excitation of the cortex. Hebb calls this the Non-specific Projection System (NPS) and indicates it operates as an arousal function. Given an aroused organism (drive), his behavior depends upon the cue function of the Specific Projection System (SPS). Figure 2.2 is a modified S → O → R model of Figure 2.1, designed to account for the arousal and cue functions. Figure 2.2 is extended a bit further in this chapter to account for response intensity.

FIGURE 2.2

A modification of S → O → R model to account for arousal

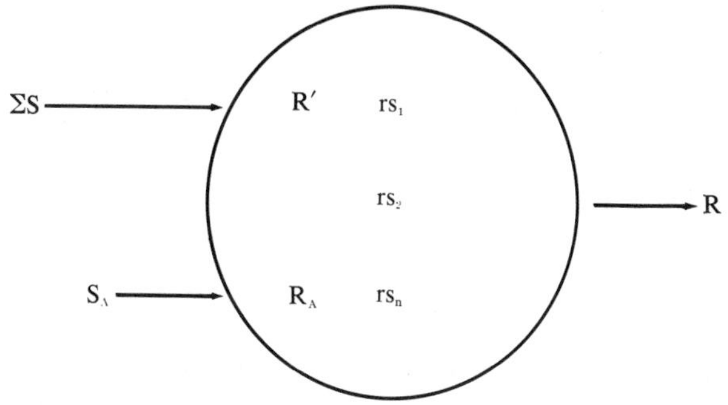

ΣS = sum of effective stimuli impinging upon the organism (e.g., excitation of rods and cones, patterned sound waves, etc.).
S_A = energy from afferents branched off through the Recticular Formation.
R′ = excitation of cortex from SPS (cue functions).
R'_A = excitation of cortex from NPS (arousal).
$rs_1, rs_2, \ldots rs_n$ = residuals of experience that modify the organism's response potential.
R = response of the organism.

In that behavior takes many forms, behavior is classified into three categories: instrumental, affective, and expressive. This taxonomy is somewhat arbitrary; however, it is introduced to impose some order upon the response domain. *Instrumental* responses take many forms — walking, writing, etc. — in essence any action that is goal-directed. *Affective* responses are visceral and vascular changes under the control of the autonomic nervous system which tend to facilitate goal-directed behavior. *Expressive* responses involve facial movement and posture that might reflect some "inner-mood" of the individual — usually a non-conscious reaction. These interpretations are arbitrary, for a smile consciously used to elicit a response from another would be an instrumental response. Little research is available regarding the acquisition of meaning in relation to expressive responses. A few studies are reported, and speculation relating to the possible educational use of this class of responses is presented.*

**Note:* A few simple notions are developed within this chapter; however, a number of studies used to support these notions are complex. If you focus upon the simple notions, the complex studies will have more meaning. It might be noted that research which is intended to deal with the simplest of concepts often requires a design which is both confusing and complex to the neophyte student of psychology.

Glossary

Please scan the terms given below before reading this chapter.

acquired need: refers to a need ascribable primarily to experience or learning, i.e. for smokers the need for cigarettes is learned.

affective behavior: visceral responses to stimuli (i.e. changes in heart rate, respiration, and blood flow). Typically associated with strong "emotion."

afferent: concerned with the transmission of neural impulses toward the central part of the nervous system (see efferent).

antagonistic cell firing: refers to the inclusion of motor cortex messages to the extremities that cause contraction of opposing muscle groups.

arousal: refers to the function of a sensory event giving tone to the cortex, of arousing the cortex to vigilance or readiness.

association: a functional relationship between psychological phenomena established in the course of individual experience and of such nature that the presence of one tends to evoke the other.

bias: the tendency to favor a particular position.

conditioning (classical): the complex of organismic processes involved in the experimental procedure, or the procedure itself, wherein two stimuli are presented in close temporal proximity. One of them has a reflex or previously acquired connection with a certain response whereas the other is not an adequate stimulus to the response in question. Consequently upon such paired presentation of the two stimuli, usually many times repeated, the second stimulus acquires the potentiality of evoking a response very like the response elicited by the other stimulus.

conditioning (instrumental or operant): the complex of organismic processes involved in the experimental procedure, or the procedure itself wherein a stimulus, having evoked a response that brings into view a rewarding stimulus, thereafter is more likely to evoke that response; or alternatively, the complex of processes or the experimental procedure wherein the stimulus, having evoked a response that prevents or removes a noxious or punishing stimulus, thereafter is more likely to evoke that response.

conditioned response: the new or modified response that is elicited by a given stimulus after conditioning.

conditioned stimulus: an originally ineffective stimulus for a given response that, by the experimental procedure, has become capable of eliciting that response.

cultural deprivation: a condition wherein the individual is comparatively deprived of the means of training or discipline by which man's "moral" or intellectual nature is elevated; pertaining to an environment having comparatively less cultural stimulation.

chance: the extent to which an event occurring within a limited system of events is due to causes wholly outside that system.

discrimination: the process of detecting differences among objects (stimuli).

drive: a tendency initiated by shifts in physiological balance to be sensitive to stimuli of a certain class and to respond in any of a variety of ways that are related to the attainment of a certain goal.

efferent: concerned with the transmission of neural impulses away from the central nervous system to muscles, etc.

environment: the sum of the external conditions and factors potentially capable of influencing an organism.

extinction: the progressive reduction in the conditioned response consequent upon either of two experimental procedures: (a) the repeated presentation of the conditioned stimulus without the unconditioned stimulus; or (b) the withholding of reward after the emission of a conditioned instrumental response.

expressive behavior: a part or aspect of an act that is particularly revealing of some internal state. Not an instrumental act. Examples are: smiling, frowning, slouching, etc.

gaiting-out: a process whereby some stimuli are admitted to awareness and others are ignored.

generalization: a process whereby one reaches a judgment applicable to a whole class, often on the basis of experience with a limited number of the class (e.g. a child has a positive experience with three cats and then generalizes that all cats are friendly).

gestation: the act or period of carrying the embryo in the uterus from conception to birth; pregnancy.

heuristic: aiding or leading on toward discovery or finding out. That which incites investigation.

input: corresponds to an adequate stimuli.

inhibition: restraining or stopping a process from continuing or preventing a process from starting although the usual stimulus is present.

inference process: a mental process whereby, on the basis of one or more judgments, a person reaches another judgment regarded as proved or established by the former. All theory is inferred from some previous observation.

instrumental behavior: behavior that purposefully effects a direct alteration in the environment.

mediation: interposition between two items or terms, making them dependent upon an intervening object or process. The intervening process between stimulus and response mediation is an inferred term.

motivation: the non-stimulus variables controlling behavior; the general name for the fact that an organism's acts are partly determined in direction and strength by its own nature and/or internal state.

neurological: pertaining to the structure and diseases of the sensory and motor nervous system.

open set: a condition lacking a predisposed tendency or disposition toward particular responses.

output: corresponds to response.

premature closure: coming to an end or conclusion before the proper time; too early completion of an unfinished act resulting in allowing a meaningless object or situation to be perceived as having meaning.

proximal receptor: in an animal body, a specialized receptor that is sensitive to direct physical contact and initiates a neural impulse. A rather arbitrary classification when contrasted with *distal* receptors. For example, heat, cold, and pressure receptors are called proximal receptors. The rods and cones (distal receptors) do not come in direct contact with the object but are sensitive to the light waves which are reflected by the object.

proprioceptive: pertaining to any receptor sensitive to the position and movement of the body and its members.

post-partum: after childbirth.

progeny: offspring (collectively).

residual: remaining after certain events and operations have been performed. An inferred term to account for the changes within the individual due to experience (essentially learned).

selective breeding: reproduction planned so as to bring about specific desired traits in offspring.

strain: a species subdivision of individuals having common lineage but not having sufficiently marked common characters to constitute a named breed.

specific projection system, SPS: a system suggesting that energy from receptors is directly and relatively quickly transmitted afferently via trunk lines to specific areas of the cortex, and that the action presented through efferent conduction, too, is controlled by the SPS.

nonspecific projection system, NPS: a system suggesting that SPS trunklines branch off through the Recticular Formation in the brainstem and carry energy which diffusely bombards the cortex, and that the intensity of response, too, is controlled by the NPS.

unconditioned response: a response evoked by a certain stimulus at the beginning of a given learning or conditioning period. A response that is species predictable.

unconditioned stimulus: a stimulus that, at the beginning of a given learning or conditioning period, evokes a certain response.

Physiological Considerations

For purposes of distinguishing psychology from other sciences dealing with organic matter, we have defined our subject matter to include complex human behavior mediated by the central nervous system. But as was indicated previously, this distinction is arbitrary, for the central mediation structure is a consequence of a genetic structure and the interaction of this structure with a chemical environment (nutrients). As a preface to the mediational problem, a few pages shall be devoted to the neurophysiological characteristics of the organism.

Historically, psychologists have been concerned with the relative contribution of hereditary and environmental factors to various human behaviors. Some earlier psychologists (Burt, 1955) claimed that intelligence was due 90% to heredity and 10% to environmental factors. Recent trends of thought regarding this area seem to ignore the question, for heredity versus environment appears to be a pseudo-problem. Apparently, heredity and environment interact in a multiplicative manner rather than in an additive function. By way of illustration:

> If we take a handful of dirt (a little heredity), feed it, love it, and send it to Harvard, in twenty years we would have a rather gooey handful of dirt.
>
> Conversely, if we take an egg from a brilliant woman — e.g., Madam Curie — fertilize it with "superior" sperm but deprive it of all environment except heat and oxygen, the result is a rotten egg.

The illustration, of course, is naive; however, it does indicate that the question is a matter of heredity *and* environment, not heredity *versus* environment.

In general, environment has also been treated as a single factor. At the present level of theory development, it appears that a closer examination of the notion of environment is warranted. Donald Hebb (1958, Chapter 6) proposed a coding of the factors related to organismic development which suggests an economical classification system. Hebb's factors are somewhat arbitrary and may distort some of the physiological data; yet they provide a viewpoint that overcomes many of the weaknesses that a two-factor (heredity and environment) code generates. (See Table 2.1)

TABLE 2.1

Classes of factors in behavioral development

No.	Class	Source, mode of action, etc.
I	genetic	physiological properties of the fertilized ovum
II	chemical, prenatal	nutritive or toxic influence in the uterine environment
III	chemical, postnatal	nutritive or toxic influence: food, water, oxygen, drugs, etc.
IV	sensory, constant	pre- and postnatal experience normally inevitable for all members of the species
V	sensory, variable	experience that varies from one member of the species to another
VI	traumatic	physical events tending to destroy cells: an "abnormal" class of events to which an animal might conceivably never be exposed, unlike Factors I to V.

From Hebb, Donald Olding, *A Textbook of Psychology,* Philadelphia: W. B. Saunders Company, 1966, p. 157.

Our mediational organism is a physical product of Factors I, II, III, and VI as modified by experiential Factors IV and V.

Physical Determinants

Factor I, of course, provides the basic structural components of the organism and indeed determines, within limits, the product of environmental interaction. The gene components contributed by the egg and sperm to a large degree determine the *potential* central neural processes of man. Experimental data with human subjects in this area are lacking, for our society does not permit the existence of primate labs with human specimens for breeding purposes. On the other hand, a significant number of breeding studies have been conducted with non-human species.*

Selective breeding of maze "bright" and maze "dull" rats by Tryon (1940) produced within seven generations distinctly different strains relative to ability to learn Lashley III-type mazes (a running alley maze with three culs-de-sac). The progeny of the seventh generation maze "bright" had very little overlap in the number of errors over 19 trials with the progeny of the maze "dull." Apparently, a rat's response to stimuli in the maze is determined in some part by the genetic structure of the organism. Further, continued selective breeding seems to have little additional effect beyond the seventh generation; thus, some limit seems to be imposed by the original gene pool.

Work conducted by McGaugh (1960) and others using Tryon's maze 'bright" and maze "dull" subjects indicated that the chemical activity in the brains of these two strains is quite different. These data suggest that some behavior which is commonly called "intelligent" is due to the organism's genetic structure. We are now inferring some characteristic of the organism as a result of differential responses (R) to stimuli (S) by two groups of animals. One can call this characteristic "intelligence," and note the neural correlate of differential chemical activity. One might call this neurophysiological concept "Intelligence A" (see Hebb, 1958, pp. 246-250); we shall soon see that intelligent behavior is also related to other factors.

The organism now has a central structure due to an inherited gene pool; however, prenatal chemical factors (II) may markedly modify the development of these potentials. (An assumption underlying Tryon's work is that adverse prenatal chemical factors are random, and the chance that the "bright" group will be influenced by these factors is equal to the chance that the "dull" group will also be adversely influenced.) The virus *rubella* (German measles) when contracted by the mother during the first few months of gestation may lead to post-partum mental defects, deafness, or cataracts. Thalidomide taken during early pregnancy has resulted in malformed limbs which modify the organism's response potential. Barbituates taken during delivery have been observed to overload the fetal bloodstream and produce destruction of brain tissue.

---

*The present text is concerned with educational psychology of humans. Animals are not ideal surrogates, but where problems arise and our moral commitments prevent the conduct of research with humans, extrapolations from animal studies will be included.

To be sure, animal results may not be entirely appropriate for humans; however, data derived from sub-humans may have heuristic value for applied psychology. If these notions provide testable hypotheses and lead to more efficient prediction of human behavior, then they have served an educational psychological purpose.

These illustrations are examples of prenatal chemical factors that may have adverse effects on the organism. The interested reader may wish to refer to Montagu (1960) for an extensive summary regarding organismic modification due to the prenatal chemical environment.

The intra-uterine chemical environment (Factor II) may facilitate the organic potential (genetic structure) or may distort it. Likewise a number of postnatal chemical factors (III) may modify the basic stuff underlying complex human behavior. Lack of oxygen during the first post-partum minutes may lead to destruction of neural tissue that can lead to severe limitations in the organism's ability to respond to stimuli.* Invasion of the brain by whooping cough bacteria can also lead to cellular destruction of brain tissue and marked behavioral handicaps in responses to stimuli. On a continuing but not necessarily irreversible basis, malnutrition and parasitic invasion may debilitate the organism's response potential.

Mediation

The above chemical considerations are significant developmental moderators, and merit notice for the individual concerned with changing or controlling behavior. Extensive coverage of these factors, however, is beyond the scope of this book. Sensory factors (IV and V) are of more direct concern for the applied psychologist. Recent work by Melzack and Scott (1957) with dogs, and by Krech and Rosenzweig (see Rosenzweig, 1963) with rats provides striking evidence in support of the influence of early experience. Factor IV (sensory constants) is proposed by Hebb to indicate that many diffuse learnings of an organism are the result of being raised in a typical environment. Humans, regardless of cultural background, have patterned visual stimulation, proprioceptive feedback as a result of movement, and stimulation of proximal receptors (heat, cold, taste, etc.). These diffuse stimuli apparently lay down traces upon the central neural mediation system so as to modify the organism's response potential. The ability to learn from experience (manifest intelligent behavior) has been assumed to be a function of Factors I-III, but let us examine the evidence that casts some doubt upon this assumption.

Melzack and Scott (1957) split a litter of Scottish terriers and raised one group in a somewhat natural environment with a number of barriers

---

*Recent evidence suggests that brain cell destruction associated with heart malfunction might not be due to the brain tissues low tolerance for oxygen deficit. These recent data suggest that the cellular destruction might be due to the cell's inability to restore circulation. (See Suda, Kito, and Adachi, 1966.)

and paths within a large cage. The other group was raised in small individual cages free of objects that could present problems for the dogs. At maturity, the two groups were presented with problem-solving tasks, and the litter mates that were raised in isolation showed performance markedly inferior to those raised in the "free" environment. These effects were apparently lasting. The isolated dogs were quite active and healthy, but also were "stupid." Responses to trivial stimuli were characteristic of these dogs, yet significant sensory information (e.g., destruction of nose tissue by a lighted match) did not provide information that would be generalized and used to modify subsequent behavior. These data suggest that "intelligence" (meaning ability to manifest intelligent behavior) is not solely due to Factors I-III, but they do not indicate that Factors I-III are unimportant. Research seems to indicate that the social environment has an effect upon animal behavior. The degree of effect remains indeterminant.

Work done with Tryon's maze "bright" rats (Krech and Rosenzweig, see Rosenzweig, 1963) provides evidence supporting the importance of early experience. These workers separated litters and provided one group with a highly varied environment for 80 days and the other group with a rather drab, isolated environment. The rats with the problem-enriched environment were greatly superior in their abilities to solve problems. An interesting extension was added to this research. The rats from both groups were sacrificed and the brains subjected to bio-chemical analysis. The brains of the rats from the enriched environment, in contrast to those from the isolated environment, were heavier, had more large blood vessels in the cortex, and had a greater number of glial cells (the sheathing on the neurons). These data are intriguing for apparently, use of the brain results in "better" adaptation and the physical correlate — a richly-nourished cortex. This does not imply that the brain is a muscle, but that the brain seems to become more efficient with use. Further work is being conducted to determine the reversibility of this process as well as the importance of the timing of the enriched experiences in the life span of the organism. Does sensory deprivation lead to a permanent loss? If so, what are the crucial times? Is the pattern different for genetically "dull" subjects? These remain interesting problems for researchers in psychology.

Educationally, these data are consonant with studies by Deutsch and by Jackson, *et al.,* which indicate that children from "culturally deprived" homes (homes where stimulus variety is less conceptual) are less ready to succeed in school than are children from less deprived homes (middle class). Thus the comparative animal studies do have some very meaningful bearing upon problems of complex human behavior.

In summary, the organism apparently has a genetic structure which is modified by chemical factors (pre- and postnatal) and early experience. If we assume that the organism has had normal chemical nutrients, then "Intelligence B" (effective problem solution) can be defined as the joint *product* of genetic factors and early sensory factors, both highly interdependent. The model $S \rightarrow O \rightarrow R$ can now be expanded to include some residuals of early experience (see Figure 2.3). S_e (early stimulation) leads to brain activity and leaves some residuals (rs_1, rs_2)

FIGURE 2.3

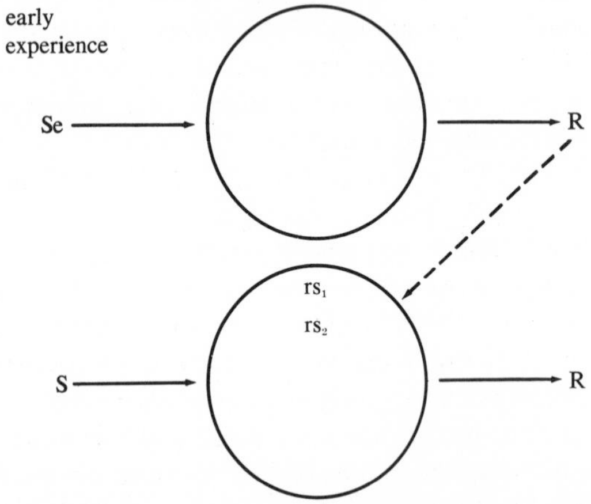

As a result of early stimulation and responses, some fraction of the R is subsequently emitted upon presentation of a similar stimulus. The inferred internal change is labelled rs_1, rs_2 (residuals).

which permit subsequent effective adaptation. Within some limits, the amount and quality of these early experiences seem positively related to adaptation.

The demarcation lines between sensory constants and sensory variables are somewhat obscured; however, illustrations of the latter are easily found. The child hearing "A, B, C, D " is certainly being exposed to a sensory variable, for not all cultures use this particular symbol system. All formal classroom learning is a sensory variable since classroom experiences vary, and all humans are not exposed to these activities. Further, the individual's processing of the sensory variables will be influenced by Factors I-IV and VI plus residuals of previous sensory variables. Thus response A in Figure 2.4 is a product of: Factor I genetic structure, Factor II chemical nutrition, Factors III and IV residuals of previous sensory stimulation (both constants and variables), and the present effective stimuli (see Figure 2.4).

FIGURE 2.4

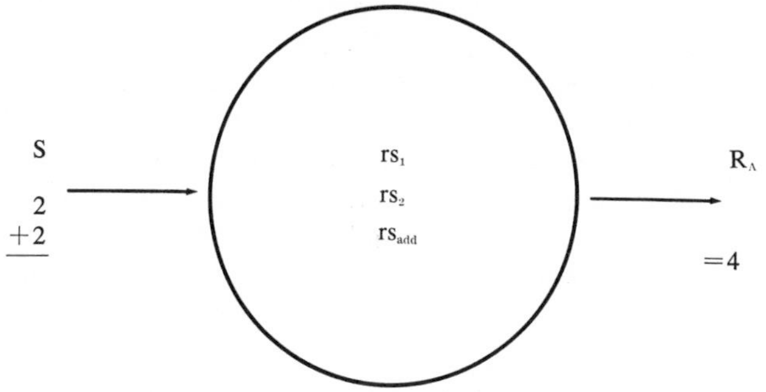

A child is exposed to a stimulus 2 + 2 and responds = 4. We infer from his response that he has some notion of addition (rs_{add}).

Since education is concerned with student response capabilities this figure shows three relevant variables; the organism (person), the problem (ΣS), and the response (R). If the organism continually provides the adequate response (that which has been determined by the teacher), we can infer that he has the effective *concept.* One may present a number of addition problems to a child, and if the child consistently provides the adequate response, the teacher infers the child has the concept of addition. Occasionally, such an inference could be faulty, because the child might have obtained the adequate response (correct answers) from his neighbor's paper. This circumstance should indicate that all inferences made by the teacher or the researcher may be contaminated and therefore periodic verification of inferences can reduce such errors.

Learning is inferred in the present frame of reference to be change in the neural structure as a result of interaction of an organism with his environment (S). Schematically, the assumed neural change (which indeed may be undiscovered) is represented as a residual (rs) which is inferred from the organism's response (R). What is learned is a joint product of the stimulus conditions and the organism.

To illustrate the importance of this notion, a return to Tryon's maze "bright" and maze "dull" should be profitable. McGaugh (1960) happened to note during his work that when the trials in the Lashley III maze were spaced (one trial a day) the dull rats performed as well as the bright rats had under massed practice. The difference between the strains is statistically significant under massed consecutive trials. McGaugh has some evidence which supports a theory that the difference is due to the facilitory influence for consolidation of the brain chemistry of the "bright" strain. These relationships are not completely filled out, but they suggest important factors for the applied psychologist. For example, a number of recent textbooks in educational psychology discuss the value of spaced learning when memorizing lines for a play. Apparently the authors noted the characteristics of the stimuli to be processed and how the stimuli should be temporally presented, yet they ignored the characteristics of the organism. In view of comparative research with animals, applied psychologists should investigate not only the stimulus characteristics but also should attend to individual differences in the processing organisms. A very "bright" person might most efficiently learn material (S) of a particular complexity with massed practice, while a "dull" person might learn the same material most efficiently with widely spaced practice. These possibilities are suggested in order to highlight the state of incompleteness of our present knowledge. Most of what is said concerning learning is based upon theory rather than evidence gathered in the complex school environment. Indeed, the future success of educational psychology as an applied science rests upon its ability to maintain an open set and to avoid premature closure.

Unfortunately, many psychologists and teachers close their minds to possibilities which seem foreign to their personal theoretical orientation. Few facts exist when the processes of complex school learning are involved. Psychologists seem better equipped to speak about the various means of inquiry (research) than they are prepared to discuss what really occurs in the classroom learning situation.

A Few Comments Regarding Trauma (Hebb's Factor VI)

The influence of Factor VI (trauma) upon behavior is quite obvious. If a person has lost an arm due to an accident, his response potential is markedly modified. Brain damage may interfere with the ascending or descending neural pathways and, as a consequence, limit the individual's response potential. These are examples of actual tissue damage. Factor VI (physical trauma), however, does not seem to allow for all the possibilities. The authors suggest that a seventh factor — "sensory trauma" — merits inclusion. Sensory variables (Factor V) include stimuli which are not common to all members of the species; however, some stimuli are of such traumatic nature that a gross change in the individual's behavior may be noted. For example, as a culmination of a week of festive wedding preparations, the bride and groom drive away from the church. A little horse play leads to loss of control of the car. An object slashes into the bride's head and splatters blood over the groom's face; the bride is dead but the groom is physically unhurt. Such bloody sensory stimulation seems likely to produce marked changes in the groom's behavior. Such an experience seems to warrant a special factor of its own, Factor VII, sensory trauma. In a non-technical sense, sensory trauma depends upon a complex set of expectations, hopes, and values. The shock that the physically unhurt groom exhibits surely would rest upon a history of courtship, planning, and anticipation of wedded bliss.

Measurement Problems

Tacitly underlying the previous discussions is the assumption that we have a means of comparing responses to stimuli. Quantification of stimuli and responses provides a means for comparison. As a result of interaction with stimulus events, the organism's response potential is modified. This modification is commonly called learning. If we control (to a degree) the stimuli (such as a test) to which the organism responds, we can quantify the responses. Then we can infer that differences in responses are due in part to the organism's previous history. For example, suppose the data in Table 2.2 represent the scores that ten students obtained on an arithmetic achievement test. If we wish to

TABLE 2.2

Arithmetic test scores for ten hypothetical students.

Person	Test Score	Person	Test Score
A	10	F	16
B	11	G	17
C	12	H	18
D	13	I	19
E	14	J	20

predict with fewest errors, students' scores with only the knowledge that they are members of the group, the safest bet would be to predict the mean (sum of scores divided by the number of scores $\frac{\Sigma X}{N} = M$).

Any other number in the long run will probably result in more errors of prediction (see Table 2.3).

TABLE 2.3

Error sum of squares made when predicting group mean (15) for each student.

X	Predict	Error		Error²
10	15	5		25
11	15	4		16
12	15	3		9
13	15	2		4
14	15	+1		1
16	15	−1		1
17	15	−2		4
18	15	−3		9
19	15	−4		16
20	15	−5	error	25
			sum of squares	110

A major concern in predicting group behavior is to reduce the likelihood of making errors. One method which can be used to check on the degree of error is to predict a behavior (in the example, a test score) and then check to see how much error really resulted. As Table 2.3 shows, when errors are computed, they are in both directions — over- and under-prediction. If errors of over-prediction are considered to result in positive errors and errors in under-prediction are negative numbers, a summation of all errors will only result in determining the direction of greatest error. One means used to reflect total error is to square each error term and then sum. In this manner all error is converted to a positive sign through multiplication ($-4 \times -4 = +16$; and $+4 \times +4 = +16$). Therefore, total error can be obtained in this manner. This is the central process underlying the error sums of squares concept. For example, with the data presented in Table 2.4, if one predicted 14, 16, or any number other than 15, the error sum of squares would be larger (see Table 2.4).

If these data represent a study in which we were investigating the effects of two teaching methods, the error sums of squares concept can

TABLE 2.4

Error sums of squares using 14 and 16 as predicted scores.

X	Predict	Error		E^2	X	Predict	Error		E^2
10	14	−4		16	10	16	−6		36
11	14	−3		9	11	16	−5		25
12	14	−2		4	12	16	−4		16
13	14	−1		1	13	16	−3		9
14	14	0		0	14	16	−2		4
16	14	2		4	16	16	0		0
17	14	3		9	17	16	1		1
18	14	4		16	18	16	2		4
19	14	5		25	19	16	3		9
20	14	6	error	36	20	16	4	error	16
			sum of squares	120				sum of squares	120

aid in determining the relative merits of the methods. Let us assume the scores for persons A through E in Table 2.2 represent the performance of students taught under method Z, and persons F through J represent students taught under method Y. If we predict the mean of group Z for those having treatment Z and the mean of group Y for those having treatment Y, we shall obtain a different error sum of squares than we found in Table 2.3 (see Table 2.5).

Obviously group Y scored better than group Z on this test, and the knowledge that we had two treatments greatly reduced our errors of prediction (from ess_1 of 110 to ess_2 of $10 + 10 = 20$). If we have been careful to eliminate bias in the selection of our groups (e.g., both groups are of similar learning ability), then apparently treatment Y (as a set of stimuli) has modified the person's response potential more favorably than treatment Z. We can infer that there are some residuals in students F through J that lead to success. Yet a problem remains. Is this difference due to chance factors? Without going into the logic behind the concept of probability, we can use the F statistic, which is a test of the probability of obtaining mean differences due to chance factors. The F value in this example is 36 and a value this high is found less than one time in a thousand due to chance (see Underwood, *et al.*, 1954).

Whenever a sample of subjects is drawn from a larger population, the sample mean will vary somewhat from the population mean. Usually one cannot obtain the population mean because the population size is too large (e.g., all seventh-grade children in the United States of

TABLE 2.5

Error sums of squares when student scores are predicted using mean for each sub-group rather than using total group mean.

Person	Test Score	Predicted Score	Error		E^2
		Method Z			
A	10	12	−2		4
B	11	12	−1		1
C	12	12	0		0
D	13	12	1		1
E	14	12	2		4
	Σ60			error sum of squares	10
	Mean $= \frac{60}{5} = 12$				
		Method Y			
F	16	18	−2		4
G	17	18	−1		1
H	18	18	0		0
I	19	18	1		1
J	20	18	2		4
	Σ90			error sum of squares	10
	Mean $= \frac{90}{5} = 18$				

America). The F statistic is designed to estimate, from the variation of scores from the mean of two or more samples, the likelihood that the obtained mean differences were due to chance factors. For example, if the mean for treatment Y was 13 and the error sum of squares remained 10, then the F statistic would be small and the observed mean difference of one (1) (mean X = 12, mean Y = 13) would likely be obtained often due to variation in sample means.

The present discussion is an attempt to suggest that if we have information regarding the previous stimulus pattern and can reduce errors of prediction with this knowledge, then we are in a better position to understand human behavior.

In the past, most educators have been concerned with the problem of which teaching method is best. Generally they might have method Y and method Z, and they would recommend either or both, depending upon the results obtained through application of the methods. Studies in education constructed so as to compare one method with another frequently provide contradictory findings, because they ignore the student variable. Figure 2.5 represents one condition that is not too uncommon.

FIGURE 2.5

Sixth grade achievement

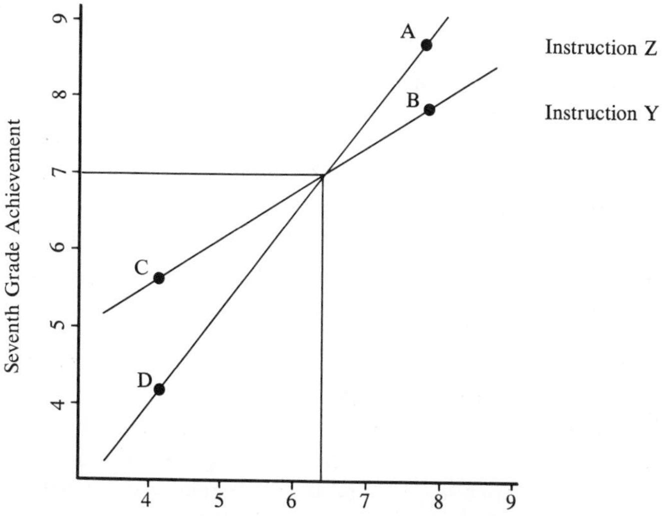

The A-D line represents the Line of Best Fit for students who received instruction Z. Note that at point A if a student had a sixth grade achievement score of 8, his predicted seventh grade achievement score would be above 9. The student represented by point B has a sixth grade score identical with student A, but his seventh grade predicted score is slightly above 8. Apparently, treatment Z is best for above average students. Note that the lines cross about 6.3. Student C achieves at a higher rate than student D. Therefore, treatment Y seems best for below average students. This crossing of lines reflects what is called interaction. The effects of treatment interact with student ability represented by previous achievement.

Two methods of instruction in a seventh-grade subject are hypothetically compared in Figure 2.5. We have added to the study the knowledge of sixth-grade achievement for each student. The hypothetical findings suggest that if a student scored below the sixth-grade placement and was given treatment Y, he improved more than the below average student given treatment Z. On the other hand, if the student scored above average in the sixth grade, treatment Z was apparently best. If the student was average, either treatment seems to have been effective.

Please note, these predictions are for groups of individuals. As long as some errors of prediction are made, then recommendations of treatment for any *particular student* might be an erroneous recommendation. In the long run however, knowledge of these relationships will reduce errors for *group* decisions.

Analyses of this sort take into account levels of ability (Factors I-VI) which might be somewhat relevant for task success. Further work will undoubtedly become more complex, taking into account other significant inter-organism differences.

Neurological Considerations

The physical correlate to the $S \rightarrow O \rightarrow R$ model is of course the sensory tracts, the brain, and the effectors (muscles, glands, etc.). Neurological inferences regarding the functioning of the organic system have been drawn from data obtained in work with animals, and with humans requiring neurosurgery. These data suggest that energy from receptors transmitted to the cortex follows two pathways. Hebb has labelled them Specific Projection System (SPS) and the Non-specific Projection System (NPS). The afferent SPS provides direct and relatively fast transmission via trunk lines to specific areas of the cortex. The ascending NPS branches off from the trunk lines through the Recticular Formation in the brainstem and then diffusely bombards the cortex. The afferent NPS apparently functions as a regulator of cortical activity (arousal) while the SPS functions to guide behavior.

Descending conduction (efferent) to the affectors also follows two paths, one controlling the action (SPS) and the other (NPS) apparently determining the intensity of response.

Figure 2.6 is a modified model of Figure 2.3 which attempts to take into account the arousal function of the NPS.

Branching from the effective stimuli (ΣS) is a set labelled S_A which accounts for the arousal function of the NPS. Note that although the efferent NPS also influences the response ($S'_{int.}$), no separate R is given, for the specific response and the intensity of the response are often measured simultaneously.

The notion of *effective* stimuli is noted by R' and R'_A within the organism, because not all receptor contact with the physical world (impingements) leads to an internal response by the organism. Apparently some gaiting-out of stimuli takes place. For example, as you sit in the lecture hall and daydream about "that big event," sound waves strike the hearing apparatus; yet the impinging sound has little or no effect upon your central processes.

FIGURE 2.6

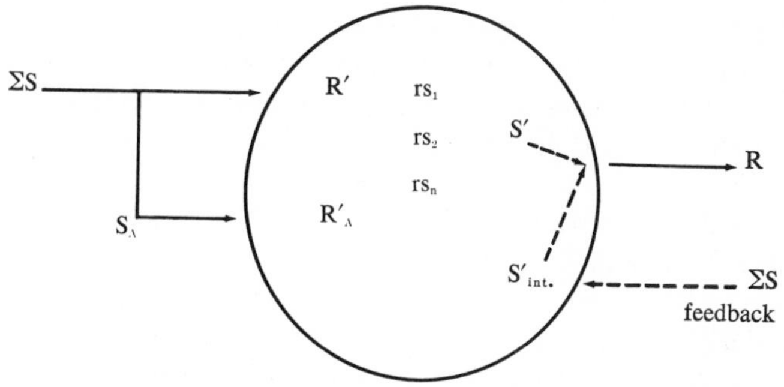

ΣS = sum of effective stimuli impinging upon the organism (e.g., excitation of rods and cones, patterned sound waves, etc.).

S_A = energy from afferents branched off through the Recticular Formation.

R' = excitation of cortex from SPS.

R'_A = excitation of cortex from NPS (arousal).

$rs_1, rs_2, \ldots rs_n$ = residuals of experience that modify the organism's response potential.

S' = stimuli from the motor cortex leading to the specific motor areas and eliciting the response of the organism.

S'_{int} = stimuli from cortex transmitted by descending NPS and controlling the intensity of the response.

R = response of the organism:
affective — visceral changes within the organism.
expressive — facial gestures, exclamation, etc.
instrumental — sequential behavior such as problem solving, etc.

ΣS feedback = proprioceptive feedback from muscles, tendons, and joints that play some role in sequential behavior.

Drive and the Notion of Arousal

In order to account for the fact that humans move first in one direction and then another, psychologists invented the concepts of "need," "drive," and "motivation." An organism was motivated to seek food in order to satisfy a "hunger need." It sought water for a similar reason. In order to account for movement of the organism during states of relative physiological satiation, psychologists invented "acquired needs" (e.g., "need achievement"). In addition, noting that rats learned mazes apparently for no reason, they formulated the concept of a "curiosity" or "novelty drive." These constructs did allow for better prediction and thus are plausible notions. But, undue emphasis on the part of the psychologists having rats run mazes in order to satisfy a "hunger need" has exaggerated the importance of reinforcement to the learning processes.

Unfortunately for the teacher, most children in the classroom are satiated with food, air, and water, and, therefore, because one cannot dispense pellets to motivate successful performance, other motivational concepts have been introduced (e.g., competition to satisfy "need achievement"). In spite of these additional concepts, some children do not respond to competition (motivation) as the teacher structures it, and these children might be labelled "lazy."

Berlyne (1958) noted that a child will respond longer to novel and complex stimuli than to common and simple stimuli. Teachers "motivate" children by having bulletin boards organized to stimulate the orienting response (the "What is it?" response) via new and complex organization. Other novel situations may occasionally be introduced. For instance, the teacher might bring fifteen different kinds of snakes into the classroom, distribute them around the room, and await the motivating effects of the novel stimuli. Yes, the children respond — running here, running there; in fact, the situation might become chaotic with diverse activity — too many "What is it?" responses in too many spatial locations.

Arousal

The above multi-drive sets have been of heuristic value; yet they have led to a rather fractured picture regarding human action. If we assume that a normal, awake person is by definition in motion because he is aroused, then the motivation problem is not focused upon from where the energy derives, but upon what stimuli the organism is processing. If one makes the additional assumption that the person is attempting to adapt to the universe, then he can make some inferences regarding what residuals of experience might be operating in the behaving situations. A few examples should illustrate the possibilities of this set.

The teacher brings in a novel picture in order to have the children focus upon an area to be taught. Many children will exhibit the "What is it?" response. Some will not. A child who has had many enriched experiences (thus a great number of residuals) may see the picture, determine that for him it is not novel, and thus ignore the presentation. On the other hand he may have also learned (rs) that he can adapt to the classroom situation by way of expressing his knowledge, and therefore his response may be to wave his hand to seek the signal (ΣS) "You may speak."

Another child might completely ignore the teacher. Upon closer investigation you might find this child examining a badly lacerated leg acquired in a recent fall. He is aroused, but the stimuli which he selects to attend to are a result of his residuals of experience (rs) regarding the meaning impulses from damaged tissue, not the stimuli from the teacher. The work of Melzack and Scott (1957) cited earlier, has shown that an avoidance response to pain does seem to be learned.

These illustrations place minimal emphasis upon arousal, for arousal is assumed to be a constant (a given). When the person is aroused, his behavior is controlled by the cue function of the stimuli plus the active residuals of experience.

Hebb (1958) suggested that when arousal is too high, the cortical activity leads to antagonistic cell firing and thus learning is unlikely to take place; but a response which leads to a lowering of arousal can be learned, since it reduces antagonistic firing. Antagonistic cell firing may include motor cortex messages to the extremities that cause contraction of opposing muscle groups. Such muscle firing does not lead to coordinated behavior. Rats given electric shocks to instigate movement often freeze or behave with uncoordinated action. But when these rats succeed in escaping the electric grid, they tend to repeat the successful response in subsequent trials. If the animal jumped to the right and escaped the grid, future escape behavior will tend to be the same — jump right.

If cortical arousal is too low (e.g., when one is in a drowsy state) learning appears to be inefficient. Action which increases arousal might also be learned because the arousal leads to adequate cell firing. Learning can take place during low levels of arousal (e.g., listening to records preceding deep sleep), but the learning is not efficient (see Simon and Emmons, 1956). Of course, if one spends an hour a day learning language preceding sleep (low level of arousal), it might be inefficient in contrast to aroused learning. This learning, however, might be more efficient than no learning.

Over-arousal may be of concern for classroom teachers, for although it is difficult to measure arousal, some child behavior appears to parallel the rat behavior. A tenuous tie might be inferred in the case in which the fifteen snakes lead to chaos. Activity on the part of children gives more ascending NPS activation by feedback, and this cycle may repeat itself; however, very seldom does one find complete uncoordination due to distal receptor stimulation. Yet, if a person has had experiences (rs) that lead to avoidance responses (i.e., fear of snakes) the arousal cycle might become sufficiently acute to result in freezing behavior. Along the same line of inferring, fear of failure (rs) might lead to freezing under testing conditions (ΣS). We shall discuss this aspect in phenomenological terms in Chapter 6.

In summary, in the usual classroom situation, arousal is commonly a given. Thus one must look to the effective stimuli when the response is judged by the teacher to be inappropriate. The "lazy" child is not a static mass of protoplasm. He probably is simply not responding to the stimuli you as a teacher are manipulating. Indeed, he may be responding to a comic book hidden under his work. The problem might be to determine why ΣS_1 (comic book) is selected over ΣS_2 (math book) as the stimulus which merits response. Subsequent chapters should provide fruitful hypotheses which the reader may desire to consider with regard to the "lazy" child.

Considerations Regarding Responses

A large portion of the responses that applied psychologists study can be classified as instrumental responses (see Figure 2.4). Examples would be: responding to test situations, seeking help and directions (verbal behavior), tripping, fighting, following directions, etc. Affective responses (such as constriction of blood vessels in the viscera, increase in heartbeat, etc.) are receiving more attention from applied psychologists. Recent use of Russian research by Americans has indicated the value of these data as hypotheses generators for the applied psychologist. We shall return to a more complete discussion of affective responses in Chapter 3.

Less easily classified responses such as expressive behavior (smiling, frowning, etc.) are observed by the teacher as indicators of conscious states within the student. From expressive responses the teacher often infers student perplexity, interest, or other states that merit a change in teacher behavior. The change in teacher behavior is of course a change in the stimulus complex for the student. The "artful" teacher has success; that is, she is able to manipulate the stimuli in such a manner as to obtain an acceptable response from the student. The less "artful" teacher apparently employs stimuli which elicit more inappropriate behavior from students. Research which critically examines expressive responses is limited and provides inadequate guidelines for applied psychology. If we wish to make the teaching-learning situation less artful and more explicit, expressive stimuli and responses need further investigation. Observation of classroom behavior suggests to many educators that a major component of classroom control is the ability of teachers to process student expressions and his or her expressive response to these data.

Speculation Regarding Expressive Responses

In that the authors perceive expressive responses to be of significance in the educational processes, *speculation* regarding why these responses seem important is presented below. Be sceptical and view this presentation with caution, for these thoughts are *not* closely tied to reliable data. Imagine that the print is red and that you have doubting responses to red.

Figure 2.1 is presented to illustrate that as a consequence of a response to an adequate stimuli, some part of this response appears to modify the organism's subsequent response potential. J. B. Watson (1921), an early American psychologist, reported a classic example of this state of affairs. A child was startled by a sharp noise (ΣS_1) each time he approached a white rabbit (ΣS_2). The adequate stimuli (sharp noise) resulted in whimpering and avoidance behavior. A nice predictable S — R situation obtained. Subsequent presentation of the white rabbit (ΣS_2) also elicited the crying and avoidance response. Apparently the response to the adequate stimuli (ΣS_1) was also associated with the paired stimuli (ΣS_2). Figure 2.7 summarizes this situation in our S→O→R model.

FIGURE 2.7

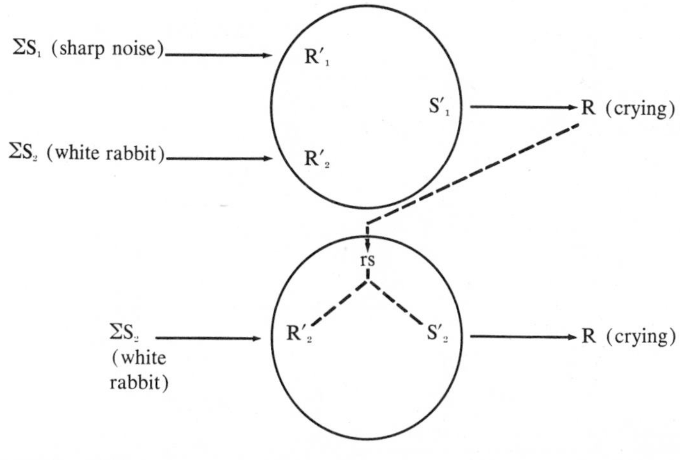

Pairing of aversive stimulus (a sharp noise) with a neutral stimulus (white rabbit) can lead to the neutral stimulus (ΣS_2) eliciting the response associated with the aversive stimulus (ΣS_1).

The crying response to the sharp noise may or may not be a learned response. If however, we assume developmental Factors I-IV (I genetic structure, II prenatal chemical environment, III postnatal chemical environment, IV sensory constants) and Factor V (sensory variables) are adequate, then we may conceive of this response as a highly probable species-predictable response. You might wish to infer that the noise is "unpleasant" and that the rabbit is now an indication of "unpleasantness." An inference of this sort might be more convenient for your symbolic system, although one need not refer to and label the suspected feelings of the individual.

When a white-bearded experimenter (ΣS_3) approached the child, the child also emitted the crying and avoidance response, while a block of wood (ΣS_4) did not elicit the response. Some fraction of the original response to the sharp noise was associated with the white rabbit (ΣS_2) and *generalized* to the white beard (ΣS_3) but not to the block of wood (ΣS_4). These generalizations can probably be extinguished with repeated

FIGURE 2.8

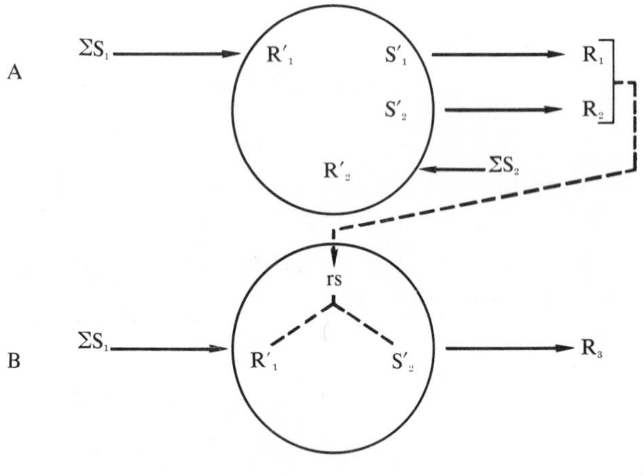

ΣS_1 = light waves reflected by a rattle.
R'_1 = cortical excitation (adequate stimuli).
R_1 = locomotion and shaking of rattle.
ΣS_2 = feedback: noise, proprioceptive stimuli from muscles, tendons, and joints.
R_2 = smiling, gurgling, etc.
R_3 = smiling, gurgling, etc.
rs = some fractional residual of total of R_1 and R_2.

non-association. The response can be greatly extended, however, through repeated intermittent association.

We have taken a rather circuitous route to get to expressive responses, but let us now relate the *smiling* expression to Watson's conditioning process. Early child behavior is composed of many responses to the novel world. As a stimulus-response organism, the child appears to seek contact with the stimulating world. Some of this contact (e.g., handling of a rattle) leads to strange noises (ΣS) which the child responds to with smiles, gurgling, and repetition of the response. Other contact with the same object (e.g., forcefully bouncing a rattle off the child's head) might lead to crying responses. Differential contact with other objects leads to either smiling or frowning. A bottle banged against the crib produces novel sounds and smiling can be associated with it. Broken glass tinkling as pieces of the bottle spread across the floor might initially produce smiling; however, mother's frowning and verbal

FIGURE 2.9

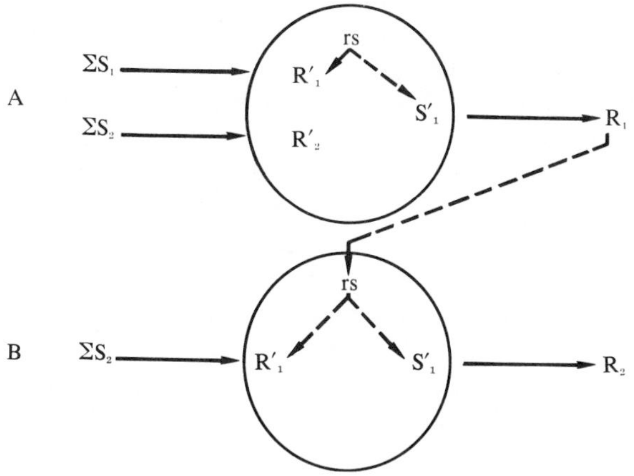

ΣS_1 = rattle.

R'_1 = cortical excitation.

rs = some fractional residual of total response associated with S_1 (smile, gurgle, locomotion).

ΣS_2 = someone smiling.

R'_2 = cortical excitation from ΣS_2.

R_1 = smile, gurgle, etc.

R_2 = smile, gurgle, etc.

response to such a state of affairs can lead to inhibition of bottle throwing.

Theoretically, if we extrapolate from Watson's data, others' smiling should lead to smiling and gurgling behavior on the part of the infant. Figures 2.6 and 2.7 represent this condition. The rattle (ΣS_1) in Figure 2.8 is assumed to be an adequate stimuli (ΣS_1 — R'_1) which activates the motor cortex (S'_1) and terminates in motor responses (R_1) (e.g., approach, pick up, and shake). This activity gives feedback (sound and proprioceptive stimuli, ΣS_2) that reaches the cortex (R'_1), and leads to motor responses (R_2) — smiling and gurgling. Some fractional part of the total response (rs) remains, and upon subsequent attention to ΣS_1, the child smiles and gurgles (R_3) simultaneously with the locomotor activities of approach (R_1). Figure 2.9 represents the association of someone smiling with the acquired response potential. A smiling and gurgling response is elicited.

In more common terms, playing and manipulating is fun. "Mommie smiles when I play. It is fun when Mommie smiles." The smile now *means* "good" feelings.

Analogous to the acquisition of "pleasant" responses to smiles (e.g., to mother), frowning is frequently associated with "unpleasant" responses (e.g., pain, spankings, restriction of activity, etc.). Frowning, if repeatedly associated with cessation of locomotion and/or avoidance behavior, should elicit some fractional part of these restrictive behaviors.

In view of the preceding speculation, smiling behavior by the teacher should elicit smiling and investigatory behavior on the part of the students. If this is so, then the stage is set for learning. What is learned, of course, depends upon the teacher's skill in the manipulation of the stimuli (e.g., introducing complexity, novelty, etc.).*

Frowning should reduce exploratory behavior and thus limit the variety of potential learnings. This is not to suggest that no learning will take place, but exploration of teacher-presented stimuli should, as a consequence of the paired frowning, be limited (see Figure 2.10).

Unfortunately, even on a speculative basis the situation is not simple. Smiling in the school context might be associated with inept stimulus manipulators (teachers). Thus smiling might elicit the diverse exploratory behaviors which are usually classified with lack of classroom control.

---

*In context of the present discussion, learning is conceived to be a modification of the individual's response potential as a result of previous response(s). Within the $S \rightarrow O \rightarrow R$ model, the modification is designated rs (residual). New responses (exploratory) to old stimuli, old responses to new stimuli, and new responses to new stimuli theoretically should maximize retention.

FIGURE 2.10

If expressive behavior is an important stimulus factor in the learning situation, then we should be able to demonstrate this influence empirically. To be sure, controlled research in the classroom is difficult for a number of reasons; nevertheless, the significance of expressive behavior can be tested.

Many educators have advocated that classroom learning activities should be conducted in a "pleasant and warm emotional climate." Our speculation has attempted to provide a theoretical rationale for this argument. In lieu of providing evidence for this position the authors suggest that you exercise caution. When you enter the classroom your expression will be hanging out; what the student response to the ΣS will be is at this stage of research development undetermined. To expect only one kind of response would be naive.

Summary and Implications

A central theme of this chapter was that human behavior is a joint product of genetic factors, chemical factors, and experiential factors. Arguments regarding heredity versus environment were dismissed because both seem necessary concepts for understanding behavior.

Probably, the only observable phenomena in relation to learning are the stimuli and the responses. In a sense, what goes on inside the learning animal is not known; the animal is like a little black box. We can, however, "shake" the black box and make a guess as to what is inside. In other words, we can manipulate the stimuli impinging upon the organism and infer from the subsequent response what is going on inside. Not only can we note responses, but we can open the box after the response and look at the goodies — rat brains, etc. One problem, however, arises regarding the inference process. Investigators tend to look at the organism from slightly different viewpoints, inventing new terms as they need them, and therefore we often have a diverse set of terms for the inferred processes. For purposes of discussion, the changes in the organism as a result of stimulation have been labelled *residuals*. One of any number of terms could have been selected (e.g., "habit," "engram," "circuit"), but "residual" is a relatively neutral term with few connotations and so has the flexibility to be molded into whatever meaning the authors define.

Responses were grouped into three classes: *instrumental, affective,* and *expressive*. The grouping is somewhat arbitrary, but it does allow behaviors to be discussed in some organized manner. Expressive behavior was selected for discussion in this chapter, since little research has been devoted to the significance of expressive responses. A theoretical discussion regarding the acquisition of meaning of smiles and frowns was presented. This acquisition of meaning was assumed to be the result of smiles being associated with pleasant conditions and frowns with unpleasant conditions. Watson and others call this process "conditioning." Teachers might wish to attend to the expressive responses of the child as they may provide information regarding the internal processes. More important (in the view of the authors), the teacher may well be directed to note her own expression, since it provides information which apparently has meaning for the child. The teacher's expression could inhibit the child's behavior or elicit inappropriate responses for the task at hand. Subsequent chapters deal in some detail with instrumental and affective responses.

Questions

1. Can we control behavior without postulating residuals or without making inferences regarding internal processes? Would it be of value to avoid postulations about internal processes? Why or why not?

2. Is your classroom behavior influenced by the expressions of your instructor?

3. What are some implications for the education of children contributed by the work done with rats by Krech and Rosenzweig? How could you modify your teaching in view of the findings?

4. If moderate arousal is to be desired (rather than low or high), how can you achieve it in your classroom? How can you raise the arousal level of a group of disinterested children? How can you control over-excited children so that they may learn more efficiently?

5. What is the role of generalization in learning? How can the principle of generalization be used to enhance your teaching?

Further Readings of Interest

Donald Hebb's *A Textbook of Psychology* is an excellent source regarding neural correlates of behavior. Chapter VI on development is especially useful for the applied psychologist.

Howard Moltz (see references) presents an excellent review regarding environmental considerations and current instinct theory.

A rather sophisticated treatment of motivation and its neural correlates is presented by Donald B. Lindsley in the 1957 *Nebraska Symposium on Motivation: Psychophysiology and Motivation.*

References

Berlyne, D. E. The influence of complexity and novelty in visual figures on orienting responses. *J. exp. Psychol.,* 1958, 55, 289-296.

Burt, C. M. The meaning and assessment of intelligence. *Eugenics Rev.,* 1955, 47, 81-91.

Hebb, D. O. *A textbook of psychology*. Philadelphia: W. B. Saunders, 1958.

Hebb, D. O. *A textbook of psychology,* 2nd Ed. Philadelphia: W. B. Saunders, 1966.

Lindsley, D. B. *Nebraska symposium on motivation: psychophysiology and motivation.* M. R. Jones (Ed.), Lincoln: Univer. of Neb. Press, 1957.

McGaugh, J. L. Neurochemical regulation of learning. Unpublished paper read at Symposium on Relations between Brain Chemistry and Learning in the Rat, San Jose, California, 1960.

Melzack, R., & Scott, T. H. The effects of early experience on the response to pain. *J. comp. physiol. Psychol.,* 1957, 50, 155-161.

Moltz, H. Contemporary instinct theory and the fixed action pattern. *Psychol. Rev.,* 1965, 72, 27-47.

Montagu, M. F. A. Constitutional and prenatal factors in infant and child health. *Human development, selected readings.* In M. L. Haimowitz & Natalie R. Haimowitz (Eds.), New York: Crowell, 1960, 124-144.

Rosenzweig, M. R. Effects of heredity and environment on brain chemistry, brain anatomy, and learning ability in the rat. Paper read at Kansas Symposium on Physiological Determinates of Behavior: Implications for Mental Retardation, Univer. of Kansas, June 4-5, 1963.

Simon, C. W., & Emmons, W. H. Responses to material presented during various levels of sleep. *J. exp. Psychol.,* 1956, 51, 89-97.

Suda, I., Adachi, C., & Kito, K. Variability of long term frozen cat brain. *Nature,* 1966, 268-270.

Tryon, R. C. Genetic differences in maze learning in rats. *Thirty-ninth-yearbook of the National Society for the Study of Education,* Part I. Bloomington, Ill.: Public School Pub. 1940, 111-119.

Underwood, B. J., Cotton, J. W., Duncan, C. P., & Taylor, J. A. *Elementary Statistics.* New York: Appleton-Century-Crofts, 1954.

Watson, J. B., & Rayner, Rosalie. Conditioned emotional reactions. *J. exp. Psychol.* 1921, 3, 1-14.

Mediation and Language 3

Overview

The S → O → R model was expanded in Chapter 2 to account for a number of research findings. Sensory input was separated into two components: 1) stimulation of the cortex by way of the Specific Projection System (SPS), and 2) stimulation via the Non-Specific Projection System (NPS). SPS transmission excites specific areas of the brain and provides the cue function for the person. Neural transmission via the NPS leads to widespread cortical stimulation and seems to control the level of arousal of the person. Since the person (organism) apparently acquires new responses as a result of action, the term residual (rs) was added to the model. Residual means that the individual has acquired a new potential response to stimuli as a result of some experience. For example, offer an infant a bar of soap, and he will likely put it into his mouth. Now offer it to him again — he will likely push it away. He has learned something. (Of course some children require more than one experience to acquire this response.) Figure 3.1 represents the summary model presented in Chapter 2.

FIGURE 3.1

An S → O → R model that includes an arousal factor and residuals (rs) of experience (inferred learnings).

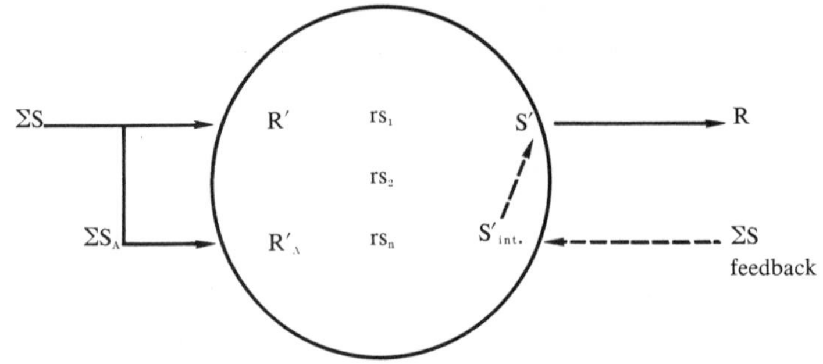

ΣS = sum of effective stimuli impinging upon the organism (e.g., excitation of rods and cones, patterned sound waves, etc.).

ΣS_A = energy from afferents branched off through the Recticular Formation.

R' = excitation of cortex from SPS.

R'_A = excitation of cortex from NPS (arousal).

rs_1, rs_2, . . . rs_n = residuals of experience that modify the organism's response potential.

S' = stimuli from the motor cortex leading to the specific motor areas and eliciting the response of the organism.

S'_{int} = stimuli from cortex transmitted by descending NPS and controlling the intensity of the response.

R = response of the organism:
affective — visceral changes within the organism.
expressive — facial gestures, exclamation, etc.
instrumental — sequential behavior such as problem solving, etc.

ΣS feedback = proprioceptive feedback from muscles, tendons, and joints that play some role in sequential behavior.

The present chapter focuses upon how the individual changes as a result of experiences (the acquisition of rs). If one observes a baby exploring his crib, room, toys, home, etc., it becomes obvious that he acquires different responses to different things. He shakes rattles, bounces balls, cuddles toys, unrolls toilet paper, and avoids hot stoves (if burned previously). In less behavioristic terms, one can say that these objects have some meaning to the child. The shaking rattle produces sound that has some pleasant meaning to the child. Conversely, the hot stove means pain. Figure 3.2 presents in a crude way the process of the acquisition of meaning (rs) regarding a rattle. Note that the ΣS_A (sum of stimuli arousal) has been deleted from the S → O → R model. All figures presented in this chapter will assume arousal in order to focus upon the relevant response acquisition.

FIGURE 3.2

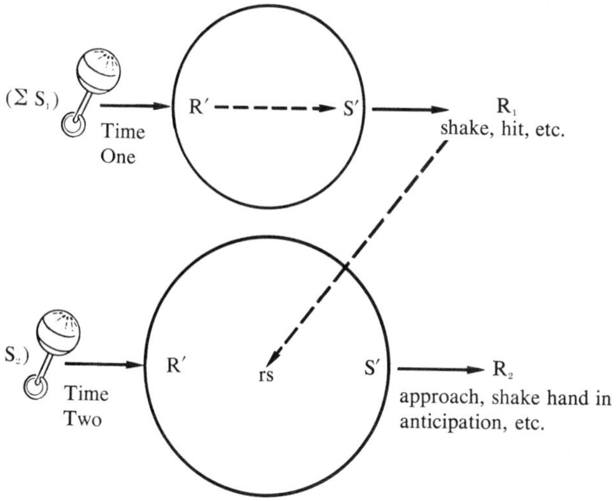

rs = the meaning acquired from experience at time one (fun, nice sound, good to shake, etc.).

Since school related behavior is often initiated not by objects but by symbols (language), the largest proportion of this chapter relates to language acquisition and usage. A central notion, that language has greatly extended man's ability to survive and that it can also add to his survival problems, is presented. The contemporary racial problem in the U.S. is a prime example of language usage having an adverse effect upon man's coping ability. Most of the illustrations we present regarding faulty language usage center around the racial problem because it is likely to be with us for decades. A number of devices are presented with the view that the reader may wish to use them in an attempt to minimize the adverse effect of faulty language usage in classroom teaching.

Another major educational problem is that children from "culturally deprived" homes tend to fail in school, drop out, and produce more "culturally deprived" children. A number of studies are reported which indicate that poverty as such does not lead to "cultural deprivation." Apparently, the language these children are exposed to is limited. The rigid symbol system is not adequate for the child to extract meaning from the complex language that the typical teacher uses. Several suggestions related to classroom teaching are presented which were taken from the work of "readiness center" programs. These programs were designed to provide the necessary background (rs's) so the "deprived" child could understand his teacher.

Glossary

Please lcok over these terms before continuing.

abstract: the ability to comprehend relationships and to react, not merely to concrete objects, but to concepts and unusual symbols.

adaptive behavior: behavior which pertains to improvement or aids in adjustment.

alternate forms: term for collection of test items so similar in content and structure to another collection, that the two are regarded, not as different tests, but as versions or variant forms of the same test.

aggressive: characterized by hostile action; action that causes fear or flight or brings the aggressor into forceful contact with another.

attitude scale: an instrument for eliciting from the person indications of the attitudes or opinions held; a number of statements represents different degrees of strength of the attitude.

causal relationship: a basic relationship in which a particular class of phenomena invariably precedes and is invariably followed by any of a certain other class of phenomena.

central neural processes: the operations of neurons in the brain and spinal cord.

concept: the idea that represents a number of individual instances, all of which are assumed to have something in common.

conceptualization: the process of inventing the appropriate notions that will put a group of facts into a useful order; or the ordering of data by means of concepts.

discrimination: the process of detecting differences in objects.

distortion: a twisting of statements or ideas, knowingly or unknowingly, so that they are not faithful to fact or to the statements upon which they are ostensibly based.

encoding: process by which a message is transformed into signals that can be carried by a communication channel (such as speech and writing in the human organism).

environment: the sum of the external conditions and factors potentially capable of influencing an organism.

expressive behavior: observable changes in expression and posture which indicate some internal state of the individual (smiling, frowning, slouching, etc.).

generalization: applying the acquired meaning of one object to another object that is seen by the person to be very similar. For example, "I like the students I have taught, therefore I like all students."

heredity: the totality of influence, biologically transmitted from parents, that in part determines the ways in which an individual will make use of his environment.

imitation: action that copies the action of another more or less exactly with or without intent to copy.

inhibition: withholding a response as a result of some mediational process, i.e., fear of punishment often inhibits a response.

input: the energy entering a system from without. In psychology, the stimulus.

isomorphic: having similar or identical structure or appearance.

intercorrelation: this value reflects the degree to which two variables vary systematically.

linguistic sign: a word that is associated with an object or act. The word "chair" is a linguistic sign, if the word has meaning. The light waves reflected by a chair would be called here a perceptual sign.

mediational processes: thinking or cognitive processes which intervene between S (stimulus) and R (response).

mnemonic: helping to improve memory.

noun referent: the object referred to by a noun.

output: that which, or the amount of that which, an organism produces in a given length of time.

perceptual sign: an object which has acquired meaning as a result of the individual's acting upon the object. For example, as a result of bottle sucking the visual presentation of a bottle to an infant often elicits sucking. The visual object has meaning to the child (see linguistic sign).

perfect negative relationship: such relation between two variables that any change in one is exactly paralleled by an opposite change in the other: correlation = −1.00.

perfect positive relationship: such relation between two variables that any change in one is exactly paralleled by a change in the other: correlation = +1.00.

process: the manner in which change is affected; a change or changing in an object or organism in which a consistent quality or direction can be discerned.

proprioceptor: any receptor sensitive to the position and movement of the body and its members, i.e., in inner ear, muscles, joints.

psychobiological: pertaining to both mind and body processes.

psychosomatic: pertaining to the interacting nature of man's cerebral processes with other physiological processes.

residual: the part remaining of certain events or after certain operations have been performed.

scales: any device for determining the magnitude or quantity of an object or event of any sort.

syntax: sentence structure; the due arrangement of word forms to show their mutual relations in the sentence.

taboo words: a solemn social prohibition of word, or social prohibition with irrational support and rather drastic penalties.

vascular orientating reactions, VOR: reactions occurring as a result of changes in the constriction and dilation of blood vessels.

vector: in regression analysis, an ordered set of numbers by rows or columns.

visceral behavior: changes in the organ system and vascular reaction due to stimulation (both external and internal).

Acquisition of Meaning

In the preceding chapter the assumption was made that the human is attempting to cope with his universe. By means of repeated associations of responses with stimulus objects in the universe, meanings and prediction of outcomes are acquired. These meanings lead to some control over the universe. In one sense, the residuals (changes in the organism as a result of stimulation) have some degree of correspondence to the outside world. The notion of *generalization* was introduced and illustrated by the case of the white rabbit and the white beard activating similar responses.

Discriminations are acquired when the response results in unpredicted feedback. To illustrate, repeated association with a docile cat may lead to formation of residuals from previous responses (rs) such that all furry four-legged objects elicit approach and fondling behavior (a complex set of responses) from the human. Subsequent contact with an aggressive tomcat theoretically results in the formation of competing residuals which inhibit the approach response, and facilitate orienting responses (the known is now the unknown — "What is it?"). These interactions result in stimulus cat (ΣS_c) activating two or more sets of residuals which lead to the seeking of more information that may bring about the acquisition of appropriate responses: ΣS_{c_1} = cat, docile →

approach; or ΣS_{c_2} = cat, aggressive → avoid. The light waves reflected by the furry animal may be associated with sound waves, snarling or purring, and two or more residuals (fractions of previous total responses) might be formed which lead to differential responses. The previously single class ΣS_c, now is refined into two subclasses, ΣS_{c_1} and ΣS_{c_2}, each with corresponding residuals.

To be sure, the illustration might not be entirely appropriate, for the discrimination between friendly and hostile animals is often difficult for children to establish.

Acquired residuals have a tremendous impact upon the organism's ability to cope with an originally unpredictable universe. The pairing of stimulus redundancies with central neural processes and the discrimination of subclasses leads to the acquisition of versatile adaptive behaviors. In Charles Osgood's (1957) language, the originally meaningless stimulus now becomes a *perceptual sign* of meaning associated with an appropriate response potential.

Our discussion to this point has emphasized the "stimulus boundness" of behavior. The emphasis has been on the cue function. Once established, the residuals may be run off in imagery and not solely by the specific cue function (e.g., dreams by humans and apparently by other organisms, such as dogs, with less complex central neural processes).

Acquisition of Linguistic Signs

The acquisition of language adds tremendously to the organism's potential coping ability, for his control processes are more liberated from the concrete impinging universe. The *perceptual sign* by necessity has some physical relation to the object while the *linguistic sign* is arbitrary. (As we shall see later, language can lead to new difficulties in coping with the environment also.)

Figure 3.3 schematically reviews the acquisition of meaning as a result of repeated contact with the "real" world (acquisition of *perceptual* signs).

Subsequent contact with the acquired perceptual sign (e.g., the rattle) often may be paired with sound waves emitted by a caretaker (mother, father, nurse, etc.). The sound (in the illustrated case, that noise resembling the word "rattle") as a result of this pairing activates some part of the central mediational process associated with the perceptual sign (ΣS_3, the rattle itself). (See Figure 3.4.)

These mediational processes are generalized through numerous subsequent interactions to develop object classes. A number of stimulus objects come to activate common residuals, and one can designate these

FIGURE 3.3

Acquisition of meaning as a result of previous behavior

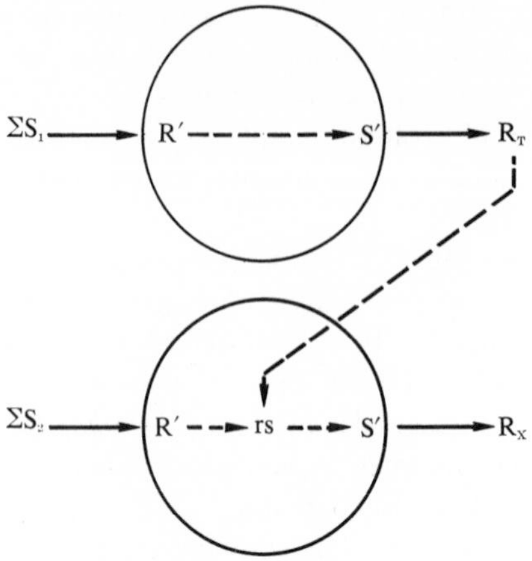

ΣS_1 = light waves reflected by a rattle.
R′ = activation of central sensory processes.
S′ = activation of central motor processes.
R_T = investigatory and manipulatory activities.
rs = some fractional part of R_T (meaning).
ΣS_2 = subsequent presentation of light waves reflected by rattle (perceptual sign).
R_X = responses determined to a degree by the meaning (rs) of rattle acquired in previous contact.

classes as a concept (e.g., "rattleness"). Also as a consequence of verbal interaction, discriminations are acquired. Although a piggy bank rattles, parents will pair the word "bank" with the stimulus pattern of the object and also an alternate activity to be related to the bank (e.g., inserting coins into the slot).

Since words are associated with a broad number of situations, meanings acquire rather complex sets of interacting residuals. To some degree the exact response residual to a linguistic sign (word) might differ from person to person, depending upon previous response patterns interacting with differing organic histories (Factors I-IV; see Chapter 2).

Two children may have the concept of "chairness." One may have been exposed to specific objects such as provincial maple chairs and acquired the meaning that a "real" chair should have a warm texture. The other child, the son of a furniture designer, may have been exposed to a wide variety of chairs and verbally instructed to note lines, configurations, etc. If these two children attend an exhibit displaying modern furniture, the son of the designer might exclaim, "My, that is an exquisite chair!" The less "sophisticated" child may reply, "That's a chair? Gad, that is *not* a chair — that's a monstrosity."

FIGURE 3.4

Acquisition of linguistic signs

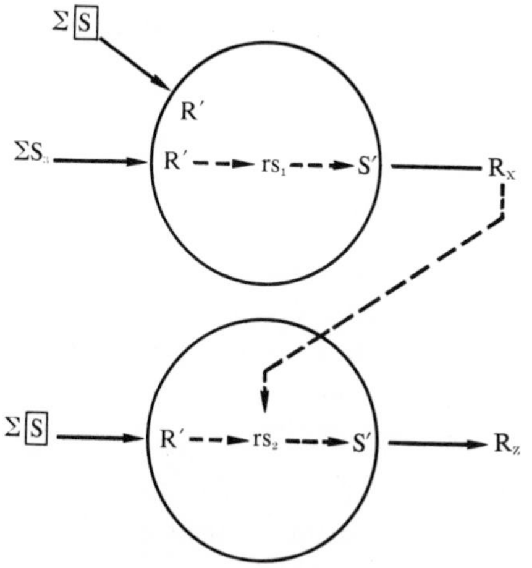

Σ S = vocalized noise by parent — "rattle" (linguistic sign).

ΣS_3 = light waves reflected by rattle.

rs_2 = fractional part of previous response to rattle (meaning) although not necessarily the same as rs_1, for the spatial location of the object is indeterminate.

The meanings of linguistic signs and perceptual signs might bear no resemblance to the real world. We shall return to this area following a brief excursion into the work of some Russian psychologists.

Meaning and the Orienting Reaction

For mnemonic purposes, responses in Chapter 2 were grouped into three categories: (1) affective (body changes), (2) expressive (smiles, etc.) and (3) instrumental (goal directed behavior). We have discussed meaning in relation to expressive responses and have indicated a number of instrumental responses. Luria and Vinogradova (1959) reported a series of interesting findings regarding vascular orienting reactions (affective responses) to words. A number of vascular response patterns to stimulation have been noted by Russian researchers, but for present purposes the vascular orienting response shall be discussed. The *vascular orienting response* (VOR) includes vascular digital *constriction* (finger) and vascular *dilation* in the forehead. These responses are found when novel verbal stimuli are presented to the subject. Conceptually, one might call the VOR a "What is it?" response. This response is also found when a person carries out an instrumental response following a key word. One of Luria's studies using VOR follows.

> Ten school children, 11 to 15 years of age, classified as "normal" in intellective functions, were instructed to press a button when they heard the word *koshka* (cat). Following a number of pairings of the word *koshka* with the button pushing, the vascular orienting response was consistently found. Subsequently, vascular orienting reactions were consistently elicited by presentation of the word *koshka itself,* without button pressing required. Apparently the orienting reactions had been conditioned to the word *koshka.* To investigate the transfer effects of this conditioning, a large number of words semantically or phonetographically (words that sound alike) related to *koshka* as well as neutral words were presented verbally to the children. Among these "normal" children the vascular orienting reaction transferred only to the semantically related words. The transfer was not to the similar stimulus characteristics of words (phonetographic) but to the words similar in meaning to the conditioned word (*koshka*).

These findings are consistent with the previous discussion regarding the acquisition of meaning. Perceptual signs paired with words produce linguistic signs. The meaning of the linguistic sign is some fractional part of the organism's previous responses to the sign. Subsequent pairings of linguistic signs build up some overlap of meanings (e.g., a lion is a member of the cat family, etc.). Indeed, these data suggest that one can map rather directly the prepotent meanings of concepts held by various individuals.

Data reported by Luria and Vinogradova regarding 13- to 17-year-old, feeble-minded children presents a different picture. Severely feeble-minded children emitted the vascular orienting transfer only to phonetographic words (words that sound like *koshka*). Moderately feeble-minded children emitted the vascular transfer to some semantically related words and also to some phonetographically related words.

These data are of importance for they support the position presented earlier that findings and treatments should take into account the variability of the nurtured organism. Among "normally" intelligent subjects, responses to verbal stimuli are a function of the central mediational (semantic) processes. Among the severely feeble-minded, whose central mediational processes theoretically are severely restricted, the response appears dependent upon the similarity in sound of the stimulus properties. (Is this due to a lack of elaborate and complex associations among the feeble-minded?)

Tangential Implications for Research

The work of these Russian psychologists has tremendous potential for problems that American educational psychologists deem significant. Specifically, the area of attitude assessment might fruitfully employ vascular orienting responses. Prediction of subsequent school behavior from attitude scales has in general produced moderate success at best. Some of this lack of success among older children is due to the fact that paper and pencil tests can be faked by an "intelligent" subject. Measurement of vascular reaction might provide a subtle quantified response pattern which would overcome many of the weaknesses of paper and pencil inventories.

Acquisition of Semantic Distortion

Pairing of linguistic signs with stimulus complexes (perceptual signs) results in the activation of meaning (rs) through the use of words. Under these circumstances, although some distortion might result, the word has some isomorphic meaning in a "real" world. When, however, new linguistic signs are paired with previously established linguistic signs, the distance between the world as referent and the new sign is theoretically greater. The *probability* of inadequately coping with a situation is increased when meaning is acquired through higher-order word pairing.

Linguistic Sign → Perceptual Sign: Distortion due to faulty application of linguistic signs to perceptual signs usually results from overgeneralization. A child surprised by the exuberance of a large dog might acquire an avoidance response to all dogs. The meaning of "dog" in this instance includes some fractional part of the previous avoidance response. The importance of this distortion of "reality" is basically inconsequential. Discrimination can be achieved through contact with small, docile dogs and thus new meanings (fractional parts of subsequent responses) regarding "dog" can be made. On the other hand, severe destructive contact with a vicious, biting dog might result in an extremely potent threat meaning which precludes approach responses and thus discrimination. Some may call this response an "irrational fear" since this meaning of "dog" is contrary to their own finely discriminated meanings of "dog." Nevertheless, the fear is rational in terms of the meaning structure of the person who interacted with the vicious dog.

Racial stereotyping can also be acquired through one highly negative interaction with a member of a specific race. Such an experience might prevent the person from differentiating individuals and thus responding only to the skin color or some other obvious physical characteristic of the perceptual sign. Translated into linguistic signs, the person may say, "Negroes are filthy, vicious, stupid people." Subsequent contact with Negroes will not modify the stereotype if the experience was traumatic, for no positive approach action would probably be carried out and thus no new positive fractional response (rs) could be acquired. Distortion of the universe due to faulty generalization in the area of race relations can have grave consequences, for that "stupid nigger" might use his intelligence to foment revolution, initiate economic blockade, etc., which may grossly disturb the world of the person entertaining the distorted view.

The late Dr. Martin Luther King, Jr. told a story which is illustrative:

> A six-foot-two, 250-pound, muscular Negro entered the bus and put his money into the box. The bus driver said, "Hey, boy, get to the back of the bus." The Negro walked up to the bus driver, looked him in the eye, and said, "Mister, you just made two mistakes. First, I am not a boy, and second, I am not one of those non-violent Negroes."

Linguistic Sign → Linguistic Sign: Pairing of two linguistic signs in a noun-adjectival sense provides a means of establishing rather broad, complex meanings and a means of representing distinguishing discriminations. "Please bring me the green, flowered vase," is a differentiated concept of vase but causes little difficulty, for there is a "real" world referent which can be checked. Distortion through word pairing is often acquired during early verbal learning. Words such as "good," and "nice" have some meaning associated with positive responses in the past. Parents might say, "Mr. Jones is a very *nice* man." Subsequent discussion might develop relating to "Mr. Jones" which means to the child (as a result of previous pairing) "the nice man," and positive responses are elicited. This acquired meaning is independent of previous responses to the perceptual sign, "Mr. Jones" (the physical entity). The acquired pairing might or might not lead to adequate prediction of Mr. Jones' behavior when direct contact is made, and unless Mr. Jones is a sexual child molester, this type of word pairing might be of little consequence.

There is a broad area of social contact where word pairing, not necessarily intentionally taught, has serious consequences for adapting to a "real" world. The pairing of "dirty" with "nigger," "no-good" with "Jew," and "vicious" with "communist" in home discussions may leave a residual of meaning which might prove deadly. As a result of this pairing, subsequent interpersonal contact with the noun referent (Negro, Jew, or communist) will likely activate an avoidant or aggressive response. On the playground Negro children might be avoided, for some meaning is previously assigned to the stimuli "Negro" (e.g., "Negroes are dirty and stink," → unpleasant stimuli → avoid). Radke *et al.* (1949) discussed in detail changes from simple imitation of parents' anti-Negro verbalizations to the final acceptance of these verbalizations into the child's meaning structure. According to Radke, very few of the verbalized meanings of "Negro" represent over-generalization from one concrete negative experience. In most cases the statements represent "indirect experience" (e.g., pairing of linguistic signs). If we disregard the personal "feelings" of out-groups (e.g., Negroes) and examine the effects of linguistic sign distortions, we may be able to consider the maladaptive consequences of such distortions. Avoidance of Negroes because "they are dirty" prevents discriminations based upon direct experience.*

In relation to linguistic sign distortions, all is well as long as the Negro is spatially distant. When he moves next door, all is not well. A number of actions can be taken, depending upon the individual's learned response potential. Legal activity, cross-burning, bomb-throwing or moving out are possible reactions. If the avoidance reaction is *not* great, casual contact with the neighbor may elicit a few mild positive social responses (e.g., "Good Morning" — "Good Morning," etc.). Some fractional part of these social responses are also part of the meaning "Negro." Further contact might lead to discriminations such as, "This Negro is not bad at all." Of course, if the avoidance reaction is strong, social contact might elicit prepotent avoidance responses, with little further opportunity for differentiating Negro behavior.

The failure to discriminate can lead to revolution on the part of the out-group and thus add coping problems for the in-group — a situation

*In context of the present discussion, *discrimination* refers to response to more than one aspect of the stimuli. In a sense, the individual attends to unique or subclass characteristics as well as the class characteristic ("discrimination" is a technical psychological term). "Discrimination" used in common language (e.g., "racial discrimination") refers to negative actions taken against a class of individuals. Ironically, the common language use of "discrimination" is the obverse of the psychological application of the term, for "racial discrimination" represents a failure to notice unique individual characteristics within the class. "Negro" is *discriminated* (psychological use) as not "white" and investigation of the stimuli ceases.

initiated primarily by distorted mediational processes. Conversely, the meaning of "Negro" as a noble, long-suffering race can lead to coping problems, for an overall non-discriminated positive response to a specific Negro might be inappropriate — apparently some Negroes *are* dirty and dangerous, just as are some "whites."

Summary Note: Apparently distortions come from (1) overgeneralizations from direct experience, (2) the pairing of words without direct experience, and (3) different meanings for the same word.

Distortion in the Educational Process

Each school day across the nation, millions of children perform a solemn rite. With hand over heart these children say:

> I pledge allegiance to the flag of the United States of America and to the Republic for which it stands; one nation, under God, indivisible, with liberty and justice for all.

Is such an act developing discrimination and the ability to notice differences? No. Is the content of the pledge true (corresponding to "reality")? Ask the Negro in Selma, Birmingham, or Harlem. The pledge might be a noble statement of *ideal,* but as presented in rote, this distinction is not specified. Logically, if justice is for all, then bombings of churches without prosecution of the offenders must be justice. Tacitly, the Negro churches must have done something wrong.

History courses which fail to detail past misadventures of American international policy (e.g., Nineteenth Century Dollar-Diplomacy) are providing meanings which are distorted through omission. The problems of capitalism in the 1930's (bread lines, etc.) and the hysteria and guilt found in the early 1950's when a person was called a communist if he knew a communist are also historical "realities" which add to a somewhat isomorphic concept of America. Often meanings of this nature are omitted for they are controversial or even "unpatriotic." Yet, if we assume accurate perception to be an aim of education, then these meanings should be attached to "America."

The school personnel often reinforce word magic initiated in the home. "Son of a bitch," "bastard," and the good old Anglo-Saxon word meaning punching seeds into the ground elicit teacher responses which can be amusing. Why are these words such a threat? If a student called you, a teacher, "a male progeny of a female dog," would this merit his expulsion from school? Likely not. However, to be called "a son of a bitch" is *horrible,* and would demand punitive action. Little children learn to say, "Sticks and stones may break my bones but words will never harm me." Yet this is for the faint of heart, for grown men fight to rebuff the name-caller, and adult school administrators expel children from school for using "vulgar" (?) words. Indeed, verbal accusations related to matters of fact may call for evidence to refute the accusation. To be called a "thief" is a matter that calls for evidence, and protestation of innocence might be an appropriate response. To be called a "bastard" does not call for the presentation of a birth certificate as contrary evidence. Evidently, the latter use of words must carry some subtle meaning. One can speculate that past response associations with this class of linguistic signs ("vulgar" words) has been avoidant in nature. Some "vulgar" words (e.g., "damn") result in mild avoidance responses and others (e.g., "son of a bitch") result in extreme avoidance responses.

A Suggestion for Future Teachers

It is quite possible that during your tenure as a teacher you might be called a "bastard" or some other such term. Further, if you are a typical "nice" person, your probable response will be to automatically rebuff and chastize. Under these conditions, who is controlling whom? We suggest that the child as the stimulus object would be controlling you. If we examine the conditions which lead to the labelling act, the meaning underlying the student's action might emerge. A translation of "You are a bastard," might be:

> Teacher, I want to do this, but you say, "No." You are on my back every time I turn around. Mr. Teacher, you (as a perceptual sign) recall all kinds of things I hate (unpleasant responses). I don't like you, etc.

If this is what the child means, expelling him from school will prevent a reoccurrence of this act at school, but the expulsion probably will not lead to discrimination learning. As a first step, you may wish to extinguish your avoidance reaction to "vulgar" words. Ask a few of your friends to call you by these words in pleasant surroundings. Or get a child with the appropriate vocabulary to tape a few choice comments and play them while you drink your beer or coke in the evening. Unless your reaction to these words is psychotically aberrant, you should be able to inhibit uncontrolled reaction, and the opportunity to investigate the antecedents to the child's action can be exploited.

These recommendations are extrapolations from theory. Due to the ruling force of "moral" people, investigation by psychologists into taboo areas is extremely difficult to carry out. Many middle-class social agents in charge of school operations would object to a procedure whereby the student is exposed to "vulgar" words in order that the psychologist may conduct extinguishing experiments.

Considerations of Syntax

Although semantic considerations have been discussed, most message units processed in adult life occur within a grammatical structure (the sentence). We acquire linguistic signs *and* language structure. In the following sentence you can predict the type of word which is missing, and many can insert the appropriate word. "He ________ to the show." The missing word is of course a verb of some sort, and the particular word that the authors have deleted is "went." According to Benjamin Lee Whorf (1956), the linguistic syntax varies among language groups. The Indo-European language, of which English is a sub-class, basically differentiates the world into things and events (nouns and verbs). We have a bi-polar division of the universe, and apparently this bi-polarity is arbitrary. In the past (and unfortunately in some cases in the present), teachers defined a noun to be "a person, place, or thing," and a verb as "a word which represents action."*

The bi-polar view of the universe, Whorf contends, determines to a degree the direction of our thoughts. For example, we classify "run," "throw," "ride," etc., as verbs and not as things. On the other hand, "wave," "cycle," and "lightning," (short term events) are classified as nouns, and thus we think of these events as nouns (things). According to Whorf, English *arbitrarily* divides the universe into things and events. An event is an action because we call it an action. In contrast to our arbitrary bi-polarization, the Hopi Indians bi-polarize in terms of duration. A cloud represents about the shortest duration for a noun. Anything shorter in duration is a verb. Thus, "fist," "lap," "lightening," and "cycle" are verbs in the Hopi language structure. Close your hand to make a fist. Look at it. How would you describe it? In English you would probably say "That is a *fist*" (a noun). The Hopi would say, "I am fisting" (a verb). This illustration *means* we see a fist as being passive whereas the Hopi interpret a fist to be active.

---

*A number of linguists advocate a structural approach to language. Within the structural framework, a noun is "a word used as a subject or as an object." Thus, a set is provided which stresses the notion that words are abstractions and that they may play different roles under alternate conceptual conditions. Indeed, this approach is not "rule-bound," but "process-bound."

The bi-polarization of thought imposed by the subject-predicate grammar leads to three laws of thought given by Jevons (1883):

1. The law of identity (Whatever is, is).
2. The law of contradiction (Nothing can both be and not be).
3. The law of the excluded third (Everything must be, or not be).

The second and third laws are restatements of the first law. In western man's thought processes, the basic law of identity leads us to an either/or resolution of questions. For example, if one says, "Bill 'is' a communist," we look at Bill to determine whether he is or is not a communist. Either he is or he isn't. Our language does not allow him to be both. A significant point can be raised regarding this example. When the statement is made, we look at Bill to see if he has the awful disease rather than looking at the person who made the statement. When a neuro-evaluational-organism (man) abstracts a number of behaviors and affixes a linguistic sign to these behaviors, he is stressing similarities and non-consciously neglecting differences. Such abstracting is not in itself dangerous, but the failure to recognize that we are abstracting can be.

To restate, the law of identity inherent in our Indo-European language structure leads to a stress upon noting similarities and a neglecting of differences. We see the world in over-simplified terms (discrimination is poor). This static picture of the universe is not in keeping with the modern notion of a universe "in process."

If the universe is "in process," then a failure to realize the distortion imposed by a bi-polarized language can unduly limit our conceptual processes. A number of changes have been introduced into our language which seem to affect the either/or problem (Byrnes, 1961). "Finalize" and "businesswise" are two examples. (Purists in language lament these developments.) "Finalize" is an attempt to account for the process involved in the act of making something final.

Indo-European linguistic classifications cause some difficulty in the field of psychology for we have "child psychology" and "adolescent psychology." The problem of bi-polarity of course is encountered when a distinction between the two classes is required. Man apparently develops from dust into dust, in a continuous process. When is a child an adolescent? A perusal of textbooks in these two areas reveals a great redundancy in subject matter which reflects the arbitrary nature of these classifications. A recent trend in psychology has been to deal with "the individual in the life cycle."

The language of set theory can add a degree of flexibility to our thinking. Korzybski (1951, pp. 186-187) illustrated this possibility with an example using apples. If two apples were before us, we would perceive them to be "touching" or "not touching." Through our habitual acts of thought, we tend to evaluate on a gross level. At a submicroscopic level the question is not "touch" or "not touch," but a matter of the number of electrons shared by the two objects (see Figure 3.5). We shall note Korzybski's solution to the problem of bi-polarity in the next section.

FIGURE 3.5

Macroscopic view and submicroscopic process level of two apples, side by side.

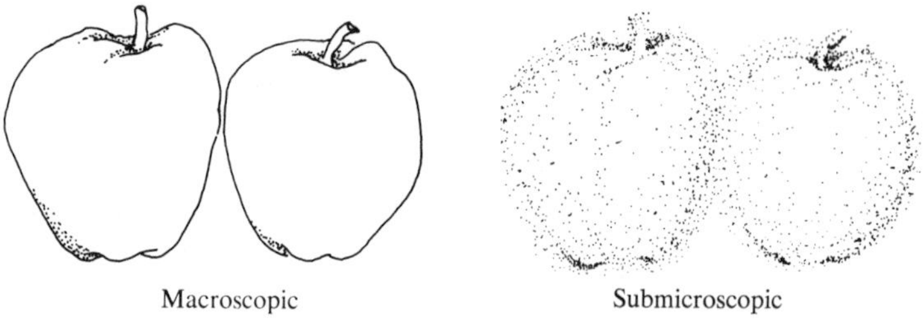

Taken from Korzybski, Alfred, "The Role of Language in the Perceptual Processes," Blake, R. R. and Ramsey, G. V., eds., *Perception — An Approach to Personality*. New York: Ronald Press, 1951.

The law of identity within the Indo-European language is most prevalent in the use of the verb "to be." Bertrand Russell (1903) identified four different uses of the verb:

1. as an auxiliary verb: It *is* raining.
2. as the "is" of existence: I *am*.
3. as the "is" of predication: The rose *is* red.
4. as the "is" of identity: The rose *is* a flower.

Korzybski (1951) indicated that the first two uses of the verb "to be" are difficult to avoid and are relatively harmless. The third use, the "is" of predication as in "The rose is red" apparently is contrary to what we now "know" about the universe. In our previous discussion regarding the acquisition of meaning, we emphasized the point that the perceptual sign is *not* the object; it is the light waves mediated by the neural organism. The rose is *not red;* it is a part of the universe and thus redness it *not* a quality of the flower, but an abstraction entertained by the central neural processes. An appropriate statement can be "I see the rose as red." Now the statement places red as an internal process of man and not as an attribute of the universe. If man were color blind he would see the rose as grey.

The "is" of identity as in "Bill *is* a communist" can be restated, "I classify Bill as a communist." Now we do not look at Bill. We look instead at the classifier and ask, "What behavioral characteristics are you grouping together?"

Vigotsky (1939) reported work with preschool children which indicated that children tended to view the name of an object to be an attribute of the object. The children were given new names for familiar objects, and then they were asked questions about the objects to which the new names were applied. In one interview the child was told to call a dog by the name "cow."

> Exp: "Has a cow horns?"
> Child: "Yes, it has."
> Exp: "But the 'cow' is really a dog."
> Child: "Of course, if a dog is a cow, if it is called a cow, then there must be horns. Such a dog which is called cow must have little horns."

Vigotsky also suggested that poorly-educated peasants as well as children retained the concept that words are attributes of the objects.

Such reports as these suggest that during the process of linguistic sign acquisition, little differentiation is being made between the perceptual sign and the linguistic sign. If adults use words as attributes of the objects, then apparently something other than age is intervening. Can this be a result of a misuse of the verb "to be" in which the neuro-evaluational aspect of the sign application is ignored?

If in fact classroom instruction is intended to develop critical thinking, it seems imperative that more importance be placed on verb usages. If a student is not made aware of the object to be observed, then the requirement of observation seems vague and perhaps unnecessary. Many problem situations would be less complex if the instructor and the student were precise in their communication. For example, how can one identify traits of a communist when the object should be to identify the traits the *accuser* holds as characteristic of a communist?

Extensional Devices

In an attempt to update our language from the elementalistic Aristotelian thinking habitually applied today, Korzybski (1951, p. 190) identified a number of extensional devices. As a preface to his devices he states:

> The degrees to which we are "conscious of abstracting," . . . becomes a key problem in the way we evaluate and therefore to a large extent may affect the way in which we "perceive." If we can devise methods to increase our "consciousness of abstracting," this would eventually free us from the archaic, prescientific, and/or Aristotelian limitations inherent in the older language structures. The following structural expedients to achieve this I call the *extensional devices,* and the application of them automatically brings about an orientation in conformity with the latest scientific assumptions.

Korzybski's last statement seems to be a bit strong, but let us withhold final judgment.

The present chapter has raised questions regarding distortions due to over-generalization, acquisition of meaning through linguistic sign pairing (indirect experience), and bi-polarization of the universe into things and events. In the following discussion let us see if Korzybski's devices moderate these distortions.

The devices:

1. *Indexing,* as in x_1, x_2 . . . x_n; chair_1, chair_2, . . . chair_n; Negro_1, Negro_2, . . . Negro_n. Indexing produces a proper name for each member of a generic class. The application of indexing stresses the fact that each individual is unique and that the classification is a neuro-evaluational act. The intent of indexing is to encourage caution in the generalization process. Indexing, as a device, retains the value of classification, but can increase the individual's awareness of the fact that he is constructing the classification.
2. *Chain-indexes,* as in chair_{1_1} (in a dry attic), chair_{1_2} (in a burned-down house); Negro_{1_1} (at home with his family), Negro_{1_2} (at work). Our modern (1969) world is a world of process; "cause-effect" chain reactions operate. Chain-indexes may linguistically provide a representation of these processes. The environmental conditions with which any object interacts determine to a large extent the meaning of the object. John Jones_{1_1} (a particular individual at church) and John Jones_{1_2} (the same individual at a fraternity "beer-bust") are two different individuals as a result of the interacting conditions. More specifically, John Jones_1 is a sum total of his response repertory. He can be both the pious young man (condition 1) and the sly young rogue (condition 2). Each *evaluation* of John is an *abstraction* from noting his behavior under specific *conditions.* The use of chain-indexing can also pro-

vide some moderation of the difficulties inherent in the use of the *is* of identity.

3. *Dates,* as in John $Jones_1^{1960}$, John $Jones_1^{1965}$, . . . John $Jones_1^{t}$ (t = time). The use of dates provides for the four-dimensional world of process, yet retains the value of arresting the process for purposes of communication, analysis, clarity, etc. We date and index our automobiles (e.g., 1964 Ford, license CAT007), but often fail to date our ideas, theories, friends, etc. Psychological journals are generously interspersed with names and dates. Scientists use dating devices to code ideas, and also to permit review of methodology. For example, Korzybski discussed the "misuse" of words such as "modern." In the *Communist Manifesto* (1848), "modern" is frequently used. The unwary reader may interpret this as "$modern^{1969}$" rather than the appropriate "$modern^{1848}$." Korzybski suggested that the reader write in by hand the appropriate date, as we have done here. Textbooks in the sciences often are out-dated within a few years, yet the unsuspecting reader may fail to realize this fact. A simple, habitual check of the copyright date can provide the time setting for the serious investigator. In chemistry the number of elements in 1940 was reported at 92; $today^{1969}$ more than 100 have been identified — the date of the periodic chart is significant. Likewise, with the advent of the computer, $modern^{1969}$ $psychology_1$ (American psychology) is becoming quite different from $modern^{1945}$ $psychology_1$. Many of us are aware of the failure of our close relatives to recognize change. Mother is notoriously guilty in failing to recognize that her little $baby^{1945}$ is $today^{1969}$ no longer a dependent child. Writers blessed with longevity are plagued by their early utterances. When a woman exclaimed to George Bernard Shaw, "But, Mr. Shaw, what you have just said is contrary to your statements in your essay," he is reputed to have replied, "Don't quote Shaw to me." He seemed to mean, "$Shaw^{1926}$ is dead; listen to $Shaw^{1936}$." How many of us are willing to defend our high school English themes?
4. *Etc.* Etc., as an extensional device, facilitates the awareness of the abstracting process. Words are not the things and there are an infinite number of aspects regarding "things" in the universe. Flexibility and conditionality of meaning are added with the use of "etc." A number of English instructors punish the use of "etc.," claiming the user is a "fuzzy thinker." The student should be aware of the different behavioral sets required in the academic $market^{1969}$.
5. *Quotes,* used to designate metaphysical or elementalistic terms (e.g., "mind," "soul," "emotion," "modern," "truth," etc.), put

the evaluator on guard, warning him that these terms might have no referent or that they are ill-defined.

6. *Hyphens.* The universe^{1969} is seen by modern^{1969} man to be a dynamic interacting process — the hyphenation of space-time revolutionized physics. Man is a biological animal with a complex psycho-neural apparatus: the interacting processes can be identified by the term "psycho-biological." Complex interaction sets man apart from other organisms, for the complexity permits time-binding via linguistic sign usage.

   The use of hyphens as a device can determine to a large part one's perception of the universe. Referring to "heredity *and* environment" leads to the perception of these as separate entities. "Heredity$_n$-environment$_n$," however, linguistically ties together the interacting nature of man as seen by science^{1969}. Hyphenating "psycho-somatic" stresses the interacting nature of man's cerebral processes with other physiological processes. For example, the "mental health" of a person can lead to ulcers which in turn can affect "mental health."

Implications: Frequent first reactions to Korzybski's extension devices are: (1) they are cumbersome, (2) they are simple, (3) they are not "really" new. At first glance the devices are cumbersome, and indeed, for adults the initial use of them takes time. Yes, they are simple, deceptively simple. A "knowledge" of the devices, however, does little for the individual's conceptual processes. If the devices are to aid "thought," they must become an integral part of the individual's mediational processes. Children can be taught these devices and possibly should be taught the process nature of the universe as we now^{1969} see it. Vigotski's (1939) observations regarding confusion of words as being attributes of the objects indicate possible failure in children's early training.

We do use these devices although we may not be making maximum use of the identifying terms. The indexing of cars reduces the number of inconveniences for police officers writing tickets. Yet we fail to index such things as "significant" characteristics of individuals.

Cast into terms of the model of human behavior, the devices are residuals of experience. If used, these devices can act as a "set" to process the input and utilize a greater portion of the mediators. Input-output time (S — R) theoretically would be greater with the use of extensional devices. Generalizations will require more mediation, for subclasses will be activated as well as the major classifications. Figure 3.6 represents two possible sequences, one in the presence of the extensional devices; the other without.

FIGURE 3.6

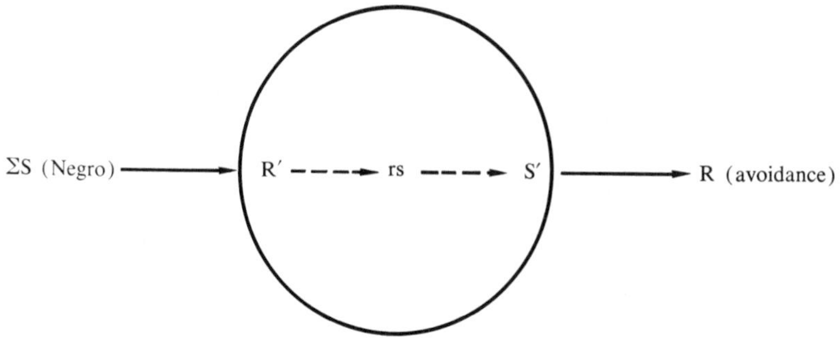

Without the set to process, "Negro," as a linguistic sign, activates the fractional part of previous total responses (Negro = dirty = stink = avoid) and may lead to overt avoidance behavior.

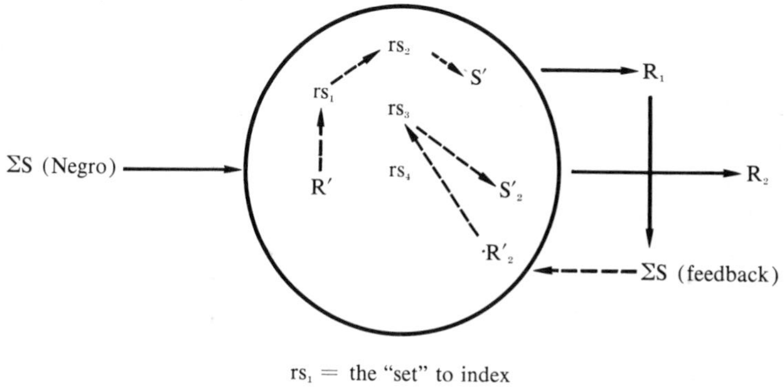

rs_1 = the "set" to index

"Negro" as a linguistic sign can activate the indexing process, rs_1, which activates a subset, rs_2, (get more information) → R_1 (orientation to look at the subject and question, "Which Negro?") → ΣS (feedback) (possibly "Dr. Ralph Bunch") → activation of rs_3 ("diplomat") → R_2 ("What about Dr. Bunch?").

We grant that these are awkward means of obtaining meaning. Yet, in the light of the gross perceptual distortions acquired by way of (1) over-generalization, (2) "faulty" word pairing, and (3) bi-polarization, the price might be right. The authors believe the cost of misperception due to the structural limitations of the language can be the over-specialization which might lead to the extinction of man. The reader is only asked to consider these matters.

Correlation

Some notion of correlation is needed to understand the following sections; therefore a brief discussion of correlation is provided at this point.

Psychologists theorize, research and write in order to develop understanding of human behavior. To most psychologists this need to understand is reinforced by a desire to predict and perhaps control human behavior. Prediction and control of human behavior suggest that knowledges of cause and effect or causal relationships have been acquired. As a result of interpretations based on statistical tests in experimental studies in psychology, some seem convinced that causal relationships have been established. To our knowledge this kind of information has not been validated in the study of human behavior.

In Chapter 2, a brief discussion of the F statistic was provided and the conclusion drawn was that one treatment was superior to the other. One might say Treatment Y caused the students to perform better on the test than those who received Treatment Z. These statements are always subject to error. Some unknown third factor might have been the determining variable. Students who received Treatment Y might have had an initially superior ability in the subject matter. Contaminating influences may at any time enter into attempts to determine causal relations and produce misleading conclusions. The knowledgeable researcher, however, attempts to anticipate contaminators and balance out these influences. The most sophisticated attempts to rule out all contaminating factors fall far short of the intended goal.

Another statistical device that deals with causal relationships is the *correlation coefficient,* which is an index representing the degree and direction with which one variable *varies* with another. Figure 3.7 shows three cases which seem to best illustrate these relationships.

Example 3.7a indicates a *perfect positive relationship* between scores on Test X and Test Y. Each of the six dots represents a person. The person who received a score of 5 on Test X received a score of 2 on Test Y. Reading across the scores on Test X you should note that an increase in X is accompanied by a constant increase in Y. A perfect positive correlation such as this is seldom found in actual research. Note "$r = +1.0$" above the diagram. The plus sign indicates that the greater the score on X, the greater the tendency to obtain a larger score on Y. The "1.0" represents the perfect relationship; thus there is not only a *tendency* to increase, there is an absolute increase. Figure 3.7(b) represents an essentially un-correlated relationship between test performances. If person_1 scores higher on Test A than person_2, no prediction of superiority or inferiority on Test B can reasonably be made.

FIGURE 3.7

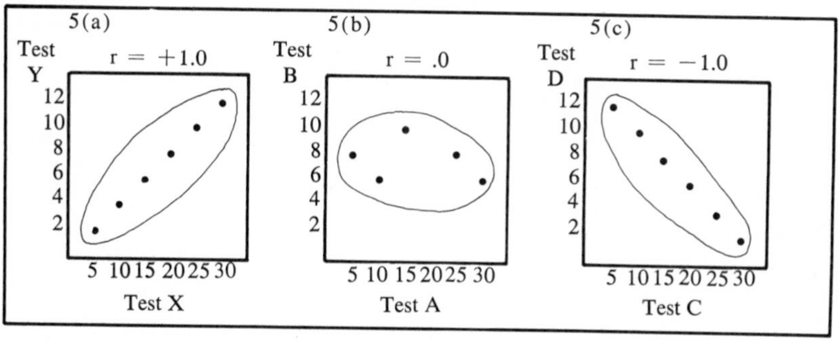

Indeed, under these conditions, the best prediction (to insure the minimum errors of prediction) for all students would be the mean score on B (see Chapter 2). Figure 3.7(c) represents a *perfect negative relationship* (r = −1.0). The sign is negative, indicating that there is a constant *decrease* on Test D performance as Test C performance increases. A perfect prediction can be made with this knowledge.

Correlation coefficients range from +1.0 through .0 to −1.0. Correlations of r = (+ or −) .20 might represent a significant departure from zero; that is, a correlation of this magnitude is very seldom found by chance. However, the predictive value is limited. The errors of prediction are significantly reduced statistically, but for practical purposes the reduction might not be of sufficient magnitude to be important.

Departures from r = ±1.0 can be somewhat misleading. An r = ±1.0 represents a 100% correspondence between the two variables. However, an r = ±.90 does *not* represent a 90% correspondence. It represents $.90^2$, or an 81% positive or negative correspondence. Further examples are: r = .70 (49%); r = .60 (36%); r = .50 (25%); r = .20 (4%).

The importance of the degree of the correlation varies from problem to problem. If we have two tests which are purported to be alternate forms designed to measure the same thing, a correlation between these tests of at least +.9 is a reasonable expectation. On the other hand, a correlation of +.4 might provide important information to theoreticians. In the latter case, a prediction of complex behavior might not be too efficient, for the causal relationship is weak. Nevertheless, if information of this size is added to other variables which also are moderately related to the behavior to be predicted, an almost perfect prediction might be made. In other words, variables which independently have little practical significance might together provide practical information.

A Note of Caution

Interpretation of causality using correlation coefficients can be tricky. We might think that performance on Test Y is due to some ability measured by Test X. Both performances, however, might be due to some third variable such as "intelligence."

To illustrate, the senior author has developed a test he calls "The Kelly Scratch-an-Ear Intelligence Test" (KSAE). The subject is asked, "Will you please scratch your right ear?" Scores are assigned on the basis of the number of fingers used, and the posture of the little pinky. One finger scratch on the appropriate ear with the little finger crooked and at a distance of one-fourth inch or greater from the others represents an IQ (KSAE) of 150 which is the ceiling. A rub with the whole hand on the *left* ear yields an IQ (KSAE) of 50, the lower limit. Other values are assigned so that the gross response receives a lower score than the "delicate, refined" response. These IQ's correlate ($r = +.3$) with grades (supposedly based somewhat upon intelligence) received in educational psychology courses. Can we say that the way students scratch an ear causes better grades in college educational psychology courses? We can, of course, say it, but most likely the performance on the KSAE and the grades received are influenced by the nature of the home background. Middle-class children learn to behave with decorum and also learn that school performance is important; thus students who scratch their ears delicately probably study more also. The r of .3, of course, indicates that the relationship is weak and therefore if you use your whole hand to scratch your ear you will not necessarily flunk educational psychology.

A coefficient of correlation indicates the level at which at least two variables relate to one another. Thus, if the observation of one variable can be used to forecast the appearance of the second variable, prediction is possible. An example is the relationship between scores on an intelligence test and grade point achievement. In order to determine a correlation score value, two different measures must be obtained for a group of individuals. We are then concerned with "the extent to which individuals or objects which are average, above average, or below average in one dimension tend also to be average, above average, or below average respectively in the other dimension" (Blommers 1960, p. 361). If such a situation is determined then prediction is possible under certain conditions.

Since correlation coefficients are based on probability theory then prediction based on correlations can be employed legitimately only when probability theory applies. Probability statements are dependent upon the possibility of an infinite number of trials. Thus predictions, based on correlational data, cannot be made for individual people or single events. In the case of Johnny, a second grader, IQ scores can give us some clues, but they cannot be used to predict his achievement. However, if Johnny's score and the scores of the rest of his classmates are taken together it might be safe to conclude that generally speaking those who scored high on the IQ test will be among the top performers in achievement also. Seldom is there a one to one correspondence. Some who scored high on the IQ test will perform poorly in school. Thus prediction for individual students based on correlational data is hazardous. For this reason attempts to work with individual students involve problems with which the teacher can find little assistance. When we are satisfied to speak collectively about groups of students, our problems seem more easily resolved.

Prediction serves two major purposes in education. First, it provides a means by which behavior can be investigated. If a teacher believes one teaching procedure is superior to others, she might predict achievement based on student behavior in the learning setting. If students perform as predicted there is some evidence to suggest that the teacher may be correct. Second, variables which can be used to predict other variables provide clues which may aid in the search for causes of behavior. In other words if a reasonable level of prediction (correct in 8 out of 10 cases) is achieved, then an investigator might begin to experiment to determine whether or not a cause and effect relationship is tenable.

Summary Note: The factor causing a high correlation is difficult to discover. A number of tests might be highly correlated ($r = +.8$), but we cannot say that one causes the other. These tests might simply be sampling some third underlying factor, such as a finely-developed central-neural-process.

It can be seen that in discussions related to psychological characteristics of human behavior, cause and effect relationships are seldom established. The reader should be aware that in the discussions which follow terms such as probably, probabilistic, etc., usually are employed to connote degrees of relationships between events. As the presentation of complex meaning is structured it seems important that the reader be aware of the limitations which are encountered when attempts are made to translate theory to practical settings. At this point an understanding of the limitations of correlational data seems sufficient background for interpreting the information to be presented.

Complex Meaning

Our previous discussion included a theory regarding the acquisition of perceptual and linguistic meaning. Language is acquired by way of pairing words with perceptual signs (residual parts of previous total responses to the stimulus object). Charles Osgood (1957) refers to this acquisition process as *linguistic decoding.* The process of acquiring the ability to *verbalize* words includes babbling → imitation → labelling → *semantic encoding.* Babbling provides a repertory of motor responses and opportunity to imitate others (e.g., mother) which in turn leads to sequential coordination of syllables. Labelling of the visual stimulus (e.g., cat) is basically a single-stage affair (imitation), whereas semantic encoding includes the mediational process of meaning. Thus the visual stimulus (cat) might elicit the verbal response "cat" as well as approach behavior that has been associated with the perceptual sign "cat." A host of linguistic meanings of "cat" might be acquired as a result of association. Thus "cat" might not only mean "approach" but it also might mean: "furry," "soft," "warm," "clean," "small," "light," "fast," etc.

As a result of associations, any stimulus object may acquire a hierarchy of meanings and a hierarchy of response potentials. Each meaning will have a probabilistic potency depending upon frequency of past associations. For a child, visual stimulation by a small cat will have a higher probability of eliciting the linguistic sign "kitty" than will "baby cat," although both meanings might have been acquired by the child. If we assume that "baby cat" is lower on the hierarchy of associations than "kitten," further stimulus input might be necessary to elicit the meaning "baby cat." One may ask the child, "What kind of cat is it?" and get the reply, "A baby cat."

At this point, schematic representations become complex and often add to confusion rather than provide clarification. At least three S — R hierarchies regarding meaning may be conceptualized:

1. A number of signs (perceptual and linguistic) might converge into one meaning (e.g., dinner (rs) may be stimulated by signs of dinner such as odor of food, sound of frying, sound of plates being placed on the table, Dad rapidly draining his beer bottle or Martini, the word "dinner," etc.).
2. One sign might diverge into many possible meanings (e.g., the spoken word "bear" may stimulate many meanings (rs) of "bear," such as "carry," "veer," "animal," "unclothed," etc.).
3. One meaning (rs) might diverge into many possible responses (e.g., dinner (rs) may stimulate "Ugh" when mentioned after the Christmas feast, salivation if the individual has been deprived of food, or spasms if one is seasick).

Measurement of Meaning

The term "meaning," as used within this chapter, is given response-like characteristics; the residuals are assumed to be some fractional parts of the previous total responses to the stimulus object. An infinite number of meanings are therefore possible, and if each meaning were independent of all other meanings, measurement would be a superhuman task. Osgood, Suci, and Tannenbaum (1957) assume that meanings are *not* independent of each other, and that meanings of concepts and objects can be represented by clusters of residuals which have similar or related meanings. The implications of their assumption are that meanings may be correlated with each other, and thus can be conceived to reflect a limited number of underlying factors.

In an attempt to develop a set of scales to measure meaning and to determine how these meanings hang together, Osgood and his colleagues asked a group of students to supply an adjective to each of 40 nouns. The conditions of response were constructed in such a manner as to elicit the prepotent meaning for the noun. Examples of responses were: TREE – "green," HOUSE – "big," PRIEST – "good." A frequency of use of certain adjectives, regardless of the noun referent, was observed. The 50 most-frequently-used adjectives were selected for further analysis. These 50 adjectives were made into sets of polar opposites and were used as a sample of descriptive scales for further study. A few examples of polar scales constructed were: "good – bad," "beautiful – ugly," "high – low," "loud – soft," "heavy – light," "wet – dry," "brave – cowardly," "rich – poor," "honest – dishonest."

Another group of subjects was asked to judge a number of concepts according to these scales. The scales were blocked off into seven partitions to indicate the degree of judgment. For example:

LADY: rough____:____:____:____:____:_X_:____smooth

This mark is placed close to "smooth" to indicate the judgment.

LADY: delicate____:_X_:____:____:____:____:____rugged
LADY: wide____:____:____:_X_:____:____:____narrow

"Lady," as indicated above, means "fairly delicate" and neither "wide" nor "narrow."

Fifty judgments were made on each of 20 concepts by the subjects. Disregarding the concepts judged, each scale was correlated with the other 49 scales, and the 50 by 50 matrix of intercorrelations were factor analyzed. *Factor analysis* is a rather complex procedure extending largely beyond the scope of a text of this nature (see Harmon, 1960). In general, however, correlations can be expressed by vectors and the angles between the vectors. Figure 3.8 shows angles representing three correlations. The higher the correlation, the closer the angles are together. If a number of scales cluster together (correlate with each other), then a new vector can be cast among the cluster. This new vector is called a factor. Figure 3.9 shows two clusters of scales and the casting of two new vectors. Each scale will be correlated with each of the two new vectors. Scales 1, 2, and 3 in Figure 3.9 correlate highly with Factor I and scales 4, 5, and 6 correlate highly with Factor II. Scale 4 correlates about .75 with Factor II and about .15 with Factor I. Scale 6 represents a high correlation with Factor II and a slight *negative* correlation with Factor I.

Essentially, if the larger pool of scales (50) can be represented by a smaller number of factors, then the meaning can be expressed in a more manageable form. The results of a number of factor analyses produced rather consistently three fairly strong factors which account for one-half of the variation among scales. On the basis of the scales which correlate highly with each other, a label can be applied which suggests the meaning of each factor. These identified factors are: *evaluative,* identified by scales such as "good – bad," "clean – dirty," "valuable – worthless"; *potency,* represented by scales "strong–weak," "large–small," "heavy – light"; and *activity,* characterized by scales "active – passive," "slow – fast."

FIGURE 3.8

Vector representation of three correlation coefficients

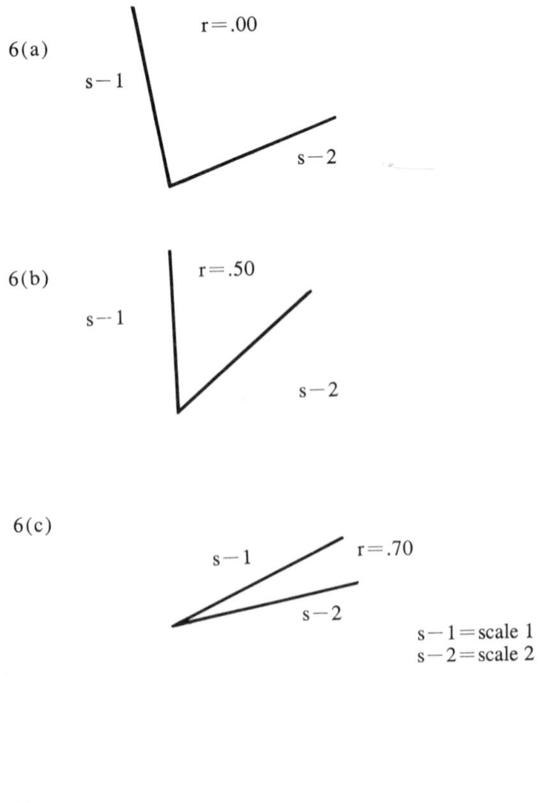

FIGURE 3.9

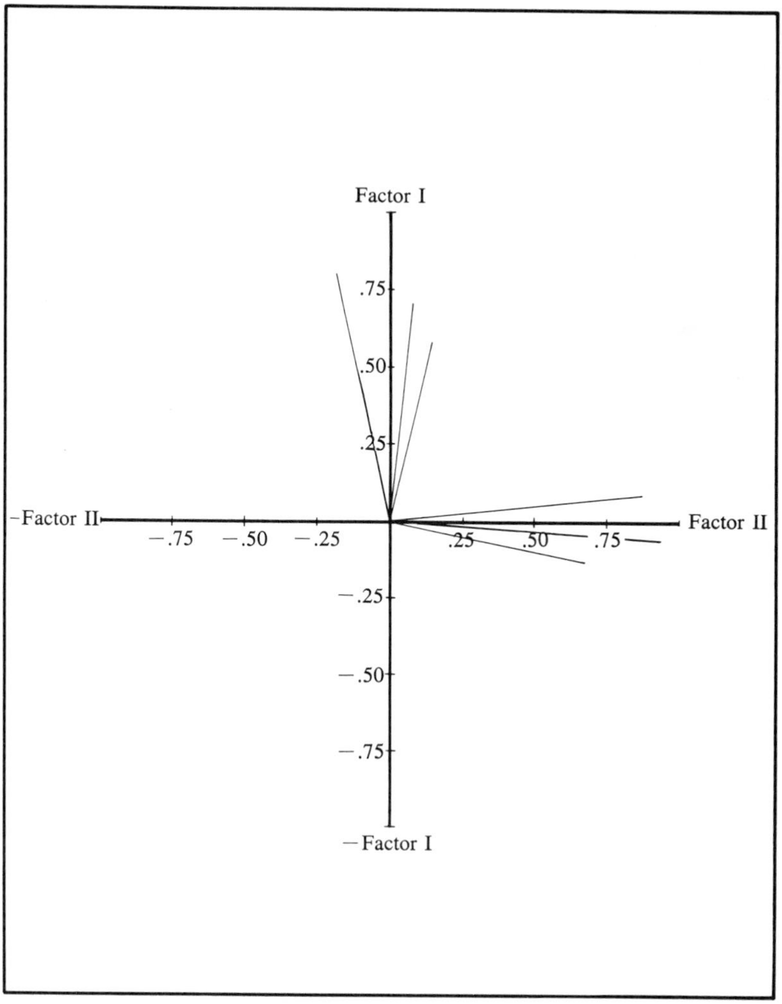

For each factor, a selection of a few scales which correlate highly with the factor and little with the other factors can provide a relatively "pure" instrument for an analysis of meaning. Indeed, an instrument of this nature cannot purport to measure all meaning (in view of Korzybski's position that meaning is in part unique). The instrument might, however, provide some assessment of prepotent meanings. Table 3.1 is an example of one *semantic differential* (the term Osgood applies to the scale combinations). The first four scales correlate with the evaluative factor, scales 5 through 8 with activity, and scales 9 through 12 with potency. Any number of subjects can be asked to judge the meaning of any number of concepts or objects on the scales. A cube of data can represent the responses by concepts, subjects, and scales (see Figure 3.10). The shaded cube represents the response of $subject_1$ to scale "a" on concept "A." To illustrate:

MOTHER: Good__X__:_____:_____:_____:_____:_____:_____Bad
(1) (2) (3) (4) (5) (6) (7)

TABLE 3.1

Modified semantic differential

Good	____:____:____:____:____:____:____	Bad
True	____:____:____:____:____:____:____	False
Kind	____:____:____:____:____:____:____	Cruel
Wise	____:____:____:____:____:____:____	Foolish
Active	____:____:____:____:____:____:____	Inactive
Hot	____:____:____:____:____:____:____	Cold
Excitable	____:____:____:____:____:____:____	Passive
Fast	____:____:____:____:____:____:____	Slow
Strong	____:____:____:____:____:____:____	Weak
Hard	____:____:____:____:____:____:____	Soft
Interesting	____:____:____:____:____:____:____	Boring
Severe	____:____:____:____:____:____:____	Lenient

FIGURE 3.10

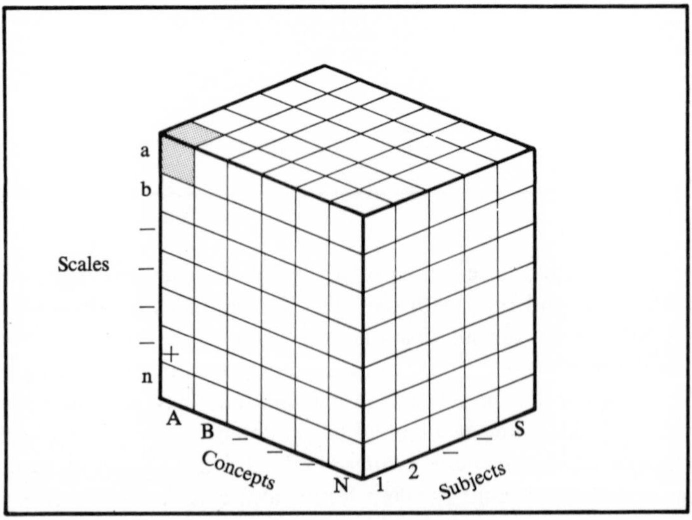

If concept "A" is "Mother," the scale "a" is "good – bad," and the "x" is the response of $subject_1$, then in the shaded cube the value (1) may

FIGURE 3.11

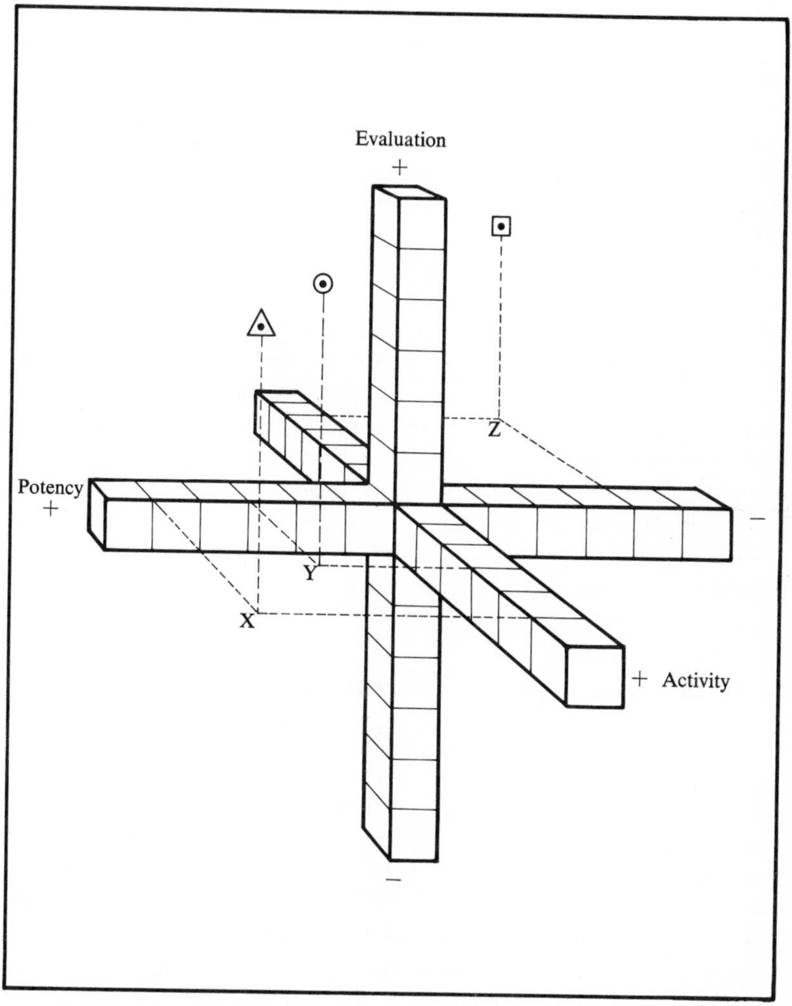

△ = Judgment of $subject_1$ on the concept "Mother." At point "X" mother is potent and active — the line up to the △ indicates a positive evaluation.
⊙ = Judgment of $subject_2$ on the concept "Mother." Point "Y" indicates $subject_2$ feels mother is less potent and active than does $subject_1$.
⊡ = Judgment of $subject_3$ on the concept "Mother." Point "Z" indicates a non-active and non-potent judgment, but mother ⊡ is also evaluated as positive.

be placed. Likewise, the concept "Mother" can be judged by $subject_1$ on all 12 scales in Table I. $Subject_2$ and $subject_3$ can also judge the concept "Mother" and a distance scale can be calculated to compare the differences in meaning of "Mother" among the three subjects. The 12 scales can be collapsed into the three factors (evaluative, activity, and potency). Figure 3.11 presents the three dimensions and the hypothetical placements of the meaning of "Mother" for each of the three subjects.

A reading of the figure shows that $subject_1$ and $subject_2$ evaluate the concept of "Mother" as being positive, active, and potent. $Subject_1$ assigns to "Mother" even more activity and potency than does $subject_2$. $Subject_3$ evaluates the "Mother" concept as positive but *not* active or potent.

If judgments of concepts are learned, then one could expect that $subject_3$ has had a fairly different experience with mother figures than has $subject_1$ and $subject_2$. The hypothetical figure (Figure 3.11) was constructed to reflect in the first two cases the "all-American" mother (sweet, loving, member of Junior League, PTA, etc.; manager of money, clothes, etc.) and in the third case, a placid, effete, nineteenth century upper-class mother.

Similar distance projections can be made *between* concepts either by one or more subjects.

Research with the semantic differential suggests that the measurement does tap some of the meaning structure.

Research and the Semantic Differential

Our previous discussion regarding distortion due to pairing of linguistic signs (prejudice, etc.) is consistent with a conditioning experiment utilizing the semantic differential. Staats and Staats (1957) simultaneously presented names of countries paired with either positively or negatively evaluative words to a number of subjects. The subjects then were asked to judge the country on a "pleasant – unpleasant" scale. Subjects who had received positive evaluations paired with a country rated that country more pleasant than those who had negative evaluations associated with the country. If the semantic differential measures meaning, then meaning can apparently be conditioned.

Osgood, Suci, and Tannenbaum (1957, pp. 155-159) reported data which indicated that extreme evaluations (1, 2, 6, and 7) on the semantic differential were related to judgmental latency (the time it takes a person to read and then respond). The subjects took less time to respond to the scales on which they provided the extreme responses. In a sense, when a person has a strong feeling and has expressed it often, he makes his judgment rapidly.

A recent study by Manson (1965) found data indicating that judgments can be influenced by subjects' postures and by movements of facial muscles. A bust of a "Prussian type" man was judged twice on the semantic differential by three groups, with a 15-minute interval between judgments. The "control" group rated the bust both times under "normal," comfortable conditions. A "Fixed Posture" (FP) group rated the bust under "normal" conditions and under conditions in which the subjects were instructed to tense the muscles in the limbs. One-half of this group judged under FP conditions first in order to control position effects. Under "Varied Facial Movement" (VFM) conditions, the group was asked to judge while rapidly moving the scalp and facial muscles. The FP group and the VFM group changed evaluations more markedly from "normal" conditions to experimental conditions than the "control" group changed from one "normal" trial to the other. Apparently, the judged meaning of a particular concept depends in part upon the proprioceptive stimuli (impulses from the muscles, tendons and joints) which accompany the visual stimuli representing the concept. Pierce-Jones (1965) reported that stereotyped response patterns can be changed by modification of posture. These data supported the notion that meanings of concepts change as the context stimuli change. Further, these data are consistent with the interaction concept of the psychosomatic process. Theoretically, habitual responses (instrumental, visceral, expressive) are elicited by linguistic signs and perceptual signs as a function of the signs' meanings (rs's). Conversely, the response to a sign might be influenced by simultaneous proprioceptive stimulation. In a sense, the meaning of a motor task can be changed through inhibition of the stereotyped response.

Although these reports are rather esoteric, they indicate a source of stimulation which is often overlooked. Documented evidence regarding proprioceptive stimuli as they apply to education is lacking; nevertheless, a number of possible educational implications can be drawn from these laboratory studies.

Classroom posture is a concern of many teachers. When Johnny slouches down in his desk the teacher may request him to sit up. The act of sitting up must mean something to the teacher. Is it that she has found that children who sit up are more attentive? Viewed from the child's point, does the stimuli from the new posture alter the meaning of the classroom situation? Pierce-Jones (1965, p. 211) suggested that posture functions like an "attitude" and the changed posture can change the habitual "attitude." The authors have noted that in their own classrooms, when the pupils were instructed to sit up to show the teacher they were ready, classroom management problems were minimized. Sitting up in the classroom might have had the effect of implying that school requires attention and decorum. For some work purposes, an attentive set may be important, although the attentiveness might not be appropriate for all school learning. In art classes, for example, movement may be desired in order to break stereotypic classroom sets so that "freedom of expression" may be facilitated. Many teachers have stated, "I have done everything and yet cannot get through to Johnny!" Possibly the wrong person was moving. Change the movements of Johnny — it might work.

Note: The authors have taken the position that psychology has no rules for the teacher to follow, for effective teaching is difficult to assess. The intent of this text is to provide psychological data and suggest *possible* strategies which the teacher might try. Little evidence, however, can be mustered to say that these strategies will make you a more competent teacher. To reiterate, these speculations are presented to draw your attention to possible stimuli and responses that you might wish to investigate in order to accomplish your goals (see Chapter 1).

Language and School Success

At the present time it is quite fashionable to be concerned with the "culturally deprived" child. A large body of recent evidence indicates that low socio-economic status and economic deprivation produce submarginal citizens (Glueck and Glueck, 1950; Cohen, 1955; Lichter *et al.,* 1962). Deutsch (1960) contended that children from lower socio-economic homes were deficient in ability to use language efficiently, to follow directions, and to extract meaning from sight and sound. As a consequence of these deficiencies, lower-class children enter school ill-prepared to meet the demands of the primarily middle-class orientation of the school. These children meet failure, and so become psychological drop-outs around age nine, and physical drop-outs as soon as the law allows.

Deutsch (1960) suggested that economic poverty is *not* the relevant variable which leads to language deficiency; it is rather the lack of language stimulation in the home. Surely, the cramped physical conditions encountered by lower socio-economic families might foster poor communication; nevertheless, many lower socio-economic homes produce linguistically competent children. Research conducted by Bernstein (1961; 1962) in Britain indicated that the language structure of the middle-class homes differs markedly from that employed in lower-class homes. Bernstein (1961) proposed two linguistic codes: *formal* (in later work, called *elaborated*), and *public* (later called *restricted*).

The restricted language code is grammatically simple and fails to permit precise statements of concepts. Bernstein lists (pp. 297-8) ten characteristics of the restricted code which are shown here in Table 3.2.

TABLE 3.2

Characteristics of the restricted linguistic code

1. Short, grammatically simple, often unfinished sentences with a poor syntactical form.
2. Simple and repetitive use of conjunctions (so, then, and because).
3. Little use of subordinate clauses used to break down the initial categories of the dominant subject.
4. Inability to hold a formal subject through a speech sequence, thus facilitating a dislocated informational content.
5. Rigid and limited use of adjectives and adverbs.
6. Infrequent use of impersonal pronouns as subjects of conditional clauses or sentences, e.g., "one."
7. Frequent use of statements in which the reason and the conclusion are confounded to produce a categoric utterance.
8. A large number of statements and phrases that signal a requirement for the previous speech sequence to be reinforced — "Wouldn't it," "You see," "Just fancy." This process is termed "sympathetic circularity."
9. Individual selection from a group of idiomatic sequences will frequently occur.
10. *The individual qualification is implicit in the sentence organization: it is a language of implicit meaning.*

Taken from Bernstein, Basil, "Social Class and Linguistic Development: A Theory of Social Learning." In A. H. Halsey, Jean Floud, and C. A. Anderson (eds.), *Education, Economy, and Society*. New York:The Free Press of Glencoe, Inc., 1961. Pp. 297-8.

The lower classes in Britain tend to use primarily the restricted code, whereas the middle classes tend to use both codes. The restricted code is often apparent in command forms such as "Shut up!" and "Go to bed!" If the child questions "Why?" to either of the above statements, the reply typically is not a reasoned elaboration but rather a statement expressing the social relationship. For example, the parent might reply, "Because I tell you (to shut up)." A gang leader's reply to the question "Why?" might be, "Because I am the leader."

Although middle-class parents make frequent use of the restricted code, they also employ the elaborated code. When the parent commands the child, "Go to bed!" and the child questions "Why?" a reply such as the following is likely: "Well honey, when you stay up late at night, you are tired the next day and you get cranky, but if you get a good night's sleep, you can have more fun." Such an elaborated statement provides information to the child as well as indicating a causal relationship in time. In one sense, the feedback directs the child to differentiate experience. Refined differentiations provide the child with a language repertory which permits the majority of middle-class children to understand the elaborated language of the middle-class teacher. Communication, however, breaks down when the middle-class teacher uses an elaborated language to direct the typical lower-class child. Subtle intent may be expressed by the teacher (e.g., "I would like you children to be less noisy"), but the average lower-class child will be unable to decode the subtle meaning, for he has not had these linguistic signs paired with previous response patterns. Likewise, the teacher might become impatient with the lower-class child who supplements his speech with action in order to convey intent. For example, pushing another child while saying, "Leave me alone," constitutes behavior to which the teacher responds negatively.

According to Bernstein, the restrictive language code provides limited differentiation of the world and a lack of basic concepts. In terms of the earlier discussion of language acquisition, generalization is difficult because the necessary residuals of experience are lacking. Bernstein recommends that school programs for children accustomed to the restricted linguistic code should *not* attempt to be "permissive," but should place emphasis upon formation of basic concepts. Programs which emphasize "discovery" (see Chapter 5) should be delayed for children having low levels of conceptualization until the basic conceptual rudiments are acquired. Bernstein further recommends that the teacher should not use solely concrete teaching, since such action would maintain the child's dependence upon discrete experience. The concrete experiences should be coupled with verbal generalizations.

A great number of programs have been developed in the large urban centers to provide preschool remedial education for children who have, because of low levels of conceptualization, a high probability of school failure. The children attend "readiness centers" where they are presented with tasks which are designed to provide a number of basic linguistic concepts necessary for school success. Often the centers require a large number of volunteers, because the intent of the program is to develop an elaborated linguistic code, which can only be done in small groups with face-to-face verbal interactions. Suggested activities include:

1. A screen is placed between the adult and a few children. The adult bounces a ball, and the children are asked to tell what is happening. An eggbeater may be operated and a verbal description of what makes the sound is required. (Such activities as these are designed to help the children attach linguistic meanings to sounds.)

2. Tricycles are available: if a child wants to ride he must first ask "May I ride the tricycle?" rather than be permitted to push off another child and command "Gimme!" (Here the purpose is to develop linguistic expression instead of physical expression.)

3. The children may be given an orange or pear and be instructed to take the fruit home, eat it, and bring the seeds back to school. (Concepts of time relationships are developed through tasks of this nature.)

Although deficiencies in elaborated linguistic codes may be found among children from middle-class homes, and conversely, elaborated codes may be present in some children from lower-class homes, the elaborated code is markedly more prevalent among middle-class children. The relevant variable is, of course, the language code to which the child has been exposed.

Jackson, Hess, and Shipman (1965) taught 60 Negro mothers of varying social class background a block-sorting task, and then asked these mothers to teach their four-year-old children the same task. The preliminary analysis of these teaching situations (which were taped) suggested that the mothers who encouraged their children to verbalize their activities had more success than the parents who encouraged action. The investigators concluded that mothers who stimulate verbal feedback from their children receive information which enables them to provide more verbal suggestions that further facilitate the child's differentiation of the task characteristics. These data are consistent with Bernstein's observations.

The fact that children from lower-class homes tend to have limited ability both to express themselves linguistically and to understand subtle meanings can cause a great deal of misunderstanding between the teacher and the children. As an initial set, the teacher would be well advised to associate the elaborated code with the concrete behavior desired. For example, if the teacher wishes the children to enter the classroom "calmly and quietly," some attention called to concrete behaviors that are *not* "calm and quiet" as well as some that *are* desirable might provide differentiation and behavioral meaning to the phrase "calm and quiet." The newly-acquired meanings might be elaborated by including verbal practice with the concepts. For example:

Teacher: "Children, how are we going to enter the room?"
Child_1: "Calmly and quietly, teacher."
Teacher: "And what does 'calmly and quietly' mean?"
Child_2: "We pick up our feet."
Teacher: "Anything else?"
Child_3: "We don't talk."

$Child_4$:	"We sit still in our seats."
	(etc.)
Teacher:	(after the children have gone for recess and returned) "How did we come in?"
$Child_3$:	"Calmly and quietly."
Teacher:	"John, do you think we came in quietly?"
John:	"*Pretty* quietly."
Teacher:	"What do you mean?"
John:	"Well, I bumped my desk a bit."
Teacher:	"Let us see if we can come in *very* quietly." (children go out and come in) "That was very nice, children. You picked up your feet, sat up in your desks, and you all kept your hands to yourselves."

Care in associating the word with subtle behaviors may seem to be wasteful repetition; however, repetitive association might be necessary to develop the desired concepts and actions.

Krech and Rosenzweig's (see Rosenzweig, 1963) studies cited in Chapter 2 may relate to the non-elaborated language typical of the lower classes. Children from these homes might have a less effective central neural process as a consequence of less symbolic manipulation of concepts. The most appropriate and most efficient time for intervention has been selected by many to be during the child's preschool life. At the present, however, little evidence is available for decision making in respect to this assumption.

Lower-class homes have been judged as a maladaptive milieu because elaborate language usage is limited. Eric Hoffer (1963), a longshoreman and social philosopher, noted, however, that the longshoremen solve rather complex problems without the sophisticated linguistic code. Since most academicians are middle-class oriented, they might fail to differentiate the subtle expressive communication, such as gesture and inflection, which Hoffer indicates is adaptive. Some persons might wish to question the importance of the dominant middle-class mode, but many educators, as socialization agents, seem to assume that "rich" conceptual processes *should* be given to all. (This assumption is itself a middle-class value.) If one wishes to produce individuals who are adaptive to change, then educators might have the "correct" position. Possibly, however, the achievement of this goal will inadvertently produce "unhappy" people. Behaviors other than school success which are a result of our educational system may merit investigation if the school is to truly be an agent of social change.

Perhaps two illustrations will provide some insight into the real problem confronting educators relating to values and school success.

Mike is a thirteen-year-old boy who has a strong attachment to his coal miner father and housewife mother. Neither of his parents completed the sixth grade in school. Mike has developed an interest and apparently a high degree of skill in writing poetry. Mike's folks refuse to read the poetry (perhaps they cannot read) and discourage him from going on in school. On the other hand, the English teacher encourages Mike to read and write more. Soon Mike finds the company of his parents dull and drab and drifts into the "arty" crowd downtown. Mike no longer communicates with his parents and he passes most of his school work and excells in English class. Is Mike now better educated? Is Mike now a better person? Was the school justified in splitting (if this was in fact the cause) the home so that Mike could rise above his environment?

Mary was almost unnoticed by her elementary school teacher. She was an average student in all of the required work. Most of her free time was spent fitting pieces of chipped glass into unbelievable places in a frame of plaster. After a sociogram indicated she was an isolate, she was counseled and the recipient of special treatment in the home and in school. She raised her school achievement to the A minus level. Now she is one of the crowd. Now she is busy with school affiliations and she has lost her interest in mosaics. Is Mary happier now? Is her teacher happier? Whose values are most important? These and several other issues that merge into real moral conflicts arise daily as a result of endeavors to improve society. Language codes are but one frame of reference for observing students.

In closing this topic it seems appropriate to cite the refreshing way a small "culturally deprived" child evaluated his school experience in the sixth grade: "School stinks like a cornered skunk on a damp day." If communication of feelings is the goal, this statement seems descriptive.

Summary and Implications

Acquisition of language and meaning has been described in this chapter as a function of direct contact with the stimulus object, or indirect contact through association of linguistic signs with previously-acquired meanings. Distortions of meaning can be acquired through over-generalization and/or by failure to recognize the evaluative nature of our abstracting processes. Korzybski's extensional devices were presented to suggest one tool that could encourage the awareness that our abstractions are derived from a particular point of view.

Habitual use of language imposes a set that the word is somehow isomorphic with the "real" world. Science recognizes that various sets regarding any object may be taken, and that these sets represent only a few aspects of a "universe-in-process." If we wish to communicate accurately, an explicit statement regarding one's set may be necessary.

Meaning apparently can be measured to some degree with the semantic differential. Research with this instrument indicates that meanings can be conditioned. Further, the posture and facial movements of a person provide proprioceptive stimuli which may influence the judged meaning of a concept.

If we desire to educate children to cope "effectively" with a "universe-in-process," then we may find it necessary to build in mediators which will delay immediate responses. Such mediators might include Korzybski's devices which were designed to emphasize that the word is not the object and that the word does not exhaust the characteristics of that object.

Avoidant responses to taboo words and jingoisms are viewed by the present authors to be potentially maladaptive. Undifferentiated positive or negative responses to stimulus objects or symbols (e.g., "America," "communism," "Negro," etc.) are assumed to be a result of distorted linguistic sign pairing. Pledges of allegiance without differentiation may prevent future processing of significant adaptive information. In view of the ubiquitous distorted sign pairing expressed by nationalism, one may become a bit cynical regarding man's future in this corner of the universe.

Questions

1. Why is the concept of discrimination essential to understanding the learning process?
2. Can you change "meaning" by changing your expression and posture? Try smiling under conditions of "anger." Try frowning at a party. Does this change the meaning of the situation? Slouch down in your chair while you read this book. What happens?
3. How can a person with a conditioned negative response to members of another race eliminate it, or modify it, if he wishes to do so? What can the classroom teacher do to help prevent pupil acquisition of such negative responses? What responses should the pupils acquire?
4. How do you react to taboo words? What shocks you? Why?
5. Are the suggested problems generated by syntax "really" problems? Are Korzybski's (1951) extensional devices "helpful," or are they excess baggage?

6. Would you teach Korzybski's extensional devices to your class? Why or why not?
7. Can you discover, in your everyday life, examples of faulty linguistic generalization or word pairing which distort or even prevent communication? Can you discern cases where middle-class values are influencing your viewpoints?
8. In what way can a teacher help children to use our language as an explicitly expressive tool and to overcome linguistic habits, which, in our particular language structure, modify and even control our patterns of thinking?
9. As a teacher in the primary grades, what would you do to help a child of lower-class background who has had limited language experiences? What would you not do with this child that you would normally do with other children? Can Bernstein's (1961) list of restricted linguistic code characteristics help you to see possibilities in the handling of culturally deprived children?

Further Readings of Interest

Regarding linguistic sign learning, C. Osgood's Chapter 16 in *Method and Theory in Experimental Psychology* (1953) provides a rather comprehensive theoretical review.

Korzybski's chapter (see bibliography) presents a more complete case than has been set forth here for the use of his extensional devices. His bibliography may provide further leads for the English major.

Bloom, Davis, and Hess (1965, see bibliography) report the summary of working papers of participants in the Research Conference on Education and Cultural Deprivation. The report includes a wide presentation regarding "Cultural Deprivation" and an excellent annotated bibliography on research and educational programs.

Bernstein's (1961) chapter (see bibliography) is quite provocative and merits reading by the teacher who may be asked to teach lower-class children.

The student with neuro-physiological interests may find Gellhorn's (1964) discussion of "Motion and Emotion" interesting. He supports a physiological case regarding the influence of proprioception on subjective emotional states.

References

Bernstein, B. Social class and linguistic development: a theory of social learning. A. H. Halsey, Jean Floud, & C. A. Anderson (Eds.), In

Education, economy, and society. New York: Free Press of Glenco, 1961, 288-314.

Bernstein, B. Linguistic codes, hesitation phenomena and intelligence. *Lang. Speech,* 1962, 5, 31-46.

Blommers, P. J., & Lindquist, E. F. *Elementary statistical methods in phychology and education.* Boston: Houghton Mifflin, 1960.

Bloom, B. S., Davis, Allison., & Hess, R. D. *Compensatory education for cultural deprivation.* New York: Holt, Rinehart, Winston, 1965.

Byrnes, R. H. The symbolization of motion. *Main currents in modern thought,* 1961, 17, 89-91.

Cohen, A. K. *Delinquent boys: the culture of the gang.* New York: Free Press, 1955.

Deutsch, M. Minority groups and class status as related to social and personality factors in scholastic achievement. New York: Soc. for Applied Anthropol., 1960.

Gellhorn, E. Motion and emotion: the role of proprioception in the psychology and pathology of the emotions. *Psychol. Rev.* 1964, 71, 457-472.

Glueck, S., & Glueck, Eleanor T. *Unraveling juvenile delinquency.* Cambridge, Mass.: Harvard Univer. Press, 1950.

Harmon, H. H. *Modern factor analysis.* Chicago: Univer. of Chicago Press, 1960.

Hoffer, E. An interview with Mr. Day, KQED TV Director, San Francisco, 1963.

Jackson, J. D., Hess, R. D., & Shipman, Virginia. Communication styles in teachers: an experiment. Unpublished paper read at the 1965 meeting of the Am. Educ. Res. Assoc., Chicago, Feb. 12, 1965.

Jevons, W. S., *The elements of logic.* New York: American, 1883.

Korzybski, A. The role of language in the perceptual processes. In R. R. Blake & G. V. Ramsey (Eds.), *Perception—an approach to personality.* New York: Ronald Press, 1951, 170-205.

Lichter, S., Rapien, Elsie B., Seibert, Frances M., & Sklansky, M. A. *The drop-outs.* Glencoe, Ill.: Free Press, 1962.

Luria, A. R., & Vinogradova, O. S. An objective investigation of the dynamics of semantic systems. *Brit. J. of Psychol.,* 1959, 50, 89-105.

Manson, G. G. Muscles and meanings: an investigation into the effects of proprioception on perception and emotion. Unpublished research report, Univer. of Alberta, 1965.

Osgood, C. E. *Method and theory in experimental psychology.* New York: Oxford Univer. Press, 1953.

Osgood, C. E. A behavioristic analysis of perception and language as cognitive phenomena. In Bruner, J. S. and others (Eds.), *Contemporary approaches to cognition.* Cambridge, Mass.: Harvard Univer. Press, 1957, 75-118. (a)

Osgood, C. E., Suci, G. J., & Tannenbaum, P.H. *The measurement of meaning.* Urbana: Univer. of Ill. Press, 1957. (b)

Pierce-Jones, F. Method for changing stereotyped response patterns by the inhibition of certain postural sets. *Psychol. Rev.,* 1965, 72, 196-214.

Radke, M.J., Davis, H. S., & Trager, H. C. Social perception and attitudes of children. *Genet. Psychol. Monogr.,* 1949, 40, 327-447.

Rosenzweig, M. R. Effects of heredity and environment on brain chemistry, brain anatomy, and learning ability in the rat. Paper read at Kansas Symposium on Physiological Determinates of Behavior: Implications for Mental Retardation, Univer. of Kansas, June 4-5, 1963.

Russell, B. *Principles of mathematics.* Cambridge: Cambridge Univer. Press, 1903.

Staats, Carolyn K., & Staats, A. W. Meaning established by classical conditioning. *J. of exp. Psychol.,* 1957, 54, 74-80.

Vigotsky, L. S. Thought and speech. *Psychiatry,* 1939, 2, 29-52.

Whorf, B. L. *Language, thought, and reality.* New York: Wiley, 1956.

Prediction and Selected Behavioral Variables 4

Overview

The discussion in Chapter 2 developed the S → O → R model and included data indicating that behavior is a function of chemical and sensory variables interacting with the organism's genetic potential. Chapter 3 was concerned with theories regarding the acquisition of meaning and the acquisition of linguistic signs. It was pointed out that the effective stimuli may be conceived of as occurring in minute units (such as contact with a small, sharp, pointed instrument), and the responses may also be measured in small units. In other cases, such as in language acquisition, the effective stimuli may involve a large number of sequential stimuli and the response (or responses) observed may be a set of coordinated actions. Applied psychologists find that the use of the sequential stimuli and extended responses is often more fruitful than the "simpler," smaller-unit sequences. The authors favor this position since school learning occurs in classrooms where small unit, highly controlled investigations are seldom possible.

Complete knowledge regarding the process of response acquisition is an *ideal* of behavioral research, but we are far from achieving this ideal. The organism manifests many responses which have unknown origins or whose origins are only partially known. When such is the case, an alternate strategy for prediction and control is to measure responses to controlled stimuli and then note behavioral correlates of the measured responses. In other words, relationships between performances in different types of behavioral situations are sought. If a high relationship can be found between performances on a 45-minute "objectively" scored test and performances in specific learning situations, then it is said that the test results can be employed to predict behavior in the other setting. If test instruments can be employed to forecast accurately those students who will perform at high, low, and moderate levels in a given situation, then the predictive devices can be of extreme importance in educational settings. Particularly, predicted failure can indicate that a special program is needed for these individuals because the typical setting leads to failure. One of the most widely-applied uses of this strategy is in the prediction of school achievement on the basis of measured "intelligence." In addition to measures of intelligence, instruments which estimate aptitudes, abilities, interests, and personality have been devised and used with some success in the prediction of academic performance.

The present chapter elaborates upon a number of measurement devices that sample rather large units of behavior to a number of stimuli. These observations suggest that some residuals of experience seem to go together and others seem to stand alone. A quasi-mathematical model is cast to note these measured sets of residuals. These independent sets include: *cognitive abilities, elements of motivation, expectancies* regarding how others will react to the individual, and *special learnings* (achievement in various subject matters, i.e., mathematics, science, etc.).

Measurement of *cognitive ability* has in the past centered around the notion of the IQ (intelligence quotient), and we have tended to view this as *one* ability. More recent investigations suggest cognitive ability is much more complex. The controversy between these two views is presented and the implication of each position for educational practice is noted.

Informal observation of human behavior seems to support some notion of *motivation.* Give two children the same problem and one may attack it with much fervor while the other dawdles along. Both children may be "bright" (high cognitive ability), but one is motivated (accomplishment on the task apparently is important to him). Some seem to learn that school success is important, others learn that athletic prowess is important, and still others seem to find most school activities unimportant.

Figure 4.1 represents the S → O → R model with a number of inferred residuals depicted.

FIGURE 4.1

The S → O → R model with the focus upon the contents of the Organism (O)

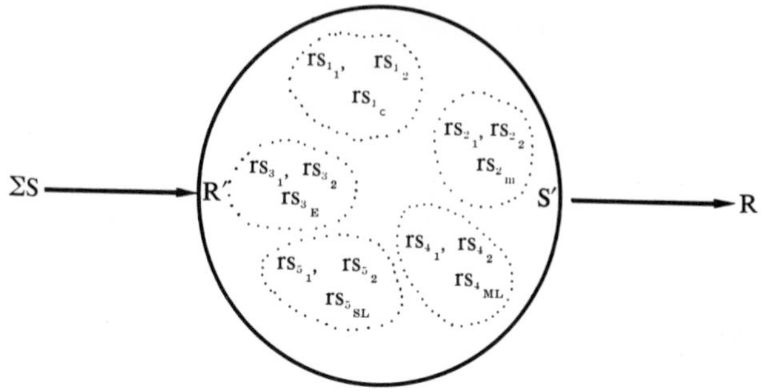

$\Sigma S \rightarrow R'$ = any adequate stimuli processed by the individual.
$rs1_1, rs1_2 \ldots rs1_c$ = residuals related to cognitive ability.
$rs2_1, rs2_2 \ldots rs2_m$ = residuals related to motivation.
$rs3_1, rs3_2 \ldots rs3_E$ = expectancies regarding how others will react.
$rs4_1 \ldots rs4_{ML}$ = previous learnings in mathematics.
$rs5_1 \ldots rs5_{SL}$ = previous learnings in science.
$S' \rightarrow R$ = response to ΣS mediated by the person.

In many behaving situations, a number of the independent sets of residuals may be necessary for an adequate response as in the following examples:

1. A boy with the necessary cognitive ability (rs_c) who desires to succeed (motivation rs_m) in a science class may fail (R is unacceptable) because he lacks the necessary previous science learnings (rs_{5_1}).
2. Another boy in the same class with similar abilities and the necessary "knowledge" may not be particularly excited about the topic and fail also.
3. A third student whose cognitive ability is marginal but who has a great desire to achieve may compensate for his limitations with much work. Thus he acquires the adequate response and succeeds.

Because complex human behavior such as school performance seems to be a function of many variables within the person, the S → O → R representation becomes cumbersome. A quasi-mathematical model is developed in this chapter to replace the S → O → R model. The quasi-mathematical model is cast into a multivariate statistical model. Such statistical models permit an analysis of behavior in which a number of human characteristics are simultaneously manipulated to predict behavior. These analyses are contrasted with univariate models in which *one* variable is compared with another.

The multivariate notions presented within this chapter depart from traditional treatments of cognition and motivation. Indeed, the theme of this chapter is based upon the assumption that cognitive factors (i.e. intelligence) cannot be discussed independently of the so-called non-cognitive domain (i.e. motivation, etc.). As a preface to the newer measurement devices a few notions underlying measurement are presented.

Glossary

ability: actual power to perform an act, physical or mental, whether or not obtained by training and education.

abstract intelligence: the ability to deal effectively with abstract concepts and symbols as contrasted with social intelligence (effectiveness in relation with people); mechanical intelligence (effectiveness in dealing with concrete objects); and esthetic intelligence (ability to appreciate and/or create beauty).

adaptive behavior: any behavior that helps the organism meet environmental demands; capacity to profit from experience and to initiate new and complex activities are two criteria frequently implied. Essentially a vague term which should be evaluated within the context of a study. If one is attending a typical school, hitting teachers and principals is *not* adaptive behavior.

adjustment: a state in which the individual is able to cope with the environment in which he is operating.

behavior correlates: refers to behavior(s) that correlates with some other set of behaviors. As used in this chapter, test behaviors (i.e., intelligence tests) may correlate with academic performance. Academic behavior is then one behavioral correlate of intelligence test behavior.

catalyst: a substance or object that alters the speed of a reaction but itself emerges unchanged.

closure: as used in this chapter, the ability to fill in gaps to make an incomplete idea complete.

cognition: a generic term for any process whereby an organism becomes aware or obtains knowledge of an object; includes perceiving, conceiving, recognizing, judging, and reasoning.

construct: a concept formally proposed with definition and limits explicitly related to data.

construct validity: when a test developed from a theory consistently relates to other variables as the theory indicates it should, the theory is said to have construct validity. As a result of intelligence testing, the notion of intelligence has some construct validity. Within the field of measurement, construct validity seems to carry several definitions. (See Cronbach, L. J., and Meehl, P. E., 1955; also Campbell, D., 1960).

continuous data: data changing by extremely small units and essentially so small as to be separately unnoticeable. Mercury measures of temperature are continuous.

creative intelligence: the ability to adopt new and often more complex behavior from previously learned behaviors. Used with quotes in this chapter because "creative" is a fuzzy term.

criterion: a behavior or a set of behaviors used as a basis for comparison. In predictive studies the criterion is the behavior that the investigator is attemping to predict. Grade point average (GPA) is used in a study reported in this chapter as the criterion. GPA is really not the student's behavior; it is an evaluation by a teacher of the student's behavior.

cross-sectional studies: a simultaneous study of a large sample of persons across a number of levels on some variables, e.g., cross-sectional studies in child development, individuals representing a number of age groups. In contrast longitudinal studies cover a number of children over a period of time making analysis of change.

curvilinear: a line that is bent that changes direction from moment to moment or of data that can be represented by such a line as distinguished from rectilinear of a line that maintains a constant direction.

deviation IQ: a standard score on an intelligence test that has a mean of 100 and a standard deviation approximately equal to that of the Stanford-Binet (approx. 16). It is held that the deviation IQ can be interpreted as having the same meaning as the familiar IQ; but since it is not a quotient between mental age (MA) and chronological age, to call it an IQ is misleading. (Standard IQ $= \frac{\text{MA}}{\text{CA}} \text{x } 100$.)

discrete data: separate, distinct, discontinuous data. For example, sex (male or female) is usually distinct (notwithstanding present dress styles).

face validity: relates to the extent to which a test is made of items that upon inspection seem related to the variable to be tested. (i.e., an arithmetic test should include arithmetic problems: $2 + 2 + ?$, $3 \text{ x } 12 = ?$, etc.)

grade point average: point-hour ratio used generally in high school or college.

independent variable: the variable whose changes are regarded not dependent upon changes in another specified variable. The variable which is manipulated or treated in an experiment to see what effects change on some other variable.

intelligence: a theoretic construct which was invented to account for the fact that some people seem to learn faster than others. (See intelligence test.)

intelligence quotient: a measure of rate of development up to the age of testing, computed by dividing the mental age (MA) as determined on a standardized test of intelligence by the chronological or life age (CA) multiplied by 100 to avoid decimals.

intelligence test: a series of tasks yielding a score which the test constructor thinks is indicative of the intelligence of the person. This definition implies that intelligence test measures that which the investigator calls "intelligence."

masochism: a sexual anomoly (deviation from common rule) characterized by erotic or sexual excitement and/or satisfaction from being subjected to pain, whether by oneself or by another.

motivation: a theoretical process that is assumed to energize the person to move in certain directions, e.g., an individual who works hard to succeed is said to be motivated to achieve. This construct is assumed in most cases to be largely learned.

need achievement: (nAch) a hypothesized need invented to account for the fact that some individuals work harder for achievement than do others. Apparently this is an acquired need which characterizes a large proportion of middle-class America.

normal distribution curve: a curve representing the frequency with which the values of a variable are obtained when the number is infinite and the variation is subject to change of the law of probability. The curve is bell-shaped; that is, the highest frequency is in the middle with a gradual and symmetrical tapering toward the extremes.

obtained score: the score a subject receives on a test or other measuring instrument.

Oedipus Complex: according to psychoanalytic theory, a universally repressed drive of a person for sex relations with the parent of the opposite sex. This term usually refers to a boy's desire for his mother while Electra Complex is the female counterpart. Oedipus is often used to refer to both sexes.

operation: an act upon some variable or object which changes the variable or object in some way. Some manipulation upon an object, e.g., $2 + 2 = 4$ is a combination operation.

personality: the distinguishing qualities of an individual. Those characteristics of an individual that give rise to his reputation or that are perceived by others; a man's social stimulus value. Some refer to the internal process or entity that determines the behavior of an individual.

predicted score: the score one applies to an individual based upon some set of information which has some relation to the score to be predicted. If the information is "very good," the difference between the predicted score and the real (observed) score will be small.

predictive validity: an empirical validity measure based on the correspondence actually found for a representative sample of persons between their test scores and their actual behavior at a given interval after testing on the task in question (e.g., test scores compared with grades received the following year; the correlation is a measure of the validity with which grades can be predicted a year later).

prejudice: a belief or judgment held regarding an object, race, or system made with insufficient direct evidence.

psychoanalytic: a theory of analysis of the psychi invented by Freud and continued with modifications by some analysists.

quantification: the process of translating responses, etc., into some numerical system. Counting the number of responses is one form of quantification.

range: distance from the lowest score to the highest score; often equals disstance from highest to lowest score plus 1.

reliability: the consistency of a measure; e.g., a reliable test is characterized by some stability. A person who scores high at time *one* should also score high at time *two*. This assumes that no force has operated upon the individual to intentionally upset the consistency.

response acquisition: the process of learning a response in association with a stimulus or stimuli.

semantic: the meaning of words or other signs; the rules that describe the way signs relate to objects.

synthesis: putting two or more ideas or things together to result in a new whole.

transfer (positive): an improvement in performance as a result of a previous act. Positive transfer would occur in changing from straight typing to IBM card punching.

transfer (negative): a change for the worse in the performance of a task as a result of performing some other task. Negative transfer might occur when changing to a four-speed manual shift car after learning to drive a three-speed (forward) manual shift car. The driving would transfer positively, but the shifting will cause some difficulty.

validity: an estimate of the degree to which a test measures what it is supposed to measure.

variability: the difference of the scores in a set from each other or from some standard; the fact that the scores or measures or values differ, or the degree to which they differ. It is measured by the *Mean deviation,* the standard deviation, or the variance (SD squared).

univariate: research study using only one independent variable, such as "test anxiety is negatively related to success on a college examination."

Measurement Notions

An earlier discussion (see Chapter 2) suggested that a quantification of behavior permits a number of statistical operations and some determination can be made regarding the statistical significance of findings. For prediction purposes, a number of considerations regarding the nature of the measurement process merit attention:

1. Measurement changes the organism. Any manipulation of the organism is achieved by presenting a set of stimuli, and therefore some residual of the response to the measurement stimuli will remain. For example, if a person performs on an intelligence test, any subsequent exposure to the test will be moderated by the knowledge (residuals) gained during the original experience. Indeed, one characteristic of the successful student is that he becomes "test wise": he "knows" how to beat the test. He has learned about tests through experience and as a consequence the same test given to the same student a second time is in reality a different stimulus than when the test was first administered.
2. All measurement relates to a static, non-existent organism. Measurement is carried out in time-space, and the responses of the person tested represent a slice of the individual's life which is in the past. To a degree, this statement is a corollary to the first statement.
3. Measurement is more likely to provide evidence to predict future performances if the measured behavior is typical of the individual. The implication here is that even though the numbers represent the responses of a static or non-existent organism, if they relate to typical response patterns, then statements 1 and 2 are less significant. Stated differently, if the measured behavior is relatively stable over time, then the probability that the measure is applicable for future prediction is enhanced. It should be recognized that either the instrument or the individual or both lack characteristics which yield a high degree of stability from one time to another.

4. The quantification and statistical manipulation must have some isomorphic relation (similar properties) to the existing state of affairs. If this criterion is not met, a reverse logic process gives nonsense. To illustrate, if a person sets out to investigate students' course preferences among a set of courses, such as mathematics, science, and English, the appropriate procedure is to count the number of students selecting each and then report, for example, that 25% preferred mathematics, 50% preferred science, and 25% preferred English. An inappropriate use of quantity would be to assign a value "3" to mathematics, "2" to science, and "1" to English, have the students check their preference, and then report the mean preference as 2.5. The 2.5 is a meaningless value. Oddly enough, some people attempt to evaluate such meaningless data. The courses presented represent categorical data, and the mean has no meaning with these data. Interval scores where the numbers represent some logical order can have meaning when means are reported. For example, the average height of man is, say 5′8″—these numbers make sense. In this situation interval scores make sense since feet and inches are representative of a quantity usually employed to indicate height.

These brief explanations of the nature of measurement should be sufficient to provide students with some basis for weighing the efficacy of the specific use of measurement.

Variability

In Chapter 2 we discussed one measure of central tendency (the mean $\frac{\Sigma X}{N}$), and others are presented in Chapter 8. Another question of importance for applied use is, "How do the scores vary from the mean?" One description of variation is the *range* which gives simply the highest and lowest scores. On a classroom examination, the mean may be 10, and the range from 5 to 15, with 15 being a perfect score. This estimate of variability is of limited value because it provides little information regarding the other scores. One very "dull" or one very "bright" child may extend the range unduly. An estimate of variability which is based upon all deviations from the mean is the *Standard Deviation* (SD or σ). Understanding the process of calculating the SD is not necessary for an understanding of its use, but it is a simple process. (It is the square root of the average of the squared deviations from the mean—see Chapter 8.)

TABLE 4.1

Normal distribution curve and selected standard scores

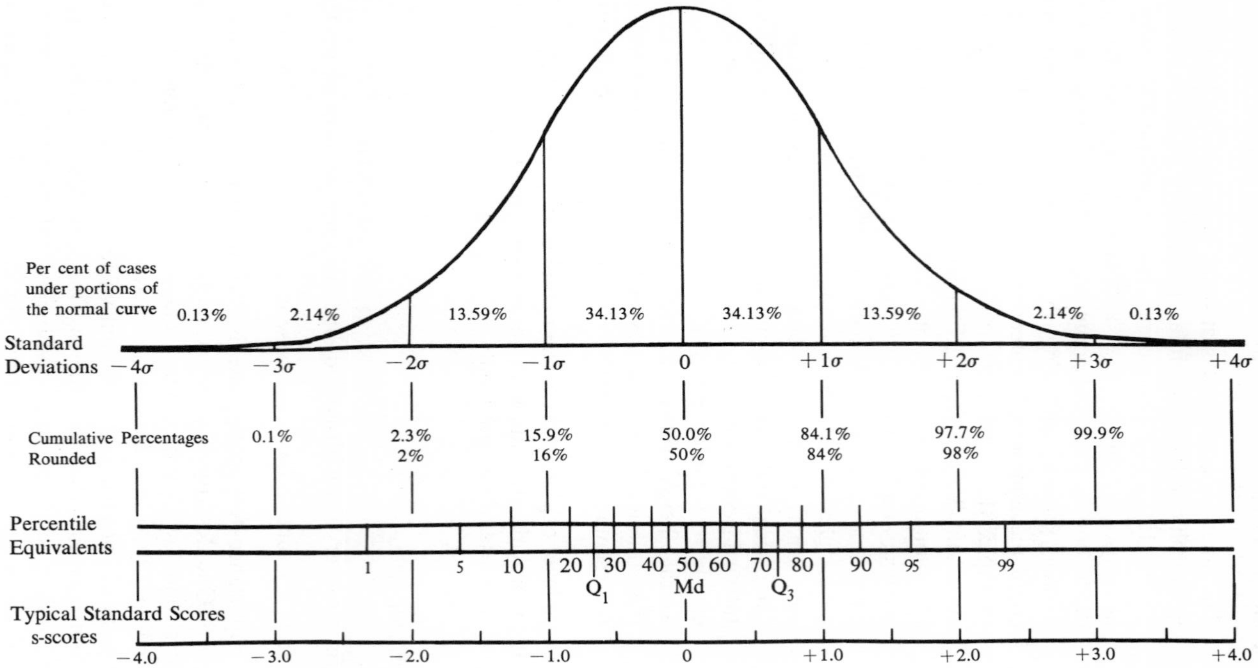

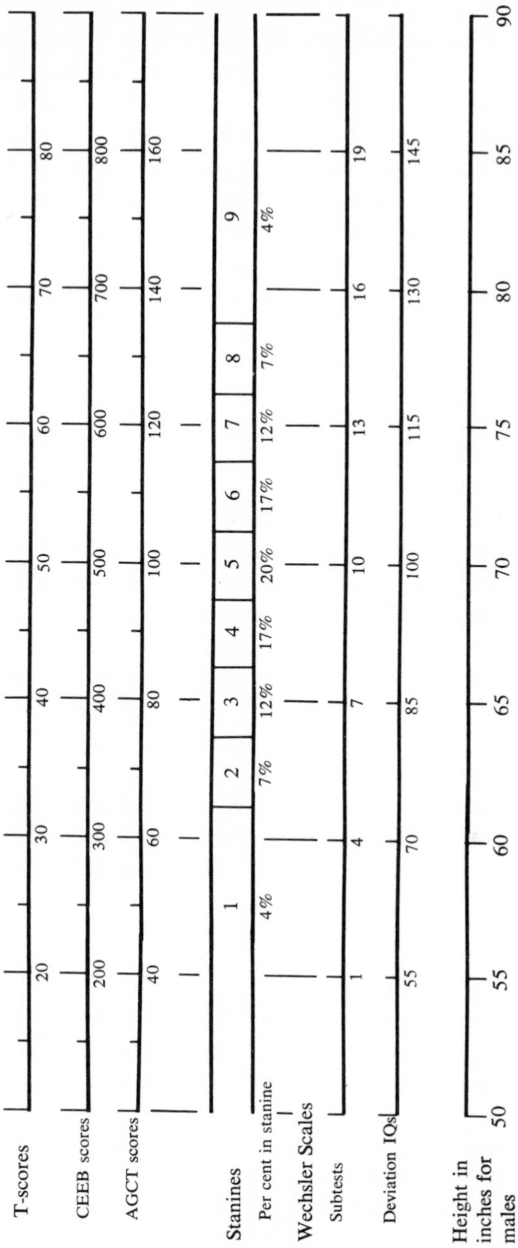

T-scores 20 30 40 50 60 70 80
CEEB scores 200 300 400 500 600 700 800
AGCT scores 40 60 80 100 120 140 160
Stanines 1 2 3 4 5 6 7 8 9
Per cent in stanine 4% 7% 12% 17% 20% 17% 12% 7% 4%
Wechsler Scales
Subtests 1 4 7 10 13 16 19
Deviation IQs 55 70 85 100 115 130 145
Height in inches for males 50 55 60 65 70 75 80 85 90

The SD is generally used in relation to the normal distribution curve (see Table 4.1). In biometrics and psychometrics, most measurements will take the shape of the bell-shaped curve. For example, if we obtain a group of 1,000 men and measure their heights, we would find that the largest proportion of men would fall close to the mean of the group. (See the last entry in Table 4.1.) *If* the mean is 70″ and the SD is 5″, about 68% of the men would fall between 65″ and 75″ in height. (Note that the area in Table 4.1 under the curve between 0 and $-$ 1 SD (σ) $=$ 34.13% and between 0 and $+$ 1 SD (σ) $=$ 34.13%. The total of these two areas is 34.13 $+$ 34.13 $=$ 68.26%.) How often would one expect to encounter a person 85″ tall or taller? The area under the curve from $+$ 3 SD (85″ $-$ 70″ $=$ 15; 1 SD $=$ 5; 15 $\div$ 5 $=$ 3 SD′ above is .13%, thus 13 times in 10,000 one would expect to encounter a man this tall (85″) or taller.

The next to last entry on Table 4.1 shows deviation IQ scores. The mean is 100 and the SD is 15. Therefore, 68% of the population falls between 85 and 115 deviation IQ points. "Mentally retarded" individuals are considered by some to fall below 70 deviation IQ points and therefore represent 2.27% of the population. Likewise, a score of 130 or greater represents 2.27% of the total population. Some people refer to individuals with scores this great or greater as "geniuses," although there is some disagreement over the use of such a term. From these illustrations it can be seen that estimates of standard deviations are employed to represent the likelihood of encountering a particular event or individual when the events or individuals occur at about the frequency represented at various points on a normal distribution curve (the usual—about ⅔ of the time and the unusual about ⅓ of the time).

Sampling

Often when we measure groups of individuals and find behavioral correlates of the measures, we wish to generalize from the sample to the overall population. For example, if we find that IQ correlates with college success in one sample of 1,000 college students and that the mean IQ of this sample is 125, one can ask how representative this sample is of college students in general. If we test five other samples of 1,000 and get mean IQ's of 123, 124, 125, 126, and 127, although we still do not have the total college population, we can estimate the mean of the total from the sample means, and from the *variability* of the sample means we can estimate the probability of how likely the sample mean of 125 is drawn from a population whose mean is really not 125, but is, for example, 127 or greater. With knowledge of the sample variability, an estimate of the population variability can be made, and a probability value can be calculated regarding the question. In this case, the probability that the sample mean of 125 comes from a population whose mean is 127 or greater would most likely be $p < .01$ (probability less than 1 time in 100). Due to errors of measurement, all estimates are subject to error.

Gross errors may be found when the sample is biased for one reason or another (by either known or unknown variables). For example, in the case discussed above, if the sample was drawn from top quality universities, the mean would be a "good" estimate for those top universities, but a generalization to all college students including those attending marginal institutions would be unwarranted because the sample does *not* represent the total group. In addition to information related to the IQ's of students, reasonable interpretations of the data would require additional information concerning the procedures employed in selecting the samples.

It is important to recognize that statements of probability are based on what is observed from a sample. Thus it is extremely important to pay close attention to the characteristics of the large population from which the sample is selected. Statements of probability based on observations of a sample can be made regarding the parent population only. Implications for populations which resemble the parent population are always tenuous.

Measurement and Intelligence

Historically, intelligence tests were developed to determine to what extent a person could benefit from education. A modicum of predictive success was obtained and, since then, the use of the inferred construct called "intelligence" has proliferated. Unfortunately, the use of intelligence tests has extended far more widely than understanding of what the tests can and cannot predict. In Chapter 2, Hebb's concepts of "Intelligence A" and "Intelligence B" were briefly discussed. "Intelligence A" is a theoretical concept regarding the potential effectiveness of the neural structure, while "Intelligence B" relates to observed "intelligent" behavior. The former is not observable and thus at the present time has little value to an applied worker. From noting that some people seem to learn more quickly than others ("Intelligence B"), we tend to make rough categorizations regarding an individual's "intelligence" (ability to behave in a more or less successful manner). We say, "Bill is more 'intelligent' than Sue." Since the reliability of such informal observations is poor, efforts have been made to formalize observation and reduce the subjectivity. Attempts to formalize and standardize observations of behavior required that (1) a group of standardized tasks, which conformed to the observation of experienced observers of behavior, be developed, (2) the tasks be presented to subjects, (3) the subjects respond, (4) the responses be quantified, and (5) those who receive the high scores be called "more intelligent," as measured by this particular test. In this way, we infer from the performances on the tasks the existence of some intervening variable we call "intelligence." (Theoretically, this inferred "intelligence" is a product of Hebb's Factors I through VI—see Chapter 2.)

The determination of the question, "Do intelligence tests *really* measure intelligence?" is meaningless. "Intelligence" is an *invented* construct designed to summarize behavioral characteristics. If a test efficiently predicts the behavior the test inventor wishes to predict, then the test has some value. In our society, the dominant cultural agents believe high scholastic achievement to be "intelligent" behavior; intelligence tests to a limited degree *do* predict level of scholastic achievement. IQ's then, reflect some of the characteristics we group under the label "intelligence."

Any interpretation of an IQ should be made in view of (1) the *reliability* of the instrument (test), (2) the *variability* of the scores, (3) the *representativeness* of the sample from whom the norms were derived, and (4) the *predictive validity* of the instrument. If the instrument is not reliable (e.g., one testing yields a score of 85 and another, with the same individual, yields a score of 145), then the predictive validity will probably be low. On the other hand, an instrument such as "Kelly's Scratch-an-Ear Intelligence Test" may be reliable but have little predictive value if social class characteristics are controlled. If the norm group (that is, the group from which means and standard deviations were derived) is representative of the overall population, then some comparative assessments can be made. Many IQ tests today standardize the scores to a mean of 100 and an SD of 15. If a person scores 130 on such a test, he does as well or better than 97.7% of the population (see cumulative percentages in Table 4.1). Care should be noted regarding the use of the mean and the SD since it is possible for a charlatan to satisfy the egos of naive parents by arbitrarily setting the mean at 150 and the SD at 10. Thus, if a child originally scored two standard deviations below the mean (that is, an IQ of 70), on the typical deviation IQ test, he would, under the charlatan's modified, deceptive scores, be given an IQ of 130 ($150 - 2$ SD $= 130$). Quoting means and standard deviations has no meaning out of context.

Intelligence Scores and Achievement

Typical intelligence tests are heavily weighted with items which relate to an understanding of linguistic signs. Vocabulary and comprehension of meaning are usually stressed. An assumption underlying the assessment of performance on the tests is that, given an equal opportunity to learn, those individuals who are more "intelligent" will understand and remember more. Of course, if a child comes from a home with illiterate parents, his exposure to linguistic signs and meaning will be a great deal less extensive than that of the child exposed to a "rich" language environment. Measured intelligence can therefore vary a great deal as a result of experience. In view of the studies cited in Chapter 2, experience might even change the organic structure, although theoretically the genetic structure imposes some limitations upon the degree of possible change. Caution should be exercised so that IQ scores are not attributed qualities which in fact they do not represent.

The fact that intelligence tests do predict school success moderately well is not surprising, for the behaviors sampled by the intelligence tests are similar to the behaviors which are required for success on other school achievement measures. To be sure, these findings provide *construct validity* for the IQ measures. If we wish to predict school success, IQs provide some information. This information, however, accounts for less than one-half of the achievement variation. More than 50% of the variability in achievement is due to variables other than measured intelligence. Although IQ scores seem to increase the probability of forecasting future behavior in given settings, it is only one of several variables which might be extremely important. We shall return to this prediction problem.

Additional Notes Regarding IQ Measurements

Intelligence tests for children assume that mental ability increases with age; empirical data support the position. A number of cross-sectional studies (where individuals are selected from different age groups) indicate that intelligence test performance increases up to age 21 and then slowly declines. Nancy Bayley (1955) reported data which indicated that intelligence test performance continues to increase (but at a much slower rate) even during the adult years. Bayley's data were derived from longitudinal studies (tests at different ages with the same individuals). Some of the discrepancies between reports can be attributed to the fact that the retested subject performs better due to practice effects, although one of the longitudinal studies Bayley cites retested the subjects 31 years later. Practice effects cannot be very significant with such a huge intervening time period.

Since cross-sectional studies measure individuals who are not contemporaries, the cultural influences are not the same. A fifty-year-old person today will have had a markedly different group of experiences than today's ten-year old child will have had when he is fifty. Educational practices and communication media change—to cite two factors which might contribute to the apparent decline in test performance observed in cross-sectional studies.

Studies following individuals (over a period of time) who are involved in very markedly differing occupations should be conducted to determine the effects of occupational stimulation upon their apparent growth (or lack of it) in intelligence. For example, teachers' activities may have different effects upon manifest intelligence than the activities of ditch-diggers.

Does mental ability "really" increase with age? If by mental ability we mean manifest "intelligent" behavior, then indeed Bayley's data would indicate that ability does increase with age. On the other hand, if we mean improvement in "Intelligence A," then no evidence is available other than the suggestive work of Krech and Rosenzweig, reported in Chapter 2. And perhaps the ability to succeed in later life does not require the same kind of intelligence which seems essential for the young. Remember—intelligence is what the test measures.

Is IQ Enough?

Historically, a controversy waged by psychologists has centered around the question of whether intelligence is a unitary cognitive process or whether it is composed of many factors or special abilities. Whether we like it or not, some single underlying factor—call it "intelligence" if you wish—seems to pervade *much* of the human's cognitive behavior. If Bill is exceptionally "bright" in mathematics, he is likely to be exceptionally "bright" also in many other areas, and conversely, if a person is "dull" in one area, he tends to be "dull" in others. On the other hand, many behaviors considered as adaptive are unrelated to measured "intelligence." Very "bright" Bill might be a social "dunce" whereas "slow" Joe may be the "life of the party." To be sure, such "social intelligence" may be learned, but it is nevertheless "intelligent" behavior. Further, an innovator may show remarkable "creative intelligence," but might not be markedly "bright" with regard to language manipulation. Again we have "intelligent" behavior unrelated to "abstract intelligence" (e.g., IQ performance). These comments should not imply that some genetic neural potential is not important for theoretically if IQ reflects in part genetic capacity to handle abstract symbols, then the high IQ innovator should be able to surpass the moderate IQ innovator. From a pragmatic view the notion that the IQ does not represent the totality of intelligent behavior should be sufficient to allow us to consider the following other intellective processes.

The Structure of Intellect

J. P. Guilford (1959), operating from a factor analytic view, (see Chapter 3 for a discussion of factor analysis) attempted to develop a theory regarding the structure of intellect. By obtaining individuals' responses to a large number of tasks representing diverse content, intercorrelating the responses, and then factoring, the various tests can be boiled down to a number of factors. Inspection of tests which load heavily on one factor and less on the others provides some understanding regarding the nature of the factor. The factors Guilford (1961) derived were assumed to be at a primary-trait level within a hierarchical model of intellective processes. The four levels of the hierarchy are: (1) *specific-action level,* (2) *hexis level,* (3) *primary-trait level,* and (4) *type level.* At the lowest level of the hierarchy, a number of *specific* actions may correlate with each other so as to indicate a higher level, which might be a "habitual" tendency to respond to certain stimuli in specified ways (he calls this the *hexis level* rather than "habitual," since these response tendencies may or may not be learned). A number of "habitual" *(hexical)* response tendencies might correlate so as to indicate a higher level in the hierarchy which would be the *primary-trait level.* For example, regarding personal behavior, *specific* acts such as cheating in cards, in exams, in love, etc., can be grouped together at the *hexis level* to represent a trait of cheating. Acts such as cheating, lying, stealing, etc., might be grouped at the *primary-trait* level as traits of honesty. Honesty may combine with other traits to form a *type* which may reflect strength of character.

The intellective factors which theoretically are primary traits are characterized by three operational facets: (1) the kind of *operation* performed, (2) the kind of *content* or material upon which the operations are performed, and (3) the kind of *products* resulting from the operation on the contents (see Figure 4.2). These "Three Faces of Intellect" are theoretically represented as a cube of data with 120 factors (of which at least 80 have been identified—Guilford, 1966).

FIGURE 4.2

Cubical model of the structure of intellect, representing categories of primary abilities with respect to three modes of variation.

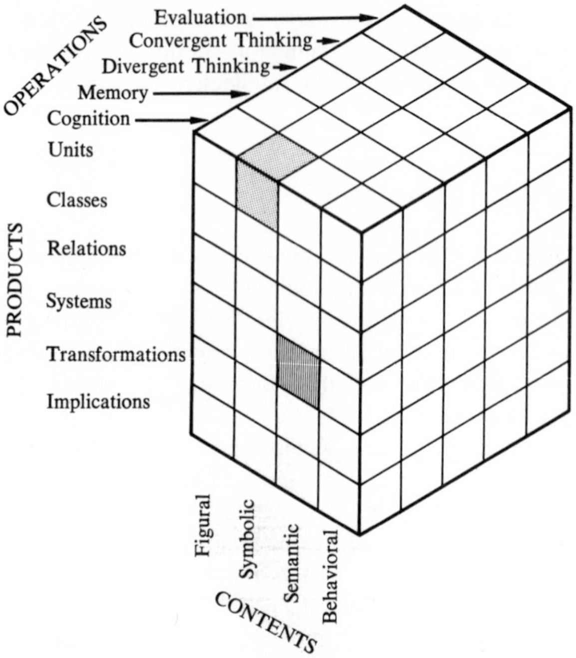

Taken from Guilford, J. P., "Three Faces of Intellect," *American Psychologist*, 14 (1959), 470.

TABLE 4.2

Structure of intellect

I. *Operational Factors*
   - A. *Cognition* – discovery, rediscovery, or recognition.
   - B. *Memory* – retention of what is discovered or recognized.
   - C. *Divergent Thinking* – thinking in different directions, seeking and searching, answers unknown and non-specific.
   - D. *Convergent Thinking* – thinking and processing information to obtain the *one right* answer.
   - E. *Evaluation* – producing decisions regarding the goodness or adequacy of the information one knows, or remembers, or produces by way of divergent or convergent thinking.

II. *Content Factors*
   - A. *Figural* – concrete material (that is, the objects producing perceptual signs) which represents itself — visual, auditory, etc.
   - B. *Symbolic* – letters A, B, C, etc., digits 1, 2, 3, etc.
   - C. *Semantic* – verbal meanings or ideas (linguistic signs and syntax).

D. *Behavioral* – (at the present time, a theoretical area) represents the general area called "social intelligence." (A possible measurement approach may be peer nomination data, where peers nominate persons to such classifications as, "Who knows how to get along with others?" etc.).

III. *Product Factors*

A. *Units*
B. *Classes*
C. *Relations*
D. *Systems*
E. *Transformations*
F. *Implications*

From Guilford, J. P., "Three Faces of Intellect," *American Psychologist,* 14 (1959), 469-479.

Because the best description of a factor is a sample item, Guilford (1959) provided a number of samples. A few are included below:

1. *Cognition of Symbolic Units* (the shaded cube in Figure 4.2) is measured by such items as:

Put vowels in the following blanks to make real words:

P __ W __ R
M __ RV __ L

Rearrange the letters to make real words.

R A C I H

T V O E S

2. *Cognition of Semantic Units* (the cube to the right of the shaded cube is represented by items included in tests called "verbal comprehension." A vocabulary test can assess this factor:

GRAVITY means____________________

CIRCUS means____________________

Guilford is saying, then, that even though the above two sets represent cognition, different abilities are required to deal with *symbolic* units than with *semantic* units.

3. *Cognition of Semantic Systems* (the dotted cube) represents the common concept of *general* reasoning. The instructions for a typical item ask what operations are needed to solve the problem:

A city lot 48 feet wide and 149 feet deep costs $79,432. What is the cost per square foot?

A. add and multiply
B. multiply and divide
C. subtract and divide
D. add and subtract
E. divide and add

This ability, according to Guilford, should be applied to all kinds of verbal conceptual systems, not solely to arithmetic types of problems.

4. *Memory of Symbolic Units* should be broken into visual and auditory facets. Tests such as number series or letter series represent this factor, which can be presented as either visual or audio stimuli. A visual example might instruct the subject to look at a group of letters for 10 seconds and then close the book and repeat the sequence:

L X B C P D F

5. *Divergent Production of Semantic Classes* is also called "spontaneous flexibility." A typical item instructs the individual to list all of the uses he can think of for some common object, such as a brick. An eight-minute time limit is imposed. If the responses are "build a house, build a garage, build a fence," etc., a high score is obtained for fluency but *not* for "spontaneous flexibility." Responses which *shift* in usage, however (e.g., "make a door stop, make a bookcase, drown a cat, make a paperweight, throw at a dog, use for bases in baseball," etc.), would yield a high score for flexibility because the individual has gone frequently from one class to another. Thus fluency and flexibility are considered components of divergent production.

6. *Convergent Symbolic Relationships* are illustrated by the analogies task in which the subject is asked to provide the missing symbolic unit which conforms to the previous relationships:

POTS STOP BARD DRAB RATS ________?

7. *Convergent Semantic Relationships* can be measured by items such as:

The absence of sound is________________.

8. *Evaluation of Symbolic Units* is represented by items included in typical clerical aptitude tests:

Are members of the following pairs identical or not?

825170493 825176493

dkeltvmpa .... dkeltvmpa

9. *Evaluation of Figural Transformations* may be measured by the "apparatus test." This test asks for two needed improvements for each of a number of common devices, such as telephones, toasters, etc.

Implications of the Structure of Intellect

Human behavior is a complex set of actions which emanate from an organism that has complex abilities. From this position, in order to make decisions regarding future "intelligent" behavior of an individual, two conditions need clarification: (1) a determination of the task characteristics regarding the content to be manipulated, operations to be carried out, and the product desired, and (2) a determination of the individual's ability to deliver the product.

Guilford claims that there are at least 80 known ways to be "intelligent." Cast into the S→O→R model presented in Chapter 2, then, there are at least 80 clusters of residuals which may be activated by a set of stimuli, and the individual who responds "well" to the stimuli (tasks) may be said to have a "superior" set of the relevant residuals. Typical intelligence tests include a large number of convergent thinking items and thus in part assess the individual's ability to derive the one correct answer to a problem. Because most achievement tests provided by the teachers or the testing staffs in schools require the provision or selection of the one best answer, intelligence tests which stress convergence can predict these assessments of achievement.

If the educational systems aim at providing the students with the necessary response strategies, then some courses and achievement tests should be geared to abilities which, Guilford suggests, involve operations upon material content. Figural content apparently relates to "concrete intelligence," development of which should be necessary for mechanics, machine operators, artists, engineers, musicians, etc.

Abilities associated with symbolic and semantic content can be called "abstract intelligence." Symbolic abilities relate to spelling, number operations, word recognition, etc. "Semantic intelligence," according to Guilford, should be important for understanding verbal concepts as they relate to facts and ideas. Much of our university training requires "semantic intelligence."

"Social intelligence" should be predictive of success in occupations which require understanding and manipulation of behavior in the social situation. At the present, no measures of this theoretical intelligence are available. The entire behavioral plane of the structure of intellect is awaiting research.

In one sense, when Guilford claims that there is a structure of intellect, he is also saying that there is structure in the subject matter to be manipulated. We shall return to this point in Chapter 5.

Educational Practice and the Structure of Intellect

The abilities Guilford delineates are theoretically a product of Hebb's Factors I through VI, and since the abilities are empirical measures, the relative limitations imposed on them by the genetic structure are unknown. Consequently, Guilford suggested that practice in exercising each of the abilities might lead to more effective development of the intellect. The learning of habits and skills should, in his view, be supplemented by practice relating to the more general abilities of discovery, invention, evaluation, and other means of information processing. At the present time, our schools seem to be giving practice mostly in convergent thinking abilities. In general, theoretical concepts relative to the way man learns and how he is expected to perform seem to have little effect on school practices.

At first glance, Guilford's writing appears to be a reversion to the repudiated school that advocates "mental discipline" and exercising of the "mind" as though it were a muscle. Guilford's intellect, however, is much more complex than the "mind" conceived by the older (1930) view. Rather than memorize geometry because it is good exercise, Guilford seems to be advocating practice in drawing implications, making transformations, evaluating divergent ideas, etc. Each of these processes are assumed to have *transfer* properties that the memorization of rules seems to lack. In other words, all subject matter can be a tool, and perhaps an essential tool, to develop the thinking processes.

A Note of Caution

Americans believe in equality, and therefore often subscribe to the notion of compensatory functions where, if a person is "dull" in, say, abstract processes, he must then be "superior" in some other area—but this notion is not supported by evidence. On the other hand, in light of the studies with "culturally deprived" children (see Chapter 3) and some animal studies, the limitations imposed upon intellective functions by the genetic structure might be less than many present-day theoreticians suggest. This is not to say that a person with relatively low abilities (theoretically in part a function of the genetic structure) can be made a "genius," but "enriched" environments and opportunities to solve problems might provide him with coping strategies which were believed impossible in the past. We still have much to learn about human learning.

Another consideration merits note. The traditional intelligence test still does much predictive work, and thus has some applied value. Also, although we may discover 120 distinct abilities, many of these might have little value for the great majority of the behaviors necessary for successful coping. A number of the factors, however, might prove to have wide applicability. Since the 120 factors are of interest to some psychologists who have theoretical inclinations, the authors suggest that we use what ideas we can and continue investigations in order to discover wider applications and understandings.

The "Creativity" Fad

American educators and psychologists are prone to be band-wagon riders. We have gone through the "whole child" phase, attending more to Johnnie's feelings and social development than to other matters. Also we have bought "learn by doing" but have discarded parts of the scheme. In the early sixties we entered into the new science, new math, automated learning, team teaching, TV teaching, and "creativity" cycle. We can be thankful, at least, that there is more than one area emphasized today. (Something for everyone, perhaps?) We shall discuss teaching machines in Chapter 8 and the new math in Chapter 5. A few words regarding the "creativity" fad are included below.

J. P. Guilford (1950) in the late forties pioneered the interest in measurement of "creativity." Lowenfeld (1958) later provided independent corroboration of Guilford's findings. These investigators have shown that "creativity" involves sensitivity to problems, fluency of ideas, flexibility, originality, redefinition, ability to rearrange, abstracting ability, synthesis and closure, and coherence of organization, all of which are included in Guilford's structure of intellect. Then, in 1957, the Russians lobbed "Sputnik 1" in orbit, and immediately wails of anguish were heard across the country. The schools were not producing scientists, were not producing "creative" people — and so "creativity" as an aim of education went into orbit with plenty of research money for fuel. "Creative" writers, "creative" engineers, "creative" scientists, etc., were studied. And indeed, they manifested originality, flexibility, etc. Unfortunately, these studies have just scratched the surface.

We now "know" (Getzels and Jackson, 1958) that among school children "creativity" and IQ correlate about +.30 (9% variation is common), but among the gifted (IQs from 132 to 186) these correlations approach zero. And we "know" that teachers tend to prefer the highly "intelligent" but moderately "creative" students to the highly "creative" and above average in "intelligence" students (Getzels and Jackson, 1958). According to Torrance (1960), the "creative" child should be identified early, since the peer group exercises severe censure against him. Torrance stated that educators should develop "creative thinking" in all children, because it is associated with "positive mental health," "vocational success," and "social welfare."

Maltzman, *et al.* (1960), reported that originality (defined as statistically unique responses to an "unusual use test" in which the subject listed unusual uses of, say, an automobile tire) can be increased for at least 48 hours when training requires a student to repeatedly provide different responses to the same stimuli. In relation to possible applications, such studies might appear to be rather trivial. The workers, however, have broached the task of defining "originality," and have systematically attempted to increase it. Many educators applaud "creativity," but fail to define what is meant by the term behaviorally. We are continually faced with objectives of education which are not testable because we do not specify what responses reflect the objectives.

The "creativity" fad now seems to be dissipating in the schools. However, the systematic development of methods and longitudinal testing of the adaptive value of the "creativity" training which has been given remain to be carried out. One might become a bit peeved with faddism and the concomitant tendency to proclaim the new idea as the "be all and end all" of educational problems, but faddism does give impetus to areas of possible research which have been neglected. In terms related to creativity, faddism seems to be the result of those less inventive souls following the lead of the original thinker because his ideas seem sound or because of the belief that a follower eventually picks up the traits of the leader.

Difficulties in the Measurement of Abilities

Test performance is assumed to be a function of Hebb's Factors I through VI. We mentioned earlier that intelligence test performance assumes some minimal educational experiences (sensory variables). Figure 4.3 is a simplified illustration of three stages related to "intelligent" behavior. As a result of early stimulation and educational exposure, some fraction of the responses remain as residuals (rs's). Theoretically, the individual with a more adequate genetic structure will build a repertory of residuals which are "superior" to those with a less adequate structure. Therefore, in the measurement situation, when the test (ΣS – test) is presented, the individual with the "superior" response repertory should exhibit "superior" test performance, and in new learning situations he should be able to exhibit "superior" achievement performance. Unfortunately, measurement is not so simple.

Sarason (1958) developed an assessment instrument which he called the *Test Anxiety Scale* (TAS). The scale asks questions regarding the

FIGURE 4.3

Three aspects of intelligent behavior

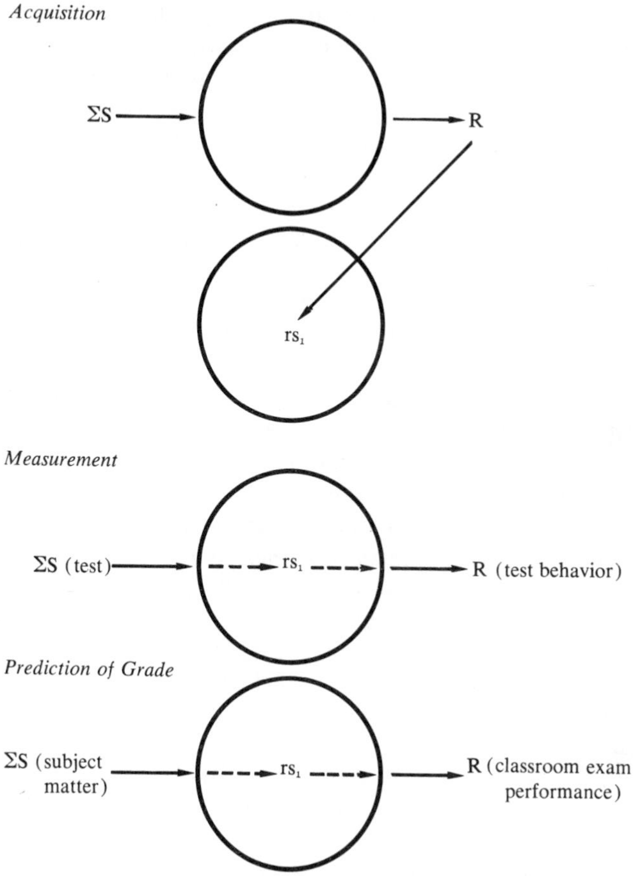

amounts of tension, etc., the person feels before or during a test. The individual indicates whether or not the situations apply to himself. Those who indicate that a large number of the items are typical of their reactions to tests have *High Test Anxiety* (HTA) and those who indicate the stated behaviors do not describe them have *Low Test Anxiety* (LTA). Sarason and Palola (1960) reported a number of studies which showed that Test Anxiety is related to intelligence test performance. If the items were easy, HTA subjects exhibited performance "superior" to LTA subjects. Conversely, if the items were difficult, LTA subjects performed better than HTA subjects.

In relation to two of Guilford's measures of divergent thinking, Kelly, Hunka, and Conklin (1965) found that HTA university subjects performed better than LTA subjects. Among high school subjects the relationship is reversed. Kelly, *et al.*, suggested that high school students as a group might take the tests more seriously than university students accustomed to being subjects in research projects.

Apparently, some other learnings are influencing performances on tests of the intellect. Intelligence test performance can be conceived of as the product of anxiety interacting with the underlying ability. Results of hard and easy tests might not correlate highly due to the contaminating effects of anxiety. For predictive purposes, the fact that test anxiety contaminates intelligence measures can be significant information. Performance under pressure, such as in classroom exams, should be best by high IQ, LTA students. Without pressure, high IQ, HTA students should excel.

A revision of the complete S→ O→R model presented in Chapter 2 could include a set of residuals (that may be called rs_{anx}) which function as moderators. Since, however, a number of other "personality" characteristics seem to influence behavior, causing the S→O→R model to become too cumbersome for illustrative purposes, the next section provides a possibly more economical model.

Prior to discussing the new model, we should point out that, theoretically, anxiety (manifest anxiety as well as test anxiety) is acquired through some learning process (Sarason, Hill and Zimbardo, 1964; Hill and Sarason, 1966). As a result of parental expectations and peer or teacher pressure, the child may acquire a fear of failure which causes him to face examinations with tension. High tension can have a debilitating effect on performance. If, as Hebb theorizes, over-arousal leads to inefficient cortical firing, then central processes, such as fear of failure, might lead to tension, which then gives feedback through the NPS (Non-specific Projection System) and brings about an over-aroused state. Anxiety may not lead to the extreme diffuse cortical firing that electro-shock provides, but the higher arousal contributed by anxiety might cause the individual to process trivial stimuli (non-task-relevant stimuli) in his environment and thus cause poorer performance.

A Model Representing the Complexities Underlying Behavior

The anxiety studies reported above suggest that central mediational processes include more than that which falls into the category called intellective processes. As a result of his work, McGuire (1960) proposed a quasi-mathematical equation to represent factors influencing behavior. Table 4.3 presents a modified version of McGuire's model.

TABLE 4.3

A modified version of McGuire's model

$$Ba = f\ (Pa, Eab, Rba, rs_{1 \ldots n})\ Sa, Cab, x$$

Ba = behavior of the person (a) to be explained or predicted.

Pa = potential cognitive, perceptual, and other relevant abilities (e.g., divergent thinking, convergent thinking, symbol aptitude).

Eab = elements of personality and motivation, especially expectations about one's own behavior and probable responses of other persons (e.g., attitudes and values).

Rba = perception of other persons' (b) expectations and pressures imposed upon the given individual (a).

$rs_{1 \ldots n}$ = acquired response repertory that is relevant to the behavior to be explained or predicted (e.g., previous achievement).

Sa = sex-role identification of the individual (a) and sex-typing of socialization pressures, both of which moderate preceding variables.

Cab = context of behavior, such as community or school setting which provides an institutional framework along with certain experiences and impersonal expectations, or the setting in which a natural or a laboratory experiment takes place.

x = unaccounted-for variations, due possibly to errors in measurement as well as due to undiscovered relevant variables; some may wish to call this "free will," but for heuristic purposes, it may be best described as the unknown factor(s) underlying behavior.

Adapted from Carson McGuire, "The Prediction of Talented Behavior in the Junior High School," Invitational Conference on Testing Problems, E. T. S. Princeton, N. J., (1960), 66.

The equation may be interpreted as follows:

> The behavior of an individual is (a) a function of his potential cognitive abilities, elements of motivation, expectations of support or non-support from others, (b) task-relevant learnings, sex-role expectations in the behaving context, plus other factors presently unknown. (The parentheses in the equation indicate factors within the individual. The other factors are external.)

We have discussed in some detail the nature of the cognitive abilities (Pa). For many school-related activities, convergent thinking abilities are of paramount relevance, although symbol aptitude and divergent thinking might be of importance for some courses of study. The following discussion will elaborate upon the remaining factors relevant to behavior.

If McGuire's model has any relevance for prediction of school success, then one would expect that measures which sample behaviors related to each of the terms in the equation should give statistically better prediction than measures of cognitive abilities alone. Whiteside (1964), using McGuire's comprehensive model in a predictive study with grade 9 Grade Point Average (GPA) as the criterion, was able to increase the predicted variation by 100% over studies with only an ability measure. Since Whiteside's work illustrates a number of points, we shall discuss it in some detail. First a brief note regarding Multiple Linear Regression Analysis, which will help us to understand Whiteside's work.

Multiple Regression Analysis

In Chapter 2 we discussed the concept of error sums of squares (ESS). The predicted score which was derived was based upon the mean of the group that the individual represented. We had for Treatment Z a mean of 12, for Treatment Y a mean of 18, and certain errors of prediction. In vector notation, the observed score for any individual can be expressed:

$Y_1 = a_1 x_1 + a_2 x_2 + e$, where:

- Y_1 = observed score
- x_1 = "1," if the score on the criterion has come from a person under Treatment Z, "0" otherwise.
- a_1 = mean for Treatment Z.
- x_2 = "1," if the score on the criterion has come from a person under Treatment Y, "0" otherwise.
- a_2 = mean for Treatment Y.
- e = error or difference between the observed score Y and the predicted score (mean of Treatment Z if the person was in Group Z).

Multiple Linear Regression Analysis is a statistical procedure where the weights (e.g., a_1, a_2) can be calculated in such a manner as to yield the smallest error sums of squares. The technique capitalizes upon the correlation of each predictor with the criterion and takes into account the correlations among predictors. Predictors are initially selected in most research because they seem to have a theoretical relationship to the performance to be predicted. The "shotgun" technique (obtain a wide variety of performances) in which many factors are plugged into a formula without considering theoretical relationships seems a waste of effort in most cases. If two tests correlate perfectly with each other, they most likely measure the same characteristics in the criterion, thus one will predict as well as two. In the above two-group case, the calculated weights will be the means of the groups; however, when one is dealing with continuous data, these weights have no direct relationship to the mean . . .

If there are five tests which correlate with the criterion (in Whiteside's study, grade 9 GPA) and they do not correlate too highly with each other, then an equation using all five tests will most likely predict better than any one of the tests alone. Such an equation may be:

$$Y = a_0 u + a_1 x_1 + a_2 x_2 + a_3 x_3 + a_4 x_4 + a_5 x_5 + e, \text{ where:}$$

a_0u = a unit vector and a weight which provide the regression constant (this adjusts the regression line so that the predicted mean equals the observed mean)

$x_1 \ldots x_5$ = scores obtained by the individual on the five tests

$a_1 \ldots a_5$ = weights for each test calculated so as to provide the minimum ESS

e = error, observed score minus predicted score

If the five tests add to the prediction, then the error sums of squares would be smaller with the test information than without. Recall that we can make a prediction for each individual using the weights times the scores on the tests. We subtract this *predicted* score for the criterion from the individual's *obtained* score, which gives us "e." Upon squaring each of these "e's" and adding them, we get the ESS. Assuming that these five test scores do not aid prediction (or, stated differently do not significantly decrease the error sums of squares) we can express the equation:

$$Y = a_0 u + e_1, \text{ where:}$$

a_0 = mean on the criterion.

u = a vector with 1's for all subjects.

e_1 = error — observed score minus the group mean.

We can square "e_1" and sum over all subjects and get an ESS which will represent the squared errors of prediction with only knowledge of group means. An F test can be calculated to determine the significance of the increased ESS as a result of throwing away the test information. (For those with an interest in this procedure, see Bottenberg and Ward, 1963.) If the F test is significant, then we have thrown away predictive information. A multiple R (multiple correlation) can be calculated to indicate the relationship. With knowledge of the mean only, the R will be "0." With eight scores, Whiteside obtained R's of .80, which is fairly good prediction.

Prediction of Grade 9 GPA

In Whiteside's (1964) study, the following information (categorized according to McGuire's model) was used to predict grade 9 averages for 580 students living in four different cities:

Pa = potential cognitive abilities, etc.

1. *California Test of Mental Maturity* (CTMM), a measure of convergent thinking. The test is a typical paper-and-pencil IQ test.
2. *Mutilated Words,* a measure of symbol aptitude. The test gives a number of words which have been partially erased. The student must figure out what the word is from the letters given.
3. *Seeing Problems,* a measure of divergent thinking. In this test of Guilford's, the student lists the number of problems he can see which are related to some everyday task (e.g., "making a sandwich").

Eab = elements of personality and motivation, etc.

4. *Survey of Study Habits and Attitudes (SSHA), Scholastic Motivation,* assumed to assess conformity motivation. The scale includes such items as "Whether I like a subject or not, I still work hard to make a good grade," and, "Unless I really like a subject, I believe in only doing enough to get a passing grade." Note that theoretically, the person learns, as a result of previous interactions with others (particularly his parents), that school success is either important or not important. These learnings should influence school performance. The scale *attempts* to assess these learnings, but may only partially tap the individual's evaluating processes regarding school activities.
5. *Co-operative Youth Study (CYS), Personal Adjustment,* assumed to measure "neurotic anxiety." The scale is composed of items such as, "Sometimes I feel things are not real," and, "I get mad and do things I shouldn't do when I can't have my way." This scale attempts to assess some learnings regarding self-control and tension states due to the inability of the individual to predict the consequences of his actions.
6. *Sequential Tests of Educational Progress (STEP), Listening,* used as an assessment of "impulsiveness." This test was developed as a measure of listening ability; however, the test is rather interesting and was viewed by Kelly and Veldman (1964) to be a test of the ability to maintain a convergent set. The test administrator reads a paragraph and then reads a series of questions

which the student is required to answer. If a person is impulsive and easily distracted, theoretically his score will suffer because there is no printed matter to which to refer.

Rba = perceived expectations, etc.

7. *Peer Nomination: Academic Model,* assumed to reflect the role others expect of the individual. The value (number) placed in this vector is the number of times the individual is named by his classmates in response to, "Name three persons you could work with or ask for help on a *school* problem."

Sa = Sex-role expectancies

8. The subject is given "1" if female, "0" if male. Females are expected in our society to be more serious and docile, and as a result of sex-role fulfillment, the females' achievement scores as assessed by teachers should therefore be increased.

Each of the eight predictors independently *contributed significantly* to the prediction. The process involves first establishing a regression equation with all eight predictors and then dropping out one. If the ESS is significantly increased, then the predictor is said to contribute independently to the prediction. The predictor which was dropped out is then replaced and another dropped out. This process is repeated for all eight predictors.

Three of the predictors, *CTMM, Seeing Problems,* and *Academic Model,* were curvilinearly related to the criterion. Curvilinearity means that the rate of increase is not constant across all scores. Figure 4.4 represents this condition. Reading across the *CTMM* scale, as one goes from low scores to high scores, the rate of increase on the GPA scale increases. Thus, a 10-point increase in IQ from 80-90 yields about a 0.2 increase in GPA, whereas a 10-point increase from 110-120 yields about a 1.0 increase in GPA. By including these three predictors and three new vectors which would be $CTMM^2$, $Seeing\ Problems^2$, and $Academic\ Model^2$, the curvilinear relationship can be expressed in a regression model. These three curvilinear vectors add to statistically significant increased prediction.

Further, *STEP Listening* was postulated by Whiteside to act upon ("interact" with) *CTMM* as a "catalyst." He reasoned that high *STEP Listening* scores represent impulse control which can markedly influence the student's application of his intelligence (CTMM) to school-related tasks. Indeed, this was the condition Whiteside found. Figure 4.5 shows

FIGURE 4.4

This figure represents a curvilinear relationship that accelerates positively.

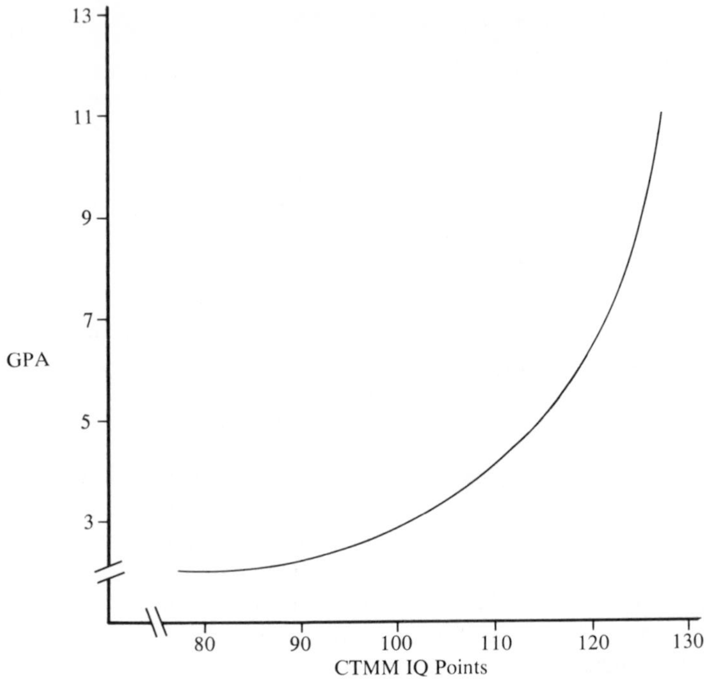

this possible relationship. Note that the slope of the high *STEP Listening* students is steeper than the slope of the low *STEP Listening* subjects. "Interaction" means only that the slopes are different for the two groups. A vector which is the product of *(CTMM)* x *(STEP Listening)* represents this condition in the regression model. However, due to the fact that *CTMM* is curvilinearly related to the criterion, a "curvilinear interaction" exists as is expressed in Figure 4.6. (For those who are interested in the final equation, see Table 4.4.)

TABLE 4.4

Whiteside's final regression model which best predicts GPA

$$Y = a_0 u + a_1 x_1 + a_2 x_2 + a_3 x_3 + \ldots a_{13} x_{13} + e, \text{ where:}$$

Y = the criterion, grade 9 GPA in standard score form

$a_0 \ldots a_{13}$ = regression weights
u = unit vector
x_1 = *STEP Listening*
x_2 = *CTMM*
x_3 = *(CTMM)*^{2}
x_4 = (*STEP Listening*) x (*CTMM*)
x_5 = (*STEP Listening*) x (*CTMM*)^2
x_6 = *Seeing Problems*
x_7 = (*Seeing Problems*)^2
x_8 = *Mutilated Words*
x_9 = *Scholastic Motivation*
x_{10} = *CYS Personal Maladjustment*
x_{11} = *Peer Nom.: Academic Model*
x_{12} = (*Peer Nom.: Academic Model*)^2
x_{13} = "1" if score on Y is from a female,
"0" if from a male.
e = observed score minus predicted score

From Whiteside, R., "Dimensions of Teacher Evaluation of Academic Achievement," unpublished Ph.D. Dissertation, University of Texas, Austin, Texas, 1964.

FIGURE 4.5

This figure represents an interacting relationship

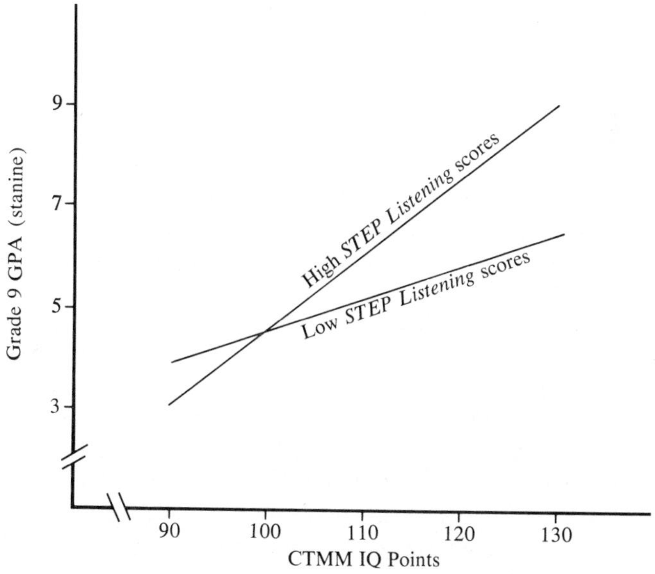

FIGURE 4.6

This figure represents a curvilinear-interaction relationship

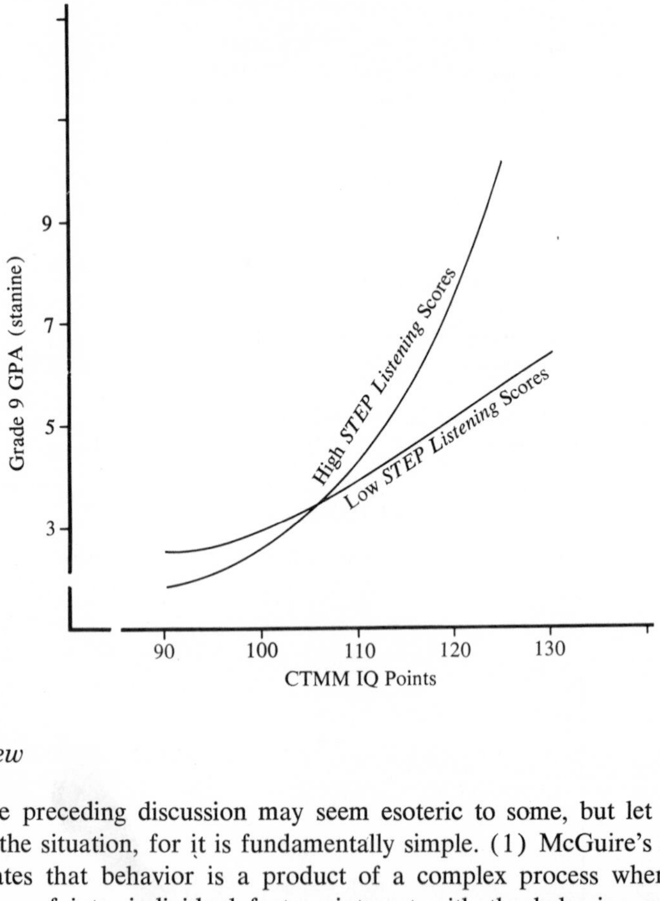

Review

The preceding discussion may seem esoteric to some, but let us review the situation, for it is fundamentally simple. (1) McGuire's model indicates that behavior is a product of a complex process whereby a number of intra-individual factors interact with the behaving context. (2) Multiple Linear Regression techniques provide one statistical method where the complex process can at least in part be numerically reflected. (3) Whiteside's study combined the theoretical model with the statistical technique and was thereby able to double the amount of predicted variation. (4) Grade Point Average is related to eight predictors, assumed to be related to some stable characteristic of the person. The relation of these eight predictors to the criterion is complex (e.g., curvilinear in some cases and curvilinearly interacting in another).

These calculations can be carried out very easily with the high-speed digital computer, and a number of excellent computer programs have been developed to carry out these operations efficiently (in less than two minutes with an IBM 7040 Computer).

Applied Prediction

The previous discussion uses a multivariate theoretical approach to the prediction of grade 9 GPA and has been presented to illustrate the fact that scores (theoretically measuring some of the individual's stable characteristics) relate in complex ways to measured school behavior.

One of the limitations of the Whiteside (1964) study is that the number used as the criterion was the grade 9 GPA which is an *evaluation* of the behavior of the student, but Whiteside did not include in his equations an estimate of teacher expectancy. A second limitation is that the eight predictors plus the five curvilinear and/or interaction vectors provide a rather cumbersome equation to manipulate, especially for school personnel who may be concerned with academic and vocational guidance.

Whiteside (1964) conducted a second series of studies to determine the feasibility of developing an equation which contains fewer variables and requires tests which are economical to administer.

Since one of the crucial periods for intensive counselling is at the end of grade 9, prior to entering high school, (in a 6-3-3 school system) Whiteside selected scores from this grade to predict total (grades 10, 11 and 12) high school GPA. Whiteside contended that if an efficient equation could be developed, guidance personnel could make some estimate of probable high school failure and then attempt to prevent the predicted failure by way of special programs designed to provide the student with efficient coping skills.

Whiteside used 580 students (297 boys, 283 girls) who finished grade 12 and who had participated in a grade 9 testing program (part of the Human Talent Research Project at Austin, Texas).

Most prediction studies lose some of their value when the equation is applied to a new sample. Since no two samples from the same population are likely to be identical, predictive equations derived from one sample will probably not work to the same degree with a second sample. Differences between samples are usually sufficiently great to yield an observable difference when prediction is attempted. To estimate this possible loss, Whiteside developed an equation for each of the four communities involved, and then cross-applied the weights obtained from Community A to Communities B, C, and D. This process was repeated for each of the equations giving a total of 12 cross-validations (three for each equation).

Predictor Vectors

In order to obtain an efficient predictor set, Whiteside selected all of the variables included in his grade 9 predictive set plus grade 9 GPA squared, and then selected the five best predictors which related to the high school GPA of the students attending school in Community A.

The final prediction equation included:

$$Y = a_0 u + a_1 x_1 + a_2 x_2 + a_3 x_3 + a_4 x_4 + a_5 x_5 + e, \text{ where:}$$

Y = Total high school GPA
$a_1 \ldots a_5$ = regression weight. (calculated so as to minimize the errors of prediction)
x_1 = grade 9 score on *Mutilated Words.*
x_2 = grade 9 score on *Academic Model.*
x_3 = "1" if subject was female, "0" if male.
x_4 = (grade 9 *CTMM* Score) x (Grade 9 *STEP Listening*).
x_5 = (grade 9 GPA)^2.
e = difference between predicted and observed GPA's.

It is interesting to note that the curvilinear *CTMM* score did not show a strong relationship to high school grade average; however, the *STEP Listening* still operates as a "catalyst." The strongest predictor by far was the grade 9 GPA square (accounting for 60% of the predictive variance). The value of this predictor is that it gives some estimate of the behaviors which teachers evaluate. Ninth grade teachers have some evaluative criteria in common with high school teachers but the relationship is curvilinear, which might indicate that grade 9 teachers give above average grades to "nice" average students and that very high grade 9 GPA's indicate students with above average abilities.

Multiple R's obtained with these five predictors for each community were:

Community A: $R = .88$, $(R^2 = .78)$
Community B: $R = .84$, $(R^2 = .71)$
Community C: $R = .89$, $(R^2 = .80)$
Community D: $R = .83$, $(R^2 = .69)$

These values represent remarkably high predictions. More remarkable was the finding that among the cross-validations (applying weights from one community to another) only four of the twelve showed statistically significant loss of information and the smallest cross-validated multiple correlation coefficients were greater than $+.80$.

A word of caution: since these data were obtained from a longitudinal study, a number of students (those who moved in and out of the communities) were by necessity excluded from the study. As such, the sample used by Whiteside represents a special (non-mobile) population. Nevertheless, McGuire's Multivariate Theory of Behavior receives substantial support from Whiteside's work. The prediction equations seem to have definite potency for practical uses. Consider a guidance worker who has student information on the five predictors. He can apply Whiteside's weights and can obtain a fairly good prediction regarding the students' high school performance. In cases of predicted failure, the guidance worker, teacher, and other school personnel might wish (should wish?) to revise the school curriculum in an attempt to upset the predicted failure. Indeed, this whole prediction business is included here for this very purpose. The concern of the educator is not to be satisfied with prediction alone, but to employ predictive devices in efforts to improve educational programs.

Single Determinants of Behavior: A Transition Note

We discussed intelligence as a characteristic of human behavior and then presented information regarding anxiety as it relates to behavior. The anxiety studies mentioned were basically what is commonly called univariate studies. That is, one variable is observed to relate to another. Univariate studies can be misleading in that they fail to represent the complexities of behavior. A case in point is the *CTMM* and *STEP Listening* interaction noted in Whiteside's studies. Multivariate studies, where a number of variables are treated simultaneously, seem to represent the complexities more adequately. In addition, when several predictors can be used and compared, those variables which contribute most significantly can be identified. In this manner many variables may be relegated to a postion of irrelevance and thus much time and effort can be spared. School specialists can ignore data which do not contribute significantly to the task at hand. On the other hand, multivariate analysis can profit greatly from univariate work, since isolation of one or two variables and intensive investigation of these variables can lead to some understanding of the acquisition process. Also, univariate studies can provide measures which theoretically relate to complex behaviors. These measures can be systematically investigated in multivariate studies which can provide further theoretic as well as applied information. The following section provides a sampling of non-intellective notions (e.g., "achievement motivation") which have contributed to the understanding of human behavior and which have some value for the applied worker. Need achievement and the authoritarian personality are discussed in detail as examples of univariate studies which appear to have some value. Other univariate studies could just as well have been chosen.

Single Determinants of Behavior: (1) "Need Achievement"

McClelland (1955) reported a number of studies related to the achievement motive or what is called "Need Achievement" ("n Ach").

McClelland, (1953) measured "n Ach" through the quantification of "free" fantasy. A picture was flashed on a screen for 20 seconds and the subject was asked to write a story about the picture. The instructions were:

> This is a test of your creative imagination. A number of pictures will be projected on the screen before you. You will have twenty seconds to look at the picture and then about four minutes to make up a story about it. Notice that there is one page for each picture. The same four questions are asked. They will guide your thinking and enable you to cover all the elements of a plot in the time allotted. Plan to spend about a minute on each question. I will keep time and tell you when it is about time to finish your story before the next picture is shown.
>
> Obviously there are no right or wrong answers, so you may feel free to make up any kind of a story about the pictures that you choose. Try to make them vivid and dramatic, for this is a test of *creative* imagination. Do not merely describe the picture you see. Tell a story about it. Work as fast as you can in order to finish in time. Make them interesting. Are there any questions? If you need more space for any question, use the reverse side.
>
> Each sheet contains four questions:
> 1. What is happening? Who are the persons?
> 2. What has led up to this situation? What has happened in the past?
> 3. What it being thought? What is wanted? By whom?
> 4. What will happen? What will be done?

The responses to the pictures were scored in relation to "achievement goals" (that is, success in competition with some standard of excellence). Assignment of scores derived from projective devices such as these requires training of interpreters and extra time to develop reliability among the judges. Although the procedure is rather costly, the test taps information which is otherwise difficult to obtain and at the same time minimizes "faking" on the part of subjects. For example, in a school setting, a statement such as "Whether I like a subject or not, I still work hard to make a good grade," may be answered, "Yes," just to please the school officials. The "n Ach" measure is obscured within McCelland's test so that supposedly little faking can take place.

The "n Ach" is reported to be positively related to performance on tasks which require subjects to unscramble words (e.g., unscramble the letters "W T S E" to get the word "W E S T"). McClelland suggests that the more highly-motivated students, as measured by "n Ach," scored higher in the tasks because they had learned better ways to solve the problems. High "n Ach" subjects also produce better than low "n Ach" subjects in tasks which require the solution of simple addition questions that presumably do not require new learnings. Under conditions which are achievement-oriented, high "n Ach" subjects recall significantly more interrupted tasks than do low "n Ach" subjects.

Achievement motivation as measured by "n Ach" seems to be a valuable inferred construct for it does predict behavior that theoretically should be related to the achievement motive.

Note: The fact that scrambled word performance is influenced by achievement motivation is interesting since unscrambling words is a symbol aptitude task. Note that this suggests again that human behavior is complex and that even test performance designed to assess abilities is contaminated by non-intellective characteristics. The authors interpret this condition to be another strong argument for the multivariate analysis of behavior.

Winterbottom (1953) reported data which suggested that achievement motivation among males was related to the mothers' reported desires regarding "independence training." The mothers were to indicate how early they thought their sons should manifest the following behaviors:

_______ To know his way around the city
_______ To try new things for himself
_______ To do well in competition
_______ To make his own friends

The mothers of boys who scored high on achievement motivation indicated the desire that these behaviors be acquired at a younger age than mothers of boys who scored low on achievement motivation. These findings indicate that mothers who encourage early independence or who are less restrictive, produce sons with strong achievement motivation. The last statement is an inference drawn by the present authors and not by Winterbottom, because his study was not longitudinal, nor did it include direct observation of parental behavior.

Using Winterbottom's items, McClelland, Rindlisbacher, and de Charms (1955) presented data which suggested that early "independence training" is related to educational level and religious affiliation of the parents. The more highly-educated parents reported that they desire early "independence training." Protestant and Jewish parents also reported similar desires. The apparent "spirit of capitalism" and its irrational need to achieve, which Max Weber theorizes has evolved from the Protestant Ethic, is interpreted by McClelland, *et al.,* to be the result of "independence training" associated with the self-reliance entailed by the new salvation, and the data seem to support their interpretations.

Since "n Ach" is reported to relate to student performance, it should therefore be a variable for teachers to note. If the student has acquired achievement motivation from his early training, he will most likely be easy to teach under the usual competitive conditions. On the other hand, if the student has not acquired strong achievement motives, a problem might arise. Not only is the potential problem an educational matter, but it may well spill over into a moral question. As teachers, most of us have a high achievement motive. We think achievement is important and our way of life is therefore "future-oriented." However, some people might not exhibit the "future-orientation" and high achievement motivation. Should we attempt to develop the achievement motive? Should we encourage hard work? extended education? If so, how? Fortunately, as psychologists, we do not have to make the moral decision, but you the teacher must do so. The work reported in Chapter 3 regarding readiness centers, etc., may answer the "How" question for you, but you should recognize that you are making a moral decision if you decide to encourage achievement motivation. (Indeed, our "War on Poverty" also encounters the same moral problem.)

Single Determinants of Behavior: (2) "The Authoritarian Personality"

A monumental study regarding attitudes was conducted by Adorno, *et al.* (1950), regarding what they called the "Authoritarian personality." Appalled by the sadistic behavior of Fascist Germany, these investigators sought to determine the underlying motivational characteristics related to the disposition to behave anti-democratically. One assumption of the researchers was that a number of learned ways of ordering social stimuli may be acquired as a result of early learning which then predisposes a person to be susceptible to anti-democratic propaganda. These learned patterns (Adorno, *et al.,* 1950, p. 228) are listed below. (Note that Adorno, *et al.,* operated from a psychoanalytical, theoretical frame of reference, and therefore, some of the terminology deviates from the neobehavioristic language which you are by now accustomed to manipulating.)

a. *Conventionalism*—rigid adherence to conventional, middle-class values.
b. *Authoritarian submission*—submissive, uncritical attitude toward idealized moral authorities of the in-group.
c. *Authoritarian aggression*—tendency to be on the lookout for, and to condemn, reject, and punish people who violate conventional rules.
d. *Anti-intraceptive*—opposition to the subjective, the imaginative, the tender-minded.
e. *Superstition and stereotypy*—the belief in mystical determinants of the individual's fate; the disposition to think in rigid categories.
f. *Power and "toughness"*—preoccupation with the dominant-submissive, strong-weak, leader-follower dimension; identification with power figures . . . exaggerated assertion of strength and "toughness."
g. *Destructiveness and cynicism*—generalized hostility, vilification of the human.
h. *Projectivity*—the disposition to believe that wild and dangerous things go on in the world; the projection outward of unconscious emotional impulses.
i. *Sex*—exaggerated concern with sexual "goings-on."

The research strategy was to first develop a personality scale (called the F scale) designed to tap anti-democratic values indirectly, and then to clinically assess the individuals who scored high or low on the scale to determine the characteristics of the two kinds of individuals. Of particular concern in the clinical analysis were the early parent-child relations reported by the subjects. Examples of scale items which were assumed to reflect the underlying learned attitudes are:

1. Every person should have complete faith in some supernatural power whose decisions he obeys without question.
2. There is hardly anything lower than a person who does not feel a great love, gratitude, and respect for his parents.
3. Sex crimes, such as rape and attacks on children, deserve more than mere imprisonment; such criminals ought to be publicly whipped, or worse.

4. What the youth needs most is strict discipline, rugged determination, and the will to work and fight for family and country.
5. Young people sometimes get rebellious ideas, but as they grow up they ought to get over them and settle down.

The subject is to mark on a six-point scale his reactions to each statement. The two poles are strong support or agreement and strong opposition or disagreement. The points between reflect varying degrees of agreement or disagreement. High scores are obtained by individuals who strongly agree with many of the statements. Note that although the items do *not* suggest political activity, anti-democratic political attitudes theoretically should be positively correlated to the attitudes reflected in the statements. These attitudes are thought to be a part of the personality structures of pre-Fascists.

As a result of the clinical analysis, the high F scale scorers were classified into six syndromes that are seen as inter-related characteristics of a higher level of personality organization. Each syndrome reflects a number of behavioral traits although there is some trait overlap among the syndromes. The six syndromes among the high scorers are: "Surface Resentment," "The Conventional," "The Authoritarian," "The Rebel and Psychopath," "The Crank," and "The Manipulative Type." Since within the study of Adorno, *et al.,* the greatest number by far of high scorers fell into "The Authoritarian" and "The Conventional" syndromes, a discussion of these two groups follows.

"The Authoritarian" is described in psychoanalytic terms as a person who manifests a sadomasochistic resolution of the *Oedipus Complex,* which involves the following characteristics: (1) The love for the mother comes under a severe taboo. (2) The hatred for the (severe) father is transformed by the reaction-formation into love for the father. (3) Since the transformation is never complete, the hatred for the father is displaced onto substitutes such as out-groups. Aggressiveness is absorbed in part by masochistic submission to the strong father or father figure (the leader), but also some of the aggressiveness is expressed sadistically—to those seen as weak outsiders (Jew, Negro, etc.). An example of the Oedipus formation is illustrated by one subject's discussion of his father:

> Well, my father was a very strict man. He wasn't religious, but strict in raising the youngsters. His word was law, and whenever he was disobeyed, there was punishment. When I was 12, my father beat me practically every day for getting into the tool chest in the back yard and not putting everything away . . . finally he explained that things cost money, and I must learn to put it back . . . But you

> know, I never hold that against my father — I had it coming (masochistic response) . . . . He laid the law down, and if I broke it, there was punishment, but never in uncontrolled anger. My father was a good man no doubt about that (Adorno, *et al.*, p. 761).

Regarding job satisfaction the same subject stated:

> Well I am the head operator — shift foreman — rotating schedules — small department — five in department — five in a shift — I get personal satisfaction . . . that I have five people working for me, who come to me for advice in handling the production that we make, and that the ultimate decision . . . is mine, and in the fact that in the ultimate decision, I should be *right* — and am usually, and the knowledge that I am correct gives me personal satisfaction. The fact that I earn a living doesn't give me any personal satisfaction. It's these things that I have mentioned . . . knowing that I am pleasing someone else also gives me satisfaction (Adorno, *et al.*, p. 760).

Note here the stress upon subordinates and superordinates, typical of masochistic submission, and also of domination of those *under* him. This subject sees the Jews as possible usurpers of authority and suggests that a religious prohibition should be imposed upon them. Social conditions of the Negroes are blamed upon their low morals and congested conditions, etc. No pity is shown for the weak—this is a dominant theme among "Authoritarians."

The conforming syndrome among high F scale scorers represents stereotypy which comes from external social factors as well as familial factors, but which is integrated into the personality structure of the individual. Prejudice among this group does not reflect a sadomasochistic personality need, but rather reflects the individual's conformity to the dominant social group. (Theoretically, this is related to lack of "independence training.") If the dominant group does not express prejudice to, say, the Negro, then the conventional person will follow the group. "The Conventional" will not condone violence and will not express his prejudice with hostility, because he has accepted the middle-class values of decency." Nevertheless, he tends to express rather intense prejudice against Negroes, presumably because their out-group identification is obvious. "The Conventional" is against extremes. For example, one subject discussed his religious choice of Christian Science: ". . . it is a quieter religion than most . . . religion should restrain you from overindulgences of any kind, such as drinking, gambling, or anything to excess" (Adorno, *et al.*, p. 757). Rejection of non-assimilated Jews by this subject reflects the degree of identification of these Jew's differences to his in-group activities. Assimilated Jews are more acceptable to "The Conventional."

Among the low F scale scorers a number of syndromes were noted. The "Rigid" low scorer manifests many characteristics similar to the high scorer. Rather than accept all authority, they reject it. They are disposed to totalitarianism, and indoctrination to social movements, as long as the social movements are against the constituted authority. Other low scorers reflect "neurotic" as well as rational liberality.

These same studies suggest that prejudice has many faces. "The Conventional" will manifest prejudice as a result of linguistic sign pairing if the pairing has been provided by the dominant group, but will inhibit the prejudice if the group provides sanctions against prejudice. "The Authoritarian" on the other hand uses prejudice to satisfy his sadomasochistic personality structure and will not respond favorably to an appeal to a sense of fairness. If one attempts to suggest that Negroes are weak and need help, a typical reply would be, "They brought it upon themselves." Indeed, to the true "Authoritarian," passive resistance is an invitation for sadistic aggression. (Films of police moving the participants of "sit-ins" show this expressed aggression.) To combat "Authoritarian" prejudice, a position of strength seems to be the most fruitful posture. Strong legal authority will not change the prejudice, but it will lead to submission to the authority on the part of "The Authoritarian." Rational education will apparently reduce prejudice within individuals who have learned the set from linguistic sign pairing, and who do not have personality needs which are met by the use of prejudice.

Limitations of the F Scale (Pre-Fascistic Scale). The F scale has been subjected to criticism on two counts: (1) Christie (1954, p. 166) reported that the F scale correlated (−.48) with a measure of intelligence and that scores also are related to the educational level of the person. The more "intelligent" and the more educated persons score lower on the F scale. (2) A number of researchers, including Bass (1955), and Jackson and Messick (1957), reported that the scale is "really" measuring acquiescence—the person's tendency to conform and thus say "Yes" to positively-stated items.

To some degree the criticisms are not valid for although the F scale might measure two dimensions (authoritarianism-liberality and acquiescence-negativism) rather than one, this is to be expected. The fact that Adorno, *et al.*, specified that high scores do express different syndromes seems to be ignored. Likewise the negative correlation with education should be expected because if prejudice is learned, then it can for some be unlearned. Theoretically, education should challenge attitudes, and as a result of the challenge, some attitudes should change. Pettigrew (1959) reported that anti-Negro prejudice has a stronger negative relationship to education among southern subjects than among northern subjects. Both educated groups show less prejudice, but education might have greater influence on the southerner since he might have more prejudice to unlearn.

The studies which criticize the F scale seem to possibly suffer from the limitations imposed by their statistical models. Multivariate equations can account for interaction effects, so as to provide differential prediction. The F scale in conjunction with a conformity measure can theoretically separate the "yea sayers" from the "true Authoritarians."

Summary and Implications

"Intelligence," as discussed in this chapter, is viewed as a summarizing construct invented to account for differential human behaviors. IQ's are the result of attempts to quantify the construct. Whether "intelligence" represents one unified underlying process or a multitude of abilities remains to be resolved. Nevertheless, some abilities appear to be somewhat unrelated to intelligence test performance. Even though some abilities may be correlated with intelligence test scores, the relationship is usually quite weak ($r = +.3$ or so).

Bayley's data suggest that performance on intelligence tests increases rapidly up to about ages 21 to 25, and then continues to increase slowly. The fact that other studies indicate decline in "intelligence" from early adulthood until death is most likely due to sampling differences obtained in cross-sectional studies. In the past education was far from universal, and therefore many of the lower scores can be attributed to lower educational levels of the older subjects.

Guilford's 120 factors of the intellect are purported to be somewhat independent of each other although some may be moderately correlated. Guilford suggests that little is known regarding the development of these 120 abilities and therefore, if we assume that they are at least in part learned, then we may be able through learning to strengthen these abilities. For example, tasks such as those requiring students to name as many different objects in a category as they can might increase divergent thinking abilities. Likewise, more practice devoted to evaluation of the goodness of pictures, music, writing, etc., might enhance the individual's evaluating processes. This may mean that less time must be devoted to such activities as memory tasks, but here again is where we are faced with a decision based upon the aims of the particular school system and the people involved in the educative process.

The suggestion made by Guilford that we should attempt to increase abilities in all areas may be unrealistic. Indeed, one might be better advised to enhance the individual's coping abilities by means of "over-training" (see Chapter 5) in a single area. This should be especially true for persons with apparently limited abilities. Surely it would be nice if all people were developed in all areas of intellective processes; however, even for those capable of being so, the time involved might be prohibitive. Not only might there be individual and personal limitations, but also some occupations require the presence of some specific abilities and the absence of others. For example, a druggist who "creatively" fills a prescription might kill the patient. Conversely in pharmaceutical research, that same originality might lead to great breakthroughs in chemotherapy.

We noted that teachers like "creative" students less than the highly "intelligent" but less "creative" students. Apparently, the "creative" student is less docile and more troublesome in the classroom. If one indeed believes that "creativity" is an aim of education, some consideration should be given to the possibility that "creativity" and quiet, predictable classroom activities are not completely compatible. At the same time, some note should be made of the fact that Lowenfeld and Guilford both cite coherence of organization as a factor associated with "creativity." If this is so, then achievement of "creativeness" may not mean complete abandonment of discipline and control. To be able to create a story, some mastery of language usage and descriptive techniques seems to be a necessity. In graphic art, the ability to master the paint and brush should be important. The problem seems to indicate that mastery of the material and techniques should be acquired in such a manner so as to permit, but not stifle, expression. A difficulty may arise, however, since impulsivity and spontaneity are also associated with delinquent behavior. The "creative beatnik" may indeed violate some trivial middle-class norms, but the "psuedo-beatnik" may use the rouge of "creativity" as an out for lack of impulse control. Unfortunately, we have no available answers for this problem.

Decisions regarding the appropriate timing of specialized training are difficult to make because complex factors seem to be operating in this matter. However, vocational training for those with limited "abstract intelligence" might be an important early branching in the student's life. But should general education cease at this time? If these individuals are to be evaluative citizens at the polls, some semantic education may need to be an important part of the future specialist's continuing education. Further, with the rapid technological changes and with the advent of automation, some degree of flexibility in training might be necessary. The ability to evaluate and to see relationships could possibly be developed within the current vocational programs so as to produce more "flexible" workers.

Programs for the "gifted child" might do well to note historical factors. Specialization in mathematics and the physical sciences for those with special abilities in these areas should be initiated early, since most significant contributions in these areas have come from young men in their early twenties. Some effort should include attempts to associate the clear thinking of laboratory research with social-political activity since many of these mathematics and physical science specialists are political "idiots" who make generalizations without data—an unthinkable laboratory behavior.*

Some reconciliation between specialization and the all-around man, as Guilford suggests, seems necessary.

The need for achievement was discussed, and the relationship between "n Ach" and intelligence test performance was cited. In our zest to have all students striving for success, we should be aware of our real motives for doing so. As was indicated in Chapter 1, our own assumptions and values might interfere with the moral values of others. If, as some religions believe, the "afterlife" is most important, and that "afterlife" does *not* require production here on earth, then we may be imposing our own values regarding production onto these people. One may take the position that our society demands production, and that if, because of faith, the individual refuses to take the productive course, then he must suffer the consequences. Of course, the matter is not easily dismissed, because even the "other-worldly" produce children and we believe all children should be fed and cared for, and because the welfare situation does not allow us to dismiss the problem. Therefore the educational leaders may feel justified in their attempts to develop "n Ach."

Achievement need and the "Authoritarian Personality" were discussed as areas where univariate studies predominate, and although such studies may provide interesting data, the areas might better be studied and applied by way of multivariate analyses. McGuire's model and Whiteside's study were presented to indicate that intra-individual factors relate in complex ways to behavior. Multiple Linear Regression Analysis was presented as one statistical method which may represent fairly accurately the complexities of these interactions. The use of this statistical model appears to be highly efficient in predicting school success when it is employed with a comprehensive model relating to human behavior. With more accurate identification of potential school failures, intervention strategies can be developed and *tested.* The stress is placed upon

---

*The authors hesitate to point the finger in such a manner, as there are three other fingers pointing right back at them. Many psychologists run rats through mazes, play with the computer, etc., but fail to note that all these accomplishments might be destroyed by a political blunder. Fortunately, some psychologists (e.g., Charles Osgood) devote ratiocinative effort to social matters.

"tested" because empirical research is one of the strongest checks we can apply to educational faddism.

Questions

1. If "intelligence" is a single, genetically-determined characteristic, how could the educational system provide for the "dull" students? The "bright" students?
2. If "intelligence" is not a single factor, but many factors that are in part due to training, how would the educational system differ from one geared to a single-factor theory?
3. Is achievement "really" important? (Remember that a thousand years from now you will be long dead.) Can you rationally defend your answer? How? Be careful that you do not use value judgments in your reasoning.
4. What are some of the possible student reactions to pressure to do well on a test? How should you as a teacher respond to these reactions?
5. Can you think of three or four factors in McGuire's model that relate to non-GPA school behaviors? State the relationship using McGuire's model. Now, can you translate the verbal model to a multiple regression model? Do you think any of the factors will be curvilinearly related to the behavior? Why or why not?
6. Are you prejudiced? Assume you are white. Given a Negro partner who satisfies your ideals regarding looks, interests, abilities, etc., would you marry the person? What are some possible problems in such a marriage? Will your answers to these questions have any implications for your teaching roles? Is prejudice an important educational problem? Why or why not? How did your attitudes toward Negroes, Caucasians, Jews, Irish, Italians, Puerto Ricans, Japanese, etc., develop? Are they adaptive attitudes?

References

Adorno, T. W., Frenkel-Brunswik, Else, Levinson, D. J., & Sanford, R. N. *The authoritarian personality.* New York: Harper, 1950.

Bass, B. M. Authoritarianism or acquiescence? *J. abnorm. soc. Psychol.,* 1955, 51, 616-623.

Bayley, Nancy. On the growth of intelligence. *Amer. Psychologist,* 1955, 10, 805-818.

Bottenberg, R. A., & Ward, J. H., Jr. *Applied multiple linear regression.* Technical Document, AD 413128, U.S. Depart. of Commerce, Wash. D. C., 1963.

Campbell, D. T. Construct, trait, and discriminant validity. *Amer. Psychologist,* 1960, 15, 545-549.

Christie, L. S., & Jahoda, M. (Eds.), *Studies in the scope and method of the authoritarian personality.* Glencoe, Ill.: Free Press, 1954.

Cronbach, L. J., & Meehl, P. E. Construct validity in psychological tests, *Psychol. Bull.,* 1955, 52, 281-303.

Getzels, J. U., & Jackson, P. W. The meaning of "giftedness"—an examination of an expanding concept. *Phi Delta Kappan,* 1958, 40, 75-77.

Guilford, J. P. Creativity. *Amer. Psychologist,* 1950, 9, 444-445.

Guilford, J. P. Three faces of intellect. *Amer. Psychologist,* 1959, 14, 469-479.

Guilford, J. P. Factor angles to psychology. *Psycholog. Rev.,* 1961, 68, 1-20.

Guilford, J. P. Intelligence: 1965 model. *Amer. Psychologist,* 1966, 21, 20-26.

Hill, K. T., & Sarason, S. B. The relation of test anxiety and defensiveness to test and school performance over the elementary school years. *Monogr. of the Soc. for Res. in Child Develpm.,* 1966, 31, No. 2.

Jackson, D. N., & Messick, S. J. A note of "ethnocentrism" and acquiescent response set. *J. abnorm. soc. Psychol.* 1957, 54, 132-134.

Kelly, F. J., Conklin, R. N., & Hunka, S. H. Further normative data on tests measuring flexibility in cognitive processes. *Psychol. Reports,* 1965, 17, 683-686.

Kelly, F. J., & Veldman, D. J. Delinquency and school dropout behavior as a function of impulsivity and nondominant values. *J. abnorm. soc. Psychol.,* 1964, 69, 190-194.

Lowenfeld, V. Current research on creativity. *NEA J.,* 1958, 47, 538-540.

McClelland, D. C., Clark, R. A., & Lowell, E. L. (Eds.) *The achievement motive.* New York: Appleton-Century-Crofts, 1953.

McClelland, D. C., de Charms, R. V., & Rindlisbacher, R. Religious and other sources of parental attitudes toward independence training. In D. C. McClelland (Ed.), *Studies in motivation.* New York: Appleton-Century-Crofts, 1955, 389-397.

McClelland, D. C. (Ed.), *Studies in motivation.* New York: Appleton-Century Crofts, 1955.

McGuire, J. C. The prediction of talented behavior in the junior high school. Report on 1960 Invitational conference in testing, Princeton, N. J.: Educ. Testing Service, 1960.

Maltzman, I. M., Licht, L., Raskin, D. C., & Simon, S. Experimental studies in the training of originality. *Psychol. Monogr.,* 1960, 493, 1-23.

Pettigrew, T. F. Regional differences in anti-Negro prejudice. *J. abnorm. soc. Psychol.,* 1959, 59, 28-36.

Sarason, I. G. Interrelationships among individual difference variables, behavior in psychotherapy, and verbal conditioning. *J. abnorm. soc. Psychol.,* 1958, 56, 339-344.

Sarason, I. G., & Palola, E. G. The relationship of test and general anxiety, difficulty of task, and experimental instructions to performance. *J. exp. Psychol.,* 1960, 59, 185-191.

Sarason, S. B., Hill, K. T., & Zimbardo, P. G. A longitudinal study of the relation of test anxiety to performance on intelligence and achievement tests. *Monogr. of Soc. for Research in Child Develpm.,* 1964, 29, No. 7.

Torrance, E. P. Explorations in creative thinking. *Education,* 1960, 81, 216-220.

Whiteside, R. Dimensions of teacher evaluation of academic achievement. Doctoral dissertation, Univer. of Texas, Austin, Texas, 1964.

Winterbottom, M. R. The sources of achievement motivation in mothers' attitudes toward independence training. In D. C. McClelland, R. A. Clark, & E. L. Lowell (Eds.), *The achievement motive.* New York: Appleton-Century-Crofts, 1953, 297-304.

Cognitive Views 5

Overview

This chapter centers around the process of knowing (cognition). Placed in relation to the quasi-mathematical model introduced in Chapter 4, knowledge is assumed to be another way to talk about the residuals of previous action ($rs_1 \ldots rs_n$). Table 5.1 shows the model.

Chapter 4 focused upon the first three elements in the formula (*Pa, Eab,* and *Rba*). Although this chapter deals primarily with the process of knowing ($rs_1 \ldots rs_n$), you should notice that the other elements relating to behavior enter into the discussion.

The initial point developed in this chapter is that knowledge may vary from highly specific action potential to very abstract symbolic behavior. For example, we know that apples are edible and we also know that the area of a circle can be derived from the formula πr^2. Apparently through contact with the elements outside our bodies we develop concepts which enable us to cope with the universe. Essentially, these concepts are abstractions which we develop from noting relationships among objects in our environment. Some concepts seem to have wider applications than others. For example, formal concepts, such as the formula πr^2, have application to a broad class of objects — they have transfer value.

TABLE 5.1

A modified version of McGuire's model

$$Ba = f(Pa, Eab, Rba, rs_{1...n})\ Sa, Cab, x$$

Ba = behavior of the person(a) to be explained or predicted.

Pa = potential cognitive, perceptual, and other relevant abilities (e.g., divergent thinking, convergent thinking, symbol aptitude).

Eab = elements of personality and motivation, especially expectations about one's own behavior and probable responses of other persons (e.g., attitudes and values).

Rba = perception of other persons' (b) expectations and pressures imposed upon the given individual (a).

$rs_{1...n}$ = acquired response repertory that is relevant to the behavior to be explained or predicted (e.g., previous achievement).

Sa = sex-role identification of the individual (a) and sex-typing of socialization pressures, both of which moderate preceding variables.

Cab = context of behavior, such as community or school setting which provides an institutional framework along with certain experiences and impersonal expectations, or the setting in which a natural or a laboratory experiment takes place.

x = unaccounted-for variations, due possibly to errors in measurement as well as due to undiscovered relevant variables, some may wish to call this "free will," but for heuristic purposes, it may be best described as the unknown factor(s) underlying behavior.

Adapted from Carson McGuire, "The Prediction of Talented Behavior in the Junior High School," Invitational Conference on Testing Problems, E. T. S. Princeton, N. J., 1960. P. 66.

Since educators lately have stressed transfer of learning and discovery learning, this chapter examines in detail three aspects of concepts that bear upon transfer and discovery. These are (1) *conditions* which facilitate concept formation and attainment, (2) *types* of concepts, and (3) *strategies* which are appropriate for different types of concepts. On the surface, concept formation (discovery and invention) appears to be messy to handle. As a means to suggest operations which can clean up the area, a discussion of operant conditioning is introduced. This discussion indicates that attention to the responses required in discovery might overcome some of the messiness.

The last fourth of this chapter examines the "New Math" and Science Inquiry Training in light of cognitive theories. Taken together, newer educational practice and newer cognitive views raise a number of questions regarding university training. The onus for educational change seems to fall upon liberal arts instructors as well as upon education faculty.

Glossary

anxiety: an unpleasant emotional state in which a present and continuing strong desire or drive seems likely to miss its goal.

aversive stimulus: a stimulus which, if applied following a response, decreases the tendency to emit that response on later similar occasions.

catechetical: designating a means of instruction in which a question is asked to which a single answer is memorized and given as the only correct response.

chaining: a process of learning wherein a sequence of behaviors proceeds semi-automatically in a determinate order, with the last previous response providing the necessary cue that determines which behavior comes next.

class: a group or aggregate of items — things, persons, abstractions — all of which manifest certain characteristics that collectively are the mark setting this group off from all others.

closure: generally, the premise that two or more operations can be combined to form a new operation.

cognitive process: refers to the way the individual sees the physical and social worlds, including all his facts, concepts, beliefs, and expectations and the pattern of their interrelation.

cognitive theory: an interpretation of the facts of learning that, more freely than other theories, postulates central brain processes.

competence motive: the premise that man, given the opportunity, will exploit his tendencies to learn more about himself and his environment.

concept attainment: the act whereby the individual is seeking the distinguishing characteristic of objects belonging to two or more *known* classes.

concept formation: the act of arranging a diverse set of stimuli into some "meaningful" relationship.

conceptual incongruity: the situation that exists when one has learned that characteristic A is unlikely to be found together with characteristic B, but is informed that a particular A also has characteristic B.

concreteness: pertains to a specific or particular item or thing, as a whole; characterizing an individual fact at a particular moment; opposite of abstract.

confusion: a condition that exists under conditions where the stimulus input is ambiguous and the ambiguity activates conflicting symbolic responses.

conjunctive concepts: concepts defined by the joint presence of specific values of a number of attributes.

cue: a signal for an action; that specific portion of a perceptual field or pattern of stimuli to which a subject has learned to respond.

cumulative constructionism: the set to impose constraints in problem solving activities, assuring a greater reduction of the problem limits and increasing the probability of problem solution.

differentiation: an experimental procedure in which a person is trained to make a distinction between two similar responses to a given situation.

discovery learning: a process by which the learner acquires knowledge by way of concrete and conceptual manipulation rather than by exposition by the expert.

discriminate: to note differences.

disjunctive concepts: concepts characterized by one of a number of attributes, or all of them.

doubt: the conflict between a tendency to believe and at the same time disbelieve a statement.

episodic empiricism: the set to ask questions which test specific hypotheses, which in turn may result in accidental correct outcomes.

epistemic behavior: refers to processes of knowledge seeking, usually initiated by a question or its equivalent.

equivalence classification: a scheme for classification whereby the relation between two terms or two sets of data is such that one can be substituted for the other in a given context without making any substantial difference.

expository mode: the conservative practice in which the teacher as a lecturer, or the text as a source of knowledge, is solely responsible for the material presented as well as the direction taken by the learner.

fixed interval: the relationship between reinforcement and responses over some fixed time basis within a schedule of reinforcement.

fixed ratio schedule: a means of maintaining a behavior based on the presentation of a reinforcer after the subject emits a specific number of responses.

focusing: the attitude or set which leads to careful effort to discriminate, to discover the exact nature of the stimulating circumstances, whether or not there is an objectively apparent demand for such accuracy.

generic codes: codes which transcend specific subject matter; codes which serve as a basis for behavior in many situations (for example, the general equation for area = πr^2).

hypothetical mode: a procedure included in teaching which fosters the development of the cumulative construction set to impose constraints in problem solving. Includes decisions of the learner as well as the teacher. The teacher reinforces student's hypothesis making.

intermittent reinforcement: a nonreinforcing or nonrewarding situation is irregularly interspersed with reinforcing situations during the conditioning period resulting in slower conditioning and slower extinction.

intrinsic motivation: a motivation in which the satisfaction or incentive conditions are obtained within the activity itself.

intuitive behavior: acts or responses based on judgment that occurs without any known process of cogitation or reflective thinking. Said to be acquired only through practice in problem solving with the intent to discover relevant relationships.

irrelevance: the notion involving the fact that humans learn to process related material; therefore, the introduction of irrelevant concepts leads to frustration and increased arousal.

iteration: refers to the premise that any number combined with itself forms a new number.

manifest anxiety: an apparent or conscious anxiety believed to be symptomatic of repression.

need state: the condition of an organism as the result of some deprivation (i.e., water deficiency → water need → thirst).

operant: any observable change (behavior) the organism carries out on the environment (e.g., walking, lifting, etc.).

operational: refers simply to a procedure about which one may talk. Thus an operationally defined object or situation refers to a procedure rather than to implications of truth, correctness or scientific validity.

overlearning: learning in which practice proceeds beyond the point where the act can just be performed with the required degree of excellence. There is no implication that the practice has been carried to injudicious lengths.

paradigm: a model, pattern, or example that exhibits all the variable forms of something.

perplexity: conceptual conflict that is experienced when evidence supports two mutually exclusive events.

relational concepts: concepts characterized by a specified relationship between attributes.

relations: that which forms a connection between two things, of such nature that what is true of one has some relevance to the other.

reversability: refers to the premise that an operation can be cancelled by an opposite operation.

set: a temporary, but often recurrent, condition of the person or organism that orients him toward certain environmental stimuli or events rather than toward others, selectively sensitizing him for apprehending them.

shaping: an experimental procedure wherein the animal is trained to make an unusual response to a certain stimulus by reinforcing acts progressively more like the act to be learned until that act finally occurs and is rewarded.

successive approximation: a variation of trial-and-error learning in which the desired performance is encouraged by rewarding any responses that approximate, or are part of, the correct performance.

symbolic behavior: organismic activity or behavior of utilizing symbols, including all communication and language.

transfer of training, transfer: a general term for change in ability to perform a given act as a direct consequence of having performed another act relevant or related to it.

variable interval: refers to the specified time interval between responses and reinforcements. The specific time interval between reinforcements may be shorter or longer.

variable ratio: a scheme for maintaining a behavior based on the presentation of reinforcement on the average at a specified number of responses, but the specific number of responses necessary for reinforcement to occur may vary.

Classification and Meaning

In Chapter 3, meaning was discussed in relation to the organism's response to the stimulus object. As a result of action upon the stimulus object, some fractional part of the response remains as a residual and becomes associated with the stimulus object. The residual is the meaning of the stimulus object (perceptual sign). Thus a rattle (ΣS) may acquire the meaning of shake, etc. Objects similar to the rattle may also activate the residuals of responses to rattles, and we call this "generalization." Words, when associated with the perceptual sign, acquire some of the meaning associated with that particular perceptual sign. Therefore, the word "rattle" becomes a linguistic sign with the fractional response potential (meaning) that the perceptual sign activates. Many objects of varying shape are called "rattle" through generalization, and the old meaning is applied to these stimuli. The individual's generalizing process might extend beyond the culturally designated equivalence classification and the individual might be asked to *discriminate* between two classifications. A new response must be acquired: a *rattle* is to shake, suck, bite, etc.; a *bank* is to put coins into. These generalizations and discriminations provide the basis of classification which enables man to adapt to the complex universe. One apple is eaten, another, and another, and then we may classify apples (similar objects, but not identical in every respect) as "edible." This is not a very profound classification; but nevertheless, it is a highly economical adaptive process. Each new instance of "apple" is *not* a new problem when we have an appropriate classification scheme. If we lack grouping, each object encountered in the universe would acquire unique meaning, which would result in an insurmountable survival task.

On Going Beyond the Information Given

Generalization of meaning as we have discussed the concept is a rudimentary form of what Jerome Bruner (1957) called "going beyond the information given." If human conceptual activity was limited to *equivalence classification,* man's horizons would appear quite limited.

A more refined case of going beyond the information given as indicated by Bruner involves *noting* the *redundancies* of the environment. Within the context of this book, an incomplete word such as ED__C__T__ON is easily recognized as EDUCATION, but within the context of a geology text recognition might be more difficult. Thus learning or overlearning enables one to go beyond the limitations prescribed by the incomplete information available and enhances the probability of making predictions. The learning of probable environmental relationships permits one to go beyond immediate information and make predictions.

Guilford's "Cognition of Symbolic Units" (see Chapter 4) is an attempt to identify this characteristic of learning (e.g., P__W__R; put in vowels to make real words). Completing P__W__R and deriving POWER are examples of recognizing and filling in missing information. One only has to observe the many phenomena in the world to verify the rationality of Guilford's attempt to isolate this aspect of human behavior. A host of redundant relationships within the "natural" world are noted and predictable consequences are anticipated. Consider man's behavior in relation to the weather. The joint occurrence of rain with dark clouds is highly probable. The noting of these redundancies leads one to predict rain. This process seems a simple extension of equivalence classification. One classifies "cloud," and stimulus objects which are similar are called clouds. Likewise rain is classified, and the probability of rain being associated with these clouds (one class predictably leads to another) can be noted.

These behaviors which at first glance seem simple should suggest the inventive characteristics of man's cognitive (knowing) process. Some elements of the environment are abstracted (grouped) and classified as being relevant while others are ignored. As in the case of the rain-cloud example, wind direction, moisture content of the air, season of the year, and temperature have been ignored. As science progresses, fewer of the most relevant variables which accompany events will be ignored.

Further, man invents mnemonic devices as codes which allow him to recall the noted relevancies (e.g., Rainbow in morning, sailors take warning, Rainbow at night, sailors' delight). Inventions such as these are fundamental; however, they are to a large degree codes that are tied to the *specific* subject matter.

Schools are apparently concerned with transmitting what Bruner called *formal codes* or generic (general) codes. Syllogistic processes (e.g., $X > Y; Y > Z; \therefore X > Z$) and numerical operations (e.g., $3 + 4 = 7$) are generic codes in the sense that they have wide applicability which transcends particular subject matter. Indeed, Bruner suggests that that which is commonly called transfer of training or generalization is basically the learning of codes which have wider or narrower application. In this view, if a person has learned $2 + 2 = 4$, but fails to see $2x + 2x = 4x$, then the code of "grouping" probably is lacking and numerical combinations have not been "genericized." A specific response is probably acquired.

Bruner concludes, from a study conducted by William Hull, that the good speller has developed a code for English while the poor speller may be memorizing specific responses. The study was conducted with fifth grade students and included subjects who scored in the highest and lowest quartile on a standardized spelling achievement test. These students were briefly exposed to pseudo-words and were asked to write these words down immediately after exposure. The list of pseudo-words included first-order approximations to English (e.g., YRULPZOC) and third- and fourth-order approximations (e.g., Mossiant and Vernalt). Third- and fourth-order words are highly similar in the probability structure of letter sequence to English words. The two groups performed equally well in writing the essentially random strings of letters (first-order), but the "good" speller showed superior performance on writing third- and fourth-order pseudo-words. Apparently the good spellers noted redundancy of syllabication and probable letter groupings as well as a *particular* letter grouping.

Conditions Influencing the Acquisition of Coding Systems

If educators wish to teach material for later use (transfer), then some concern for the acquisition of generic coding (codes which transcend specific subject matter) might be of value. The fact that there are good spellers under the conditions outlined above, suggests that some individuals invent generalizable codes. Bruner proposes four general sets of conditions which might be relevant to the acquisition of generic coding systems: (1) set, (2) need state, (3) degree of mastery, and (4) diversity of training.

Set. The influence of set or attitude upon performance is grossly apparent. Ask a person to memorize the following list of numbers: 371014172124. Ask another person to learn these numbers, but also suggest that there is a pattern which can help (a set). Let the individuals work until they can repeat these without aids. (The pattern is: anchor at three and successively alternate the process: add 3, and 4, add 3, $3 + 4 = 7 + 3 = 10 + 4 = 14$, then 37101417, etc.). If the second individual has learned the pattern, his retention should be longer *if* he practiced the pattern. Give another group of numbers with some similar pattern and his learning behavior will be quite different from the memorizer's. Of course, the set can be made debilitating by introducing a random pattern.

These situational sets (instructions) might be temporary; more permanent sets (e.g., noting structural properties of English spelling) are theoretically acquired through life experiences (a very equivocal phrase). One student sits in class and blindly adds $3 + 2 = 5$, etc.; another notes that $2 + 3 = 5 = 3 + 2$.

Bruner (1961) reported that some ten- to twelve-year-old children, given a 20 question problem, ask questions which impose constraints on the task which insure reduction of the unknowns. The following is a typical problem:

> A car has gone off the road and hit a tree. Ask questions which can be answered with a "yes" or "no" to discover the cause of the accident.

An example of the constraint question would be, "Was there anything wrong with the driver?" A question of this nature provides a marked reduction in the unknown factors. A "yes" answer indicates the subsequent focus should be upon the driver, and a "no" answer rules out the driver's condition.

Other children tend to ask questions which test *specific* hypotheses, such as "Was the driver rushing to the doctor's office for an appointment and the car went out of control?" A "yes" answer is highly improbable for an incorrect element in any one of the conditions would make the hypothesis wrong. The set to impose constraints has been called "cumulative constructionism" by Bruner and the specific hypothesis testing mode is called "episodic empiricism." Cumulative constructionism does *not* provide the spectacular results which a fortuitous correct specific hypothesis provides. On the other hand, as a set or strategy, cumulative constructionism assures a greater reduction of the problem limits and increases the probability of problem solution more often than does episodic empiricism.

A recent informal presentation of the above mentioned problem was conducted by the senior author with a group of 30 graduate educational psychology students. Over 50 per cent of the student responses were episodic in content. The experimenter was somewhat surprised. One might conclude that university training may not assure the acquisition of systematic strategies, or for that matter, other learning strategies which many apparently believe are automatically associated with usual classroom experiences.

Apparently, if one has a set to look for generic codes, he behaves differently from one who does not have the set. Further, if we assume that acquisition and formation of codes is important for adaption to a complex universe, then some attention should be directed to the question, "How do individuals acquire the set to seek underlying uniformities?" The following section on "need state" and a later discussion regarding the "act of discovery" might provide tentative answers to this question.

Need State. Bruner (1957) proposed that the tendency to generically code new information depends upon an optimal motivational level. Very high drive or very low drive increases the probability that the cognitive processes will increase in concreteness (note the similarity to Hebb's concept of arousal discussed in Chapter 2). To support this proposition, a comparative study conducted by Bruner, Mandler, O'Dowd and Wallach (1958) is cited. Two groups of rats were run through a maze with a left, right, left, right (LRLR) pattern. Each group ran the maze until it learned the pattern (criterion) and then was given 80 further trials (overlearning). The two groups differed in one respect: one group was run under conditions of 36-hour food deprivation (high drive?) and the other under 12-hour food deprivation (moderate drive?). The 36-hour deprived rats tended to perform in the maze with fewer errors; however, the difference was not statistically significant. When, upon overlearning, the task was changed to a pattern of RLRL (reversal); the 12-hour deprived rats learned the shift with fewer errors than did the 36-hour deprived rats. These data were interpreted by Bruner, *et al.,* as an indication that moderate deprivation might provide an opportunity for generic (generalized) learning. These data seem to be consonant with the notion of arousal discussed in Chapter 2 and Chapter 4 (Anxiety and Arousal). Apparently when the stakes are too high learning is less efficient.

In a sense, the high drive rats appear to have learned a specific set of responses (this path to this goal), whereas the moderately driven rats might have learned this *kind* of response for this *kind* of a task. Furthermore, the rats performing under moderate levels of deprivation exhibited vicarious trial and error (VTE) behavior upon encountering the blocked left alley for the first time. If one anthropomorphizes the activity of the rat, his VTE behavior could be interpreted as his asking: "Hey! What's up? Now what has happened here?" These moderately driven rats spent more time in the first unit under transfer conditions than did the highly driven rats, but less VTE behavior was exhibited by the 12-hour deprived rats in the other units. In contrast, the 36-hour deprived rats blundered on through the maze, making error after error. In another experiment, rats which overlearned under 36 hours of deprivation and were presented with the transfer task under 12 hours of deprivation exhibited three times as many VTE's as did the 12-12 hour group. However, the 12-12 group exhibited most of the VTE behavior in the first unit, while the 36-12 group distributed the VTE behavior among the four units. Apparently, the 36-12 group was generalizing during transfer, whereas the 12-12 group learned generically during the original learning.

In view of these data, one may speculate that students who learn to spell generically may have done so because early spelling learning was conducted under moderate arousal during response acquisition. Of course, additional research data need to be collected to substantiate this speculation and probably other factors can be identified which operate to influence the results of such experiments.

In dealing with human behavior, it should be noted that the matter might not be as simple as might be inferred if studies concerning rats only are considered. The research with manifest anxiety (Castaneda, Palermo and McCandless, 1956) and test anxiety (Sarason and Palola, 1960) suggested that external pressure, assumed to be drive or arousal inducing, functions differently for various individuals. Individuals classified on the basis of a test anxiety scale to be "low test anxious" perform better on "difficult" tasks than do "high test anxious" subjects. Conversely, high test anxious subjects perform better on "easy" tasks when compared with low test anxious subjects (Sarason and Palola, 1960). These data do not contradict Bruner's proposition that moderate drive might facilitate generic coding; however, these data do suggest that external measures of drive must take into account the individual's internal state of drive or arousal. Apparently, some individuals, due to any number of factors, become highly aroused under testing conditions and others do not; thus, the external pressure has differential effects upon the test performance. Indeed, some students become so highly aroused that little appropriate behavior is exhibited. These performance blocks during testing also seem manifested during learning sessions for some students as well. These and other forms of behavior can be easily observed in the day-to-day behavior of students in the classroom. Mary, ordinarily a calm and confident student, when confronted with a test setting, might flush, perspire profusely, bite her fingernails or wring her hands. Nancy, on the other hand, usually displays a degree of hesitancy during a class period. When confronted with a testing situation, she seems to become more attentive, difficult to distract and her eyes might glisten. It seems equally evident that some students appear flustered in one test situation and at ease in another test situation. The assumed fact of individual differences is usually re-affirmed by carefully examining data obtained in experimental settings.

Degree of Mastery. Whether an individual codes generically or memorizes specific information depends not only upon *set* and *level of arousal,* but also upon the amount of training. In the rat study just mentioned, Bruner noted that the animals which ran only to criterion (no overlearning trials) did not exhibit the transfer. Apparently the noting of regularities is a function of familiarity with the components of the task to be coded. First, perhaps each turn in the maze must be mastered before the single alternation principle can be recognized and coded. In one sense, then, it is as if attention is directed to the immediate stimuli (reach the food) until mastery, then attention can be directed to the total task. The units of turn L, turn R can be grouped into the higher unit single alternation. It might be hypothesized that the shortest route to the food can be determined by the rats only after they are secure ("know" they can find the food when the need arises).

Of course, human learning can be greatly accelerated because of early overlearned symbolic behavior (language, etc.). If one wishes students to learn the area of a number of circles, he can ask the students to memorize the specific values, or he can provide the generic code: Area $= \pi r^2$. Indeed, the practice for each of these sets would be different and one would expect greater savings with the code if the component parts were overlearned. Likewise, if the code for determining the area of circles was overlearned, transfer to problems which require finding the volume of cylinders could be expected. This example highlights the importance of prior learning upon subsequent coding activity.

Piaget's concepts relating to the growth of logical thinking apparently depend in some degree on mastery of parts (in agreement with the inference made from rat studies described above). Within the period that Piaget calls "concrete operations" (roughly between ages 7-11), operational thought is developed as a result of conducting physical manipulation of objects. With extensive practice in grouping objects (e.g., all blocks, all green blocks, all triangles, etc.) the concept of *class* is formed. The child can think of the class of objects operationally (i.e., all triangles), and theoretically some fractional part of the physical manipulation is activated within the individual's neuromuscular apparatus.

Concepts of *relations* are acquired through practice in ordering objects (e.g., stick A is longer than stick B — a physical comparison; Mary is taller than Sue, and Sue is shorter than Bill, etc.). Practice (operational) and mastery are the key factors which lead to the concept.

Mastery of class and relations are prerequisites to adequate *number* concepts. Grouping ten objects and comparing the group with others (e.g., 8, 9, 15, etc.) are the operations which apparently lead to effective numbering. In order to have stability of numerical operations, at least five notions should be acquired by means of concrete manipulation:

1. *Closure.* Two or more operations can be combined to form a new operation (e.g., $5 + 5 = 10$; $10 + 2 + 3 = 15$).
2. *Reversability.* An operation can be cancelled by an opposite operation ($1 + 1 = 2$ and $2 - 1 = 1$).
3. *Associativity.* The order of combining of three or more grouping operations does *not* matter [e.g., $3 + 4 + 5 + 6 = (3 + 4) + 5 + 6 = 3 + (4 + 5) + 6$, etc.].
4. *Identity.* A "null operation" is obtained when one operation is combined with its inverse (e.g., $1 - 1 = 0$; $10 - 10 = 0$).
5. *Iteration.* Any number combined with itself forms a new number (e.g., $10 + 10 = 20$; $3 + 3 + 3 = 3 \times 3 = 9$).

Theoretically, failure to master any one of these notions will lead to instability in the numbering process.

Diversity of Training. The significance of diversity in students' training or background has been noted in relation to linguistic sign learning. Numerous exemplars of rattle are often available in the child's world, but a more generic and differentiated notion of rattle is formed when the negative case is encountered (e.g., a rattling bank). The school difficulty encountered by the "culturally deprived," which was discussed in Chapter 4, is theoretically a case where early learning lacks the diversity to develop the broad linguistic repertory (formal code) which middle-class teachers expect of all children who enter the school. This is not to say that the "culturally deprived" lack formal codes, for these children might have acquired codes which are different from those usually expected. Perhaps a few examples will serve to accentuate this point. Jerry, a first grade student from the slums in suburbia, might interpret a teacher's use of the word "honesty" to mean "you don't take something from someone else without his knowing it unless you need it." "Honesty," thus defined, is a formal code; however, it is different from the middle-class teacher's formal code. Similarly, recognition of words which associate with pictures have little meaning unless the words and phrases hit upon some familiarity among Jimmy's past experiences. To him, ministers may be cranks; beautiful might mean something he likes — candy, knife, comic book or toy. Arrangement of colors, decor, and middle-class preference for style may be neglected references in Jimmy's background.

Piaget's notions regarding logical thinking are also based upon some amount of diverse training before the grouping concept is formed.

A Transition Note

Bruner's ideas regarding the conditions which influence generic coding seem worthy of consideration by teachers. Some of these ideas will be expanded and related to the classroom.

1. If a person accepts the notion that developing an attitude to seek relationships is a worthy educational process, he should be aware that this notion assumes that *relations exist.* Restated, from Bruner's framework, the universe is *not* an arbitrary collection of discrete happenings; interacting and interdependent uniformities exist. In order to facilitate efficient seeking behaviors, the teacher should have a firm grasp of the subject matter under investigation. The typical self-contained classroom in elementary schools may place an unrealistic expectation upon teachers since overlearning in five or six disciplines seems to be required of them. Team

teaching has some promise for mitigating the expectation just mentioned.

2. The post-Sputnik drive for excellence in education may hinder generic coding behavior if the pressure becomes too great (high drive). Unwise use of extrinsic reinforcement or aversive stimuli (poor grades) theoretically can stifle the realization of the excellence goal, since learning of specifics, which is usually the method employed to grade students beyond third grade, might be the product.
3. Overlearning combined with the set to seek uniformities and moderate drive appear to be interacting. Each aspect apparently cannot be viewed independently. Many educators mistakenly grasp at one idea or procedure and fail to consider the ramifications when this procedure fails to yield anticipated results.
4. In view of the host of concepts a child acquires in the home and elsewhere, the notions which Bruner proposes can only be viewed as tentative first statements. The following sections present views on how teaching modes might influence the learning style of students in respect to a few selected concepts currently emphasized in education.

The Act of Discovery

Bruner's notions tacitly assume that there are underlying structures and uniformities in the universe and that generic codes can approximate or represent these uniformities. As a result of early learning, some individuals acquire strategies of information processing (cumulative constructionism) which are based upon a search for uniformities. Bruner (1961) theorized that teaching procedures which include a "hypothetical mode" foster the development of cumulative constructionism.

The writing of the present text and the typical lecture session are examples of the "expository mode." As such, the expositor (writer or lecturer) makes decisions regarding the content which follows sequentially. These decisions are based upon a problem-solving approach (e.g., How can these ideas be most efficiently presented?). You as the reader are not required to entertain nor provide alternative ordering of data. In contrast to this mode, the *hypothetical mode* includes decisions of the audience (learner) as well as the leader (teacher). Consider a problem such as, "What permits an airplane to get off the ground?" Utilizing the expository mode one may discuss airfoils, differential air speeds, lift, etc., or one might permit the learner to generate hypotheses and place restrictions upon the problem which lead to seeking evidence which confirms or disconfirms the particular hypothesis. Bruner hypothesized that the search for the relevant variables via discovery within the school is the vehicle which fosters "constructionism." In essence, practice in seeking relevant variables leads to the acquisition of strategies which are successful and the elimination of less robust strategies.

Knowledge acquired through discovery is obtained by way of concrete and conceptual *manipulation* rather than by means of exposition by the expert. Presumably, knowledge of this sort is subject to change as further manipulation and evaluation are carried out. Concepts thus are *not* arbitrary dictates of some demi-god, but are related to some notion of universal uniformity. In other words, learning by discovery is not a chance or haphazard approach to classroom management. Teachers who employ this procedure must be experts in subject matter, in knowledge of student experiences, and in directing a mode of inquiry. Under these conditions a teacher must have a "complete" understanding of subject matter in order to provide students with meaningful clues. Not only must subject matter be mastered, but a teacher should also have a deep understanding of students. If a teacher knows students and subject matter well then discovery learning seems a worthy pursuit. Too frequently, discovery learning is depicted as a "leaderless situation" or as a situation in which teachers have responsibilities to provide freedom to discover alone. Discovery apparently is learned just as other skills and knowledges.

Discovery and Motivation

Bruner (1961) also proposes that learning by discovery brings about a condition in which the solution to the problem (rather than teacher approval or approval of other social agents) is rewarding. Catechetical procedures of listen, recite, recall, and reinforcement (grade) are supplanted by hypothesize, question, seek, verify and master. Thus learning by discovery theoretically should result in what has been called "intrinsic motivation." An assumption underlying this position is that a large part of human behavior is controlled by a *competence motive*. This means simply that man, given the opportunity, will exploit his tendencies to learn more about himself and his environment. A number of writers have proposed similar notions of motivation although the terms vary (see Rogers, 1951; Angyal, 1965; Kelly, 1958).

Page, in his work within the Illinois Mathematics Projects, demonstrated the possible value of discovery learning. Among a class of fourth graders he posed a problem: "Suppose you have two red beads and two white beads. How many different closed chains can you make from them?" Students were asked to create an answer after manipulating beads on a wire. Various answers were proposed and evaluated, and the students finally concluded there are two different chains (see Figure 5.1).

FIGURE 5.1

Possible number of different closed chains when 2 red beads and 2 white beads were placed on a wire that formed a closed circle.

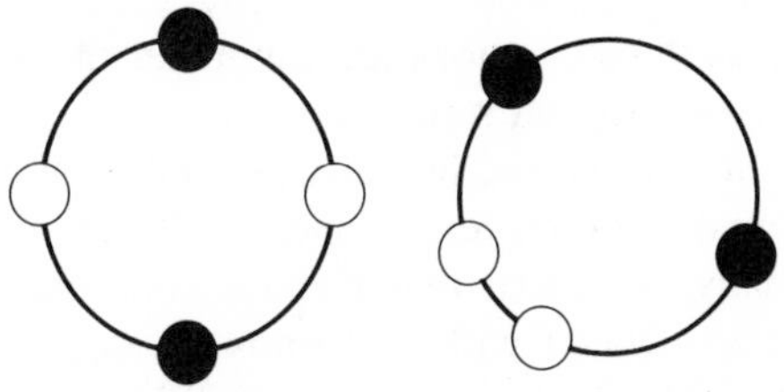

A third white bead is added and a number of different chains are proposed as answers and evaluated. Again, the conclusion is derived (see Figure 5.2).

FIGURE 5.2

Possible number of different closed chains when 2 red beads and 3 white beads were placed on a wire that formed a closed circle.

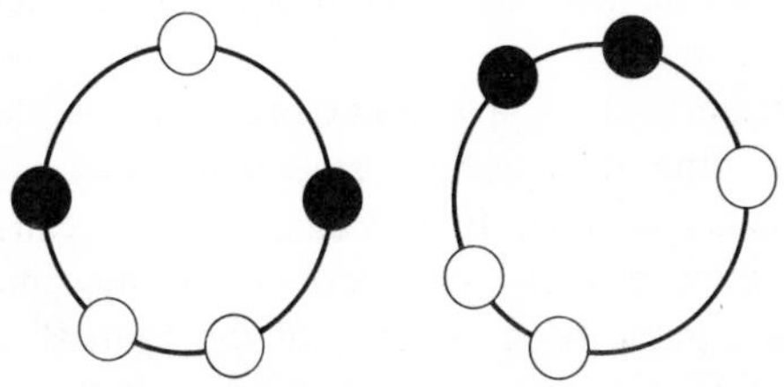

More white beads are added, one at a time, and with practice, less concrete manipulation is necessary. Ultimately, the children can provide the answer without demonstrating the cases and can formally derive a rule or theorem which applies to the possibilities. These activities represent work in permutations and the derived theorems are not included in textbooks. Observers report that these sessions generate excitement and interest among students. One can infer that learning under these conditions simulates the discovery mode which takes place at the frontiers of knowledge. Note, however, that the instructor has selected the relevant variables for manipulation as well as the problem.

These considerations parallel some concepts proposed by Berlyne (1960) regarding "Conceptual Conflict" and "Epistemic Curiosity." In that Berlyne's notions provide, in more detail, suggestive factors which might provide the motivation generated by discovery learning, a number of his formalized concepts seem worthy of consideration.

Conceptual Conflict

At the base of Berlyne's notions are a number of assumptions which seem to coincide with Bruner's thoughts on coding. As a consequence of interactions with objects and humans, the individual assigns meaning to the universe and acquires expectancies of how the universe goes together. Specifically, we learn that night is contrasted with day; lung cancer is seldom associated with non-smokers; dogs never talk; communists are bad; Eisenhower is good; etc. When concepts which are incompatible or which are highly improbable occur jointly, conceptual conflict is a result. For example, if you hear, "Eisenhower is a communist," you will most likely find this statement hard to believe. You can ignore the statement or you may be aroused to seek more information (epistemic curiosity). If the statement is important, denial is difficult to maintain without logic or data and induced arousal (motivation) is the usual result of conceptual conflict.

Berlyne tentatively proposes six somewhat overlapping types of conceptual conflict: doubt, perplexity, contradiction, conceptual incongruity, confusion, and irrelevance.

Doubt is characterized by a conflict between a tendency to believe and at the same time disbelieve a statement. The credibility of the speaker is a crucial variable. If J. Edgar Hoover calls Eisenhower a communist, one is more likely to experience conflict and doubt than if the statement were made by a member of the John Birch Society. One is likely to believe Eisenhower is a "good" American, but the stature of the accuser might cause one to doubt his convictions.

Perplexity. The second type of conceptual conflict is experienced by the individual when the evidence supports two mutually exclusive beliefs. Albert Einstein must have experienced perplexity when the evidence supporting a quantum theory of light was presented. A more common example is in evidence during political campaigns. An individual might become convinced that a particular democratic candidate is by far the best man for the job. On the other hand, the same voter might be equally certain that the Republican Party is the only party which he can support. To him evidence dictates a commitment to a particular candidate and a particular party. Since the political beliefs of the individual are mutually exclusive, perplexity results.

Contradiction. In most literate societies, the child is taught in a number of ways to behave logically and to resolve contradictions (i.e., through ridicule by parents, teachers and friends). Not all learning regarding a particular object takes place at one time; therefore, the individual may maintain logically contradictory concepts regarding a specific topic. When the contradiction is recognized, an increase in arousal will follow. In such a situation the businessman has learned to be honest at all times and that he is, in fact, responsible to protect his neighbor. At the same time he has been taught business tactics which demand that a good businessman take advantage of others who lack his skill and knowledge of the business world. When these two beliefs are brought to light the man can see the contradiction, and high arousal is a likely result of this awareness.

Conceptual incongruity exists when the individual has learned that characteristic A is unlikely to be found together with characteristic B, but is informed that a particular A also has characteristic B. Such incongruity may arise the first time a religious fundamentalist encounters a wine drinking priest. A similar case may occur when a Catholic child encounters a married Episcopalian or Eastern Rite priest.

Confusion arises under conditions in which the stimulus input is ambiguous and the ambiguity activates conflicting symbolic responses. A speech which never quite gets to the point can elicit conceptual activity which attempts to put together the ambiguous input, but confusion occurs because the point is not discernible. Another case of possible confusion is when faulty transmission distorts the input just as a faulty loudspeaker or smudged printing distorts or obscures a crucial passage. The noise which creates the ambiguity leads to a higher arousal and an attempt by the individual to reduce the confusion. Of course, extended confusion due to faulty transmission might lead to a tuning out of the signal.

Irrelevance as a trigger for conceptual conflict causes Berlyne some descriptive difficulty and a second hand interpretation surely compounds the problem. Apparently, this notion involves the fact that humans learn to process related material; therefore, the introduction of irrelevant concepts leads to frustration and increased arousal. Irrelevant concepts are often encountered in group discussions, particularly at P.T.A., faculty, council, and political meetings. If the problem under discussion is important to the receiver of messages, he will experience a desire to get on with the presentation of relevant information. Cody and Rothney (1963) reported that some superior high school students limit their problem-solving performances since they bring information to the problem which might be related to the topic but irrelevant to reaching a correct conclusion. In one of the problems presented in this study students were given the following problem:

> There are six white socks and six black socks in a drawer. If one reaches into the drawer in the dark so that he is unable to see them, how many socks must be removed to make sure he has a pair of matching socks?

Those who failed to solve the problem considered reaching for pairs of socks rather than numbers of socks. Since socks are usually thought of in pairs this connection would normally have been useful. In this particular situation the association led to an incorrect response. If the problem solver considered socks in pairs only, there was a possibility that after he retrieved a pair of socks one might be white and one might be black. Since there was an even number of socks in the drawer, it might be impossible to be sure he retrieved a "pair" of matching socks. Other students, who considered socks as individual items gave the correct response: three.

Conceptual Conflict and the Act of Discovery

Conceptual conflict is set off by either external message units (ΣS) or by the activation of internal processes (thoughts or rs's). Conceptual conflict may be reduced by non-knowledge-seeking behavior, as we shall see in Chapter 6. However, for present purposes, we shall be concerned with the reduction of conflict by way of epistemic behaviors (knowledge seeking). Berlyne proposes that all specific epistemic behavior is initiated by a question or its equivalent, but one must conclude that not all questions elicit conflict and epistemic behavior. Catechetical teaching such as, "Who are the five most important Greek dramatists?" might or might not initiate epistemic curiosity and/or conflict. Observation in history classes has led the present authors to conclude that a large proportion of the students tune-out the message. Few students are overwhelmed with learning who the "best" author, historian, or dramatist might be. It seems reasonable to assume that instruction must go beyond memorizing five names on the basis of some authority unknown to the student. Within the catechetical setting, if knowledge-seeking occurs, the activity will most probably lead to reading the authoritative text which provides the answer. Under these conditions, epistemic curiosity surely is not present.

On the other hand, if the students have been exposed to the works of the dramatists under consideration, a question such as, "Who are the five most important Greek dramatists?" should lead to: confusion (due to ambiguity) → conceptual conflict → epistemic curiosity > epistemic behavior. Here problems are involved which require knowledge. "What does one mean by the greatest?" Each student can propose definitions; these can be contrasted with "traditional conclusions" and evaluations of the several conclusions may be made. Learning of this nature can be truly discovery learning, but the excitement and maximum value are not assured. The teacher might direct the activities in such a manner that the outcome is predetermined — everyone agrees with some authority chosen by the teacher. Furthermore, lack of resources might limit the diversity of information which is necessary for extended epistemic behavior and a resolution of the conflict.

In the example just discussed, theoretically there is no one correct answer. One might define "greatest" in relation to a number of frames of reference (e.g., who is the sexiest, most profound, humorous, etc.). Other questions may have answers which are "true" or "false" in view of present day "knowledge." Epistemic behavior does not assure that the resolution of the conflict will be "correct." A question in chemistry regarding the number of known elements might be answered by reading an outdated book with the satisfactory conclusion being 96 elements. Of course, such a resolution can be upset upon encountering a more recent text. The new information can cause a conceptual conflict and initiate a new cycle of epistemic behavior. Indeed, one might deliberately provide informational sources which differ. Such a practice might lead to the expectancy that one can be fairly certain of change in almost all areas of science.

By way of emphasis: Success in creating conceptual conflict depends greatly upon some knowledge of the concepts and expectancies entertained by the target population. Apparently, no conflict can be induced if the student has not acquired the necessary concepts.

A brief summary note: The hypothetical mode involves the learner in the problem solving process. Theoretically, the process leads to cumulative constructionism and seems likely to develop intrinsic motivation. The initiation of discovery learning might be provided by means of a question designed to create conceptual conflict.

Discovery and Inquiry

Behaviors which distinguish the productive scientist from the non-productive have been classified as intuitive. He can "tease-out" the relevant variables and ignore the irrelevant or noisy variables. Model building by these individuals results in powerful notions based upon a minimum of constructs. Bruner hypothesized that these intuitive behaviors are acquired only through practice in problem solving with the intent to discover relevant relationships. Knowing the subject matter in only a formalized manner apparently is not sufficient. Learning by inquiry is an attempt to transcend this difficulty for it is not assimilation of second hand conclusions. Rather, it involves a direct attack upon critical problems and issues. As such, learning by inquiry approximates the behavior of researchers.

A Moderating View

The foibles of professional faddism were noted in Chapter 1. To some degree, "learning by discovery" is "bullish" on the educational market. Unfortunately, many educators ignore Bruner's explicit statements that his notions are tentative propositions. Further, the statements of Bruner are necessarily vague with very minor mention of operational procedures regarding the response characteristics of productive inquiry. These statements are vague since the behavior involved is complex, but this is not intended to imply that the desired operationalism is impossible. In his presidential address to the American Psychological Association, Bruner (1965) specified the ignorance of psychological theorists regarding the growth of intelligence within the schools. Indeed, he admonishes the psychologist to look at the school setting if he wishes to foster and "understand" learning. One might conclude that we should look twice before buying nothing but discovery learning. We shall return to a discussion of this matter in a later section of this chapter.

Operant Conditioning

The cognitive and/or neo-behavioristic orientation up to this point in the text has emphasized three variables: (1) the *conditions* (ΣS) under which the organism is behaving, (2) the *organism,* and (3) the *response* (R) of the organism. From noting regularities of $\Sigma S - R$ conditions, some inferences regarding central neural-conceptual processes were made. Little attention has been given to "reinforcing states" except on a feedback or informational basis. A rather attractive alternate view of behavior is provided by B. F. Skinner in his voluminous writings regarding *operant conditioning.* Since Skinner's ideas are both simple and powerful, a digression regarding his basic notions follows. Subsequently, these notions will be applied to Bruner's ideas relating to discovery learning.

Response and Reinforcement ($R \rightarrow S^{rein}$). Most discussions regarding learning emphasize the S-R connection or various intervening variables. Skinner's presentation directs the focus of concern away from the unobservable internal state to the *response* → reinforcement conditions ($R \rightarrow S^{rein}$). In this sense, Skinner is concerned with performance rather than learning, which is *not* immediately observable. An operant (R) is any change the organism carries out on the environment (e.g., walking, lifting, etc.). A reinforcer is any stimulus that follows a free response and increases the probability of the response occurring again. To a food deprived rat, a pellet of food is usually an effective reinforcer. Place a 24-hour food deprived rat in a box with a stirrup lever and arrange the lever so that a press releases a pellet of food in a small container. The rat will move around (free operants) and possibly strike the lever, releasing a pellet (S^{rein}). As a consequence of S^{rein}, the operants preceding the stimulus are more likely to re-occur. Within a short time the rat will acquire a lever-pressing response activity. Of course, if the rat never presses the lever under these conditions, no S^{rein} is presented and operant conditioning cannot take place. The animal, however, can be *shaped* by means of successive approximations. A pellet might be released when the rat is facing the food dish. When this facing response is established, the pellet is only released when he approaches the dish. Within a short time, the animal acquires the desired response. Skinner demonstrates his ability to shape a pigeon to turn figure 8's within a short training period using successive approximation.

The emphasis in these activities is upon response and consequence. For a 24-hour deprived rat, food is a reinforcer only if the preceding response increases in frequency. In general, pellets are effective for food-deprived rats, grain for food-deprived pigeons and M & M's for children under low levels of food deprivation. Occasionally, Skinner talks about a "hungry" rat, but only in times of weakness, for "hungry" implies some internal processes.*

---

*Reinforcement is *not* intended by Skinner to mean the same as reward. Reward implies some external incentive defined independently of the behaving organism. A reinforcer is any stimulus which follows a response and is observed to increase the rate of the response.

Once an operant response is established, the behavior might be maintained efficiently by establishing one of four reinforcement schedules:

1. A *fixed ratio* schedule is based upon presenting a reinforcer after the subject emits a specified number of responses. Thus in a 5:1 ratio the subject is reinforced after each set of five responses.
2. A *variable ratio,* schedule presents reinforcement on the average at a specified number of responses, but the specific number may vary. An average 5:1 ratio with a variable schedule may be set such that reinforcement is presented after two responses, then seven, four, six, eight, three, etc.
3. A *fixed interval* provides reinforcement to responses on some fixed time basis, e.g., a five-minute delay after the preceding reinforcement.
4. A *variable interval* schedule has a specified average time interval, but the specific interval may be shorter or longer. (This interval is concerned with the mean time between reinforcements while variable ratio is concerned with a mean number of reinforcers).

The fixed schedules tend to produce scalloping effects; that is, the response rate diminishes after each reinforcement. The variable schedules do not manifest the scalloping phenomena primarily because the variable schedules do reinforce, at times, contiguous responses. On a work output basis, the variable ratio is superior to all schedules, for rapid responding pays off. Responses acquired under conditions of intermittent reinforcement are more resistant to extinction than those acquired under continuous reinforcement conditions. Continuous reinforcement, however, provides a more rapid extinction of learned behavior.

Discrimination. In the operant conditioning paradigm, the preceding stimulus conditions do *not* elicit responses as in the case in classical conditioning (e.g., Pavlov's dog salivating at the presentation of a buzzer). The preceding stimulus conditions are, however, important as cue signals. One might establish a lever pressing operant in a rat and pair the response with a red light. The experimenter might turn off the light and withhold reinforcement for lever pressing. He might turn on the light and then reinforce lever pressing. With careful manipulation the S (light on) becomes a cue that the lever pressing response is appropriate. Note, the red light does *not* elicit the response; it is only a *cue* that lever pressing responses are appropriate. This is called operant discrimination. Figure 5.3 provides a scheme that might illustrate the case.

FIGURE 5.3

Formation of cue discrimination

S^D (red light)	————————	R—S^{rein}
S^{Δ} (no light)		R—no S^{rein}

In the presence of the red light the response is reinforced. Responses emitted without the light are not reinforced, and as a consequence diminish in frequency.

The cue is called S^D (ess dee) by operant researchers and the stimulus which is not the cue is called S^{Δ} (ess delta). Thus, although the operant frame of reference stresses the response reinforcement area, the stimulating conditions are discussed. The role of the stimulus conditions, nevertheless, is essentially of lesser importance from this frame of reference.

Differentiation. The stimulus conditions are *discriminated.* Response shaping is called response *differentiation.* One starts with a relatively gross response and gradually differentiates it by means of reinforcement manipulation until a highly specific response is obtained.

By putting *discrimination* and *differentiation* together, one obtains a total unit as shown in Figure 5.4.

FIGURE 5.4

S^{Δ}		R^{Δ}		
S^D	————	R^D	————	S^{rein}
S^D		R^{Δ}		

Responses in the presence of S^{Δ} (stimulus delta) are never reinforced. In the presence of the red light (S^D) responses are reinforced. The S^D becomes a cue that response is appropriate and the S^{Δ} that response is not appropriate. Note R^{Δ} is never reinforced and response differentiation is acquired, that is R^{Δ} is extinguished in the experimental setting.

The S^D is a cue that R^D is appropriate and the reinforcing condition obtains. R^D in the presence of S^{Δ} is not reinforced and the behavior in the presence of S^{Δ} is extinguished. R^{Δ} in the presence of S^D is not reinforced and the response is extinguished. These responses can be *chained* so that one response may produce the stimulus (S^D) for the next response. This is the more typical state of affairs.

Negative Reinforcement. Pellets, grain and M & M's are examples of stimuli which are often positive reinforcers. Negative reinforcement occurs when the response leads to cessation of an aversive stimulus. An example might be cessation of shock following lever pressing. Negative reinforcement is *not* punishment, for the latter is presented as a consequence of the response; negative reinforcement is obtained by a response leading to cessation of the aversive stimuli. Negative and positive reinforcement increase the probability of the occurrence of the response. Punishment decreases the response rate and often has side effects which disrupt other sequential behavior. As a means of controlling school behavior, punishment might be a poor method since avoidance of school is reinforced (by way of negative reinforcement). Thus, one can prevent talking in school through use of punishment, but one may prevent any school learning also, for the child may not be present. To editorialize, the behavior of some teachers seems to reflect the desire to get the child out of one's hair at school. If you wish to encourage school dropouts, indeed frequent punishment is an effective stimulus to present. Please note, we do not wish to imply that punishment should never be used for there might be cases where the information value of punishment is productive. On the other hand, exclusive control of behavior by means of presentation of aversive stimuli seems to be self-defeating.

Skinner's notions are simple, but many elaborations upon the basic structure have been devised. For the interested student, a number of references are available in the bibliography of this chapter.

Implications of Operant Conditioning

The operant view emphasizes the response and the contingent consequence. In order to teach any subject, a close examination of the terminal behavior is mandatory from this viewpoint. Furthermore, if the terminal response is complex, the sequential set of responses must be specified. When this specification task is complete, the student must be analyzed to determine which stimuli will operate as reinforcers. These may be a smile, praise (very good), M & M's, or the generalized reinforcer, money.

Armed with these data, learning (response acquisition) can commence. A much used procedural tool is the teaching machine. Material is presented, a response is required, and reinforcement follows in the form of blinking red lights or knowledge of correct response. In that programmed learning and teaching machines are significant educational tools, Chapter 8 discusses this area in more detail.

An auxiliary implication of the operant frame is that it makes the teacher "think." If we want children to "appreciate good music," what terminal behaviors exemplify "appreciation?" If the terminal behavior is attendance at concerts, then one may wish to take children to concerts and reinforce the child upon entering and every time he sighs in "appreciation." Of course, one might desire to change the reinforcement schedule once the behavior is acquired so that he is reinforced every third time he enters the concert hall. This suggestion is made only half in jest.

The present authors believe the operant view and Bruner's cognitive view can be complementary. Bruner states the "beautiful thoughts" and Skinner presents the elegant techniques. Skinner lacks the answer to what *should* be learned and Bruner, to a large degree, slights the *how* problem. Thus, if we wish to develop cumulative constructionism, we must note the responses relevant to constructionism.

To illustrate, consider the "Twenty Questions" problem cited earlier. Cumulative constructionists ask questions which impose constraints upon the problem. Let us subject constructionism to a *loose* operant analysis. First, free responses to the problem will be somewhere on the continuum between absolute episodic empiricism (specific questions) and perfect cumulative constructionism (questions which impose constraints by means of ruling out large areas). Therefore, analysis of the problem, by the behavior modifier (teacher), can specify the response type (constructionist) to be conditioned. Second, an analysis of the student should be made to determine what class of stimuli are reinforcers for that student. In the actual problem situation, reinforcement, plus the yes or no, can be paired whenever the more cumulative constructionist response mode is provided. The reinforcer might be: "No, but that is a good question." Of course, the successive approximation method might be employed to shape an extreme episodic empiricist. Theoretically, diversity of training and overlearning might be necessary to obtain this mode of inquiry as a predominant response tendency. In Skinner's terms, we would want to tie the operant response mode to a wide range of S^D's. This presentation is *not* a rigorous functional analysis (an operant term for the process outlined); however, it does represent some possibilities which a marriage between cognitive theory and operant technology might provide for the educator.

Maintenance of cumulative constructionism in day-to-day problem solving at first glance appears to pose a problem, for an outside agent might not be present to provide an effective reinforcement schedule. Greenspoon (1955) increased the frequency of plural nouns in speech by means of saying "mmhm" whenever the subject included a plural noun in his conversation. When the experimenter discontinued the reinforcer the number of plural nouns decreased in frequency. Can the same fate be predicted for the carefully developed constructionist mode? Evidence needs to be gathered on this matter. If behavior is so short lived that it is not expressed outside the classroom, perhaps something is missing in the education process.

Theoretically, there are a number of indications that external reinforcement can be internalized such that the individual supplies his own reinforcement schedule. Hunt (1963) developed a theory of *intrinsic* motivation using Piaget's observations as well as his own informal observations. In brief, the theory suggests that during the second year of life, the human infant develops "motivation inherent in information processing and action." Stated differently, "the more a child has seen and heard, the more he wants to see and hear" (Hunt, 1963, p. 273). Hunt's theory proposes that problem solving activity is reinforcing, but he does *not* imply that the efficient approach will necessarily be employed. Berlyne's (1960) ideas regarding conceptual conflict also do not insure efficient problem solving; nevertheless, under both views the theory can be molded into an operant view which increases the theoretical probability that operant research regarding discovery learning will pay off.

Consider the notions that problem solution is reinforcing and that responses which are more frequently reinforced are more likely to reoccur. Once cumulative constructionist behavior is acquired, problem solution (reinforcement) should be more likely to follow. Episodic empiricism will pay off less frequently and, thus, to some degree be extinguished, although intermittent reinforcement might prolong the extinction period. This state of affairs supports the need for an overlearning provision.

By Way of Summary

Discovery learning is not a mysterious spark which vitalizes thinking. Essentially, we learn specific responses and habitual modes of responding. Apparently those responses which remain are the ones that have been most frequently reinforced. In order to teach learning by discovery effectively, the reinforcing agent (teacher) must examine the response sequence which reflects the terminal behavior desired. If these notions are "true," it is then obvious that the teacher must know something more than *how* to reinforce (teach); she must know *what* responses to reinforce. The implications for teacher training are apparent. First, the training should include intensive preparation in examining the *structure* of her subject matter specialty. Second, the training should provide intensive practice in shaping procedures and in analysis of selection of reinforcing stimuli. Apparently there is no substitute for knowledge of subject matter and knowledge of behavior for the classroom teacher.

On Concepts

The noting of redundancies in the environment was previously discussed as a classifying (coding) task which imposes conceptual order upon the universe of experience. Essentially the classifying act is an abstracting process and, as such, the derived code is a function of the stimuli *and* the individual's habitual coding patterns (see Korzybski in Chapter 3). The product of classification is frequently called a *concept* in psychological literature. A few additional notions regarding concepts merit discussion in this chapter. The present discussion is in part abstracted from "A Study of Thinking" (Bruner, Goodnow and Austin, 1956). Two terms which seem ambiguously used in the literature are concept *formation* and concept *attainment*. Bruner, *et al.,* (1956) distinguished between the two processes on the basis of operations. Concept *formation* from Bruner's frame of reference is defined as the act of arranging a diverse set of stimuli into some "meaningful" relationship (inventing classes). Concept *attainment* is the act whereby the individual is seeking the distinguishing characteristics of objects belonging to two or more *known* classes (in essence, seeking the defining attributes of a class).

Consider the task of the early biologists. Faced with a myriad of living organisms, "how can these organisms be ordered to form classes which will convey 'meaningful' relationships?" Initially each school of biology invented its own taxonomy (classification system). As the field became larger and communication among schools occurred, the investigators were faced with tremendous difficulties because uniformity was missing. Controversy developed regarding which system was most nearly correct. Each school argued the merits of its own system. Eventually Linnaeus' taxonomic system survived as the dominant code. The resolution does not imply that Linneaus' system is "true"; it only means that his taxonomy is accepted for utility.

Once the classification is *formed,* the defining characteristics of the classification may or may *not* be known. Nevertheless, the problem is now one of *attaining* a concept. Let us entertain two examples.

First, consider a biology student faced with the problem of determining the defining attributes (characteristics) of a vertebrate. Of course, the student might look in a text for the definition of a vertebrate (defining attributes) or the instructor might require some discovery mode. Under the discovery approach, the student may be presented with various organisms, some which belong to the class *vertebrate* and others which do not. Through a careful noting of the attributes of the positive and negative cases, the student can employ various strategies in order to attain the concept (solve the problem). He might attempt to memorize all the attributes of the positive case and determine those which are always present. Memorizing will succeed if the number of attributes are few, but memory storage will break down when a large number of attributes are present. In the presence of multiple attributes, a more successful strategy might be to select a positive example of the class *vertebrate,* and then choose an organism which differs in only one respect. If the chosen case is positive, the deleted attribute is not a defining characteristic and, therefore, can be dropped from consideration. Such a strategy sequentially employed assures a high degree of success and reduced memory strain. (This latter strategy is called *conservative focusing* by Bruner, *et al.,* (1956) and approximates Bruner's notion of cumulative constructionism noted earlier.) The example just mentioned is a case in which the defining attributes of a concept are known to man. Concept attainment under these conditions might be acquired either by means of the *expository* mode or the *discovery* mode.

A second case may occur in which the class is known but the attributes or common characteristics are unknown. Present day investigation into the causes of schizophrenia is a case in point. On a descriptive basis, schizophrenia can loosely be stated and individuals can to some degree be placed in a category relating to schizophrenia on the basis of manifest behavior. Research is being conducted to determine the common elements which underlie the overt behavior patterns. Some findings note that a correlation with environmental conditions and other findings suggest hereditary factors. Unfortunately from the point of view of science not all people from a schizoid environment manifest schizophrenic behavior. Likewise, when one monozygotic twin manifests schizophrenic behavior, it is *not* always observed that the other twin with "identical" inheritance follows the other's behavior pattern. Apparently schizophrenia is *not* a simple class. Recent theorizing (a tentative unverified concept) includes the possibility that the defining characteristic might be a genetic deficiency operating within a hostile environment (Meehl, 1962). Concept attainment in this case as well as the previous vertebrate problem represents the seeking of the defining attributes even though the schizophrenia definition is not as yet resolved.

Categories of Concepts

Bruner, *et al.,* (1956) discussed three categories of concepts: *conjunctive, relational* and *disjunctive.* For purposes of classifying subject matter structure in education, the distinction among these types merits consideration.

Conjunctive concepts are defined by the joint presence of specific values of a number of attributes. The concept vertebrate is conjunctive for it includes being an organism and an animal, and having a *back-bone*.

Relational concepts are characterized by a specified relationship between attributes. Skinner's definition of a "reinforcer" is an example, for it is defined as any stimuli that follows a response which increases the probability of the recurrence of the response. This relational term is often confused with the conjunctive term *reward*. Reward is defined as an object used to reinforce a response. It is conjunctive for it is defined independently of the consequences upon the individual's behavior. As such, a *reward* might not work. Therefore, it is possible to say, "Johnny will not work for the rewards I give him." The relational term "reinforcement" would lead to a statement of failure such as: "I cannot find an effective stimulus which is reinforcing."

Another relational concept in psychology is the notion of an effective stimulus. It is defined in psycho-physics as an energy change at the receptor that is capable of discharging the receptor. The stimulus is effective when it works. Both definitions of reinforcement and effective stimulus are cases where the determination of the state is made after the fact. Some individuals might feel uncomfortable with these ex post facto definitions; nevertheless, they provide a basis for lawful description and prediction of behavior. For example, a hundred candlepower unobstructed light source, 10 feet distant from the rods, is an effective stimulus for an aroused intact human. As long as this relationship holds, behavior is lawful. When it does not hold, the investigator looks for the missing relevant variable.

A *disjunctive* concept is characterized by one of a number of attributes or all of them. The typical concept of a noun is a disjunctive case. A noun is either the name of a person, a place, or a thing. Bruner, *et al.,* (1956, p. 43) classified the *strike* in baseball as a disjunctive concept. A strike is a pitch which crosses the plate between the batter's knees and the armpits, *or* a ball that is swung at and fails to enter the playing field. An obvious characteristic of a disjunctive concept is its arbitrary nature. No common elements describe a disjunctive concept, and it appears to be quite messy. Bruner points out that in our western culture we tend to avoid disjunctive concepts. He raises the question that Korzybski raised regarding the noun centeredness of the Indo-European language structure (see Chapter 3). When confronted with disjunctive notions we attempt to transpose them to common elements or to common relationships. Structural linguists have redefined a noun to be the relation the word plays in a sentence. Thus, "to run" might be a verb or a noun (e.g., To *run* is fun, or they *run* fast). The strike in baseball can also be cast into a relational definition. A strike can be defined as a ball that is thrown in the direction of the batter and the relevant characteristics of a strike depend upon the trend in baseball to maintain some balance between pitcher prowess and batter prowess as these factor-relate to a definition of "interestingness" of the game. The definition of the strike and the strike zone changes as any one of the several relationships change. This relational definition is not more economical than the disjunctive definition; however, it is somewhat more lawful.

An evaluation of why disjunctive concepts are difficult to entertain presents no ready answer. The constriction of thought imposed by our language structure might be one possible factor. We may be forced to habitually think in conjunctive and relational terms. Another possibility might be that disjunctive concepts are only first statements which reflect imperfect "knowledge." Furthermore, the inelegance of disjunctivity violates our basic assumption of universal uniformity (a relational world view). If the history of science is any guide, specific disjunctive categories might well fall to the invention of more lawful relational categories as representations of the specific concept. Of course, the initial assumptions of uniformity might be false, and we may ultimately be forced to revise our world view.

More Regarding Strategies

Conservative focusing was presented as a strategy which leads to an efficient selection of the common elements constituting the conjunctive concept. When time limits are imposed, conservative focusing may be unsuccessful since the systematic processing of each variable might exceed the limits established. *Focus gambling* increases the probability of success under rigid time limits; however, it does not assure success. For example, consider the concept vertebrate presented earlier. We have before the subject an array of plants and animals. Given the first example, a cat which is a vertebrate, the focus gambler would change many attributes at once — he might select a fish (no legs, habitat water, no fur, etc.). In this case, many irrelevant attributes are eliminated at once because the fish is a vertebrate. Focus gambling does not provide information if the new case (fish) is negative because *fur, legs, surface habitat, etc.,* might be the defining attribute or some combination of these characteristics. Conservative focusing assures a small amount of information on each trial for only one attribute is changed at a time (e.g., eliminate fur, select a crawling child, if positive fur is not a defining attribute).

The appropriateness of a strategy apparently depends in some degree on the nature and consequences of the problem. Furthermore, strategies appropriate for conjunctive concepts are not appropriate for disjunctive categories. A strategy called *negative* focusing apparently leads to the successful attainment of the disjunctive concept. Recall that the disjunctive concept is characterized by: this attribute, *or* this one, *or* this one, *or* all of them. In contrast to conjunctive strategies which pay off when the focus is on the positive case (joint presence of two or more attributes), successful disjunctive strategies require focus on the negative case and then add an attribute. Any added attribute which makes the case positive is one of the defining attributes of the concept. Sequential negative focusing will identify the defining attributes whereas positive conservative focusing will not. Consider the disjunctive concept "a strike in baseball." Given a positive instance — batter in box, ball over the plate, ball between batter's armpits and knees, and ball *not* swung on — a positive conservative focus strategy would proceed to eliminate the irrelevant variables. First let's assume the problem seeker focuses on the plate and asks the ball to be thrown away from the plate. This would give a negative instance; therefore "ball over the plate" is one necessary attribute and should be replaced. The focus might then go to the batter, and then to the height dimension and finally to the swing characteristic. The concept derived would be: a strike is a pitch which crosses the plate between the batter's knees and armpits. The foul strike and swinging strike would not be found using this conjunctive strategy. From a conjunctive view, a strike can be broken into two concepts, strike and swing strike, rather than one. If the concept strike is cast into two concepts, the conservative focusing strategy would be appropriate.

The notions just presented are rather complex; nonetheless they are central to the educational process for concept attainment is a large educational activity. Present day medical practice relating to the identification of allergens is based upon a disjunctive notion; therefore, negative focusing should be a strategy that is taught to allergists. The researcher, however, may pursue a conjunctive or a relational concept in order to seek the uniformities missing on the practitioners level. Perhaps educators should plan lessons so that students would learn how to select problem-solving strategies which are appropriate to the problem and the situation.

Creativity Revisited

The demand for developing creative people has resulted in new pressures upon the schools to incorporate creativity as an aim of education.

In the presence of the diverse use of the term, one must conclude "creativity" is a disjunctive concept. Psychological research into the nature of creativity specifies characteristics of creative people which include *originality, fluency, flexibility, etc.* (see Chapter 4). Within these vast sets, research becomes messy unless some restrictions are imposed in the design. A series of studies conducted by Maltzman, *et al.,* (1960) represents one restricted design which reduced the ambiguity. These studies involved training for "originality." Original responses were defined within the studies as statistically infrequent responses to a Word Association Task and an Unusual Uses Task. A typical Unusual Uses Task follows:

> In this test, you will be asked to consider some common objects. Each object has a common use which will be given to you. You are to list six other uses for which the object or parts of the object could serve.
>
> List six possible uses for each of the following objects:
> A newspaper (used for reading)
>
> ______________ ______________ ______________
>
> ______________ ______________ ______________
>
> Answers might be: to start a fire, to wrap garbage, to swat flies, to hang for curtains, to wash windows, etc.

Within the criterion group, a low originality classification represents the individual who provided uses which many others gave. Conversely a high originality score indicated that the individual gave uses which few others gave. Originality defined in these terms is a *relational* concept. A response is original only if few others provide the same response. Once originality is operationally converted into a relational problem, the search for defining underlying attributes gains focus. The results of the study by Maltzman, *et al.,* supports the position that originality so defined is a function of operant learning. Apparently original responses (as defined) can be increased by means of reinforcing "original" (statistically unique) responses.

Barron and others (1965) conducted a number of studies to determine the differences between "creative" writers, architects, authors and the "less-creative." Individuals called creative were identified by their peers. The peer selection procedure is an evaluative act which is often overlooked in discussions regarding creativity. Figure 5.5 is presented in an effort to specify a number of variables contaminating the concept of creativity.

Figure 5.5 includes four dimensions: simple-complex, common-unique, good-bad, and time. Acts or products called creative usually involve complex, unique, and good characteristics (region A in the figure). A product occupying region A at time one (t_1) can shift to any position in time two (t_2). Consider the invention of the first A Bomb in 1944-45 — it was complex, unique, and good, *and* was considered creative. In 1969, the A Bomb is *common,* less *complex* (in relation to other bombs), not evaluated to be good (the Chinese have some) and we consider it destructive, *not* creative.

FIGURE 5.5

Four dimensions of evaluated creativity

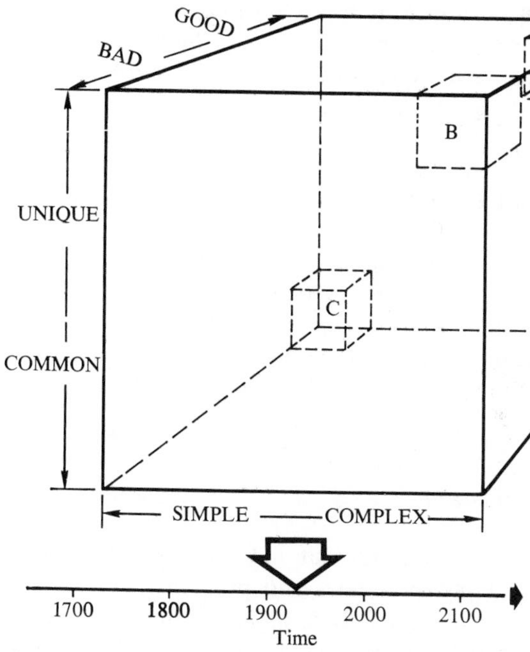

Van Gogh in 1880 produced a number of "works of art" whose characteristics were undoubtedly unique and complex, but evaluated by the critics to be bad and, therefore, *not* "really" art. These canvasses were labeled as the works of a mad man, yet today (1969), Van Gogh is considered to have been a "creative" artist. Van Gogh moved from region B to region A as a function of time and the change in culture and critics.

A child repeats for the first time the ABC's, a common-simple-good response (region C) — this is usually not considered to be creative;

however, the inventor of the alphabet (whoever he may have been) must have been creative.

The point of this brief digression into creativity is that a number of people with diverse backgrounds and understandings label behavior in creative categories. When this situation obtains, the concept is fuzzy and disjunctive. Some consider pop groups to be creative, while others praise country singers as creative artists. Essentially a person is creative if someone calls him creative. Salvador Dali, the flamboyant surrealistic painter, is creative because he tells everyone he is.

If, as a teacher, you are required to develop creativity, you may well ask for some specific behavioral definitions before proceeding. Indeed, you might be able to establish several types of creativity, each of which may have lawful attributes. It seems obvious that the use of the term "creativity" may be just another addition to educational jargon. In order to insure that this term connotes some specific and intended meaning, it should be defined as well as presented.

Applications of Cognitive Theory

This chapter has dealt with the cognitive frame of reference in theoretical terms. The suggested educational implications of these theories are preceded by modifiers (e.g., possibly, this might mean, etc.). The following discussion presents a selected review of some of the newer educational practices which are influenced by or reflect these cognitive concepts.

Mathematics Education

The "New Math" has recently hit and perhaps dominated the educational scene. The number of texts and programs with this orientation have proliferated, and the influence of Piaget and Bruner is apparent. One example of textual material that attempts to bridge the gap between concrete operations and formal operations is a book series on Sets and Numbers (Suppes, *et al.,* 1963). The introductory book in this series exemplifies the detailed attention devoted to easing the transition from thing manipulation to number manipulation. To illustrate, the following examples are drawn from Suppes, Boyle, and Hill (1963, pp. vii).

Consider the notion of grouping. One may obtain a family of toys and group them into sets such as a pencil and a ball. A descriptive representation of this set can be words, letters, etc. Words and letters, however, are complex abstractions; therefore, these authors use pictorial representations. They are less complex and retain some features of the object:

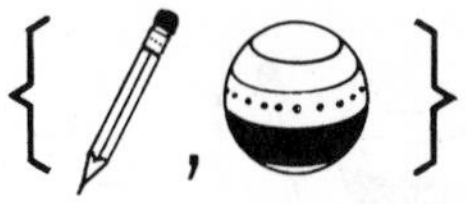

The curly brackets indicate a set. In order to specify a focus on the number of objects rather than the properties of the *objects* an N is added:

The figure represents the name of two objects just as the arabic numeral 2 indicates a name. The arabic equivalent can be introduced as:

$$N\{ \ /, \ \bigcirc \ \}=2$$

These notations permit numbers to be introduced as properties of *sets* and they provide precise definitions of numbers. Discrimination at this semi-abstract level is apparently more easily accomplished than by means of more abstract representation. For example:

$$\{ \ /, \ \bigcirc \ \} \neq \{ \ \square, \ \bigcirc \ \}$$

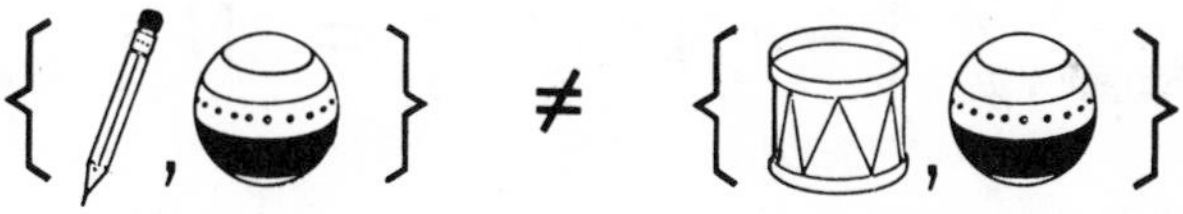

Set one does not equal set two because the properties of the objects in the two sets are not identical; however,

$$N\{ \ /, \ \bigcirc \ \} = N\{ \ \square, \ \bigcirc \ \}$$

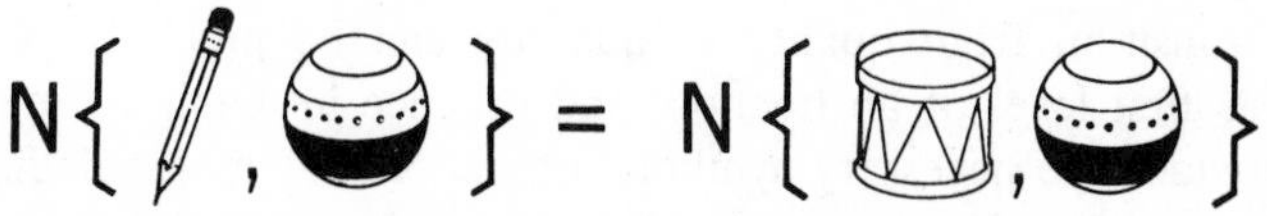

since the numbers associated with the sets *are* equal. The first group of sets are descriptions and the properties of the content within the sets are important whereas the second sets are preceded with the N which focuses upon quantity.

Union of sets and set differences provide opportunities to introduce closure on a semi-abstract level:

and

Furthermore

$$1 + 2 = 3$$

The difference of sets operation may be expressed:

and

and

$$2 - 1 = 1$$

The transition from quality to quantity can be precisely presented using this first level of abstraction, and practice in manipulating at this level provides the necessary symbolic operations for manipulating more abstract symbols. Furthermore, abstract symbols can be reduced to semi-abstract symbols whenever problem confusion obtains.

The Madison project under the direction of Robert B. Davis has developed a set of films and textual material which are designed to foster *discovery* learning in mathematics. These materials are intended to supplement the existing mathematics program. Davis (1964, p. 21) listed a number of accomplishments which he hopes will result from using these materials:

> We want children to *enjoy* mathematics.
>
> We want children to have successful experiences with mathematics.
>
> We want children to approach mathematics problems *creatively,* and not to think in terms of following rote procedures.
>
> We want children to approach mathematics problems with determination and with persistence and with optimism.
>
> We want children to approach mathematics problems, even hard problems, with confidence.
>
> We want children to have extensive experience with mathematical ideas and materials.
>
> We want them to have the familiarity which comes from such experience.
>
> We want to proceed carefully in building readiness for future mathematical experiences. In the past, traditional mathematics programs have expected this readiness to appear suddenly out of nowhere, and it has *not* tended to do so.
>
> We want younger children who are *creative* in dealing with abstract ideas, who are eager, original, and very honest in their logic, to preserve this ability and enthusiasm. Under traditional curricula it has usually been lost, and the high school student or college freshman no longer exhibits the clever resourcefulness of the fifth grader when dealing with abstract mathematical ideas.
>
> But we are not aiming for a specified level of achievement. We do not care whether every fifth grader can graph conic sections, or solve quadratic equations, or make a derivation of the binomial theorem for $(a + b)^2$ directly from the field axioms.
>
> Teaching abstract mathematics to children is, as Max Beberman of the University of Illinois Committee on School Mathematics projects recently remarked, "like giving candy to children." Nothing is gained by intruding into this paradise the apple of adult compulsiveness and the belief that work is work is work and must be inherently unpleasant. Adults may think that medicine must be painful in order to be efficacious. Children are perfectly happy to enjoy mathematics. Adults may think that the good things of life are either illegal, immoral, or fattening.

Children believe that thinking about interesting mathematical questions in a creative and intelligent way is fun.

The paid attendance at baseball games would not be increased if we required every fifth grader to memorize the current batting averages of every player in the Red Sox line-up, nor would understanding of the game be increased. The true flavor of mathematics, like baseball, is subtle and elusive. It is not derived from memorized facts. Rather, it is like Mark Twain's remark about his wife's swearing, "She knows all the words, but somehow she can't get the right tune." And a standardized test covering four-letter Anglo-Saxon words would not help her a bit.

We have included this lengthy quotation for it captures the "flavor and enthusiasm" behind the Madison Project. One can easily project a number of Bruner's, Piaget's and Berlyne's notions onto these procedures and desired outcomes, for example (1) readiness for concepts (Piaget), (2) lack of pressure to learn (Bruner's need state), and (3) questions raised to establish epistemic curiosity.

Davis' last paragraph merits comment, and we shall return to a discussion regarding the implicit problems which it raises.

Davis attempts to accomplish his objectives by means of presenting problems in a non-testing setting where the task at hand is to explore a set of problems. The teacher is instructed to play various roles which are intended to be a bit ludicrous. The incongruous or oversimplified questions apparently are designed to elicit epistemic curiosity. An example of this is provided in the following problem taken from the initial lesson in the guide for teachers (Davis, 1964, p. 35).

Teacher: Suppose we are operating a pet store, and we come into the store on Monday morning. We unlock the door, unlock the cash register (which has quite a lot of money in it), and feed the animals. Now, somebody comes in to buy something.

Teacher: (1) What does he buy?

A Child: (1) A dog.

Teacher: (2) How much does he pay us for it?

A Child: (2) $5

Teacher writes 5 on the board.

(A suggestion is given to the teacher that she might want to round off decimal fractions by saying, "Well, let's call it $5. I don't want to get into *hard* numbers." Davis suggests this will be a good joke. Along with this joke, the teacher implicitly communicates "this is fun.")

Teacher: (3) Is there now *more* money in the cash register than there was when we opened up this morning, or is there *less?*

Children: (3) More

(This is a "stupid" question to the students according to Davis for it is so simple, but also he claims this fascinates children. Is it due to the conceptual conflict, "Teachers usually don't make simple statements?")

This set continues with customers returning animals and the notation for positive (+) and negative (—) signs are developed. For example:

Teacher: (5) Now somebody comes in to return something. What does he return?

Child: (5) Parakeet

Teacher: (6) How much money do we give back?

Child: (6) $25

Teacher writes on board 5 $^{-}$25

Teacher: (7) Is there now *more* money in the cash register than there was when we first opened up this morning, or is there *less?*

Child: (7) Less

Teacher: (8) Do you know how much more or how much less?

Child: (8) $20 less

Teacher writes on board 5 $^{-}25 = {}^{-}20$

Teacher: (9) Do you know how to write this?

Children: (9) $^{-}$20 (which we read "negative twenty")

Notice the negative sign is *not* centered, this is to provide less confusion when operations later in the book are carried out with signed numbers, e. g., $^{-}2 \times {}^{+}3$.

The materials provided by Davis cover a wide range of mathematical concepts which are discovered by means of practice with games and exercises. External pressure is intended to be low throughout these exercises — the teacher is continually admonished not to block exploration, although she certainly is asked to encourage and adjust the pace such that "satisfaction" is "experienced" by the child.

Discovery learning also underlies the University of Illinois Committee on School Mathematics (UICSM) projects. Hendrix (1961a) reported on the discovery orientation of the elementary program. New concepts are introduced with a problem. The task is to bring past learnings to bear upon this new problem. For example:

½ of ¾ might be approached graphically

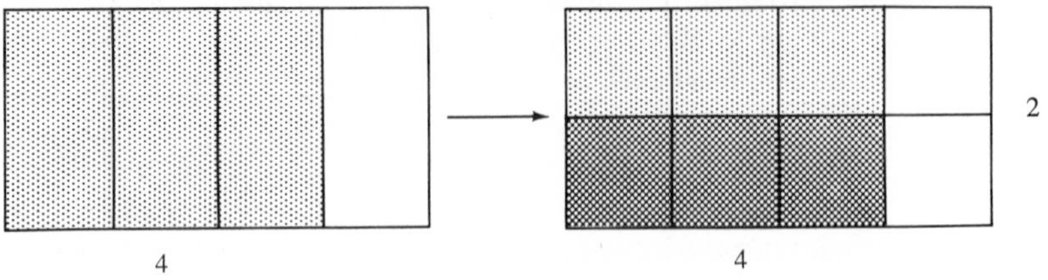

to result in ⅜.

A number (3 or 4) of these problems might be solved graphically with the total class and then seatwork problems may be assigned. As a result of prior sets to find "shortcuts," some children will "discover" a non-graphic solution to the problems and zip along. Others, noting that someone has discovered a shortcut, will return to work seeking the shortcut. Under these conditions, numerical operations are derived from practice with graphic representation. The fact that the child can solve ¾ x ½ = ⅜ is sufficient. Hendrix maintains that non-verbal understanding is demonstrated and that stating a verbal rule at this early age either results in incorrect statements (due to an inadequate vocabulary) or nonsense that hinders generalization. This approach parallels Piaget's notions that formal operations are not efficiently learned prior to age 11 or so. The UICSM program also pushes formal mathematics (using deductive proof) down to the ninth grade and in some instances (where a number of bright children are ready) to the seventh and eighth grades (Hendrix, 1961b).

The intended result of these programs is to develop precision and enthusiasm in mathematics learning. UICSM and Davis both provide films which demonstrate these outcomes. A recent review of research on the "new" mathematics program (Brown and Abell, 1965) indicated that students entered in these programs did at least as well on standardized tests as those who were enrolled in traditional programs. Furthermore, "new math" students acquired concepts not included in the traditional programs. Nonetheless, little research is available to answer the question "What mathematics should what children learn at what age?" (Brown and Abell, 1965, p. i). An apparently further relative point and caution here is that teachers who find mathematics dull are unlikely to develop enthusiasm in their pupils.

The promise of "new math" as it reflects awareness of cognitive theory is great. If we wish to avoid faddism, ways and means of assessing the "subtle" and "elusive" flavor of mathematics need to be developed. Demonstration and enthusiasm are not sufficient. Perhaps, the mathematics educator can obtain precision in defining behavioral outcomes by employing a trained functional analyst. On the other hand, it may be expecting too much from the math educator to demand that he become also a research psychologist. Indeed, rather than criticize these enthusiastic innovators, the researcher might join the innovator. The researcher can ask the innovator to identify student behaviors which he thinks express the spirit of the "new math." With these data the researcher can test children who express the spirit and those who do not. Such studies might lead to some generalizable data which specify the outcomes of the teaching procedures.

Science Education

Suchman and his colleagues constructed programs for inquiry training based upon Piaget, Bruner, and Berlyne's notions. Films have been developed in biology and physics for intermediate grade students which were designed as discrepant events which require inquiry in order to resolve the discrepancy (Suchman, 1964). One such film, "The Bimetallic Strip" (not the film title), is described by Suchman (1961, p. 154):

> The apparatus is made of two thin strips of metal, one steel, one brass, fused together into one strip that looks rather like a long narrow spatula. It is held, steel side down, in a Bunsen burner flame by means of a wooden handle. Almost immediately the strip begins to bend downward in an increasing arc which approaches 90°. Next, the strip is dipped into a large tank of cool water whereupon it straightens out quite abruptly. The strip is flipped over and once again held in the flame. This time it bends upward, forming the identical arc, as before, but inverted. Once again it straightens out when placed in the water. The problem question: "Why does the strip bend and then straighten out again?"

In order to go beyond concrete operations, Suchman limits the inquiry operation to verbal questions which can be answered with a yes or no. An additional value to verbal inquiry is that the instructor can make some assessment of the strategies the child employs. Suchman finds that early inquiry behavior without guidance is inefficient for the child apparently has not previously acquired an adequate repertory of inquiry responses. He attributes this lack to the fact that typical school experiences do not provide for autonomous problem solution.

A typical example of low autonomy is provided by Suchman (1961, p. 156) in this discussion concerning the bi-metallic strip:

Examiner:	What made it go up? I'm here to answer questions.
Mark:	Yes, I know. I can't think of any to ask.
Examiner:	I see. Think. Try.
Mark:	[Pause] Well I can't think of any questions.
Examiner:	What is it you want to know? What would you want to know?
Mark:	Why it bended upwards.
Examiner:	What could you do to find out what things were necessary?
Mark:	Try it. Ask someone who knew.
Examiner:	Yes, you could ask someone that knew, but that would just be getting somebody else to tell you, wouldn't it? I mean, finding out for yourself.
Mark:	Just try different things.
Examiner:	What?
Mark:	Well, you could get the materials and things, and then try holding the thing at a different angle.
Examiner:	What do you think would happen?
Mark:	I don't know.
Examiner:	Can you ask me some questions to find out?
Mark:	No, I can't ask you any questions.
Examiner:	You're completely stumped? You have any ideas now for any rules at all that would explain it?
Mark:	No.
Examiner:	None at all. It's a complete mystery to you? No hunches? And no ideas as to what you could ask me to get some hunches?
Mark:	No.

There is a lack of order in Mark's approach to experimentation. Lack of precision and use of pseudo-scientific language are employed by Henry in the following sequence (Suchman, 1961, p. 157):

Henry:	Did it straighten in the water because the atoms of the heat molecules on the knife changed?
Examiner:	The atoms on the . . . (Interrupted)
Henry:	Changed from a minus to a plus.
Examiner:	How could you possibly find that out?

Henry: Well, it would be kind of hard, unless you did it with a telescope or a microscope.

Examiner: I can't answer that question then.

Henry: It seems that this is just another fact of science, even though it is amazing, but sometimes it takes weeks to figure out answers. I'll do the best I can to find out an answer. Did it straighten because of the quick change of temperature?

Examiner: How could you find out?

The inquiry training employed by the Illinois group used three techniques: (a) the structuring of an operational schema, (b) guided practice, and (c) feedback and reinforcement.

The *schema* (or response repertory) includes three stages. Stage I is called *episode analysis.* This involves an analysis and verification of the facts which isolate the *objects* and the *conditions* of the objects at the significant stages of the viewed experiment. The ability to conduct an *episode analysis* was guided in group settings, and when the objects and conditions were isolated, an Episode Analysis Matrix was cast and written on the board (see Figure 5.6). Practice with new films each week built up the response repertory of the students which increased the efficiency of inquiry.

Stage II focuses upon the *determination* of *relevance.* Among the set of objects and conditions, the relevant variables are to be isolated. Strategies might be episodic or cumulative constructionist. Reinforcement and redirection are provided within the program by means of feedback. At the end of a session or the beginning of a new session, the instructor plays back a tape of the concluded session and critiques the session. A line of questioning might be evaluated or the effectiveness of an employed strategy might be discussed. These procedures are designed to develop efficient problem solving and attempt to assure some success. Indeed, a class composed of episodic empiricists may never improve without direction. One advantage of the group procedures is that cumulative constructionists can provide models of problem attack that others might not possess.

When the relevant variables are isolated, the discovery of why they are relevant is the goal of Stage III *(induction of relational constructs).* This stage requires the generation of hypotheses and the casting of the crucial experiment to test the hypotheses. Suchman indicates that this stage is more difficult to obtain because it depends upon some creativeness and intuition. Apparently, the creativity, to some degree, can be facilitated by practice and observation of others.

FIGURE 5.6

Episode Analysis Matrix — Film No. 18: "Bimetallic Strip"

Objects/Systems	Conditions/Events								
	At Start of Demonstration			After Blade is Held in Flame			After Blade is Placed in Water		
	Temperature	Size	Shape	Temperature	Size	Shape	Temperature	Size	Shape
Bimetallic Strip	Room Temp.	Normal	Straight	>Room Temp.	Normal	Curved	Room Temp.	Normal	Straight
Metal A	Room Temp.	Normal	Straight	>Room Temp.	Normal	Curved	Room Temp.	Normal	Straight
Metal B	Room Temp.	Normal (A=B)	Straight	>Room Temp.	Normal (A>B)	Curved	Room Temp.	Normal (A=B)	Straight
Tank of Water	Water Temp. = Room Temp.			Water Temp. = Room Temp.			Water Temp. = Room Temp.		
Bunsen Burner	Produces Heat			Produces Heat			Produces Heat		

From Suchman, J. R., "Inquiry Training: Building Skills for Autonomous Discovery." *Merrill-Palmer Quarterly*, 7 (1961), p. 160.

An example of a bright fifth grade student after 15 hours of inquiry training is given as follows (Suchman, 1961, pp. 165-166).

Steve:	Was this plain water in the tank?
Examiner:	Yes.
Steve:	Was this a special kind of flame?
Examiner:	No.
Steve:	If you had used a wood flame would it work?
Examiner:	Yes.
Steve:	Was the blade hot when the film was going on?
Examiner:	When it was being heated, certainly.
Steve:	Did it melt?
Examiner:	No.
Steve:	I have a hypothesis. Wait a minute, I'd better start testing before I give it. Could this be done in a vacuum?
Examiner:	Yes.
Steve:	If this had been left to set for five days would it work?
Examiner:	Yes.
Steve:	Could this have been made—was this made any different way than any other knife you would think it would be like?
Examiner:	Yes.
Steve:	Did that have any effect on it?
Examiner:	Surely.
Steve:	Was there some chemical in the metal that did it?
Examiner:	No.
Steve:	Had this thing been dipped before it hit the water?
Examiner:	No.
Steve:	Had it been heated before? Was it heated the second time?
Examiner:	Yes, many times.
Steve:	Could you have done it without heating it once?
Examiner:	Yes.
Steve:	Could you keep on heating this and the knife would keep bending?
Examiner:	Yes.
Steve:	Would it ever break from going up and down?
Examiner:	No, not from that—not from going up and down.
Steve:	Did the water have anything to do with it bending the second time?
Examiner:	Find out.
Steve:	If you had put this thing over a cold vent of air would the thing have gone back down?
Examiner:	Yes.
Steve:	Was the water in the thing cold?
Examiner:	Yes.
Steve:	Would the same thing happen if it was hot?
Examiner:	If what were hot?
Steve:	The water—to the boiling point.
Examiner:	No.

Steve:	It would stay the same?
Examiner:	Probably.
Steve:	If she had just dipped it down—if it was a shorter knife and she just dipped it down so it didn't touch anything but the water would it straighten out?
Examiner:	Yes.
Steve:	Could I have bent it—as I am now, no stronger or no weaker, could I have bent that metal?
Examiner:	Oh, sure.
Steve:	Was it aluminum?
Examiner:	No.
Steve:	Steel?
Examiner:	No.
Steve:	Was it made of the same substance that these knives are made of—regular table knives?
Examiner:	No.
Steve:	Was it made out of asbestos?
Examiner:	No.
Steve:	If she had let it cool—just let it cool down to room temperature would the thing straighten back?
Examiner:	Yes.

Earlier Steve had some of the problems indicated in the previous examples. His questions are clear and fluent. Suchman notes that Steve's responses are typical for bright fifth graders and reflect an impotence and a desire for early closure. Further training should bring about a more cumulative constructionist approach. This does not mean that creative leaps should be extinguished, but it does mean that the leaps might be more efficient if they were based upon solidly collected data.

Suchman does *not* advocate that *all* learning should be acquired via discovery. Nevertheless, inquiry training will *not* provide competency motivation unless the skills lead to competency in other areas. Cast into operant terms, the set of inquiry responses will not be maintained unless they are reinforced (via the stimulus of problem solution) in the natural setting. If school is essentially rote learning, inquiry skills will not be employed and sharpened.

Summary and Implications

We suggested earlier that teachers may need to know how to teach and also they may need to know what to teach. If we assume that mathematics, science and inquiry strategies lead to effective coping (and we have little evidence to support this assumption), then how should we train teachers? Apparently, a definite answer is not available.

A number of questions and problems are given below which are of some concern to the present writers. You may wish to examine your teacher training program in the light of these statements and ask a few questions of your own.

1. In the typical training program a sequence of coursework precedes student teaching. Then the student is assigned to a resident master teacher for supervision. Usually the student makes a lesson plan specifying objectives (e.g., "appreciation of good music"), teaches the plan (hopefully to students) and sometime later is evaluated by the supervisor. The neophyte might receive praise for her plan and clean fingernails. She may be asked to improve her handwriting and attempt to maintain better "discipline." Unfortunately, such global feedback does not reflect the complex sequence of responses that constitute teaching. In educational psychology courses, the prospective teacher "learns" that *immediate* reinforcement of a "good" response increases the probability of the response recurring (frequently praise is a reinforcer, especially for solid middle-class children). When placed in the classroom with a large number of required novel responses, she might "forget" to use reinforcement. Furthermore, the selection of correct response on a multiple choice test is *not* the same response as using reinforcement in the classroom. How can we restructure our training to bridge the gap between "knowing" reinforcement works and effectively *using* reinforcement?

   Possibly, we can use the same type of shaping procedures on you, the prospective teacher, that Skinner uses on his pigeons. For example:

   We might place you in a short five-minute teaching session and hook you up with an ear plug walky-talky. If you praise a student for a good response, we praise you. If you fail to use reinforcement, we can give you verbal instructions to do so. If you make the reinforcing response as directed, we reinforce you (e.g., that was great, or that's two more points for an "A").

   Indeed, successive approximations might be necessary and reinforcement schedules may be changed once the response has been acquired. Theoretically, once the "effective" responses are acquired, mastery in management of the classroom itself might be reinforcing. Immediate feedback relating to teaching behavior may be used for a wide number of responses from such simple matters as a smile, to important matters such as reminding the pupils to bring their milk money to school.

If we ask you to use immediate reinforcement and successive approximation to shape pupil behavior, we may well practice what we preach.

2. Suchman recommends some *guided* practice in inquiry as a means of acquiring effective inquiry strategies. Can we assume that prospective teachers have acquired these appropriate strategies? We certainly cannot get an adequate assessment of these modes from the tip of an electrographic pencil. How would you provide for inquiry training in this educational psychology course? With what problem would you start? Does it initiate epistemic curiosity? What objects and conditions would your episode analysis include?
3. Regarding content, should you have a better background in your subject specialty? What types of concepts predominate in your specialty field (relational, disjunctive and conjunctive)? Will more arts and science courses provide the mastery or can your present courses in your major field be taught more effectively? Consider any one of your present major subjects; can you improve the instruction? How? Remember, not everything needs to be discovered.

Further Readings of Interest

Keller's little book provides a highly readable account of the operant framework.

Chapter 3 in *Learning* (Hill, 1963) presents an assessment of Skinner's views in relation to other reinforcement theorists. Of course, the best account of Skinner is provided by Skinner himself in his *Cumulative Record.*

Bruner has been prolific as a writer; however, the interested student might wish to review his most recent book of essays (1966).

Palmer's article is an attempt to interpret cognitive conflict as it relates to science education.

Barron gives an overview of the work done in creativity which might merit critical reading.

References

Angyal, A. *Neurosis and treatment.* New York: Wiley, 1965.

Barron, F. *The psychology of creativity,* In F. Barron (Ed.), *New directions in psychol.* Vol. II. New York: Holt, Rinehart, Winston, 1965.

Berlyne, D. E. *Conflict, arousal and curiosity*. Toronto: McGraw Hill, 1960.

Brown, K., & Abell, T. Analysis of research in the teaching of mathematics. *Bull. U. S. Dept. of Hlth, Educ. & Welfare,* 1965, No. 28.

Bruner, J. S. On going beyond the information given. *Contemporary approaches to cognition.* Cambridge, Mass.: Harvard Univer. Press, 1957.

Bruner, J. S. The act of discovery. *Harvard Educ. Rev.,* 1961, 3, 21-32.

Bruner, J. S. The growth of mind. *Amer. Psychologist,* 1965, 20, 1007-1017.

Bruner, J. S. Toward a theory of instruction. Cambridge: Belknap Press, 1966.

Bruner, J. S., Goodnow, Jacqueline J., & Austin, G. *A study of thinking.* New York: Wiley, 1956.

Bruner, J. S., Mandler, J., O'Dowd, D., & Wallach, M. A. The role of over-learning and drive level in reversible learning. *J. comp. physiol. Psychol.,* 1958, 51, 607-613.

Castaneda, A., McCandless, B. R., & Palermo, D. S. Complex learning and performance as a function of anxiety in children and task difficulty. *Child Developm.,* 1956, 27, 328-332.

Cody, J. J., & Rothney, J. W. Oral problem-solving performances of superior high school students. *Personnel & Guid. J.,* Jan., 1963, 425-429.

Davis, R. B. *Discovery in mathematics.* Reading, Mass.: Addison-Wesley, 1964.

Greenspoon, J. The reinforcing effect of two spoken sounds on the frequency of two responses. *Amer. J. Psychol.,* 1955, 68, 409-416.

Hendrix, G. Learning by discovery. *Math. Teacher,* 1961, 54, 290-299.(a)

Hendrix, G. The psychological appeal of deductive proof. *Math. Teacher,* 1961, 54, 515-520.(b)

Hill, W. F. *Learning: a survey of psychological interpretations.* San Francisco: Chandler, 1963.

Hunt, J. McV. Piaget's system as a source of hypotheses concerning motivation. *Merrill-Palmer Quart.,* 1963, 9, 263-275.

Keller, F. S. *Learning: reinforcement theory.* New York: Random House, 1954.

Kelly, G. A. Man's construction of his alternatives. *Assessment of human motives.* G. Lindzey (Ed.), New York: Grove Press, 1958, 33-64.

Maltzman, I. M. On the training of originality. *Psychol. Rev.* 1960, 67, 229-242.

Meehl, P. E. Shizotoxia, Schizotypy, Schizophenia. *Amer. psychol.,* 1962, 17, 827-838.

Palmer, E. L. Accelerating the child's cognitive attainments through the inducement of cognitive conflict: an interpretation of the Piagetian position. *J. res. in sci. Teaching,* 1965, 3, 318-325.

Rogers, C. R. *Client-centered therapy.* Boston: Houghton Mifflin, 1951.

Sarason, I. G., & Palola, E. G. The relationship of test and general anxiety, difficulty of task, and experimental instructions to performances. *J. exp. Psychol.,* 1960, 59, 185-191.

Skinner, B. F. *Cumulative record.* New York: Appleton-Century-Crofts, 1959.

Suchman, J. R. Inquiry training: building skills for autonomous discovery. *Merrill-Palmer Quart.,* 1961, 7, 147-169.

Suchman, J. R. The Illinois studies in inquiry training. *J. of Res. in Sci. teaching,* 1964, 2, 232.

Suppes, P., Boyle A., & Hill, S. *Sets and numbers,* Bk 3A. Stanford: L. W. Singer, 1963.

Phenomenology in Education 6

Overview

The concepts regarding human behavior advanced in the previous chapters have centered around an $S \rightarrow O \rightarrow R$ model with an emphasis upon observed behavior. Intervening variables such as intelligence, anxiety, and strategies were presented as notions inferred by means of noting $S \rightarrow O \rightarrow R$ functional relationships. The quasi-mathematical model presented [$Ba =$ (Pa, Eab, Rba, $rs_1 \ldots rs_n$) Sa, C, X] was used to represent the numerous intervening variables necessary to account for the many variations in behavior. Chapter 4 centered upon intelligent behavior (Pa) and also touched upon elements of motivation (Eab). Chapter 5 stressed generalized learnings (rs) and the stimulus variables (C–context) which incite epistemic curiosity (Eab). In all cases the interaction of the several intervening variables was noted. For example, manipulation of the stimuli designed to create cognitive conflict depends upon some previous learnings with which the question can conflict. Likewise a person may have the necessary potential cognitive ability (Pa) to succeed at a task, but he may not think the task is worth the effort (Rba).

The present chapter centers around a theory of human action that is *not* derived from experimental data. The theory presented is comprehensive and relates in many ways to the individual's expectations (Rba) and elements of personality (Eab).

The specific theory (Carl Rogers, 1951) represents an approach to psychology that falls under the generic (general) classification of "phenomenology." Phenomenology relates to the individual's unique (phenomenal) world of experience. Since this frame of reference uses man's subjective conscious experiences as a source of information, notions of *self-concept, conscious awareness,* and *interpersonal knowing* are expressed. The departure from observation of external behavior to an internal frame is radical and at first may seem inconsistent with the data orientation of the text. We include these phenomenological notions because a strict experimental orientation, by necessity, neglects broad areas of complex human behavior .Thus, the global picture provided by phenomenological theorizing should suggest leads to relevant variables which may be included in an "objective" analysis of behavior.

An extensive discussion is devoted to Roger's 19 formal propositions. These propositions attempt to account for: (1) the development of the individual's picture of reality; (2) the forces which lead him to action; and (3) the development of the individual's concept of himself as a behaving person. A central theme of Rogers' theory is that man attempts to *grow*. Positive growth, however, may be thwarted if the individual's unique world picture is not congruent with reality. If given a nonthreatening environment, the individual will tend to change his world picture toward congruence with reality. In essence, Rogers has faith in man's ability to adapt.

The educational implications of Rogers' ideas are discussed, and they are compatible with the notions of discovery learning presented in Chapter 5. Rogers' theory points to possible school practices; nevertheless, no definitive data are available to lend credence to the theory. On the other hand, educational psychology today leaves great gaps relating to the complex school learning situations, and Rogers' notions might provide the teacher with an alternate way of looking at children that can help in her task of teaching *today*.

Glossary

actualization: to realize in action; to become all that one is able to become; fulfilling potentialities.

consummatory behavior: responses which enter into the action of fulfilling body needs (i.e. salivating, chewing, swallowing, etc.).

differentiated: the process whereby relatively unspecialized activities develop into relatively more specialized activities.

ethnocentrism: the attitude that one's own race, nation, or culture is superior to all others (one's "ethos" is better than others).

global: all inclusive.

internal: subjective; having to do with the inner nature of man's experience.

molar behavior: a large unit segment of the total behavior stream that possesses essential unity.

perception: an event within the person or organism, primarily controlled by the excitation of sensory receptors, yet also influenced by other factors of a kind that can be shown to have originated in the life history of the person.

phenomenal: that which is perceived in contrast with that which is real.

psychogenic: impairment in physiological functioning with no known pathological change in organic structure and with assertion of a causal antecedent in the psychological history.

rationalization: the process of concocting plausible reasons to account for one's practices or beliefs when these are challenged by oneself or others.

reality: the totality of all conditions imposed by the external world upon an organism (a hypothetical concept).

regression: a return to earlier and less mature behavior.

subception: reacting to a stimulus object that is not fully enough perceived to be symbolized in any detailed manner.

Phenomenology

Historically, one can find antecedents of the phenomenological frame of reference in Plato, Bishop Berkeley, Hume, and in existential philosophy. At the present time, phenomenological psychology has its greatest strength among counseling psychologists and is peripherally represented in social and child psychology. A host of theoreticians has presented phenomenological views often emphasizing one or two aspects of the orientation. In that each theorist coins his own terms and a sampling of viewpoints can be confusing, the following presentation shall center upon one man's collected theory, Carl Rogers'. Rogers' discussions are derived from his own experience as a psychotherapist and statements of a number of other phenomenological theorists. By necessity the presentation will to some degree distort Rogers' position since the present authors are not Rogers himself. If the reader, upon completion of this chapter, is disposed to accept or to explore in depth the phenomenological approach, he should read Rogers. A number of primary references are provided in the readings section of this chapter.

Rogers' Propositional Statements of Phenomenology

The following discussion is based upon Chapter 11 in Rogers' *Client-Centered Therapy* (1951) and includes nineteen formal propositions regarding behavior.

I. EVERY INDIVIDUAL EXISTS IN A CONTINUALLY CHANGING WORLD OF EXPERIENCE OF WHICH HE IS THE CENTER.

As you sit reading this book, a large number of sense receptors are stimulated. You are consciously aware of some of these impingements and others are ignored although they might be admissible to awareness. For some brief moments the light waves reflected from this page are of central concern and the background sound as well as the stimuli from the gluteus maximus are ignored. These data constitute your phenomenal field — the figure (conscious experience) as well as the *ground* (that which is ignored). Because of internal states of change, that which is in the background might become the figure. In your present reading activity, the content might seem senseless; therefore, a conversation in the background might readily become the center of your attention. Or, if you are cramming for an exam and have been hitting the books hard, you may suddenly realize that it is past your mealtime. The messages from your viscera suddenly are predominant (ground to figure).

One significant feature of this phenomenal world which you are experiencing is that it is private. Only you really know your experiences. I can ask you what you are experiencing and you might attempt to tell me by way of verbal symbols; nevertheless, these symbols will not completely describe your world. You have a toothache, and I might conceive of my own experiences with toothaches and thus have some concept of what you are experiencing, but this conception is incomplete — this is *your* tooth. In a phenomenological sense we *are* islands unto ourselves.

II. THE ORGANISM REACTS TO THE FIELD AS IT IS EXPERIENCED AND PERCEIVED. THIS PERCEPTUAL FIELD IS, FOR THE INDIVIDUAL, "REALITY."

A fundamental point raised in Chapter 1 is the problem of what is "real." Rogers' conclusion coincides with that which was presented in the first chapter. If you think the instructor is "out to get" you and the failing grades you receive are *your* evidence, this will influence your perception of the instructor's behavior. He might "really" be unaware of your existence; however, this "reality" is not part of your world and therefore does not exist.

Consider the often observed "stupid" behavior of seventh and eighth grade boys (usually acted out in the spring of the year). Apparently, these boys become interested in girls and in their attempt to get attention they ritualistically hit the girls and run. Interpreted from an external frame of reference, these boys are behaving stupidly. From the internal world, the boys might perceive these actions as appropriate. Fortunately for the propagation of our species, more subtle approaches are eventually acquired and the "stupid" behavior is usually extinguished. To be sure, boys have no corner upon "stupid" behaviors. Girls often engage in hit and run tactics also.

Small children often interpret a parent's restrictive actions to reflect rejection and the child will say, "You hate me." This is his perception and his actions are based upon this "reality." The parent may or may not "hate" the child, but again this alternate "reality" is not relevant to the child's world of behavior.

An important implication of proposition II: The phenomenal orientation presents us with a finite number of realities corresponding to the number of experiencing organisms. If this assumption is "true", then we probably cannot resolve the question of what is "really" real. However, we can establish a referent group for testing purposes. For example, most of us would agree (in our phenomenal perception) that a chair and people are real and do exist. But yet, others may form a consensus group with an entirely different definition of reality. This proposition reflects back to the epistemological considerations introduced in Chapter 1. We make assumptions regarding what is real and tend to associate with people who hold similar assumptions.

Behavioral scientists form one consensus group. They agree that data must be observable and a number of rules regarding data recording are followed. They *believe* such constraints will allow them to more closely approximate reality. Of course, such consensus groups do not assure success. Each behavioral researcher evaluates the consequence of his field of research from his own phenomenal frame of reference. Usually the evaluation leads to a reconfirmation of his position. Occasionally, a behavioral scientist will decide that his scientific consensus group does not pay off and he may form a new group. For example, Timothy Leary after a few psychedelic trips into himself (via LSD), tuned out of the behavioral science "truth" and "turned on" his own psychedelic consensus group. The action of Professor Leary disappointed some behavioral scientists because they "lost" a good fellow researcher. Nevertheless as behavioral scientists we cannot say he is wrong, because he no longer plays the epistemological game according to our rules. He has rejected our act of faith and therefore is not compelled to conform to our rules.

Apparently, forming consensus groups does not permit us to escape the singularity of our unique world of experience. This discussion seems "far out" even to the authors, yet we believe that an awareness of this phenomenological orientation may help you become a "better" environmental manipulator. Upon completion of this chapter, you might wish to evaluate this belief.

III. THE ORGANISM REACTS AS AN ORGANIZED WHOLE TO THIS PHENOMENAL FIELD.

Proposition III directs the attention away from reflexology and molecular behaviors and focuses upon molar behavior; a molecular reaction to cold might be shivering whereas a molar action might include getting more clothes or entering a warm room. Psychogenic illness is another molar phenomenon. Digestive processes which are autonomically controlled can be upset by thought processes which can result in heartburn and/or ulcerous lesions in the stomach or lower digestive tract. Conversely, physical illness can change the individual's attitude toward life. If Pierce-Jones' notions (see Chapter 2) are "true," posture also influences attitude. These holistic concepts cannot be accounted for on the basis of simple reflexology. Recent theorizing by behaviorists (the traditional reflexologists) to a large degree account for the holistic notion by means of introducing S-R chains and mediating responses (see Staats and Staats, 1963; Osgood, 1953, pp. 392-412; and Kendler and Kendler, 1962). To most phenomenologists presentations of S-R symbols tend to oversimplify the complexities which are involved in human behavior.

IV. THE ORGANISM HAS ONE BASIC TENDENCY AND STRIVING: TO ACTUALIZE, MAINTAIN AND ENHANCE THE EXPERIENCING ORGANISM.

Motivation theorists have invented a host of needs, drives and motives to account for the push in human behavior. Rogers holds the position that all of the specific forces can be subsumed under proposition IV. To *actualize,* the organism tends to become more differentiated. The individual strives to walk, to use his hands and extend himself by means of tool and symbol invention. A key notion within this context is the idea that the individual's perception of the behaviors which lead to self-actualization is the basis for his action. Therefore, a distorted perception may lead the individual to destruction rather than actualization. Later propositions shall provide elaboration of this point.

An implied view of human behavior held by Rogers is that man is attempting to be "good." This is an awkward way to present the concept, but it does contrast with Freud's notions of the licentious id and the tyrannical super-ego. If man can perceive clearly or be given the opportunity to modify distorted perceptions, his goal-directed activity will lead to greater positive self-actualizations. This idea leads to the point that the environmental manipulator (e.g., teacher, parent, etc.) should not provide conclusions; he should only provide the opportunity for reducing distorted perception. In essence, given the opportunity, the individual will select goals which are self-actualizing and the individual is in the best position to determine which goals meet this criterion. Please note, this is *not* a pleasure principle; it is a "growth" principle.

George Kelly (1958), a phenomenological psychologist, took a more extreme view than Rogers. He maintained that all notions regarding motivation are superfluous because man is vital. By definition he is moving. Therefore, the only concern should be the direction of movement, not why he moves. Kelly comes to a conclusion similar to Rogers', for he attempts to investigate how the individual anticipates the future, an internal individual process.

By way of emphasis: within Rogers' framework, man is attempting to move forward; the movement might not be smooth and perceived progress might indeed be regression (when viewed by an outside source). Nonetheless, given the opportunity to move ahead or backward, the forward tendency will usually prevail (subsequent propositions will clarify observed regression). It should be noted here that phenomenologists place greater limitations on what can be inferred from observed behavior. The discussion of Rogers up to this point should indicate the essential quality of uniqueness of the individual. Thus, what you and I might observe concerning another's behavior might not be a "true" picture of what the individual is doing. In everyday living it is well known that crying might be an outward sign of a biological disturbance (peeling onions), a sign of grief (in the case of a family death), or a sign of happiness (emotional display of a bride at her wedding). Phenomenologists emphasize the personal internal frame of reference of individuals, while other theorists tend to generalize observable behavior so that it (or its cause) is descriptive of most humans.

V. BEHAVIOR IS BASICALLY THE GOAL-DIRECTED ATTEMPT OF THE ORGANISM TO SATISFY ITS NEED AS EXPERIENCED IN THE PERCEIVED FIELD.

This proposition is a corollary to IV in that behavior reflects the self-actualization process. Functionally goal-directed behavior might seem to the outside observer as negating need satisfaction; nevertheless, from this theoretic view, the individual perceives the behavior to be appropriate goal-directed behavior. Consider the subject of suicide. Murdering oneself does not appear on the surface to be a case of self-enhancement or maintenance, but from the internal view even death might be more desirous than living in a world one is unable to handle. Enhancement must be considered in relationship to the individual's phenomenal world. A person suffering from metastasized cancer might wish to escape experienced pain through death just as others wish to escape the mental horror due to thoughts of inadequacy. These are positive acts bearing upon a problem although the acts may or may not be appropriate for the "real" world.

VI. EMOTION ACCOMPANIES AND IN GENERAL FACILITATES SUCH GOAL-DIRECTED BEHAVIOR, THE KIND OF EMOTION BEING RELATED TO THE SEEKING VERSUS THE CONSUMMATORY ASPECTS OF THE BEHAVIOR, AND THE INTENSITY OF THE EMOTION BEING RELATED TO THE PERCEIVED SIGNIFICANCE OF THE BEHAVIOR FOR THE MAINTENANCE AND ENHANCEMENT OF THE ORGANISM.

This statement is rather complex; therefore, we shall deal with each section in turn. Emotion in this setting is *not* the debilitating state which is commonly thought. Performers in various fields "get up" for the act. Heartbeat and respiration increase along with a number of other physiological changes and these changes permit excellent performance. To be sure, some individuals get too "high" and become "tied-up." However, this is usually the exception, not the rule.

Seeking behavior is usually associated with action situations which can accompany emotions such as fear, states of excitement, or unpleasantness. Consummatory behaviors accompany feelings of calmness and/or satisfied states. Eating, laughing, and resting are examples of the latter, and running, escaping, and competing are examples of the former.

Under conditions of intense excitement or intense joy, the resulting behavior might not facilitate goal-directed behavior. Consider the often observed case of "buck fever" where anticipation overexcites the hunter to the point that when a buck enters the scene little coordinated action is expressed. The essential point is that the appearance of the buck does not produce the intense emotion. It is the individual's perception or meaning which is ascribed to the presence of the buck, and it is this perception which is related to overexcitement, not the appearance of the deer.

Let us consider a few more examples appropriate for proposition VI. As you sit in your chair suppose you glance up and see a huge brown bear five feet away. Now if you were Davy Crockett, you might smile and salivate a little in anticipation of consuming a few chunks of bear steak. But you and I are not Davy. We would most likely jump up and seek refuge in fear, and a number of body changes will accompany this action. We react intensely to the stimuli "bear" because we perceive it as a great threat. Given a small mouse rather than the huge bear, we might be startled, but usually the intensity of the fear would be quite low (except in the case of a female who has learned that fear of mice is a sign of femininity).

Emotions are usually appropriate and facilitate the goal-directed behavior but at times might debilitate adequate functioning. Not only can the intensity of the emotion debilitate, but also an inappropriate emotion can interfere with goal-directed behavior. An after-dinner speaker might be threatened by the large audience and want to escape and the body will manifest changes in preparation for action. The speaker has a stomach full of food to digest but manifests the autonomic reactions for action. He experiences a heavy, lead-like ball in his stomach and little saliva flows in his mouth. If he is an inexperienced speaker, a "flub" or two can result in an almost complete cessation of saliva flow and a frequent need to lubricate the mouth. A practiced speaker might start with a joke, get a laugh and thus reduce fear and regain an appropriate saliva flow. This frame of reference seems to be consistent with the notions of anxiety and high need state discussed in Chapter 5.

Note emotion as viewed by Rogers is a phenomenological condition. A number of "objective" theories regarding emotion have been proposed using measures of physical change and measured excitation of the thalamic and other regions in the lower brain. Hebb (1958, p. 156) called emotion a common sense notion rather than a scientific term. Indeed, for a physiological investigation into observed behavior, perceived states of emotion might be superfluous baggage. Nonetheless, from an internal frame of reference such as is presented by Rogers, experienced emotions must be of concern. An excellent comprehensive, but a bit outdated, discussion of emotion was presented by Lindsley (1951). An up-to-date review of the literature regarding emotion and learning was presented by Berlyne (1964); however, the orientation is directed toward "arousal" as a substitute for emotion.

VII. THE BEST VANTAGE POINT FOR UNDERSTANDING BEHAVIOR IS FROM THE INTERNAL FRAME OF REFERENCE OF THE INDIVIDUAL HIMSELF.

In view of the preceding six propositions this statement seems redundant. Rogers apparently wished to emphasize the notion that each of us has a unique view and one must be careful when he evaluates another's behavior from the external view. The word *best* should be underlined, for one can empathically understand another's behavior, but *not* completely. Partial understanding of the other seems possible for apparently humans from similar backgrounds have similar experiences. Unfortunately, our own value system of good and bad often gets in the way of communication with others. We tend to classify a person and then perceive subsequent information (verbal reports and behavior) in light of the earlier construction. If I think Negroes are dirty and lazy, I will tend to see all Negroes as such irrespective of the "true" behavior.

When the *other* person communicates, the conditions under which he speaks must be considered. Under high threat conditions (i.e., in an oral examination) the individual is unlikely to reveal his perceptual field while in a private, confidential discussion much of his "inner-world" might be verbalized.

In view of proposition VII, a Rogerian would *not* attempt to diagnose another's problems since the other is in the best position to make this diagnosis.

The subject for propositions VIII through XIII is the development and process of the "self-concept." This conscious awareness of being is a central aspect of Rogers' theory.

VIII. A PORTION OF THE TOTAL PERCEPTUAL FIELD GRADUALLY BECOMES DIFFERENTIATED AS THE SELF.

The previous propositions have centered around the behavior of the "organism." An extension of these considerations is that developmentally the organism becomes aware of being and functioning. This awareness of being (independent existence) is called the "self." That which is labeled the self depends to a large degree in Rogers' thinking upon whether or not the individual perceives the object to be under his control. Therefore, a bicycle or car might be included as part of the self while under certain circumstances a part of the body, such as an anesthesized limb, might not be included in the awareness of self. The subsequent propositions shall elaborate upon the notion of the development of self.

IX. AS A RESULT OF INTERACTION WITH THE ENVIRONMENT AND, PARTICULARLY, AS A RESULT OF EVALUATIONAL INTERACTION WITH OTHERS, THE STRUCTURE OF SELF IS FORMED — AN ORGANIZED, FLUID, BUT CONSISTENT CONCEPTUAL PATTERN OF PERCEPTIONS OF CHARACTERISTICS AND RELATIONSHIPS OF THE "I" OR THE "ME" TOGETHER WITH VALUES ATTACHED TO THESE CONCEPTS.

Observation of infant play suggests that some nonverbal concepts are formed by these infants and that values are attached to these concepts. The baby plays with his toes and laughs, bumps his head and cries. He likes to play and dislikes pain. He will play with the bottle, hit his crib and laugh at the noise. Conversely, he will hit his head with the bottle and cry. In one sense he learns the head is "me," the crib is "not me." It is good to hit the crib with a bottle; it is not good to hit "my" head with the bottle.

Certainly the preverbal child does not linguistically symbolize these evaluations; nonetheless, his behavior suggests some consistent patterns of notions regarding "me" and "not me" as well as good and bad evaluations of action.

Evaluational interaction with others leads to further elaborations of the self structure. Most children hear from their parents, "You are such a sweet, lovable little baby," and conceive of themselves as "lovable." Of course, some children learn they are not lovable by living with parents who reject them.

X. THE VALUES ATTACHED TO EXPERIENCES, AND THE VALUES WHICH ARE A PART OF THE SELF-STRUCTURE, IN SOME INSTANCES ARE VALUES EXPERIENCED DIRECTLY BY THE ORGANISM, AND IN SOME INSTANCES ARE VALUES INTROJECTED OR TAKEN OVER FROM OTHERS, BUT PERCEIVED IN DISTORTED FASHION AS IF THEY HAD BEEN EXPERIENCED DIRECTLY.

Eating ice cream, being bounced, and making noise are usually evaluated as good and are *direct* experiences. *Direct* experiences of being burned, are evaluated as bad. The seeds of possible psychological maladjustment are planted when a large number of introjected values are incorporated into the self-structure which might oppose direct experience.

To illustrate, consider a child who symbolizes himself as being loved and lovable by means of direct contact with his parents. At times hollering, hitting the cat, and spitting out foul tasting food are conceived to be self-enhancing experiences. "It feels good" to holler, hit and spit. These behaviors might upset the parent and he might say, "You are nasty" or "Don't be such a baby." These statements might communicate to the child that he is not lovable when he performs these acts. Spitting and "being lovable," originally might be compatible; however, when the parent negatively evaluates such a self-enhancing behavior (spitting), the child experiences conflict. The child is confronted with a threat to his self-concept (I am lovable) when he is behaving in a self-enhancing manner.

A number of alternative solutions are available to reduce the conflict. The child might correctly perceive the situation and symbolize this experience accurately. A possible symbolic resolution might be: "I like spitting but it upsets my parents. Now if I keep upsetting them, things might get rough. I guess I'll only spit when my parents are not around." Such reasoning resolves the conflict on the basis of "reality."

An alternate symbolization for the child might involve incorporating his parents' value system by distorting his *own* direct experience. Such a symbolization might be: "I don't like to spit because it does not please *me*" and later this might be shortened to: "Spitting is nasty" (a complete acceptance of his parents' value system and a denial of his direct pleasurable experience). Spitting as a pleasure thus becomes lost to awareness for it is inconsistent with his introjected value system.

To be sure, spitting avoidance is not a very profound distortion. But consider the host of introjected values which might lead to difficulty: (1) Denial that some Democrats are "good" by a child raised in a Republican home, (2) American rejection that communists might have a viable social system, (3) The notion that atheists cannot be trusted, and (4) Negroes are dirty and inferior. Seldom are such evaluations experienced directly. The fact that individuals perceive the same occurrence differently is not debatable. From a Rogerian reference this is a result of the individual interacting with evaluations of others and the values attached to self (the "I" or "me").

XI. AS EXPERIENCES OCCUR IN THE LIFE OF THE INDIVIDUAL, THEY ARE EITHER (A) SYMBOLIZED, PERCEIVED, AND ORGANIZED INTO SOME RELATIONSHIP TO THE SELF, (B) IGNORED BECAUSE THERE IS NO PERCEIVED RELATIONSHIP TO THE SELF-STRUCTURE, OR (C) DENIED SYM-

BOLIZATION OR GIVEN A DISTORTED SYMBOLIZATION BECAUSE THE EXPERIENCE IS INCONSISTENT WITH THE STRUCTURE OF THE SELF.

Experiences symbolized, perceived, and organized into some relation to the self are experiences which reinforce the self-structure or satisfy some need. For example, when a person is thirsty he will notice a water fountain. Likewise, if a person thinks of himself as a "B" student, a "B" on an examination will be perceived and accepted for it is consistent with the self-structure. In the classroom setting the student might ignore the grades received by others for they are of no significance to the self-structure. Of course, if the individual's self-structure includes a competitive need (self-enhancement via being best), he might well notice all grades within view.

Denial or distortion in the symbolizing process occurs often when the experience is inconsistent with the self-structure. The "B" student who receives a "D" might distort the experience by saying "I really didn't study for the exam" or "He's a stupid instructor." These distortions are rather trivial and most often provide little difficulty. Repetition of "C" or "D" grades can lead to a re-organization of the self-structure so that the individual conceives of himself as an average student. To be sure, some students will not accept these new experiences, and they might develop a set of responses which consistently distort the impact. These excuses are perhaps more familiar to you as "rationalizations."

Denial of stronger organic experience can be the source of anxiety and grave coping problems. Rogers explains "sexual frigidity" in terms of a denial mechanism. The girl might be taught a rigid moral code which includes the notion that sexual activity is base and not entertained by "good" girls. These introjected teachings precede physiological development and when the development occurs, the natural organic experiences are totally denied (repression). The notion of "subception" was used by Rogers (1951, p. 506) to account for the ability to deny to awareness "true" experiences. Apparently we are able to subceive experiences which are threatening to the self-structure and marshal the central thought processes to block symbolization of the threatening stimulus. Furthermore, experience and anxiety might be accounted for by a number of subceived experiences which threaten the organized self-structure and tension mounts due to the pressure to distort or deny consistently.

XII. MOST OF THE WAYS OF BEHAVING WHICH ARE ADOPTED BY THE ORGANISM ARE THOSE WHICH ARE CONSISTENT WITH THE CONCEPT OF SELF.

The man in the battlefield might consider himself a "real man"; however, walking through the jungle infested with snipers is a "real" threat and he might wish to hide or not go into the field. Avoiding the task consciously would be inconsistent with his concept of being a "real man." He might get sick and thus escape the danger and still maintain the "real man" concept, for "real men" cannot be expected to fight when ill. During World War II a number of men at the front "hurt their back" lifting ammo boxes. Upon return to the U.S. these "hurts" disappeared. These notions seem similar to Freud's observation with "hysterics," where women became paralyzed from the waist down. (One characteristic of hysterics is that the patient seldom expresses great concern over the affliction.) Freud asked, "What can this affliction serve?" Usually the onset of paralysis occurred after childbirth. To avoid reimpregnation, apparently the woman could not deny her husband for it is inconsistent with "good wifely" behavior. Of course, if she were ill, then denial is consistent with the organized self-structure.

Many of us are honest, and must accomplish our goals by means of honest practices. Sometimes a grade is important and dishonest students have copies of the examination (this happens often with "lazy" professors). To succeed the individual might distort cheating behavior by saying, "Well this is really not dishonest because this is not a fair situation." Another individual might be so honest that he works exceptionally hard to pass the course. Then there is the "spoil sport" who tells the instructor his exam is out and everybody must work, even those of us who are not honest. In each case Rogers assumes that the action taken is consistent with the individual's self-concept.

XIII. BEHAVIOR MAY, IN SOME INSTANCES, BE BROUGHT ABOUT BY ORGANIC EXPERIENCES AND NEEDS WHICH HAVE NOT BEEN SYMBOLIZED. SUCH BEHAVIOR MAY BE INCONSISTENT WITH THE STRUCTURE OF THE SELF, BUT IN SUCH INSTANCES THE BEHAVIOR IS NOT "OWNED" BY THE INDIVIDUAL.

Office party acts often result in some rather childish behavior by "mature solid citizens." They drink a little juice, put on lampshades and dance on tops of desks. The next day one of these actors might be confronted with his acts by a colleague. A response may be: "Well that *really* wasn't me. I was tight." Under influences of fatigue or alcohol the defenses might be lowered, and the non-symbolized organic needs can be acted out.

More serious problems arise when the released behavior is highly disvalued socially such as homosexual acts and acts of child molesting.

The community is shocked when this occurs and often excuses are made that the individual was operating under pressure and he was *not* really himself. When this happens with political figures, the case is publicized and sensationalized. Often such behavior leads individuals to realistically claim that they don't know what affected them. The behavior exhibited seems completely out of tune with their usual "self."

The following five propositions relate particularly to concepts of adjustment or mental health which might be beyond the purview of the present text. These notions, however, relate also to the conceptual process and as such theoretically bear upon the educational process.

XIV. PSYCHOLOGICAL MALADJUSTMENT EXISTS WHEN THE ORGANISM DENIES TO AWARENESS SIGNIFICANT SENSORY AND VISCERAL EXPERIENCES, WHICH CONSEQUENTLY ARE NOT SYMBOLIZED AND ORGANIZED INTO THE GESTALT OF THE SELF-STRUCTURE. WHEN THIS SITUATION EXISTS, THERE IS A BASIC OR POTENTIAL PSYCHOLOGICAL TENSION.

XV. PSYCHOLOGICAL ADJUSTMENT EXISTS WHEN THE CONCEPT OF THE SELF IS SUCH THAT ALL THE SENSORY AND VISCERAL EXPERIENCES OF THE ORGANISM ARE, OR MAY BE, ASSIMILATED ON A SYMBOLIC LEVEL INTO A CONSISTENT RELATIONSHIP WITH THE CONCEPT OF SELF.

XVI. ANY EXPERIENCE WHICH IS INCONSISTENT WITH THE ORGANIZATION OR STRUCTURE OF SELF MAY BE PERCEIVED AS A THREAT, AND THE MORE OF THESE PERCEPTIONS THERE ARE THE MORE RIGIDLY THE SELF-STRUCTURE IS ORGANIZED TO MAINTAIN ITSELF.

Propositions XIV and XVI highlight the effects of denial or distortion of experiences. An individual with a large number of introjected values which are not consistent with experiences, must mobilize his defenses to maintain the "unrealistic" self-concept, for a large number of experiences threaten the self-structure.

Consider the girl from a highly moralistic home. "Good girls" do not: smoke, drink, dance, play cards, or have sexual desires. As our girl enters puberty and socializes at school, she comes into contact with music, dancing, boys and schoolmates who are experimenting with "life." These contacts might arouse organic experiences, which if symbolized, would be a threat to her self-concept as a good girl. To prevent symbolization of these threats, the girl might avoid boys, wear severe clothes and develop a repertory of defensive concepts. She might condemn cigarette ads as a monstrous plot to undermine the morals of our youth. Alcohol might be pictured as the tool of Satan and "All right thinking people should ban together to defeat these malicious sources of corruption." These are rigid conceptual organizations designed to protect the self-structure. The more defenses that are constructed, the farther the individual's focus of attention is directed from the original threat. The defense then must be defended.

Proposition XV indicates adjustment obtains when all sensory and visceral experiences are admissable to symbolization. *Note*, to be "adjusted" the person must *only* symbolize his experiences; he does not necessarily act out the desire. The "moralistic girl" does not need to promiscuously indulge in sexual activity in order to be adjusted by Rogers' definition. She only needs to recognize the presence of the urge. Likewise, the individual attracted to members of his own sex would be able to cope with the desire if he could symbolize it rather than establish elaborate defenses to maintain an "unrealistic" concept of masculinity. For emphasis: from Rogers' framework, distortion and denial of experiences cause tension and anxiety for the individual is living in a real world which constantly provides contradiction to the self-structure.

XVII. UNDER CERTAIN CONDITIONS, INVOLVING PRIMARILY COMPLETE ABSENCE OF ANY THREAT TO THE SELF-STRUCTURE, EXPERIENCES WHICH ARE INCONSISTENT WITH IT MAY BE PERCEIVED, AND EXAMINED, AND THE STRUCTURE OF SELF REVISED TO ASSIMILATE AND INCLUDE SUCH EXPERIENCES.

This notion is central to Rogers' "Client-Centered Therapy." In the presence of an accepting person (one who does not provide threatening stimuli by way of verbal or expressional communication) the individual can drop his defenses. The accepting other might not be necessary for somewhat superficial distortions of self. An individual's self-structure might be threatened by a comment inconsistent with the structure, and defensive behavior might be expressed. When the individual is alone, he might reflect upon the threatening comment and recognize the content to be "true"; as a consequence he can modify the self-structure and therefore eliminate the need for the particular defense. More generalized deep-seated distortions and denials cannot be faced alone, and the accepting other (therapist) is needed to facilitate growth.

More recent theorizing by Rogers (1957 and 1961) has elaborated upon the necessary and sufficient conditions for positive therapeutic movement. The therapist must manifest, and the client perceive, the following therapist behaviors: (1) *genuineness*, (2) *unconditional positive regard*; and (3) *sensitive, accurate, empathic understanding.*

Genuineness on the part of the therapist is viewed by Rogers to be crucial. The therapist cannot play a role and also effectively provide a climate which allows the client to examine threatening experiences. This also means the therapist must have a process self-structure which permits all organic experiences to be admissible to awareness; otherwise the therapist himself might express defensive behavior.

Unconditional positive regard includes a non-judgmental attitude. This positive regard provides the non-threatening climate which allows the client to explore his internal turmoil in the absence of threat which typically sets off defensive behavior. The client can freely express and explore feelings of hatred, fear and doubts without the fear of being downgraded or losing support. Experience with unmotivated schizophrenics and individuals of low socio-educational level has led Rogers to modify this point somewhat. He suggests that for these individuals, a first step might be to say, "I don't like you as well when you do that. I like you better when you pay attention," etc. For complete "maturity" to be realized even for these people, the nonevaluating therapist should be most effective. In one sense Rogers' experiences might suggest that differentiation between acceptance (nonevaluation) and condoning (approval or support of the act) needs to be acquired. Incidentally, new psychology students often fail to make this discrimination. Acceptance as used here implies recognition of a state of affairs without the acceptor's evaluation of the state.

Empathy is a genuine feeling *with* the client; it is not sympathy (feeling for), nor is it diagnostic. This sensitive "feeling with" provides an understanding of the client as a subject, not as an object. To some degree, empathy permits communication or feedback to the client so that someone else can understand his internal state.

These three conditions are the antithesis of the conditions which lead to distortion and denial (see propositions IX and X).

XVIII. WHEN THE INDIVIDUAL PERCEIVES AND ACCEPTS INTO ONE CONSISTENT AND INTEGRATED SYSTEM ALL HIS SENSORY AND VISCERAL EXPERIENCES, THEN HE IS NECESSARILY MORE UNDERSTANDING OF OTHERS AND IS MORE ACCEPTING OF OTHERS AS SEPARATE INDIVIDUALS.

XIX. AS THE INDIVIDUAL PERCEIVES AND ACCEPTS INTO HIS SELF-STRUCTURE MORE OF HIS ORGANIC EXPERIENCES, HE FINDS THAT HE IS REPLACING HIS PRESENT VALUE SYSTEM — BASED SO LARGELY UPON INTROJEC-

TIONS WHICH HAVE BEEN DISTORTEDLY SYMBOLIZED—WITH A CONTINUING ORGANISMIC VALUING PROCESS.

The individual who can accept and symbolize his own experiences can view and accept others as they are, for the behaviors of these others are not likely to be threatening. This observation is supported clinically and seems to be confirmed in the everyday setting. Consider the teacher who is the "student-selected counselor." Usually he is the person who can listen to the student without being defensive. These notions are not new for there are biblical references to: "Know thyself."

Proposition XIX re-emphasizes the process nature of Rogers' theory and reflects a dynamic view of the universe. Old truths become false; therefore, values are to be acquired through direct experience and modified when consistent new experience indicates present values are inadequate.

Educational Implications of Self-Theory

Self-theory implies a positive regard for the student's growth potential and his possibilities for self-direction. As a philosophy of education, self-theory focuses upon self-appropriated, self-discovered learning. Rogers (1965) suggested that self-appropriated experimental learning is the only learning that has a significant influence upon behavior. Consider the typical expository classroom. The school day is broken into six or seven segments with a particular subject assigned for each segment. Within each segment the teacher might have prepared a number of readings and assigned problems — these problems are her problems, not the students'. From a self-theory frame of reference, what is wrong with such an arrangement? (1) The procedure assumes that all children should be ready to start work on all problems at the same time and that they are ready to stop at the same time. (2) Teacher-prepared problems might not be "real" problems for many of the students. (3) The responsibility for planning resides in the teacher's hands and little opportunity for significant student planning is allowed.

Rogers (1965) proposed that experimental learning takes place when the learner is confronted with a meaningful problem. This notion corresponds to Berlyne's concept of epistemic curiosity (Chapter 5). The self-orientation places more focus upon the fact that the problem confrontation might mean different things to different learners. Indeed, for some students a well-controlled presentation designed to arouse conceptual conflict might create no problem at all.

Given a problem which the student wishes to resolve, Rogers (1965) suggested that the learning facilitator (teacher) can increase the probability of experimental learning if she is: (1) genuine, (2) accepting, and (3) empathic. Note that these three facilitator characteristics are the same three that Rogers indicated should be therapist behaviors. These similarities are not surprising when one recalls that therapy *is* considered a learning situation.

If the facilitator (teacher) is *genuine*, then his behavior provides information to the learner. The facilitator might not like a student's product and say so, but in such a learning situation the statement does not imply censure — it is a statement of one person's genuine reaction. Student-teacher interaction is direct interpersonal contact. The student need not look beneath a professional role to figure out what the teacher "really" means or feels.

An *accepting* teacher first accepts *his own* feelings of frustration or concern with personal adequacy, and if he accepts himself, he is less likely to impose his own solutions upon his students. A student might express dissatisfaction, apathy, or the joy of achievement — the accepting facilitator can recognize these feelings without possessively desiring to jump in and manage the student's affairs.

Empathic understanding involves an understanding of the student's reactions to the problem setting. When the child is puzzled, the teacher can communicate "I know you are puzzled," and this communication must be non-judgmental.

In this view the learning facilitator is a real person with whom one can interact. Furthermore, this facilitator should provide rich learning resources which permit experimental learning. In essence, the school and the facilitator should provide the environment which allows the student to go about *his* business of learning. College students who pay a high price for the privilege of attending classes should be aware of the concept that "learning is their business."

Considerations Which Demand Mention

The student enters your classroom with a particular set of cognitive abilities and a large number of residuals from past experience. These residuals involve expectancies and attitudes toward school and learning as well as a response repertory which bear upon problem solving (see Chapter 4). If students have been consistently exposed to a learner-centered school environment, you can go about your facilitating business. Unfortunately, for the learning-centered teacher, this is not the ideal world. Students will not enter your class with highly autonomous learning skills, although a few might possess an adequate response repertory. Furthermore, a significant proportion of students might enter this classroom with a set of negative attitudes acquired from former teachers who use aversive stimuli to maintain classroom control.

You have an extensive history of school attendance and have a set of rather specific expectancies regarding teacher behavior. How would you react to a university professor who indicated that you are to pursue problems *you* choose, and that he will help you when you need resource information? Undoubtedly, a number of uncertainties will immediately arise, and you will engage in epistemic behaviors. You might inquire about the assignment of grades and also ask "Must I attend class?" The answer might be, "Not if you don't want to." We think you can list a number of initial reactions which have little to do with learning — or do they? You might not learn much about the stated course content, but you certainly might learn a great deal trying to figure out "this nut's" motivation. Given sufficient time, you might discover that "the nut" respected your ability to formulate your own problems and your ability to carry out problem-solving strategies. One such exposure within the context of the expository university would likely have little influence upon the learner. In the press to acquire the inconsequentials (e.g., grades, degrees, etc.) the typical learner might ignore the work in the learner-centered class in order to work on well defined problems and solutions given by exposition. Indeed, the new class will become "Mickey Mouse."

Rogers (1965) provided case data from a sixth grade class which shifted to a learner-centered orientation. The following account illustrates that learner-centered teaching is *not* non-directed teaching.

> Miss Shiel became unhappy with the progress of her class of "difficult students" and decided to try a student-centered approach. She told the class they were going to try an experiment. They could do anything they wanted to do and they were *not* required to do anything they did not want to do for the whole day. The students engaged in a variety of projects. A large number worked on art and drawing, but some read, worked mathematics problems and other projects. An *evaluation* at the end of the day indicated that the great majority liked the idea although some were confused without direction. The majority prevailed upon the teacher to continue the experiment for they liked to do their own planning and to be able to work on a task until completion. Most of the children "felt" they had worked well, although some were concerned with the higher noise level as well as the fact that some did no work. Miss Shiel agreed to continue the experiment for two more days and then re-evaluate.
>
> For the second day, Miss Shiel introduced a "work contract" notion. A ditto sheet was made which listed each of the subjects with suggestions and space left for student-made plans. The student was *directed* to write in *specific* activities in his plan. The contract was in a folder, and the student corrected his own work from manuals and placed these materials in his contract folder. The teacher met with each child to discuss his

plans. Some completed the plan early and class discussion suggested that plans might be revised.

The program was continued for the year. A few went off the contract and returned to complete teacher direction since they were not able to cope with the non-teacher-directed program. Miss Shiel's account described successes, failures, and doubts. Some students wasted time, but she realized they did under the old program also. They just looked busy before. She found it difficult not to interfere when the student was not working but apparently she was able to keep out of the students' way. Some boys who had previously read little, read books on cars and made a mural chronologicalizing the history of the automobile. Some who returned to teacher-direction made plans to return to self-direction.

Much of Miss Shiel's activity reflects an intuitive attempt to develop self-direction by means of successive approximation. Recall *she* introduced the work contract and *she* lead the evaluation. Essentially, the teacher was attemping to lay the setting and develop successful strategies which might lead to reinforcement by means of competency.

Rogers' rather broad phenomenological language is upsetting to some of us who like neat and tidy little theories. Student-directed facilitating and Suchman's inquiry training (see Chapter 5) rely heavily upon a flexible, knowledgeable teacher, and research based upon either "method" must involve the teacher variable. This is messy and furthermore, how can we assess the outcomes? Is Miss Shiel's "success" due to the "Hawthorne Effect" or is it indeed a product of self-actualization? (The "Hawthorne Effect" is a label used to describe a reaction found in a study at the Western Electric Hawthorne Plant. Essentially the study was conducted to determine the effects of improved working conditions upon production. Greater production was realized after each innovation was introduced. Upon completion of the study the workers were returned to the old conditions — and production *continued to increase!* Apparently special attention by supervisors produced the increased production. Likewise, special attention to students, disregarding methods, might account for increased achievement.)

Self-discovered learning includes the acquisition of a number of behaviors which lead to subsequent problem solution. A functional analysis of student behavior and a specification of behaviors which reflect self-actualization can arm the teacher with the ingredients necessary for implementation. One can learn what some of these terminal behaviors might be from a reading of Suchman (1961) and Bruner (1966).

Implications for Curricular Change

The preceding discussion centered upon the teacher role and the process within the classroom. As the teacher's role changes from the authority figure to being herself (essentially a non-role) the content also changes. United States history books cannot provide conclusions for all because they are static sources. Indeed, when a child wishes to investigate government he should have numerous sources from which to draw. He might acquire a set of facts (someone else's conclusions) and attempt to simulate what has occurred. A group might set up a model United Nations, State House, etc. Explorations via simulation might provide some direct experience regarding political operation.

Guetzkow (1959) presented the results of a study using human simulators at the college level, to develop a theory regarding international relations. Five countries with one, two and three decision makers were simultaneously simulated. The decision makers were required to conduct international affairs with facts regarding the expectations of the internal pressure groups. The trick was to conduct external affairs and remain in office. The most effective set appeared to be a situation where one decision maker was responsible for internal affairs and one for external affairs. When a clash of interests occurred, internal affairs took precedence. When more than two decision makers were used, confusion was more prevalent. Such simulations were designed to understand international decision-making and possibly train future statesmen. Similar plans have been conducted at the secondary level. Research leading to and preparation for making decisions might be an exciting affair.

Simulation regarding investment by means of establishing a brokerage in the classroom and providing students with a simulated investment account which includes a base fund for investment purposes might provide some insight into our economic system. The effects of internal and external political affairs upon the confidence of the investors can be noted and the shrewd investor can realize a large paper profit. Within such a program not all students will desire to participate and under the tacit philosophy of a learner-centered class all students should not be required to do so.

One problem regarding educational innovation should be anticipated; schools do not operate within a vacuum. The political pressures which international studies simulate are also operating at the local level. If you deviate from the pattern of indoctrination in ethnocentric nationalism and attempt to expose your students to a "process value system" you might find yourself and the school in trouble. Highly "patriotic societies" can make a big issue over the matter. Charges of "un-American" practices can be made, etc. Usually these "patriotic" ones are few in number but loud in voice. Perhaps in our teacher-training we need to simulate the school and community interaction in order to develop strategies which facilitate the implementation of new programs.

Summary and Evaluation

Rogers' self-theory focuses upon the conscious experience of the individual and the meaning structure he develops. In some of his writings, especially the work discussed here in detail, Rogers suggests that a value system is acquired by means of interaction with a real world. Lawful relationships obtain and the interaction with the environment can easily be interpreted as information regarding predictable relationships within the environment. In other writings Rogers (1956) introduced the notion of individual choice, which appears almost mystical. As was mentioned in Chapter 1 we interpret Rogers' notions regarding choice as a lawful phenomenon. In this light, we re-interpret Rogers' choice to mean that he wants individuals to acquire a set of strategies which enable the individual to process stimuli and modify behavior when old specific responses do not "pay off." Such a reinterpretation permits us to analyze self-actualization as a set of inquiry strategies (e.g., Suchman's training programs). Of course, circularity is built into this re-interpretation for we must select (choose?) some strategies and call them self-actualizing and reject others. Apparently we must stick with our original *act of faith* (or assumption) that our own behavior is a consequence of our interactions (or reinforcement history) just as our fellow humans are a product of theirs.

Evidence to support the claims of student-centered teaching is not available. Autonomy in learning should provide marked behavioral change; however, the aims of self-directed learning are long term. Therefore standard criterion measures (i.e., achievement test scores) seem trivial. Apparently longitudinal studies which assess the long term effects of the various approaches to education (operant, cognitive, and phenomenal) on some criterion of success (e.g., number of inventions, self supporting vs. government support, contribution to mankind, etc.) are needed. Lacking evidence, we *cannot* prescribe, but we are still faced with the task of educating children. We reiterate — you should examine the theories and the small scale evidence available and make your choice based upon your field of experiences or imperfect reinforcement history. (Ours is imperfect, also.)

Questions

1. Rogers believes that adjustment occurs when the individual replaces his introjected value system with "a continuing organismic valuing process." What implications might this have upon teaching United States history? Government? Economics?

2. If man is "self-actualizing," what might be the consequence of the present school practices upon the self-actualization of: (1) a middle-class suburban child; (2) a Negro in the ghetto of Chicago; (3) the Negro in Alabama; and (4) the lower-class Caucasian in Alabama?

References

Berlyne, D. E. Emotional aspects of learning. *Annu. Rev. of Psychol.* Palo Alto: Annual Reviews, 1964.

Bruner, J. *Toward a theory of instruction.* Cambridge: Belknap Press, 1966.

Guetzkow, H. F. A use of simulation in the study of inter-nation relations. *Behav. Sci.,* 1959, 4, 183-191.

Hebb, D. *A textbook in psychology.* Philadelphia: W. B. Saunders, 1958.

Kelly, G. A. Man's construction of his alternatives. *Assessment of human motives.* G. Lindzey (Ed.), New York: Grove Press, 1958.

Kendler, H. H., & Kendler, T. S. Vertical and horizontal processes in problem-solving. *Phychol. Rev.,* 1962, 69, 1-16.

Lindsley, D. B. Emotion. *Handbook of experimental psychology.* S. S. Stevens (Ed.), New York: Wiley, 1951.

Osgood, C. E. *Method and theory in experimental psychology.* New York: Oxford Univer. Press, 1953.

Rogers, C. R. *Client-centered therapy.* Boston: Houghton Mifflin, 1951.

Rogers, C. R., & Skinner, B. F. Some issues concerning the control of human behavior: a symposium. *Science,* 1956, 124, 1057-1066.

Rogers, C. R. The necessary and sufficient conditions of therapeutic personality change. *J. consulting Psychol.* 1957, 21, 95-103.

Rogers, C. R. *On becoming a person.* Boston: Houghton Mifflin, 1961.

Rogers, C. R. How can the teacher facilitate significant learning? *NEA Handbook,* 1965.

Staats, A. W., & Staats, Carolyn K. *Complex human behavior.* New York: Holt, Rinehart, Winston, 1963.

Suchman, J. R. Inquiry training: building skills for autonomous discovery. *Merrill-Palmer Quarterly,* 1961, 7, 147-169.

Social Learning and Imitation

7

Overview

Learning that takes place in the social setting is focused upon in this chapter. In previous chapters meaning (rs) was defined to have response-like characteristics. Indeed, meaning was seen to be the consequence of the individual's action upon the meaningful object. Data are presented within this chapter which suggest that *novel* response potentials can be acquired by way of observation of other's actions. This is called *imitation.* Whether or not the person will imitate the observed actions seems to rest upon the individual's expectations regarding the consequences of the performance. If the individual expects (Rba) to be rewarded (e.g., be given praise, candy, etc.), he will *tend to* imitate. Conversely, if punishment seems likely, the individual will tend to inhibit the observed act. Other factors enter into the matter of learning by observation (i.e., attention to the model) and these are discussed. Since the classroom is a social setting with a number of opportunities for the individual to learn from the actions of others, a number of educational applications of social learning are presented.

A review of Soviet character training is presented and the obvious use of imitation is noted. *Character* training relates to what we have called elements of motivation (Eab) and expectancies of support and nonsupport by others in the social environment (Rba). Both are assumed to be acquired as a result of interacting with friends, teachers, parents, etc. In order to develop a "character" consonant with the goals of the state, collective competition is liberally used. These notions have some value also for the American educator.

Character training in the United States is diverse and not amenable to a simple analysis. One reason for this diversity is the fact that responsibility for education is held by the states and local governments and therefore valued character traits may change from state to state or locale to locale. American plurality is further confounded by the fact that the composition of local school boards (i.e., plumbers, doctors, salesmen, etc.) influences educational practice. In order to provide some order to this diversity, a discussion of David Riesman's *Lonely Crowd* is presented. Riesman's notions apply to the dominant middle class. Riesman contends that the American character is changing from an orientation for production to an orientation for consumption and social skills. A number of implications for the neophyte teacher are noted. Riesman's observations have little empirical support; however, a few studies based upon his framework seem to lend credence to his position.

Glossary

Please look over these terms before continuing.

acting out: the overt performance of abnormal impulses, as the acting out of a deviant impulse.

anomie: the state of being without organization or system, esp. without natural law and uniformity, also used by Riesman as a person with a highly rigid organization of moral values.

autonomy: independence, self-regulation.

aversive stimulus: a stimulus which if applied following a response, decreases the tendency to emit that response on later similar occasions.

compulsive: refers to the tendency to repeat over and over a certain kind of behavior, despite its inappropriateness, and to be unable to inhibit the behavior.

consequence: the fact that two propositions, the antecedent and the consequent, are so related logically that the former validates the latter.

contiguity: the general principle that togetherness in time is a necessary condition under which psychological phenomena become dynamically connected.

demography: the statistical study of populations as to births, marriages, mortality, health, etc.

deviant: refers to those behaviors or attitudes that are not in accord with the prevailing patterns or moral standards of the dominant group.

disinhibition: the temporary removal of an inhibition through the action of stimulation.

imitation: action that copies the action of another more or less exactly, with or without intent to copy.

incentive: an object or external condition, perceived as capable of satisfying an aroused motive, that tends to elicit action to attain the object or condition.

intention: a formulated purpose to follow a course of action when favorable opportunity arises.

model: used in this chapter to indicate a person who acts and whose actions are imitated by another person.

performance: a personal activity considered as producing a result; more abstractly, a class or set of responses that alters the environment in a way that is defined by the class, the class itself being discovered and specified only by observing responses in two or more situations.

punishment: in experimental terms, any dissatisfaction imposed on the animal for performance of the response chosen by the experimenter as incorrect.

response hierarchy: the arrangement of a class of behaviors in the order of probability in which they will be elicited in a certain situation.

response repertoire: all the responses possible for a given individual or available under specified stimulus conditions, irrespective of hierarchical order.

super-ego: a system within the total psyche developed by incorporating the parental standards as perceived by the ego; or somewhat more broadly, developed by incorporating the moral standards of society.

Imitation

The earlier chapters have focused upon a number of variables relevant to understanding and predicting human behavior (e.g., stimulus characteristics, mediation variables, organismic variables, etc.). Although some mention has been made of the social factors, most considerations regarding response acquisition have stressed differentiation. The person acts and notes the consequences of his action. Essentially, the person is considered to be making an attempt to adapt, and responses which "pay off" usually are retained in the individual's response repertory. Indeed, data are reported which indicate that pigeons can be shaped by means of successive approximations to turn figure eights and humans also can be shaped to emit and maintain novel responses by means of contingency management. Furthermore, data indicate that people engage in inquiry to resolve incongruities (epistemic curiosity). But is this really the whole story?

Consider the young boy who crawls under his brand new peddle car with a hammer in hand. He bangs a part of the undercarriage, says, "Damn!" crawls out and peddles away. If we assume this is novel behavior, how has this complex set of sequential behaviors been acquired? Certainly not by means of a painstaking shaping process. Another example for consideration is the often observed behavior of a young girl playing with her new doll. She picks up a bottle, "feeds" the doll, puts it over her shoulder, and "burps" the "baby." She might even remark, "My, that was a big burp. Do you feel better now?"

The most plausible explanation regarding these two cases is that the children have imitated the behavior of their parents or some other person. Early behavioristic social learning theorists (e.g., Miller and Dollard, 1941) proposed that imitation is dependent upon three factors: (1) a motivated subject (child or adult), (2) who is positively reinforced, (3) when he matches the behavior of a model who is positively reinforced. Presumably the matching behavior is originally emitted by the child in a series of random trial and error responses and by definition, the positive reinforcement increases the probability that the imitative response will occur again. Bandura (1965) suggested that the reinforcement in the trial and error imitation situation adequately accounts for the maintenance of previously acquired matching responses but fails to account for the original acquisition of the behaviors.

In the case of the boy and his car, theoretically the boy continues to imitate the behavior of his father because he has been positively reinforced in the past for doing so. How the child initially acquired the emitted serial set of responses is *not* explained. Bandura (1965) reported data which support a notion that (1) *acquisition* of matching responses takes place through *contiguity* and that (2) *performance* of the model's behavior depends upon the *consequence* of the act upon the model.

Bandura conceptualizes the notion of acquisition via contiguity as: " . . . when an observer witnesses a model exhibit a sequence of responses the observer acquires, through contiguous association of sensory events, perceptual and symbolic responses possessing cue properties that are capable of eliciting, at some time after the demonstration, overt responses corresponding to those that had been modeled" (Bandura, 1965, p. 590). Simply stated, if a person watches another perform he can remember the performance and has the potential to match the response (limitations shall be mentioned later). For example most of us have not paced out a figure as illustrated below on the floor. Picture a person before you and he says, "Watch me." You watch him as he paces thusly.

FIGURE 7.1

Do you think you can do it? Sure you can, but do you want to? You have acquired the potential to match the response but under what conditions will you perform? For example: (1) if immediately after walking off the figure 8 your imaginary model was hit in the mouth with a baseball bat, would you likely imitate him? (2) would you imitate him if many people complimented him for his brilliant performance? (3) if he offered you ten dollars to do the act would you do it?

Of course, your answer to each situation depends upon many factors. If you are a habitual "aggressive rebel," you might try to imitate the toothless model and dare the bat swinger to try his act again. If you like to be praised, you might imitate the praised model, and if you are the typical student ten dollars would be sufficient incentive, although some suspicious students might "look a gift horse in the mouth."

Bandura's study (1965) illustrated these points regarding the influence of incentive conditions. Thirty-three boys and thirty-three girls enrolled in a nursery school were individually exposed to a five-minute film in which a male model acted out *four* novel sequences of aggressive responses upon a large adult size plastic Bobo doll (e.g., ". . . the model laid the Bobo doll on its side, sat on it, and punched it in the nose while remarking, 'Pow, right in the nose, boom, boom!") (Bandura, 1965, p. 590). The other three aggressive acts also were accompanied with distinct verbalizations.

The consequences to the model were broken into three conditions (with 11 boys and 11 girls randomly assigned to view one of the three treatments):

1. Condition one was a *model-rewarded* condition where upon completion of the enactment of the aggressive performance an adult entered the room, praised the model for being a "strong champion" and gave him Seven-Up and "generous" amounts of candy, etc. As the model consumed the "goodies" the adult continued with the praise.
2. The *model-punished* condition was initiated with the reinforcing agent verbally admonishing the model not to be such a bully and was concluded with the model receiving a spanking.
3. The *no-consequences* condition including only exposure to the filmed aggressive acts.

Immediately following the exposure period the children were taken to an experimental room filled with a number of diverse toys, including a Bobo and the materials used by the model to aggress upon Bobo. Each child was given ten minutes of free play while two observers in an observation room recorded at five-second intervals the number of imitative aggressive responses freely emitted by the children.

At the end of the ten-minute period the experimenter entered the room and gave each child (in the incentive group) a juice treat and told him that for each physical or verbal response of the model he imitated he would be given additional juice and pretty sticker-pictures. These later suggestions were designed to provide incentives for acting out the aggressive acts. The experimenter asked the child to "show me what Rocky did in the TV program; tell me what he said," and the child was immediately "rewarded" following each matching response. Figure 7-2 shows the mean number of different imitated responses reproduced by the several groups under free play and incentive conditions.

In free play (no incentive) the boys emitted more matching responses than did the girls. The boys who observed the model being rewarded

FIGURE 7.2

Mean number of different matching responses reproduced by children as a function of positive incentives and the model's reinforcement contingencies.

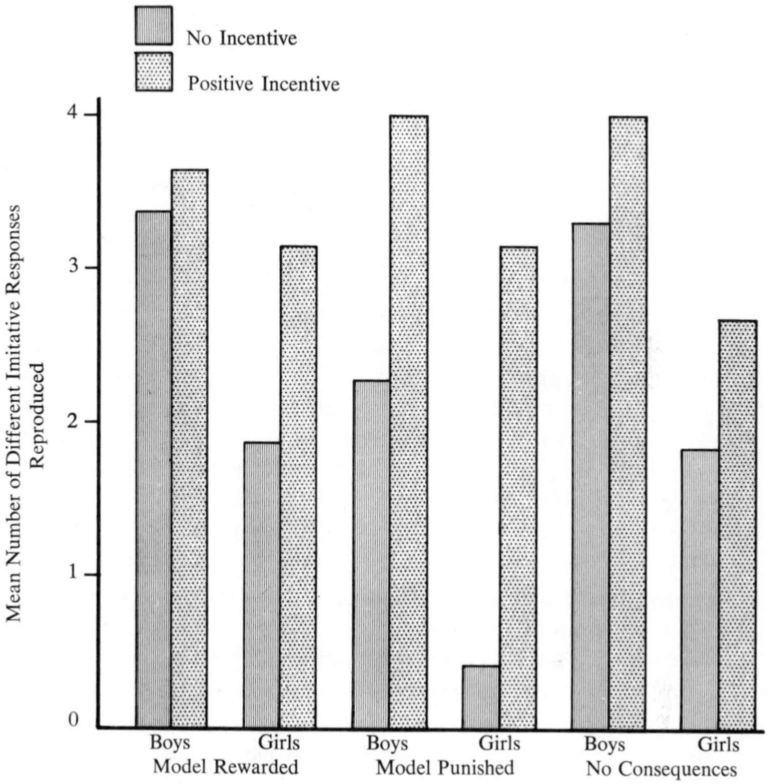

From: Albert Bandura, "Influence of Models' Reinforcement Contingencies on the Acquisition of Imitative Responses," *Journal of Personality and Social Psychology,* Vol. 1, No. 6, June, 1965, page 592. Copyright (1965) by the American Psychological Association, and reproduced by permission.

with no consequences tended to match more aggressive acts than those who observed the model-punished condition. Upon introduction of positive incentive contingent upon successful modeling, the three male groups emitted essentially an equivalent number of matching responses.

Among the girls, those who observed the model-punished situation emitted significantly fewer modeling responses under free play conditions. This difference was completely washed out under the incentive conditions.

If one infers learning from performance, a focus upon the no-incentive performance could lead to an inference that girls do not *learn* these behaviors as well as boys, and that boys who observe a punished model do not *learn* well the series of behaviors. In the presence of the positive incentive evidence, an alternate inference must be cast.

Apparently: (1) males who observe sequences of aggressive acts by a model who is subsequently punished, are inhibited from making matching responses. But when these boys are offered a positive incentive to match the aggressive behaviors, they demonstrate learning. Therefore, positive incentives might have a disinhibiting effect. (2) Girls follow a pattern similar to the boys'. Girls under both no-incentive and positive-incentive conditions perform significantly fewer modeling responses than their male counterparts. Although the sex difference was significant, the introduction of incentive conditions markedly reduced this difference. Mallick and McCandless (1966) reported data that indicate three- and four-year-old girls are as aggressive as three- and four-year-old boys if they believe no one will find out. Possibly due to a social history in which aggression is likely to be systematically nonrewarded, girls as a group have a generalized inhibition regarding aggression which can be broken down.

By way of summary: Acquisition of potential novel response patterns apparently can be accounted for in part by observation (contiguity). Performance of the observed novel responses can be inhibited or disinhibited depending upon the consequences to the model. Furthermore, the introduction of a positive incentive to the *observer* can disinhibit and lead to matching performance.

Limitations: Observational learning and imitation does not necessarily lead to perfect matching of response. Many tasks which require a basic physical structure are difficult to complete when the structure is limited. One might watch Arnold Palmer swing his driver and be praised by the gallery, but even with much practice the imitator may fail to obtain the same results. Many boys imitate Willie Mays, Mohammed Ali, Bill Russel, etc., but few come through.

Other Factors Influencing Imitation

Two crucial factors underlie imitation: (1) the individual must observe the behavior and (2) the individual must be willing and capable of performing the act. Bandura's study which included manipulation of incentive conditions bears upon the S's willingness to perform the act. A study by Lefkowitz, Blake, and Moulton (1955) demonstrated that pedestrians more frequently disobey a WAIT signal at a crosswalk when a "high status" person (suit, tie, hat, etc.) violates the signal than when a "low status" person (patched pants, denim shirt, scuffed shoes, etc.) violates the signal. Furthermore, under normal conditions (no experimental model introduced) pedestrians exhibit fewer violations than when contrived models are present. Apparently the "high status" models disinhibit traffic violations more than "low status" models, and violation by even a "low status" model disinhibits.

Grusec and Mischel (1966) reported data which suggest that model characteristics not only influence the willingness to act, but also the degree to which the individual observes the model's acts. In a play instruction situation, one group of nursery school children were individually exposed to a model who was "rewarding" in the introductory session and who was verbally introduced as the child's future teacher. Another group of children were exposed to a low-reward model who was introduced as a visiting teacher. Both models performed four distinct acts. Upon completion of the session the models played an additional five minutes with each child, and the future-teacher model told the child she just found out she was needed elsewhere and could not be his teacher after all. The teacher models later left the room and a confederate told each child that she wanted to find out how good he was at remembering the things that had happened during the play instruction session. The child was given a cookie or a picture-sticker for each correct recall of the four acts. Essentially all children were offered an incentive to recall the acts. The children who were instructed by the rewarding future-teacher as a group were able to recall more of the four acts than those who were exposed to the low-reward model. Apparently the fact that the first model was previously rewarding and possibly the child's future teacher resulted in more attention to her acts. Probably the model was viewed as being more important and therefore the child watched her more carefully. To be sure other factors are operating since some children exposed to the low-reward model recalled more than some children exposed to the high-reward model. Of importance is the recognition that imitation learning cannot be used to describe the total behavior of the group. As with other discussions of behavior some responses cannot be accounted for within the context of the topic being discussed.*

Greenspoon's (1955) study mentioned in Chapter 5 showed that a comment "mmm-hmm" following the emission of a plural noun led to

---

*Acquisition of novel serial response potential via observation is not limited to visual receptors. Due to man's extensive language history, verbal instructions to chain a number of previously acquired individual responses can lead to effective modeling. The little footprints provided for your imaginary model could just as well be replaced by the verbal instructions, "Pace a figure 8 on the floor."

a significant increase of plural nouns by experimental subjects. Furthermore, when the contingent stimulus (mmm-hmm) was omitted the experimental subjects returned to the control group baseline within two five-minute blocks.

Control subjects emitted an average of 56.6 plural nouns in a 25-minute period, whereas the *experimental* subjects emitted 109.9 on the average during the same time period. These data demonstrate the power of some contingent stimuli upon verbal behavior. To extrapolate from such studies to classroom situations might lead to success; however, time consumed can be prohibitive. Bandura (1962) speculated that a polite straight-forward verbal request for plural nouns would provide an immediate high rate of plural noun responses, and that a request to stop would lead to immediate extinction. To check this speculation an abbreviated one-subject study was conducted by the present authors. A subject was asked to emit one word using Greenspoon's (1955, p. 410) instructions, "What I want you to do is to say all the words you can think of. Say them individually. Do not use any sentences or phrases. Do not count. Please continue until I say, 'Stop'. Now go ahead." During this baseline five-minute period the subject emitted 102 words, *eight* of which were plural nouns. The subject was instructed to stop at the end of five minutes and told, "I now want you to proceed as before, except now would you please use only *plural nouns*. Go ahead." The subject emitted 110 words during this five-minute period, 109 of which were plural nouns and one was a plural pronoun. Upon completion of the second five-minute period, the subject was told, "Now give me all the words you can think of that are *not* plural nouns. Go ahead." During this extinction period, the subject emitted 71 words, none of which were plural nouns. Apparently, Bandura's prediction held.

The point of this digression is that humans have a long history of language and symbol usage. To extrapolate hastily from animal studies might lead to a focus upon one class of learning and therefore lead to omissions of other powerful classes of learning and cue utilization. (This is not intended to mean one should ignore animal studies; the intent is expressed as words for caution.)

Socialization versus Maturation as Determinants of Moral Judgments

In this chapter the notion has been presented that social behavior is a product of learning. Piaget (1948) proposed that two clear-cut stages of moral development exist (a form of social behavior), separated from each other at approximately age 7. Before age 7, the child employs *objective responsibility* in judging the severity of a moral deviation. Children in this stage tend to judge an unintentional breaking of a cookie jar more severely than an unsuccessful act with malicious intentions (e.g., if a child took a hammer to a jar but failed to succeed in breaking it he would have less concern than if he accidentally tipped the jar and it fell crashing loudly on the floor). After age 7 the *subjective responsibility* stage emerges. At this latter stage of development, the child judges the severity of a deviant act not by the consequences of the act but by evaluating the *intention* of the actor.

Such an age-specific notion of moral development tacitly implies a physical maturation component and also assumes that moral judgment is a unitary and uni-directional function. Bandura and McDonald (1963) conducted a study to check Piaget's notions and to test the malleability of modes of judgment. Children representing five age groups (age range, 5-10) were given twelve pairs of stories, one representing *intentions* and the other *consequences*. Sample stories:

Consequences: "John was in his room when his mother called him to dinner. John goes down, and opens the door to the dining room. But behind the door was a chair and on the chair was a tray with fifteen cups on it. John did not know the cups were behind the door. He opens the door, the door hits the tray, bang go the fifteen cups, and they all get broken."

Intentions: "One day when Henry's mother was out, Henry tried to get some cookies out of the cupboard. He climbed up on a chair, but the cookie jar was still too high and he couldn't reach it. But while he was trying to get the cookie jar he knocked over a cup. The cup fell down and broke." (Bandura and McDonald, 1963, p. 276).

The children were asked "Who did the naughtier thing?" and to provide a reason for the choice.

Consistent choice of the *consequences* would place the child high in objective moral judgments. Conversely choice of *intention* stories reflects subjective moral judgments. Five-year-old children provided subjective judgment in about 30% of the cases and ten-year-old children emitted subjective judgments about 60% of the time. Mode of judgment was related to age; on the other hand this relationship was far from perfect. The older child uses *subjective* moral judgment in more instances, but he also uses *objective* moral judgment; therefore, these modes exist together without clean lines of demarcation. It is apparent that placing age limits on the development of moral judgment among children is a difficult and perhaps unrealistic task (see figure 7.3).

FIGURE 7.3

Mean percentage of subjective moral judgment responses produced by boys and girls at different age levels.

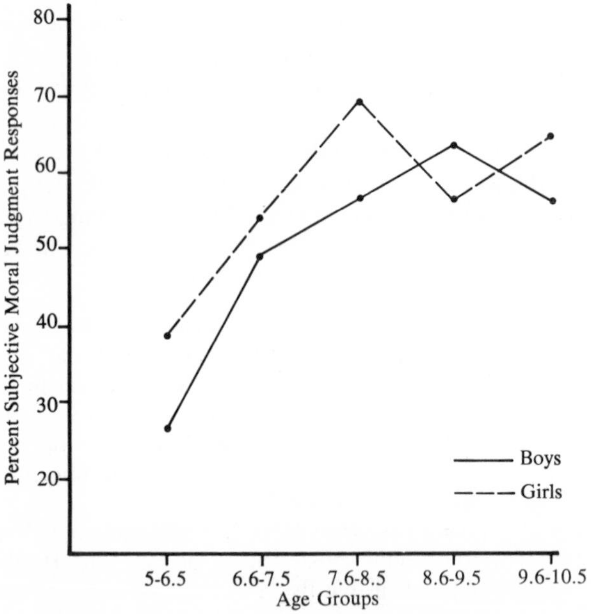

From: Bandura, Albert, and F. J. McDonald, "Influence of Social Reinforcement and Behavior of Models in Shaping Children's Moral Judgment," *Journal of Abnormal and Social Psychology,* Vol. 67, 1963, page 278. Copyright (1963) by the American Psychological Association, and reproduced by permission.

The second phase of this study included an experimental intervention condition conducted about two weeks after obtaining the baseline data. Forty-eight children who were primarily subjective in moral orientation (mean baseline subjective responses 80%) and 36 children who were decidedly objective (83%) were selected for treatment.

The *subjective* children were assigned to one of three treatments:

1. Model Reinforced—Child Reinforced
   A model and child took turns evaluating a set of 12 pairs of stories. The model got the first story. The model consistently emitted objective judgments and was praised. Whenever the child emitted *objective* responses he also was praised.

2. Only Model Reinforced
   Same as 1 except the child was not praised for his responses.
3. Operant Conditioning
   Child evaluated all 24 stories and was reinforced verbally for objective responses (no model present).

Under all conditions the reinforcement was given for responses opposite to the child's dominant judgmental mode. The objective children were given similar treatment with the exception that subjective responses were reinforced (opposite mode).

Figure 7.4 shows the percentage of objective moral judgments emitted by the three *subjective oriented treatment* groups over three phases of

FIGURE 7.4

Mean percentage of objective moral judgment responses produced by subjective children on each of the three test periods for each of three experimental conditions.

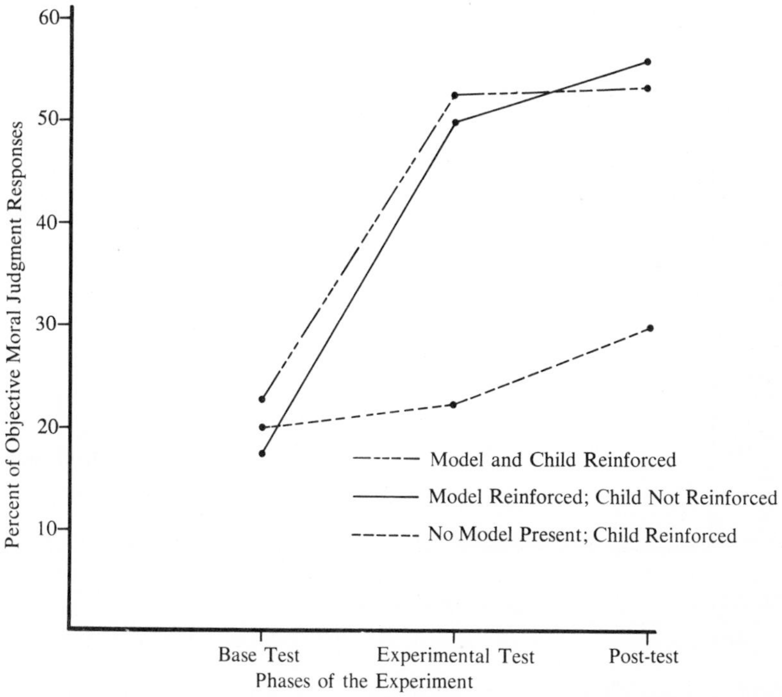

From: Bandura, Albert, and F. J. McDonald, "Influence of Social Reinforcement and Behavior of Models in Shaping Children's Moral Judgment," *Journal of Abnormal and Social Psychology,* Vol. 67, 1963, page 278. Copyright (1963) by the American Psychological Association, and reproduced by permission.

the experiment (base test, experimental test, and post test). Under the base test conditions the mean percentage of objective moral judgments for the three treatment groups was 20%. The two model-present groups emitted over 50% objective moral judgments on the experimental test and maintained this level on a post test conducted by an independent investigator. The operant group showed no appreciable increase in objective judgments.

Figure 7.5 shows the percentage of subjective moral judgments emitted by the *objective oriented treatment groups* over the three treatment conditions. The results tend to parallel those obtained for the subjective group; however, the operant group tended to increase in objective responses during the experimental test.

FIGURE 7.5

Mean percentage of subjective moral judgment responses produced by objective children on each of three test periods for each of three experimental conditions.

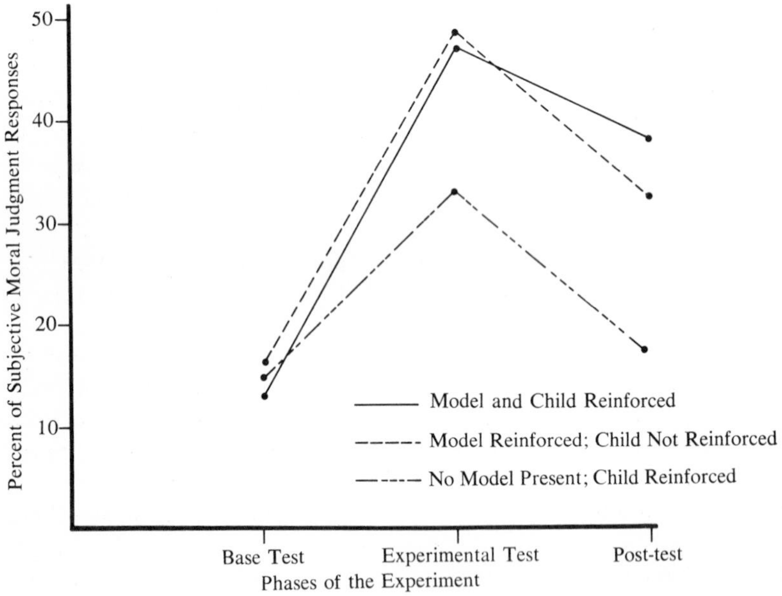

From: Bandura, Albert, and F. J. McDonald, "Influence of Social Reinforcement and Behavior of Models in Shaping Children's Moral Judgment," *Journal of Abnormal and Social Psychology,* Vol. 67, 1963, page 280. Copyright (1963) by the American Psychological Association, and reproduced by permission.

These data give strong support to the notion that moral judgments can be modified as a function of models who provide cues regarding "appropriate behavior." Once acquired, judicious reinforcement theoretically should maintain the newly acquired response mode. In view of these data age-specific uni-directional moral development notions are counterviewed. The trend toward subjective moral judgment parallels the child's increasing involvement in a peer culture. Can this trend in judgmental subjectivity be a function of observing peer models rather than authority figures?

The fact that operant conditioning procedures did not result in clear-cut modification of moral judgments is not surprising since the responses which were reinforced were low on the individual's response hierarchy. The dramatic effectiveness of both modeling conditions can be attributed to the fact that the models provided cues regarding appropriate responses (socially valued) within the experimental context.

Educational Implications of Social Learning

Within the classroom a number of possible peer models are available who can facilitate learning and performance. Some of these peer models might facilitate performances that coincide with performances which the teacher values and others might facilitate performances which are antithetical to the teacher's values or educational objectives. Of course, the teacher herself is a model and has some control over potential reinforcers. She can excuse the class to go out to play, praise the child for work or "good behavior," facilitate competency by means of "effective" teaching, withhold free play, spank the child, verbally admonish and attempt to humiliate, etc. How the teacher initially uses these reinforcers might have a marked effect upon whom the children imitate.

If the child attends to models who are rewarding and/or have high status, it might be best for the teacher to establish herself as a positively reinforcing agent. In general, a smile and "pleasant responses" to the children might be effective initial teacher behaviors. Social control (often called discipline) might be facilitated by discussing how one should behave in the classroom and developing a rationale for why these behaviors are valuable. Such presentations prior to violation might help avoid a punishing situation which can result in the school and the teacher being an aversive stimulus for the punished child. Furthermore, praise of individuals and groups within the classroom can point out positive models which might provide cues for other class members. Of course, care should be exercised. If a few individuals get all the praise (the nice conformers) they can be perceived by the students as being the teacher's "pets" and thus will not be imitated. Some teachers use models effectively by liberally praising students for "good work habits," and spreading the praise to all students. To be sure, the praise should be used discriminantly—the student should be emitting a desired behavior. Such verbal reinforcement not only maintains the reinforced behavior but also increases the probability that students will observe the desired behavior.

Although punishment to a negative model decreases the probability that others will imitate the behavior, it might also result in the school or the teacher becoming an aversive stimulus to the punished model. If the school becomes a generalized aversive stimulus, the student might well avoid school and be reinforced for doing so because he has avoided the aversive stimulus. One might be able to avoid the use of punishment for minor infractions by praising an exemplary model seated near the violator and thereby providing a positive model for him. Often the violator will observe the model and then "get to work." If so, the teacher can then praise the violator for his "good work habits." If the violator does not imitate the model, a quiet and polite admonition can often get the child back to work and thereby provide the opportunity for praise.

The use of positive reinforcement and models is stressed as a possible means of initiating and maintaining desirable classroom behaviors. This is not to imply that punishment should necessarily be avoided. In a case of major violations the consequence to the violator can be instructive to others. Suppose a child hits another with a book. Would you praise his neighbor for keeping his books on his desk? If there are no consequences for such infractions, the others might well imitate these aggressive acts. One might find it necessary to punish the child and thereby risk the loss of this student's attraction to school in order to save the group.

Another powerful reinforcer at the teacher's disposal (for elementary school children) is dismissal for recess, lunch, etc. Rows can be praised for getting ready quietly and can be excused first. The opportunity for observational learning and possible performance might be enhanced.

These applications of social learning theory imply teacher awareness of the diverse behaviors emitted by the students. To be sure, they are time and energy consuming; nonetheless these applications might well increase the probability that students will learn what the teacher desires them to learn. Tacitly, underlying these considerations is the assumption that the teacher can designate, in rather specific terms, the behaviors she wants to be acquired and maintained.

Success in problem solution also can operate as a reinforcer that can make school a desirous place to be, and therefore increase the teacher's contingency units. This again means more work and attention to student academic behaviors and a matching of appropriate materials that lead to success. It should be noted also that teacher activity which relates to techniques alone might have little meaning for reinforcement or developing models for student behavior. As an example, an elementary school teacher might employ the "best row first for recess" technique mentioned above and accomplish little or nothing. Each technique should be preceded by an identifiable purpose and accompanied with observation and specific teacher cues in order to ensure usefulness of the technique. Perhaps too much time is spent by teachers imitating model behavior demonstrated in methods courses without understanding what the method should really accomplish and under what conditions it is likely to be successful.

Imitation and Inquiry Modes

Suchman's inquiry training (see Chapter 5) included group problem solving which provided opportunities for others to learn successful inquiry strategies. The students were asked to emit questions which would help identify the variables relevant to problem solution. Theoretically, under group inquiry conditions two sets of behaviors are desired: (1) verbalization of one's problem solving sequence, and (2) verbalization of successful strategies which reflect acquisition of an appropriate inquiry mode.

In view of Bandura's studies, the consequences to the child who emits an inadequate strategy might determine, to a great degree, the amount of subsequent verbalizations expressed in class. A negative consequence (e.g., "that's a poor question") can inhibit not only poor questions but also other students' willingness to verbalize any questions. Some praise to the student for an attempt including feedback that the question follows a blind alley might maintain participation and also provide cues regarding the identification of relevant variables. For students who are highly dependent, a successful inquirer might be presented (a positive model) followed by an analysis of the strategies which the model used. Such initial inquiry sessions can focus upon the problem of "How did he do it?" rather than focusing upon the physical problem. Follow-up sessions could include opportunities to imitate the model's inquiry modes by means of presentation of simple problems and then increasing problem difficulty as success is obtained.

Classroom Resources

Other model sources available to the teacher are books, socio-political figures, films and television. Biographies provide rich sources of exemplary models regarding culturally valued behaviors. Stories of George Washington's exploits are often used to praise the value of honesty and integrity. Your grandparents may have read Horatio Alger books which illustrated that hard work is always rewarded. In some sections of the United States, Abe Lincoln stories are liberally used to foster humanitarian beliefs. The fact that Lincoln stories are used less frequently in some parts of the South reflects a degree of cultural diversity within the United States.

In the presence of local control of the educational endeavor, bans on school library books vary from locale to locale. Apparently, the community condones some models and rejects others. Some schools ban *The Catcher in the Rye* and *Forever Amber* since it is assumed that they are not "fit reading" (models?) for adolescents. A number of nationalistic groups dislike any positive mention of the United Nations in the schools — *One Worldism* is not a venerated model of politics. There are books which represent a wide range of models. A judicious selection can provide models which foster ethnocentrism, humanitarianism or any number of other moral positions. The teacher has, to a large degree, the control of these materials, and she might wish to select books which support her aims of education.

Television is also a powerful source for observational learning. Socially approved aggression is rewarded liberally on many series. The "bad guy" is always punished while the "good guy" gets the girl, the car, and the praise. Since the children probably watch television, the teacher might select some programs for homework thus exercising some further control of models for observation.*

Character Training

If one examines objectives of public school education he will find references to personal human qualities which apparently are believed

*The preceding applications are extrapolations from theory and in view of human complexity they surely oversimplify the complex that we call a classroom. Furthermore, some "effective" teachers have intuitively used imitation learning. Many of these intuitive practices antedate the formulation of theory. Theory as presented here, might provide the novice teacher with a conceptual process that will enable her to cope with problems without extensive trial and error learning. Furthermore, the theory might have broader application than just a listing or a "cookbook" of teacher practices. No evidence is available to support this possibility.

related to some common character of American manhood or womanhood. There can be little doubt that the school is charged with developing or maintaining a portion of the character of its students. Seemingly this is a trait which is noticeable in varying degrees in most societies.

Soviet Character Training

Complex societies provide a diverse set of potential models. Within the United States where a cultural plurality exists, character training is generally a major function of the home. Some parents stress aggression inhibition and others reinforce aggression. Likewise, some parents encourage academic achievement and inculcate long-term professional goals while other parental behaviors lead to "deviant" child behaviors. This cultural plurality undoubtedly is maintained by the American belief in individualism, the sanctity of parental control and the historical artifact of local control of school systems which tends to maintain regionalism. Such diverse character training can provide the teacher with problems especially from children whose home reinforces aggression and/or extinguishes academic behaviors.

In contrast with American character training with the stress upon individuality, Bronfenbrenner (1962) described Soviet character training which stresses collective competition. A central thesis by Makarenko (the leading Soviet authority on moral training) is that the highest personality development can only be realized through *productive activity* in a social collective. The home is the primary collective and the parent's duty to his child is a case of duty to society. When the values of the home conflict with the values of the collective society, the home must take second place.

Within the Soviet school system character training apparently holds a central role. The systematic program of socialization in the school is well defined in teacher manuals and reflects a judicious use of models and collective competition which appear to define behaviors for the children. Bronfenbrenner reviewed a widely used manual which spelled out a number of recommended procedures.

Recommendations for the first grade suggest that direct commands such as "All sit straight" do not involve all the children. Rather than provide direct commands the teacher is admonished to say, "Let's see which row can sit the straightest." Theoretically such activities introduce, at an early level, the notion of *collective competition* and an evaluative attitude toward members of his collective (row). First grade children are reported to respond with enthusiasm to such requests. In order to maintain the competition and energy, records are kept for each small collective for a diverse set of tasks which include cleanliness, deportment, neatness in body and work, etc. These records provide information on the degree of excellence for each collective. Peer pressure is applied to those who hold the group performance down.

Monitors are selected to help make evaluations which reduce the burden of record keeping for the teacher. Of course, for the monitor to be effective he must attend carefully to the teacher's behavior when she makes evaluations (imitation?). Once the monitors have well-established evaluative reporting (about grade 3) the monitors make their evaluations publicly and the rows are encouraged to find errors of omission which the monitor failed to note. Therefore, competition between evaluators and the evaluated is established. Note that such stress upon evaluation should facilitate discrimination learning. Furthermore, pointing out the errors of others and self is *not* viewed as negative behavior. It is an opportunity to point out the individual's duty to his collective.

The highly evaluated rows are from time to time "rewarded" (variable interval reinforcement?) by being photographed for recognition on wall newspapers which show "Who is the best." Later, competition between classes is recommended, and the "winner" is visited by the other classes to learn how to become excellent (the positive model is pointed out). Positive reinforcement is the main basis of this training. When negative acts continue, the teacher can ask the class "Is this behavior helping us?" Solutions for the problem are solicited and this provides the teacher with the opportunity to teach the children procedures which might work. Harsh punishments are *not* humane — children must learn to live together on a friendly basis.

Not only does the evaluation lead to discrimination but students learn to be responsible for members of their collective. If a child fails to solve a problem and thus reduces the rating of a row, a row member might help the child after school in order to increase future ratings of the row.

Collective competition in performing productive activity extends to all social groups from the pioneers on up to factories and farms. Of course, the effectiveness of the broader competition is a product of early and constant focus upon small group collective competition.

Parents are required to report evaluations of the children at home and some check of the parents is made by members of the parents' worker collective. If the visitor notes inappropriate parental or child behavior he reports this to the collective. The parent is not permitted to abuse his child. How effective these measures are is unknown. Parenthetically it would be interesting to contrast the number of child deaths due to parental maltreatment in the Soviet Socialistic states with that of our "open" society. A recent (1966) AMA report indicated that three children a day die in the United States due to parental maltreatment.

The use of group reinforcement and competition is *not* unknown here in the United States. Many teachers make "Standards Charts" in some detail and encourage children to evaluate. Also graphs showing "Which group is best" are used here; however, the *systematic* use of collective competition is lacking. To a large degree the teacher, as the parent, is master of his domain. Therefore, the second grade teacher might use a quite different mode of character training from that used by the first grade teacher. Some school administrators attempt to foster a consistent mode within their schools.

An evaluation of the Soviet character training program is difficult to make. Many of the practices appear to use modeling and reinforcement effectively. Control of classroom deportment apparently can be obtained by using these methods, and therefore, the business of learning can be facilitated. But as was pointed out earlier, the teacher must know specifically what behaviors she wants, and then she must systematically employ evaluative procedures to provide discrimination acquisition and response differentiation. The reader might consider these procedures and make a decision to "buy" some — no recommendation shall be provided herein.

One point should be noted — due to centralized control of Soviet education, practices might change rapidly. Bronfenbrenner's comments were derived from data obtained when Khrushchev was in power. Change in political leadership might redirect educational practices. The evidence seems to indicate no such change has taken place recently.

The American Character

In the process of examining the components of response acquisition and performance, the focus has been upon a small scale micro-system. The micro-system permits an investigation into subtle interactions between stimulus conditions, response conditions, and individual differences, etc. — this is psychology. Bronfenbrenner's survey of Soviet character training describes a larger sphere of cultural training which illustrates a possible Soviet interest in a larger system. Character education as described by Bronfenbrenner emphasized the obligation of school to society. Character education within the United States does not seem amenable to an easy analysis.

Because of a number of historical factors, character training in the United States is less systematic on a national basis. Our Constitution places stress on individuality and relegates (by omission) education to the several states. Viewed jointly, these two factors lead to a degree of cultural plurality in character training. In general, character training is a function of the family, although some change is apparent. Furthermore, with few Federal constraints, the state and local school boards determine the educational activities. A few states will not allow the schools to discuss particular topics (e.g., Theories of Evolution, The United Nations, sexual matters, etc.) and the Federal government restricts the religious activity of the schools.

Although responsibility for character training resides in the home, the school officials usually demand conformity to a norm of acceptable social behavior. This standard often reflects the values held but not necessarily practiced by the dominant middle class within the particular community.

In order to point out some of the cultural diversity which exists in the United States the following discussion is presented. This discussion centers around an analysis of the American character presented in *The Lonely Crowd: A Study of the American Character* (Riesman, Glazer and Denney, 1953). Riesman's theorizing provides views of America which can point to variables which might aid prediction. This latter belief shall be reconsidered following a summary of Riesman's notions. (Caution: such a brief summary shall by necessity simplify Riesman's concepts; the skeptical and those interested in the topic might wish to read the primary reference).

The S-Shaped Population Curve

Demographic data related to our Western world suggests that the population growth of countries takes the form of an S-shaped curve. The bottom horizontal section represents a high growth potential where the birth rate is high and the death rate is also high. This section is called a "high growth potential," because innovations which might reduce the death rate (e.g., new means of production, medical breakthroughs, etc.) can lead to a population explosion. The vertical section of the S-curve represents what demographers call the period of "transitional growth" which reflects a reduction in the death rate while the reduction in birth rate lags behind. This state existed in Western countries following the sixteenth century. When the birth rate approximates the death rate, the top horizontal section of the curve is reached on the period of "incipient population decline." Prior to World War II, America approached the decline stage. The post World War II baby boom upset, to a degree, this fine smooth representation; nevertheless the trend seems to hold for most western countries.

The main thesis presented by Riesman is ". . . each of these three different phases on the population curve appears to be occupied by a society that enforces conformity and molds social character in a definably different way" (Riesman, *et al.,* 1953, p. 23). (Figure 7.6 summarizes these three phases of the S-shaped curve.)

FIGURE 7.6

The S-shaped population curve and the associated character types.

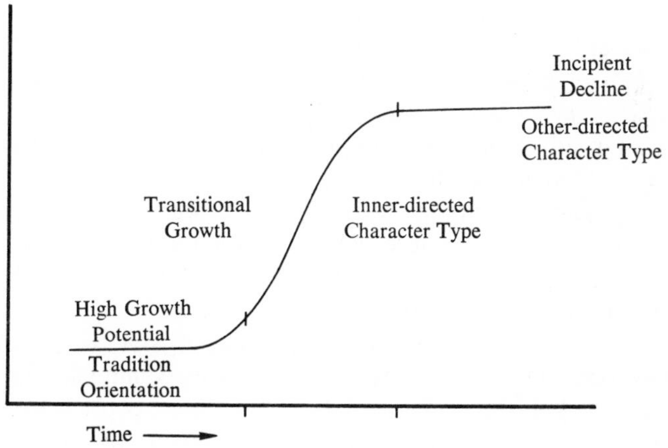

Character types are below the curve.

High Growth Potential: Traditional Directed Character Types. High growth potential cultures have in common a relatively rapid turnover in generations. Individual life expectancy is short due to a precarious balance between production and consumption. Europe in the Middle Ages, and to some degree present-day South America, Asia, and India, are examples of such a culture. In order to maintain a viable culture, stable institutions developed. These stable institutions demanded conformity from the accepted adult members of the culture. Within this stable society, social and geographic mobility was extremely limited and caste or status systems of sorts were present. For example, in medieval Europe the child who lived to adulthood succeeded his father. The son of a cobbler became a cobbler and was a valuable member of the producing community. Due to the limited number of adults in comparison to children, few adult models were available, and they usually enacted behaviors which were appropriate for future adult behavior.

Stability during the "High Growth Potential Stage" was maintained by means of elaborate ritual and relatively rigid standards of conduct for each strata of the society. Marked deviation in belief was not tolerated, but in that all productive members were valued, institutional means to bring pressure upon the deviants were prevalent. For example, Galileo Galilei was given the choice to recant his blasphemy or die — he chose the former. Parallels among the non-literate Zuni Indians of southwestern United States were noted by Ruth Benedict (1934). Among the Zuni, the appropriate character trait was non-competitiveness and the individual was expected not to stand out from the group. Deviants who continued to win all races and thus make a "spectacle of themselves" were encouraged to enter the priesthood which required a great deal of public display (a low valued position but acceptable). In pre-communist China, where a high man to land ratio was present, stability of production and consumption was somewhat controlled by means of institutionalized female infanticide.

The character orientation of this phase was labeled "Tradition directed" by Riesman because change is minimized and children are taught by word and by action to follow the traditions of the forefathers. The theme of this period is "don't upset the balance."

Transitional-Growth: Inner-Directed Types. "Mercantilism," the "Industrial Revolution," and improved sanitation and communications upset the traditional balance in Western Europe. More people were present and more production provided a continued spurt in population growth. As a consequence of these changes "the old ways" were no longer applicable. New problems had to be met and greater mobility brought together conflicting traditions. Furthermore, inventiveness was required to resolve and meet the new demands. As the primary social group (i.e., the clan) declined in control over the socialization of children and the control of adult behavior, Riesman proposed that a new psychological mechanism was invented to cope with the new freedom. This mechanism he likens to a psychological gyroscope. Rather than external institutions controlling behavior, the family as the focus of socialization inculcated *within* the child life goals which enabled him to retain some stability when he was confronted with a diverse external environment. These internal goals among Northern and Western Europeans were primarily consistent with the Protestant ethic of honesty, integrity, and hard work. Although the inner-directed man is not immune to the press of his environment, he has within his value system a core of values he might maintain in the face of aversity. The stereotype of the Englishman with a conscientious addiction to good form is an example. "Only mad dogs and Englishmen go out in the noon-day's sun."

In general, these internalized values were in keeping with the demands of the economy, for hard work led to production.

Incipient Decline: Other-Directed Types. In the latter stages of transition with the increase in capital and less dependence upon large numbers of the population working on the farm, children were no longer economic assets. Also the independence and the belief in one's own control of his destiny led to plans for his progeny's future. Taken together, these factors led to a decrease in the birth rate leading to the stage of incipient population decline. The capitalization accumulated by the fervent, hard working, frugal, inner-directed man led to abundance (especially in North America), shorter working hours, and more leisure time. The ethic of industry and frugality was no longer appropriate because the social problem was less one of production than one of coping with diverse sub-cultures reflected by others. In the United States more leisure means that Polish, Irish, and German as well as Catholics, Protestants, and Jews are faced with getting along with each other. (Note the change in tense — we are discussing some areas of present day America.)

Many adults attain higher social status during the latter stages of transition and also maintain an inner-directed ethic of achievement. The adults are unsure of themselves within the new status group and probably rely upon leaders of their "in" group for cues on how to conduct themselves properly. As parents, these mobile people want their children to succeed, but really lack tried and true rules. The old which worked in the past no longer works. Therefore, the parents apparently select peer models who represent the upward bound and whom the parent wishes his child to emulate. Rather than introject a psychic gyroscope, Riesman suggests these parents inculcate a psychic radarscope. The child is socialized to attend to what specific others do. He becomes sensitive not to moral judgments, but more to what the others do, and evaluates these acts in view of conformity of his "in" group's standard. This character type is called "other-directed" by Riesman.

Inner- and Other-Direction in Contemporary America. Riesman viewed contemporary 1950 America as a mixture of *inner- and other-direction.* Other-directedness was reported to be more characteristic of upper middle class urban America. The trend toward other-direction was seen to be expressed more in dynamic cities such as New York and

Los Angeles but less in Boston. The socialization of taste transcends the simple emulation of dress and homes — the emulation extends to values and belief systems. No strong internalized belief system is given to the other-directed child, but a strong internalized belief in "belonging." Others (the valued "in" group leaders) provide cues to indicate what beliefs are in fashion. Contemporary 1969 America seems to continue the trend noted by Riesman.

By Way of Moderation

The ideal types proposed by Riesman are not to be found in reality. Individuals maintain both inner-direction and other-direction, the degree dependent most likely upon the stress experienced by the parents and the generality of the individual's insecurity. Theoretically, the high upward socially mobile will foster other-direction more than the less mobile.

These three types describe those who *adjust* to the dominant cultural theme. Within the *inner-directed* society the *adjusted* person *compulsively* follows his interjected values. He may bend with the demands of his environment, but limits are placed upon his conformity. A gross pressure to change is met with resistance and men die for "principle." The *other-directed,* adjusted *compulsively,* follows the leadership of his reference group. This might mean he will change his dress, recreational, political, sexual and religious behaviors as his reference group changes its fashion.

Two other modes of reaction to the dominant character type possible are *anomie* and *autonomy*. NOTE: The term anomie was invented by Durkheim, an early sociologist, and was defined as a ruleless person. Riesman uses the term to refer to what may be called maladjustment. The anomic might be the ruleless rebel or the overcontrolled, overadjusted person. (See Riesman, 1953, p. 281.) Anomie is the product of an overly tight control of one's social behavior such that the "gyroscope" is tuned to a very narrow ban or the "radarscope" is continually "on." Within the inner-directed anomic person the "super-ego" is so strong that the individual overly represents the character type or he might compulsively rebel against the type. In the former case, the individual is driven by his political or religious values and can be what is called the fanatic. In the latter case he might be a fanatic against his parental values. If the parent is a theist he becomes an atheist, or he becomes a Catholic if the parent is a Protestant, etc.

Anomie within the *other-directed* person might be reflected by the person who is "chameleon like" — he changes his views to express every nuance which the leaders enact. In the case where the "in" group values "sophistication" and a "cool" attitude toward life, the anomic might become apathetic and withdraw from any human feeling.

Autonomy as presented by Riesman parallels what Rogers calls *adjusted*. The individual can accept the dominant mode, but is *not* compulsively driven by his inner values nor the dictates of his peer culture. In a sense, he profits from experience and attempts to cope with changes in his environment. For example, if supernationalism seems to lead to human destruction, he might readily consider some international control agency even though internationalism may be contrary to his early value system and also contrary to the fashionable mode of his peers. Riesman proposed that autonomy is the desired mode of character structure, for regardless of the predominant character type, autonomy permits the individual much wider latitude of choice than the adjusted is able to express. Theoretically autonomy leads to a higher probability that the individual can adapt to gross environmental changes. This is not to say the autonomous person is valueless. He is, however, able to change when the evidence indicates change is *necessary*.

The School and the Inner-Directed Society

The theme of inner-direction is accomplishment. Interpersonal relations are minimized. As an arm of the parents, the school also reflects the middle-class dominant mode. In Riesman's words ". . . school starts relatively late — there are few nursery schools. The teacher's task is largely to train the children in decorum and in intellectual matters." (Riesman, *et al.,* 1953, p. 77).

As universal education develops, the school is charged with the task of teaching middle-class, inner-directed values to lower-class children. Those who conform in speech and drive ascend the socio-economic ladder. Those who do not conform either drop out or are invited to leave. In one sense, the teacher reinforces the child who emulates the middle-class, inner-directed models.

Physical characteristics which typify the inner-directed school include an orderly arrangement of chairs in straight rows often bolted to the floor, and cultural displays (e.g., a picture of the Acropolis), and great sayings (e.g., "Time waits for no man," and "Know ye the truth and the truth shall set ye free") which exhort human industry hanging on the wall.

In essence, children go to school to learn the curriculum and are expected to work.

The School and the Other-Directed Society

Other-direction demands social skills and this is reflected in the school. Children enter school early. Two- to five-year-olds are sent to nursery schools and kindergartens. School is fun and the early school years stress learning to *share* and *cooperate*. The teacher is not a cruel task master, but a pleasant social director who is sure to encourage the isolate to play with others. "Extra-curricular" activities multiply to accommodate further cooperation and round out the student's social self.

Physically the school also changes. Desks are arranged informally and often are movable for small group "interaction." Student work is on the walls rather than classic materials. Few children are held back in grade; therefore a homogeneous age group forms a class unit. The age homogeneity leads to academic heterogeneity, and the teacher is forced to form learning groups.

The teacher is the opinion leader and provides information to the children regarding which opinions and tastes are in vogue. She encourages democratic practices as long as they lead to socialized goals. The emphasis, however, is on the process, not on significant problems. Often the teacher subtly directs the democratic process so that the outcomes reflect a predetermined choice, which again reflects the importance of getting along socially rather than solving real problems.

Support for Riesman's Theory

The Lonely Crowd presents a wealth of elaboration and illustration upon two predominant character types. As ideal types they only partially reflect "reality." Blake (1965) conducted a study to determine whether notions of inner-other direction explain career choice. A survey of University of Alberta students revealed that 92% indicated a career in science was a socially valued occupation. Among 200 high school students who chose physical science as a career, Blake selected the 54 who had a *Strong Vocational Interest Blank* profile most like physical scientists and 54 students with profiles least like physical scientists. Blake hypothesized that students who choose physical science as a career and express interest least like physical scientists are more *other-directed* than students who choose physical science as a career and express interests most like physical scientists. Scores on the *I-O Social Preference Scale* (Kassajian, 1962) were used as indicators of inner- or other-direction. The content of the items used in this scale were, in general, taken from descriptions provided by Riesman (1953) to suggest a typical situation in which inner- and other-directed people would respond differently. Such items included:

It is more desirable
- a. to be popular and well liked by everybody.
- b. to become famous in the field of one's choice or for a particular deed.

Blake found that the non-scientist interest group who chose science as a career, significantly selected items like "to be popular," etc. more often than the scientist interest group. If many continue to enter physical sciences with an other-directed character type, we might find the interests of scientists become more variable. Indeed, future physical scientists might be characterized as socially interested people, or physical scientists might be broken into two categories, e.g., (1) research physical scientist (2) administrative (other-directed) physical scientists.

Educational Implications of Riesman's Notions

America is becoming a middle-class urban society and other-direction is apparently becoming more prevalent. Even though the mass media (especially television) is a force for cultural homogeneity, the prevalence of large numbers provides plurality because almost anyone can find an "in" group.

Consider the "beat" sub-group. Dress is not individual within the group. Sandals, sweatshirts, and jeans are the accepted uniforms of this group. They deviate from the "great adult middle class," but not from their "in" group.

"Mod" groups wear hip-huggers (at least in 1969) and long hair. Each member is reinforced within his group; however, school administrators do not value these modes of dress. Whenever these two "in" groups meet they often clash. Edicts are often handed down by school administrators such as "Cut your hair before you return to school." The strongest "in" group usually wins. Sometimes the administrator backs down, sometimes the "deviant."

If such plurality exists, the teacher might well "turn on a radarscope," not necessarily for purposes to conform, but to determine which group dictates school values. In selecting a school for employment such an analysis can reduce future problems. For example, a teacher who believes that students should work hard and complete homework might be "unhappy" in a school where only "squares," "cubes," (or some other fashionable term which means "outsiders") take books home.

Some administrators expect male teachers to wear a suit and tie at school and female teachers are expected to wear heels and hose. If the teacher dislikes this mode of dress, he or she might wish to look elsewhere for employment.

These illustrations reflect differences within "other-directed" communities. A more violent clash can come when the "other-directed" and "inner-directed" meet. Consider a social studies teacher, Mr. "Y", who has accepted an internationalist's view of the world and also agrees with the recent (1954-1969) Supreme Court's decisions. Let us also say the teacher attends the National Council of Social Studies Teachers for direction regarding the content of his course material. He goes to community "X" to be interviewed for a job. On the outskirts of town Mr. "Y" notices three billboards, each calling for the impeachment of Chief Justice Warren. Upon entering the superintendent's office he notes a number of pictures on the office wall: General Douglas MacArthur, Barry Goldwater, Governor Wallace and a picture of some hooded character. Further investigation should be unnecessary. Mr. "Y" has enough information, and he may as well leave the office and the town. Of course, if Mr. "Y" is anomic he might choose (compulsively) to stay and fight.

Such illustrations exaggerate the differences; however, they are not completely farfetched.

A Return to: $B_a = f\,(P_a, E_{ab}, R_{ba}, rs_{1 \ldots n})\ S_a, C_{ab}, X$

The several notions presented in this chapter can be cast into the quasi-mathematical model introduced in Chapter 4. The model is re-introduced in order to provide a summary construct which ties these diverse data together.

To review:

B_a = the behavior of individual "a" to be explained or predicted;

P_a = potential cognitive, perceptual, and other relevant abilities;

E_{ab} = elements of personality and motivation especially expectations about one's own behavior and probable response of other persons;

R_{ba} = perception, by individual "a," of other persons' (b) expectancies and pressures imposed upon the given individual, "a";

$rs_{1 \ldots n}$ = acquired response repertory that is relevant to the behavior to be explained or predicted (e.g., previous achievement);

S_a = sex-role identification of the individual, "a" and sex-typing of socialized pressures, both of which moderate preceding variables;

C_{ab} = context of behavior, such as community or school setting which provides an institutional framework along with certain experiences and impersonal expectations; or, the setting in which a natural or a laboratory experiment takes place;

X = unaccounted for variations.

Bandura's (1965) study showed that girls do not freely model aggressive responses as frequently as boys. Aggressive modeling behavior (B_a) is apparently moderated by sex-role identification (S_a). Furthermore, Bandura's data indicated that an introduction of a positive incentive increased the number of modeling aggressive responses (B_a). Therefore, the "expectancies about one's own behavior and the probable response of other persons" (E_{ab}) seem to apply to modeling of aggressive responses. Of course, some residual (rs_1) must have been acquired from observation. Otherwise modeling could not follow.

Within the context (C_{ab}) of Bandura's experimental laboratory, aggressive modeling behavior is a function of sex-role identification, elements of motivation and residuals from observation: $B_a = f(P_a, E_{ab}, R_{ba}, rs_1)$ S_a, C_{ab}, X. P_a and R_{ba} were not analyzed. The X might be reduced if:

1. measurement of sex-role identification is more refined, because some girls identify with male roles and some boys identify with female roles. (Nonetheless, sex-role identification is often sufficiently sex specific that prediction can be made with only knowledge of the subjects' sex.)
2. the "reward" is individualized such that all subjects are highly motivated to act.
3. the observed model is important to all subjects (refer to Grusec and Mischel discussed earlier).

In the event that wide cognitive ability variations are present among the experimental sample, knowledge of these variations might be necessary for "effective" prediction of imitation.

Riesman's concepts regarding the acquisition of character types, indicated that types of personality (E_{ab}) can in part be accounted for by the institutions to which individuals are exposed (his history of experience). Blake's investigations into career choice suggested that measured inner- and other-direction plus knowledge of the individual's peer groups' valuation of a particular career (R_{ba}) can in part explain career choice.

Summary and Emphasis

Theory is used within this text as summary concepts which might provide order to the observed diverse human behaviors. Some of these theories deal with micro-systems (e.g., Bandura) and others with macro-systems (Riesman). Analysis in some cases is highly refined and in other cases, crude. These theories are inventions of men and therefore are not "holy" (some however are more hole-ly than others). Of further significance is the fact that attempting to draw upon several theories as a means of describing and predicting behavior is a difficult task. The intent of the previous discussion has not been to oversimplify psychological theory. Instead, it was the intent of the authors to focus the reader's energy in a direction which seems most meaningful to the reader. Educational psychology is not so much a collection of facts as a study of inquiry into educational practices.

The most significant concept presented in this chapter is the notion that acquisition of many response potentials can be accounted for by observation. Performance of the acquired response potential apparently depends upon the "perceived" payoff. Tangible objects such as money, etc., often are sufficient payoffs for action.

Attention to the model, of course, is relevant for response acquisition. If the model is made attractive or important for the observer, then the probability that learning and performance will occur is enhanced.

Moral development is apparently highly dependent upon the models who are available to the child. Soviet character training apparently is more systematically treated in the school when contrasted with the diverse school practices within the United States.

Questions

1. Under what conditions would punishment be an appropriate way to control undesirable behavior? (Be sure to check Bandura's study regarding no consequence to the model.)

2. What books would you select for a group of tenth-grade boys to have available for pleasure reading? List these books. What are the characteristics of the protagonists? If we assume these protagonists are possible models, what values are you tacitly supporting? Are they honesty, aggressiveness, competitiveness, cooperativeness, etc.?

References

Bandura, A. Social learning through imitation. *Nebraska symposium on motivation.* Lincoln: Univer. of Neb. Press, 1962.

Bandura, A. Influence of models' reinforcement contingencies on the acquisition of imitative responses. *J. pers. soc. Psychol.* 1965, 1, 589-595.

Bandura, A., & McDonald, F. J. Influence of social reinforcement and the behavior of models in shaping children's moral judgment. *J. abnorm. soc. Psychol.* 1963, 67, 274-281.

Benedict, Ruth. *Patterns of culture.* Boston: Houghton Mifflin, 1934.

Blake, V. E. *Career choice in science education.* Unpublished doctoral dissertation, Univer. of Alberta, 1965.

Bronfenbrenner, U. Soviet methods of character training. *Religious Educ.,* 1962, 57, (4, Res. Supplement), S45-S61.

Greenspoon, J. The reinforcing effect of two spoken sounds on the frequency of two responses. *Amer. J. Psychol.,* 1955, 68, 409-416.

Grusec, J., & Mischel, W. Model's characteristics as determinants of social learning. *J. Pers. soc. Psychol.,* 1966, 4, 211-214.

Kassarjian, W. M. A study of Riesman's theory of social character. *Sociometry,* 1962, 25, 213-230.

Lefkowitz, M. M., Blake, R. R., & Moulton, Jane. Status factors in pedestrian violation of traffic signals. *J. abnorm. soc. Psychol.,* 1955, 51, 704-706.

Mallick, S. K., & McCandless, B. R. A study of catharsis of aggression. *J. pers. soc. Psychol.,* 1966, 4, 591-596.

Miller, N. E., & Dollard, J. *Social learning and imitation.* New Haven: Yale Univer. Press, 1941.

Piaget, J. *The moral judgment of the child.* Glencoe, Ill. Free Press, 1948.

Riesman, D., Glazer, N., Denney, R. *The lonely crowd,* Garden City, N. Y.: Doubleday, 1953.

References

Technological Consideration 8

Overview

Unlike the previous chapters, this chapter is not concerned with theory. The multi-variate view of human behavior developed within this text suggests that attention to individual differences is not a simple matter. In order to cope with the educational challenge of the future, this chapter presents a number of technological developments which might be used to realize an adequate education for all. First, a brief discussion is devoted to linear programed learning materials. Second, a linear program in descriptive statistics is presented for two reasons: (1) to provide you with first-hand experience with a program; and (2) to complete some notions regarding descriptive statistics which were not presented in other sections of this text. An evaluation of linear and branching programs follows the descriptive statistics program. A suggestion is made that having students work the same linear program at the student's own pace is a weak substitute for individualization. Computer-assisted instruction is also discussed; however, like programed instruction, it can provide the desired individualization only when a multi-disciplinary approach to curricular construction is instituted.

If one reflects upon the content of the previous chapters, one obvious notion should emerge: human behavior is complex and individuals vary in abilities, interests, motivations, values, and achievement. A view of humans through the wrong end of a telescope might suggest humans are highly similar; however, one does not need a microscope to note human differences. Look around in your dorm or classroom. Some are hard workers who receive C's and B's, and others loaf but get the same grades. Some are cynical; others, optimistic. Some like to play and others like to read. To be sure, discovering how these differences emerge might require a microscopic investigation. This text should attest to this point.

The apparent fact that we "really" do not "know" completely why individuals vary need not prevent the teacher from attending to differences which can be noted. Indeed, if one holds a view that human resources need to be conserved, then the inefficiency of education evident in school drop-outs and failures might lead one to re-examine our school practices.

Consider some of our educational practices and the underlying assumptions. Often in our secondary schools the day is broken into six or seven fifty-minute sessions. All students within a class are competing with each other for grades which often conform to a normal distribution curve. Some receive A's and some fail. The content of a particular course of study centers around the learning device called a textbook. In a ninth grade social science course the text might be written at an eighth or ninth grade reading level. This assumes all have attained this reading level. In reality, at least one-sixth have not and one-sixth far excel this specified reading level. Under these circumstances school might be a bore to the "bright" and frustrating to the motivated slow learner. In an effort to account for these variations some schools have initiated a track system. The "brighter" student is assigned to one section, the "average" to two or more sections and the "slow" to another section. (Quotes are used for the descriptive adjectives because the student might not "really" be slow — he might not value the content the school has selected for him.) What happens in the "homogeneous" classrooms? Do the students receive different materials? No! Often the "bright" go through the book rapidly and the "slow" "read" the text at a slower rate! The "slow" must read material that is too difficult and, to wrap up the whole bundle, these students are often expected to perform well on the same tests taken by the "bright" student. The slow learner is doomed to failure! No wonder many choose to leave the schools where all the positive value is usurped by the bright conformer. We wish that we could say this verbal description presents an extreme distortion of most schools; unfortunately the description is eminently typical. Individualization might look good on paper, but in reality most school programs fall far short of the stated goal.

Let us briefly consider the individual child. Theoretically, the child has a number of abilities, acquired interests and values, a response repertory (learnings) and a physical structure. Sometimes he feels like working and other times he does not. Furthermore, he often develops a burning interest in a problem he would like to pursue (epistemic curiosity). Why must he work the same problem at the same time as his age mates? Why must he put aside inquiry just because a bell rings? Apparently a number of factors operate (e.g., historical precedent, economic considerations, school management problems, etc.). This chapter reviews a number of technological developments which have entered the educational scene within the last 10-15 years. Some have promise for greater educational individualization.

Audio-Magnetic Tape and Video-Tape Recorders

The versatility of the audio-tape has finally been realized and is being employed in a number of interesting ways. In modern language laboratories students have the opportunity to hear exemplary speech models and also to record their own speech in the language under study. Comparisons can facilitate auditory discrimination and psychomotor differentiation. Early labs were conducted in groups as a teaching aid, but as recording systems have become less expensive, the break from the old was made. Some students make discriminations readily while others must practice long and hard. Individual carrels have been developed with "dial access" to a central audio input and output. The student can now practice at his own rate. In a sense, a teacher is available to each student and available on demand. Lunch breaks, study periods, etc., provide opportunities for tutoring without overtaxing the non-mechanical teacher. She can have lunch while students learn individually. Not only can the teacher be relieved, but the students can learn at their own rate.

Audio-tapes have other possible uses for individualization. A student who does not attend too well at 8 a.m. might escape the lecture (apparently an inefficient learning technique) and listen when he is fully functioning. Furthermore, primary school children apparently tend to learn more through auditory communication (Budoff and Quinland, 1964). Books as well as lectures can be taped for presentation and replay.

Video tapes are being used more widely. Educational television permits demonstrations difficult to conduct in the classroom. Also, eminent scholars and teachers can be available to a wide audience. Such usage, however, is still *group* oriented. Costs for video-tape recorders are being reduced and learning labs with "dial access" terminals might provide visual information on an individual basis which parallels the audio-tape usage. Students will be able to receive multiple presentations if they so desire.

Programed Learning*

Textbooks with headings and periodic questions are crude programed materials. Because text reading is often a passive activity the attention of the reader might wander even though his eyes scan the material. Programed textual material initially was introduced in relation to the "teaching machine" (Pressey, 1932). This early machine presented questions with multiple choice answers, the correct answer being presented along with misconceptions that seemed tenable. Pressey (1963) maintained that multiple choice answers can promote differentiation. For example a child's response to a question (e.g., 2 x 3 = ? with possible answers 1, 5, and 6) can facilitate differentiation. The operator *x* gives an answer of 6. Faulty differentiation of the mathematical operator (— or +) provide the other answers.

Although the first programed teaching machine was invented well over thirty years ago it did not have any marked influence on American education. The present popularity of programed instruction apparently received its impetus from B. F. Skinner's article "The Science of Learning and the Art of Teaching" (1954). One is almost inclined to say *Bombastic* B. F. since his criticism of preprogramed instruction is indeed devastating. Skinner's criticisms focus upon the ineffective use of "reinforcers" in schools. Skinner maintained that knowledge provided by feedback in the natural world is reinforcing and one needs only to observe the child operating in his free environment for confirmation. In the schools, knowledge acquisition as a reinforcer is available; however, Skinner suggested that school in general becomes aversive due to incomplete success since complex material is not well ordered nor broken into components and this confusion often leads to failure, an aversive

*Early programed learning writers spelled programing with two *m*'s (programming). Because some confusion developed between programming for computers and programed learning, a recent convention has been adopted to spell programing of educational materials with the single *m*. You will note some references use the two *m*'s.

stimulus. How can this state be resolved? Of course, teaching machines! Machines with *well* programed material, *linear programed* material (the term applied to "Skinnerian" type programs).

Efficient linear programs are theoretically constructed with the following factors taken into consideration:

1. Material should be presented in an *ordered sequence* such that the logic of the subject unfolds.
2. Material should be presented in *short steps* (a frame) to minimize errors.
3. The student should *construct responses* for each frame and the response should focus upon significant items. He should make *few errors* so that:
4. *Immediate knowledge of results* can act as a reinforcer.
5. The student should work at his *own pace.* This theoretically allows for individual differences.
6. The behavioral objectives of the program (things the student should be able to do upon task completion) should be known to the student before the program is introduced.

Linear programing has been in many cases developed for presentation *without* the machine. A notable case is Holland and Skinner's *The Analysis of Behavior* (1961), a programed college text covering "operant psychology." The text presents a bit of information and a significant word presented in the frame or a previous frame is left blank. The student is to write his response and then turn the page where a new frame is presented as well as the correct response for the previous frame. A number of frames are presented on one page; however, the sequence is: frame 1, page 1, frame 2, page 2 . . . frame f, page n. The student works through to the end of the section (frame f, page n) then returns to page 1, second frame (f + 1) to continue the sequence.

A further discussion regarding programed instruction is to come. Before you become contaminated, a program of 151 frames covering some notions of descriptive statistics follows.

Descriptive Statistics Program

(A revision upon an original mimeographed program written by Garret Foster, Florida State University. Permission for use granted.)

Objectives: Upon completion of this program you should be able to do a number of things.

1. You should be able to write a short definition for the following terms:
   a. statistics, samples, data, datum, and variable.
   b. measure of central tendency, mean, median and mode.
   c. measures of dispersions, range, average deviation and standard deviation.
   d. types of distribution, normal curve, normal distribution, skewed distribution (positive and negative skew), bimodal distributions.
   e. discrete attributes, continuous attributes, class interval and unit interval.
   f. Bar Graph, Frequency Polygon, Frequency Histogram, Frequency Curve, frequency.
   g. correlation coefficient, scattergram.
   h. f, ΣX, cf, S.D., M, r, and N.
2. Given data, you should be able to complete:
   a. a frequency distribution table (including intervals, observed frequency, and cumulative frequency).
   b. a Frequency Histogram.
   c. a Frequency Polygon.
   d. a scattergram.
3. Given data and formulae, you should be able to calculate:
   a. mean
   b. standard deviation

Directions: The following program includes 151 frames. Each frame has one or more blanks. To the right of the frame is a column with the correct answers. Take a piece of 8½″ x 11″ paper and make three equal folds lengthwise. With this strip, cover the answers on the first page.

Your strip is now in place? You should read the headings and the first frame. Write the word that should fill the blank. (If you plan to keep this book, you might wish to write in the text; otherwise use a separate piece of paper for your writing.) When you finish writing for each frame, move your strip down to check your answer. Follow this procedure for the 151 frames. You may work at your own pace. You might wish to complete the program in two sittings — some students found a natural break after frame 73.

DESCRIPTIVE STATISTICS

Section 1: Introduction	
1. Statistics are numbers which have to do with groups of objects, organisms, or events. Descriptive statistics, then, are (1)________ which describe (2)________ of objects, organisms, or events.	(1) numbers (2) groups
2. A synonym for group is "sample," so we can define (1)________ statistics as numbers which describe groups or (2)________.	(1) descriptive (2) samples
3. Descriptive statistics are (1)________ which (2)________ (3)________ or (4)________.	(1) numbers (2) describe (3) groups (4) samples
4. But how do you describe a sample? Suppose we wanted to describe a group or (1)________ of 15 college students.	(1) sample
5. The first question that arises is "What are the facts?" Or, in scientific terminology, what are the data used to describe the sample? Note that the term "data" is synonymous with the term (1)________, and is (2)________ (plural/singular) in form.	(1) "facts" (2) plural
6. Since the word "data" is plural, you might surmise that "datum" is the (1)________ form, meaning "fact." It is correct to say that the datum (2)________ (is/are) recorded, or the data (3)________ (is/are) recorded.	(1) singular (2) is (3) are

7. To get back to the original question of getting the facts or (1)______________, assume that the following data concerning height (2)______________ (was/were) reported by the sample: 64″, 67″, 63″, 67″, 64″, 63″, 66″, 65″, 64″, 66″, 68″, 68″, 65″, 67″.	(1) data (2) were
8. The first step in describing the group or (1)______________ in terms of heights is to organize these (2)______________ in summary fashion so they can be more easily understood.	(1) sample (2) data

Section 2: Tables

9. The data are usually organized into a frequency table. The (1)______________ table reports the number of times each score occurs in the sample.	(1) frequency
10. In the set of data below, the score of 70 occurs (1)______________ times and therefore has a "frequency" of (2)______________. Data: 61, 63, 63, 69, 70, 70, 71, 74.	(1) 2 (2) 2
11. The data in Table 8.1 are organized in a frequency table. The information given in this table includes: a. Table number (1)________ b. Title (2)____________________________ c. A height column giving the (3)________ in rank order from (4)______ to (5)________ inches. d. A column "f" indicating the (6)________ of the score. e. A column "cf" indicating the (7)________________	(1) 8.1 (2) Frequency Distribution of Heights (3) heights (4) 61 (5) 68 (6) frequency (7) cumulative frequency

11. (*Cont.*)

TABLE 8.1

Frequency Distribution of Height

Height	f(Frequency)	cf(Cumulative Frequency)
68 inches	2	2
67	3	5
66	2	7
65	2	9
64	3	12
63	2	14
62	0	14
61	1	15

12. There are three important facts to note about the height column in Table 8.1 First, the scores or heights are listed in (1)________ (rank/random) order.

TABLE 8.1

Frequency Distribution of Height

Height	f	cf
68 inches	2	2
67	3	5
66	2	7
65	2	9
64	3	12
63	2	14
62	0	14
61	1	15

(1) rank

13. Second, scores or heights which were not observed in this sample were listed and given a frequency of (1)____________(zero/one) as long as they were between the two extreme (2)____________.

TABLE 8.1

Frequency Distribution of Height

Height	f	cf
68 inches	2	2
67	3	5
66	2	7
65	2	9
64	3	12
63	2	14
62	0	14
61	1	15

(1) zero
(2) scores or heights

14. Third, the height (1)__________ (column/row) is listed in unit intervals; that is, intervals of (2)__________(two inches/one inch).	(1) column (2) one inch

TABLE 8.1

Frequency Distribution of Height

Height	f	cf
68 inches	2	2
67	3	5
66	2	7
65	2	9
64	3	12
63	2	14
62	0	14
61	1	15

15. "One" and "Unit" mean the same thing, so an interval of one inch, one pound, one year, or one anything is called a (1)__________ interval.	(1) unit
16. On the other hand, intervals of 4 inches, 10 lbs., or 2 years are all (1)__________ (class/unit) intervals because they extend over 2 or more units of measurement. For example, in Table 8.2, (2)__________ __________of (3) __________(4/5) units have been used rather than unit (4) __________.	(1) class (2) class intervals (3) 5 (4) intervals

TABLE 8.2

Distribution of I.Q. Data

I.Q.	f	cf
125.5-130.5	1	1
120.5-125.5	2	3
115.5-120.5	5	8
110.5-115.5	3	11
105.5-110.5	2	13
100.5-105.5	1	14
95.5-100.5	1	15

17. If the second column heading, f, stands for frequency, then the third column heading, cf, stands for cumulative (1)________. The frequency column tells us the number of people of a given height and the (2) ________frequency tells us how many people fell at or above a given height.	(1) frequency (2) cumulative

TABLE 8.1

Frequency Distribution of Height

Height	f	cf
68 inches	2	2
67	3	5
66	2	7
65	2	9
64	3	12
63	2	14
62	0	14
61	1	15

18. We can tell from the data below that the blank in the frequency column of Table 8.1 should be filled with (1)________ and the blank in the cumulative column should be filled with (2)________. Data: 64, 61, 63, 67, 67, 64, 63, 66, 65, 64, 66, 68, 68, 65, 67.	(1) 2 (2) 15

TABLE 8.1

Frequency Distribution of Height

Height	f	cf
68 inches	2	2
67	3	5
66	—	7
65	2	9
64	3	12
63	2	14
62	0	14
61	1	—

19. Now that the height data has been organized in a (1)________ ________, let's look at the grades for a group or (2)________. The following semester averages were recorded: 60, 66, 69, 70, 75, 76, 77, 77, 77, 77, 80, 81, 84, 88, 90, 94.	(1) frequency table (2) sample
20. We could use unit (1)________ in organizing these data, as in Table 8.1. We need not complete the table since it is obvious that the use of unit intervals (2)________ (is/is not) efficient when you have more than 10 or 15 different unit intervals.	(1) intervals (2) is not

TABLE 8.3
Distribution of Grades

Score	f	cf
60	1	1
61	0	1
62	0	1
63	0	1
64	0	1
65	0	1
66	1	2
etc.	etc.	etc.

21. Grouping unit intervals into class intervals is not only (1)________ (more/less) efficient, but is often a more meaningful way to organize the (2)________.	(1) more (2) data
22. For example, in Table 8.4 below, we have used (1)________ intervals which are more (2)________ and efficient to assign letter grades rather than numerical scores.	(1) class (2) meaningful

TABLE 8.4
Grade Distribution for Sample X

Score	Grade	f	cf
92-100	A	1	1
83-91	B	3	4
74-82	C	7	11
65-73	D	3	14
56-64	F	1	15

23. Likewise, the following I.Q. scores are best organized in a (1)________ distribution with seven (2)________ intervals: 99, 102, 106, 110, 111, 113, 113, 116, 118, 118, 118, 119, 121, 122, 126.	(1) frequency (2) class

TABLE 8.2

Distribution of I.Q. Data

I.Q.	f	cf
125.5-130.5	1	1
120.5-125.5	2	3
115.5-120.5	5	8
110.5-115.5	3	11
105.5-110.5	2	13
100.5-105.5	1	14
95.5-100.5	1	15

Section 3: Graphs

24. Once we have organized the data into a frequency (1)________, we can describe the sample graphically by drawing a (2)________ (graph/table) of the distribution.	(1) distribution or table (2) graph
25. While the purpose of a frequency table is to (1)________ (organize/record) the data, the purpose of a *graph* or *diagram* is to present a clear and simple picture which can be understood at a glance.	(1) organize
26. For example, the diagram or (1)________ below gives a clear (though not complete) picture describing the sample in terms of grades. To complete the diagram we would represent the three B's in the sample by drawing a bar over the B interval to the same height as the (2)________ (F/D) bar. Sample: 95, 90, 87, 85, 81, 81, 79, 78, 77, 77, 73, 71, 69, 67, 57.	(1) graph (2) D

26. (*Cont.*)

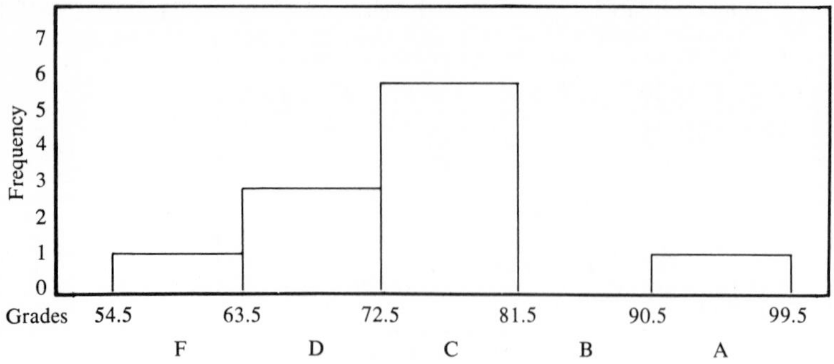

FIGURE 8.1

Frequency Histogram or Bar Graph of Grade Distribution.

27. Just as tables have a specific table number, diagrams have a specific (1)________ number. Looking at the diagram, you can see that unlike table numbers, diagram or figure numbers appear at the (2)________ of the diagram, and are followed by the title.	(1) diagram or figure (2) bottom

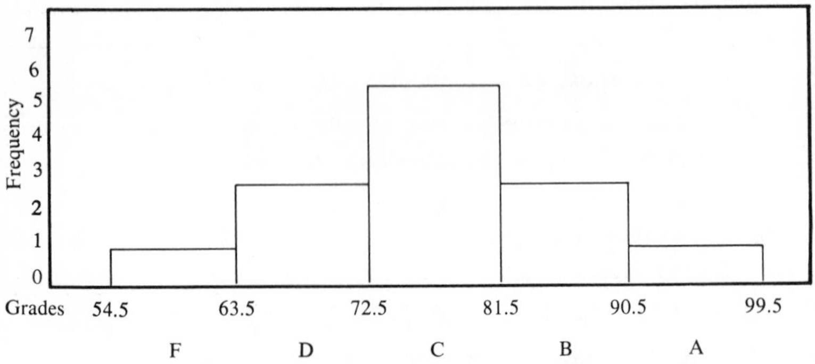

FIGURE 8.1

Frequency Histogram or Bar Graph of Grade Distribution.

28. By reading the title below the figure, you know that this kind of diagram is called a Frequency (1)________, or simply a (2) ________ Graph.	(1) Histogram (2) Bar

28. (*Cont.*)

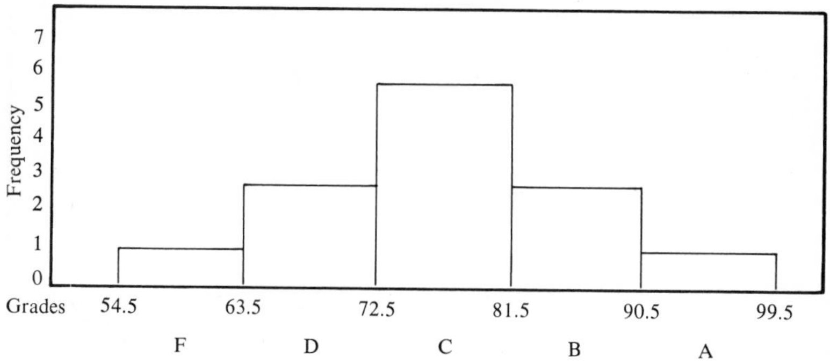

FIGURE 8.1

Frequency Histogram or Bar Graph of Grade Distribution.

29. The Bar Graph, or (1)________ ________ has two scales, a base-line scale for (2) ________ and a vertical scale for (3) ________.	(1) Frequency Histogram (2) scores (grades in this case) (3) frequency

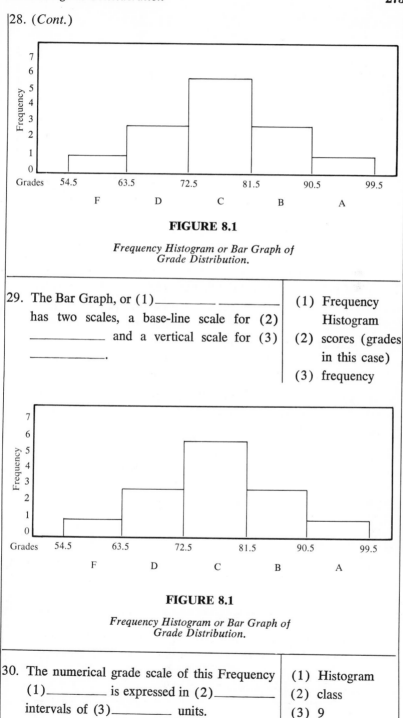

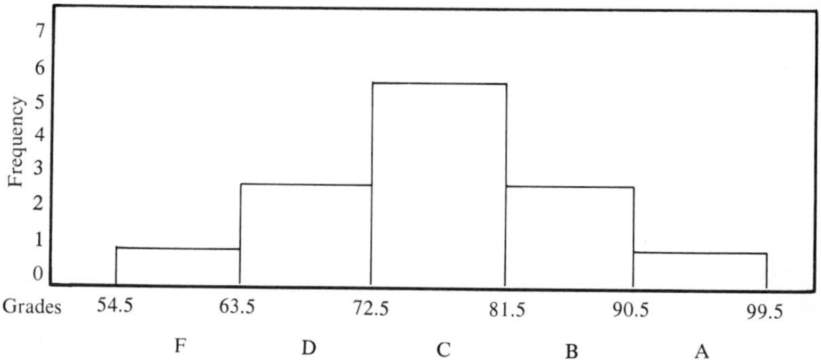

FIGURE 8.1

Frequency Histogram or Bar Graph of Grade Distribution.

30. The numerical grade scale of this Frequency (1)________ is expressed in (2)________ intervals of (3)________ units.	(1) Histogram (2) class (3) 9

30. (*Cont.*)

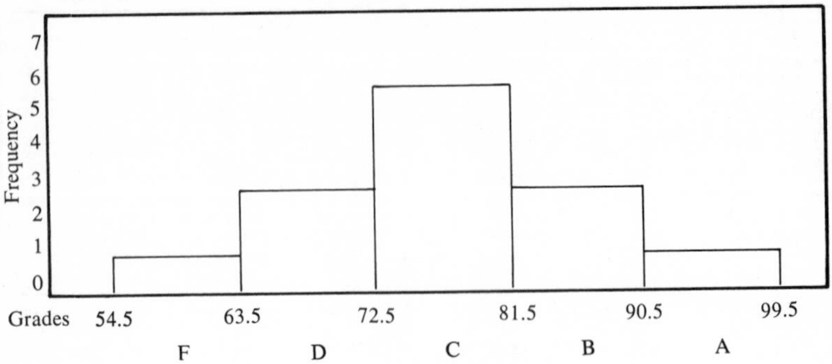

FIGURE 8.1

Frequency Histogram or Bar Graph of Grade Distribution.

31. It was previously pointed out that the purpose of graphs or (1)________ is to present a clear and simple (2)________ which can be understood at a glance.	(1) diagrams (2) picture
32. However, as you can see from Figure 8.2, it is (1)________(easy/difficult) to present a clear picture comparing two samples in one Frequency Histogram or (2)________ ________.	(1) difficult (2) Bar Graph

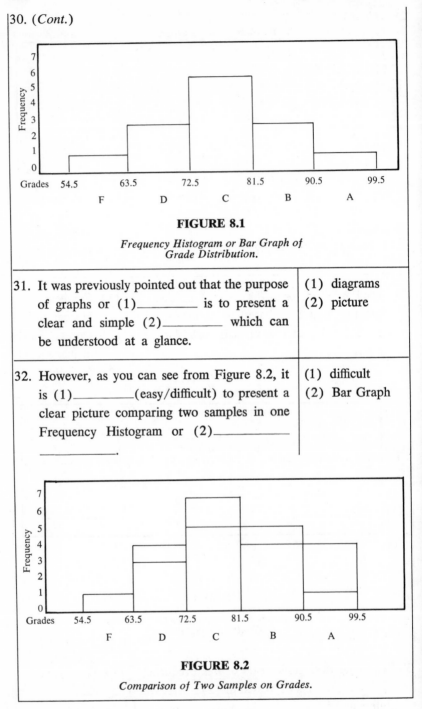

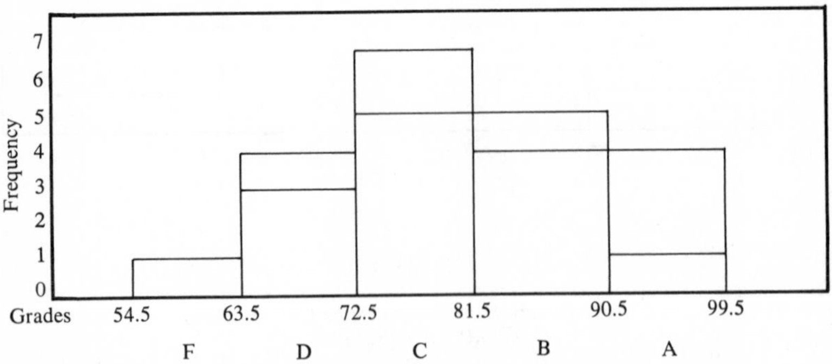

FIGURE 8.2

Comparison of Two Samples on Grades.

33. In order to compare two or more (1)______ we use a Frequency Polygon rather than a Frequency (2)________.	(1) samples (2) Histogram
34. Actually, there are many instances other than those of comparison when it is appropriate to use a (1)________ Polygon, and the (2) _______ ________ can always be used as an alternative to the Frequency Histogram.	(1) Frequency (2) Frequency Polygon
35. In fact, any Frequency Histogram can easily be converted into a (1)_______ _______ by connecting the (2)________ (midpoints/ endpoints) of the bars or class intervals.	(1) Frequency Polygon (2) midpoints

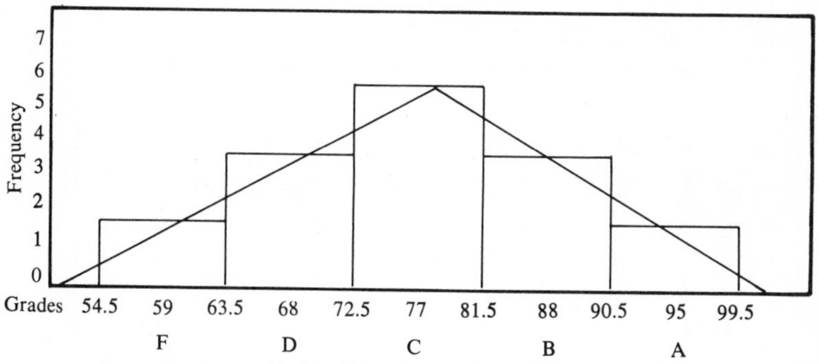

FIGURE 8.3

Frequency Histogram Converted into a Frequency Polygon.

36. Of course, the bars are not ordinarily drawn in a (1)_______ _______, and the upper and lower class interval limits are replaced by the (2)________ of the class intervals.	(1) Frequency Polygon (2) midpoints

36. (*Cont.*)

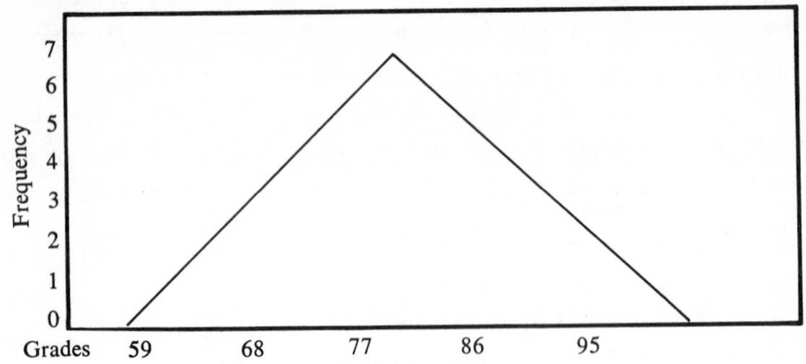

FIGURE 8.4

Frequency Polygon of Grade Distribution.

37. The diagram below illustrates the advantage of the (1)________ Polygon over the (2) ________ ________ in making comparisons of two or more samples.	(1) Frequency (2) Frequency Histogram

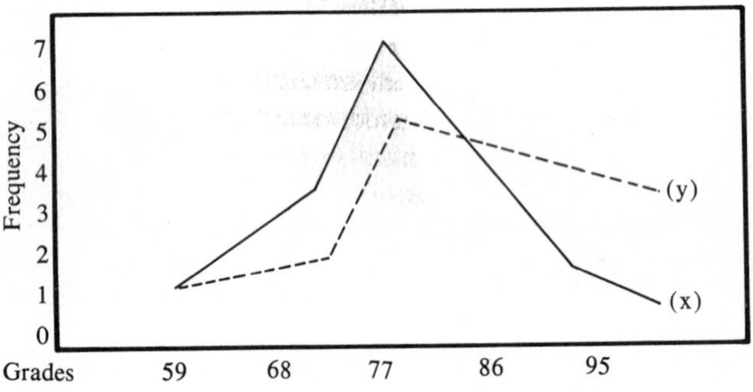

FIGURE 8.5

Comparison of Grade Distribution of Samples X and Y.

38. Besides the Frequency (1)________ and (2)________ ________, there is yet another type of (3)________ (diagram/table) used to present frequency distributions, i.e., the Frequency Curve.	(1) Histogram (2) Frequency Polygon (3) diagram

39. As you can see, a (1)________ Curve is simply a (2)________ (curved/straight) line drawn to fit the distribution.	(1) Frequency (2) curved
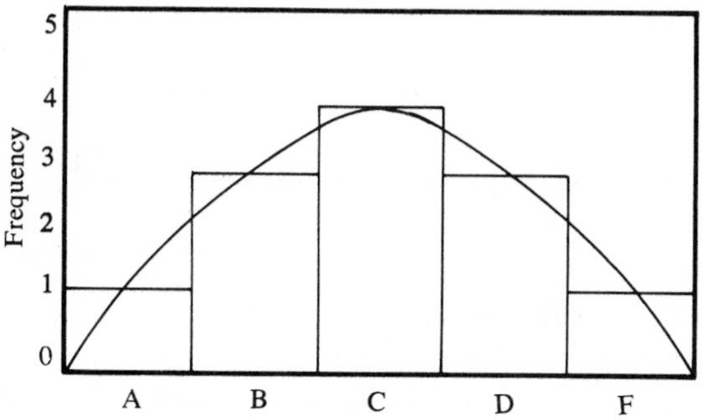 **FIGURE 8.6** *Frequency Curve for Grade Distribution.*	
40. The Frequency (1)________ is usually used to describe a larger or theoretical population.	(1) Curve
41. The advantage of the (1)________ ________ is that it takes into account the fact that many attributes are "continuous" rather than "discrete."	(1) Frequency Curve
42. Discrete characteristics are those which can be represented precisely in whole units. For example, the most precise way to represent a characteristic such as number of children is to count them in (1)________ (whole/fractional) units of one, two, three, etc. Thus, number of children is a (2)________ characteristic.	(1) whole (2) discrete
43. The best way to represent (1)________ characteristics is with a (2)________ ________ such as the one below.	(1) discrete (2) Frequency Histogram

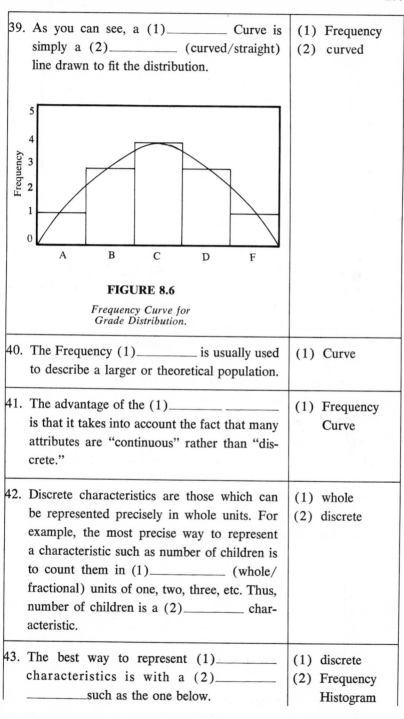

43. (*Cont.*)

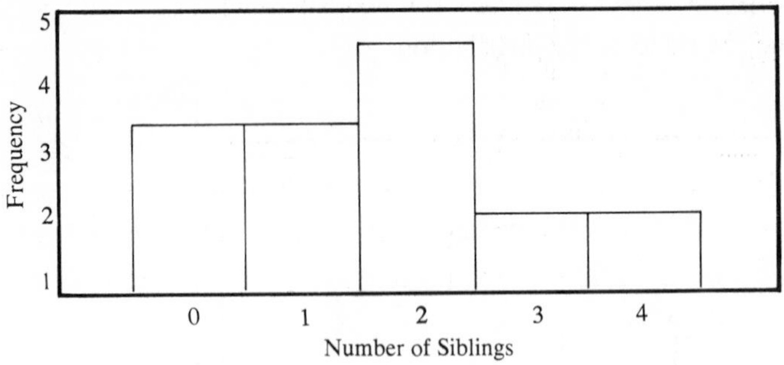

FIGURE 8.7
Number of Siblings in Fifteen Upper Class Families.

44. On the other hand, many characteristics are "continuous." For instance, while a family grows in whole or (1)________ units and is increased by one with the arrival of a new infant, each member of the family physically grows (2)________ by such a slow process that change can only be measured over a period of time even though this change is continuous.	(1) discrete (2) continuously
45. Thus, the most accurate way to represent a (1)________ characteristic, as opposed to a non-continuous characteristic, is to plot a continuous Frequency (2)________ on which all possible scores are represented at their approximate frequencies.	(1) continuous (2) Curve

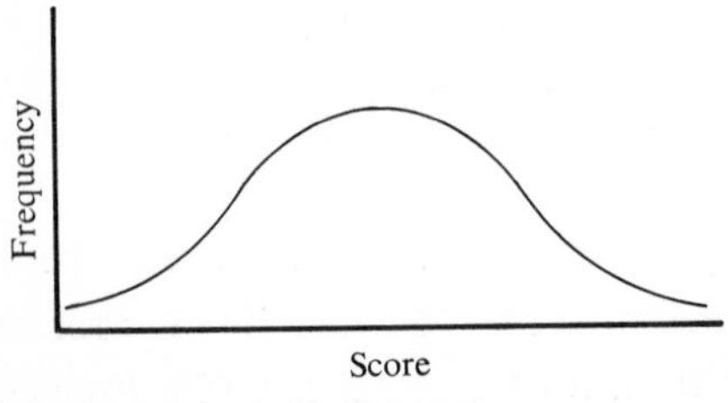

FIGURE 8.8

46. To review briefly, we have seen that the first step in describing a sample is to organize the (1)________ (students/data) into a (2) ________ ________.

(1) data
(2) frequency table or frequency distribution

47. Next, we discussed three ways by which a frequency distribution can be graphically represented.

(1) Histogram
(2) Polygon
(3) Curve

1.

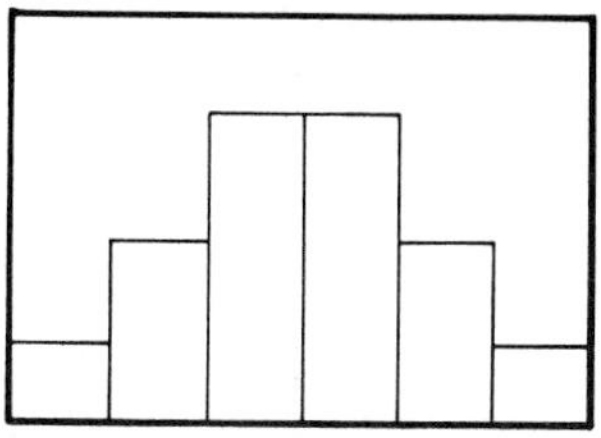

FIGURE 8.9

(1) Frequency__________
(2) Frequency__________
(3) Frequency__________

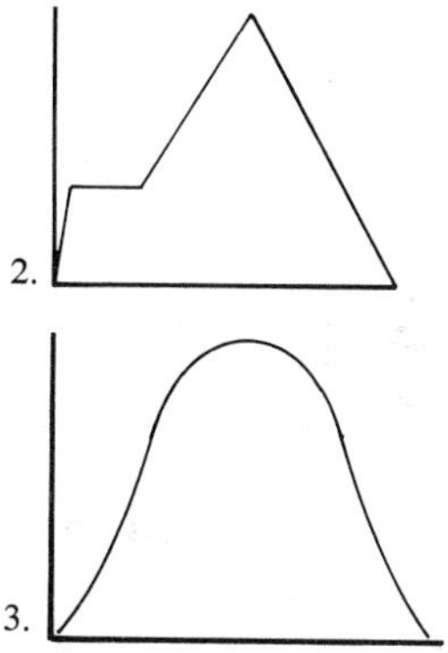

48. Now let us consider three aspects which characterize any and all (1)________ distributions.

a. Shape
b. Central Tendency
c. Dispersion

(1) frequency

Section 4: Frequency Distributions. General Shape

49. Looking at the (1)________ Curves below, we can see that they differ markedly in general (2)________.

(1) Frequency
(2) shape

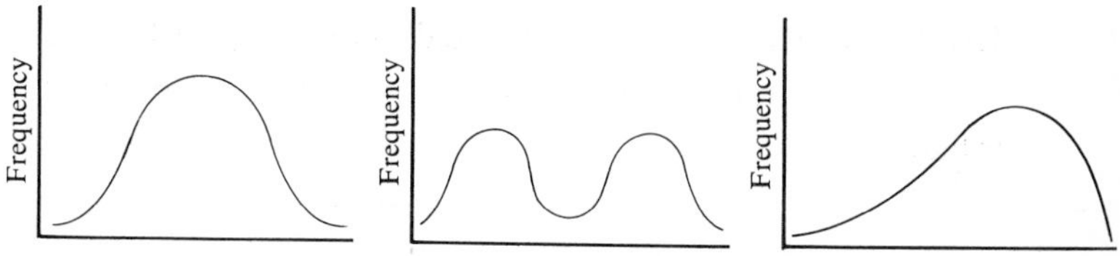

FIGURE 8.10

50. The bellshaped curve is called a "normal" frequency curve and describes a "normal" distribution. Note that the highest frequency, i.e., the "mode," is at the (1)________(end/middle) of the curve and parts A and B (2)________ (are/are not) symmetrical as they taper off toward the extremes. 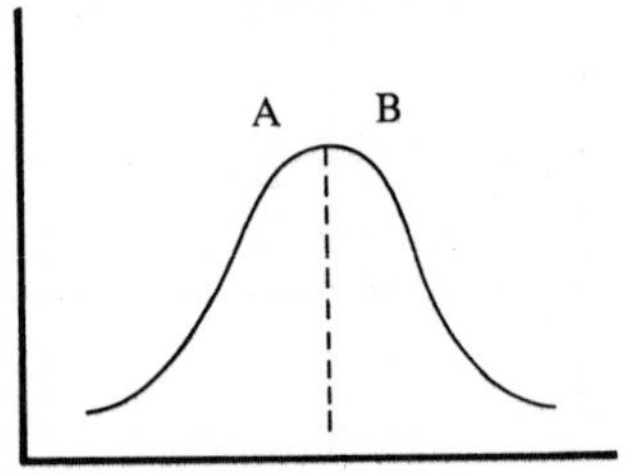 **FIGURE 8.11**	(1) middle (2) are
51. The (1)________ frequency curve is very common because many characteristics are normally distributed; i.e., most people are about average in regard to a given characteristic. But we (2)________ (do/do not) find some who are above average and some who are below average and a few at each extreme.	(1) normal (2) do
52. There are, of course, exceptions to this rule; i.e., not all characteristics are (1)________ distributed.	(1) normally
53. A few characteristics have a "bimodal" (1) ________ rather than a (2)________ distribution.	(1) distribution (2) normal

54. The prefix "bi" means two (e.g., a unicycle has one wheel and a *bi*cycle has two wheels). Therefore, a bimodal distribution has (1) ________ peaks or modes instead of one peak or (2)________ as in the normal distribution.	(1) two (2) mode
55. The height data on our sample represented in Figure 8.12 provides an example of a (1) ________ distribution although height has a normal distribution in the population at large. As you might suspect, the first peak represents the average or mode for girls while the second peak represents the average or (2)________ for boys in our sample. 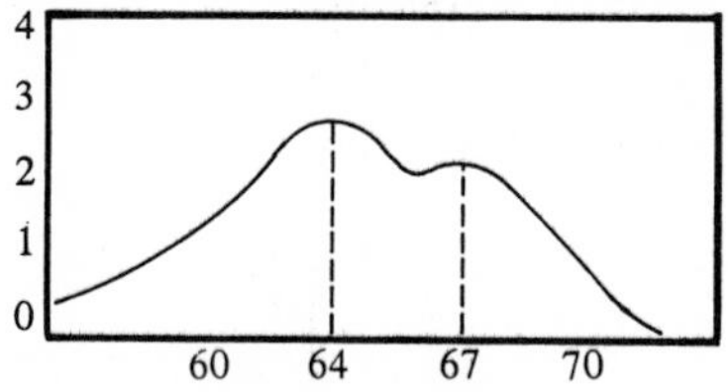 **FIGURE 8.12**	(1) Bimodal (2) mode
56. Any frequency curve which has two separate peaks, even if they are not of equal height or frequency, is considered (1)________. 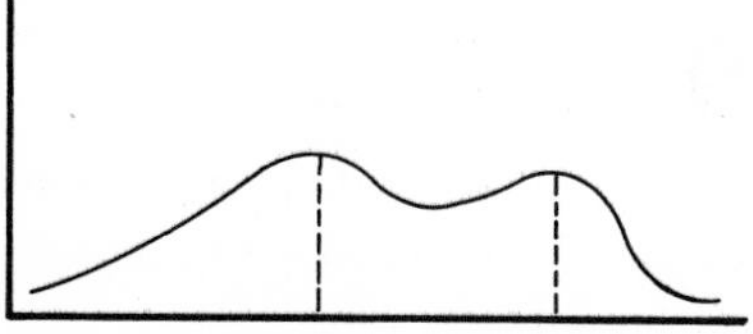 **FIGURE 8.13**	(1) bimodal

57. A third shape not uncommon among distribution curves is the "skewed" distribution. This distribution has one (1)________, but, unlike the normal curve, it (2)________ (is/is not) symmetrical. 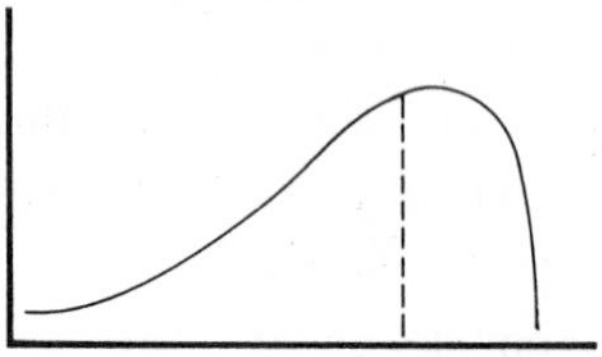 **FIGURE 8.14**	(1) peak or mode (2) is not
58. Notice that the scores pile up at one extreme but are sparse along the other extreme or "tail." It is this long "tail" which marks the frequency curve with (1)________ distribution. The tail on the left is called negatively skewed. 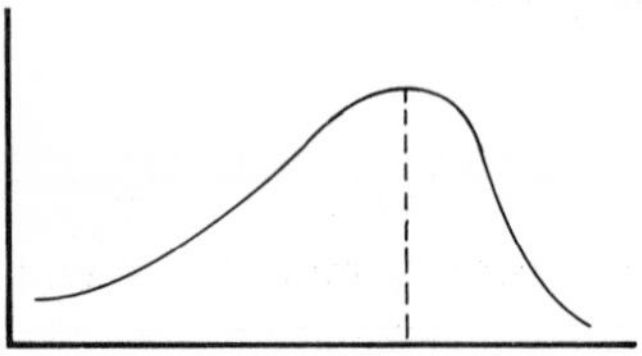 **FIGURE 8.15**	(1) skewed
59. A distribution can be either positively or negatively skewed. It is also said that the distribution is skewed right or skewed left. A distribution is named by the direction in which the tail is found. Distribution A is (1)________ skewed or skewed (2)________ and distribution B is (3)________ skewed or skewed (4)________.	(1) positively (2) right (3) negatively (4) left

59. (*Cont.*)

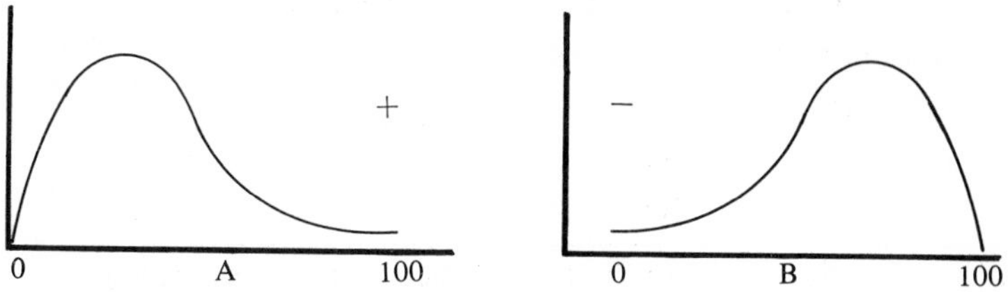

FIGURE 8.16

60. Looking at the (1)________ (Histogram/ Polygon) below, you would conclude that it is (2)________ ________.	(1) Histogram (2) positively skewed

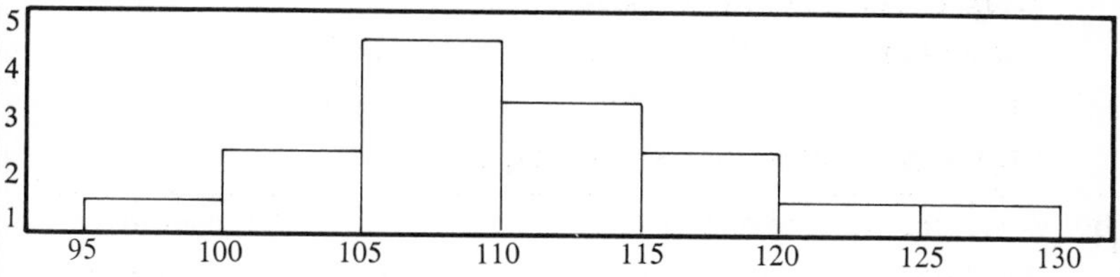

FIGURE 8.17

Distribution of IQ Scores in Sample X.

61. To summarize, the bellshaped or (1)________ distribution curve is most common, but some frequency distributions are (2)________ and still others are (3)________.	(1) normal (2) bimodal (or skewed) (3) skewed (or bimodal)

Section 5: Measures of Central Tendency

62. Another aspect of the frequency distribution which can be described statistically is that of central (1)________. In other words, it is important to know where the scores tend to center or cluster on the baseline scale.	(1) tendency

63. Measures of (1)_________ tendency are commonly known as "averages." There are three important kinds of averages: 1. Mean 2. Median 3. Mode	(1) central
64. The "mode" refers to the score which occurs most frequently in a given distribution: 65, 75, 60, 85, 65, 80, 75, 65. The (1)________ in the above distribution is (2)________.	(1) mode (2) 65
65. The bimodal distribution of height below demonstrates that there (1)________ (can/cannot) be two or more modes in a given distribution. The two modes in the height distribution are (2)____________ and (3)____________. Height: 61, 63, 63, 64, 64, 64, 65, 65, 66, 66, 67, 67, 67, 68.	(1) can (2) 64 (3) 67
66. A second measure of (1)________ ________, the "median," is that value in a ranked distribution which has half the scores above it and half the scores (2)________ it.	(1) central tendency (2) below
67. In some cases, the median value coincides with one of the observed scores. For instance, given the scores 1, 3, 4, 5, 6, 8, 9, the (1) ________ value would be (2)________.	(1) median (2) 5
68. The median does not always coincide with one of the observed scores. Remembering that the median is that score which has the same number of scores above and below it, we see that, if we have an even number of scores, as in the distribution 7, 8, 9, *10, 14,* 15, 16, 17, there is no single middle score. The median, in this case in found by averaging the "two" middle scores, and for this distribution, the median is (1)________.	(1) 12

69. In other instances the (1)________ will lie halfway between two adjacent scores. For the data 2, 2, 3, 4, 5, 6, 6, 6, the point above which four scores fall and below which four scores fall is (2)________ (4/4.5).	(1) median (2) 4.5
70. The most common and most useful measure of (1)________ ________ is the "mean." The (2)________ is calculated by adding all the scores in the distribution and dividing this sum by the number of scores in the distribution. The "mean" is the familiar average.	(1) central tendency (2) mean
71. The formula for the calculation of the mean is $M = \frac{\Sigma X}{N}$ where $M =$ the (1)________ $\Sigma =$ the sum $X =$ the scores $N =$ the number of scores Thus, "ΣX" means the (2)________ of the (3)________.	(1) mean (2) sum (3) scores
72. 1, 0, 5, 2, 2, 4, 6, 4 For the data above the sum of the scores (ΣX) = (1)________, the number of scores (N) = (2)________, and the mean (M) = (3)________.	(1) 24 (2) 8 (3) 3
73. The mean is the most useful average because it is the most stable from group to group and it is useful in further statistical calculations. However, the two other averages, i.e., the (1)________ and the (2)________, are also useful in describing our sample.	(1,2) median and mode

Section 6: Measures of Dispersion	
74. Measures of central tendency tell us where the scores tend to pile up. Measures of (1) ________, on the other hand, tell us the extent to which the scores cluster closely around the mean or deviate away from the (2)________.	(1) dispersion (2) mean
75. The two curves below illustrate what is meant by dispersion of scores. While the mean is the same in both samples, the (1)________ of scores around the mean is quite different. That is, the scores are more widely spread out or dispersed in (2)________ (Curve A/Curve B). 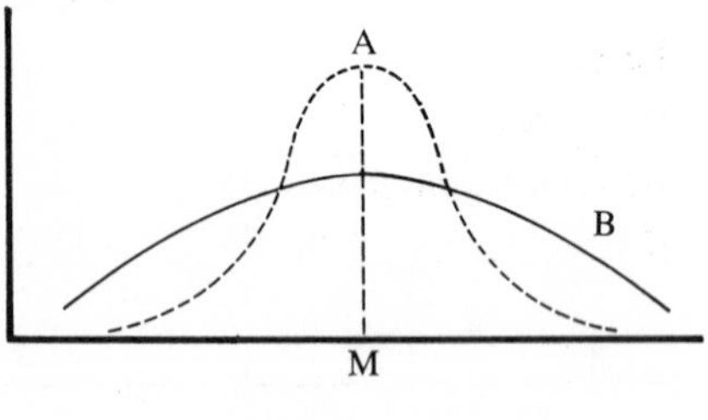 **FIGURE 8.18**	(1) dispersion or distribution (2) Curve B
76. The range is the most simple of the various measures of (1)________. It represents the distance along the baseline scale between the highest and lowest score in the distribution and is calculated by subtracting the lowest score from the (2)________ score in the distribution.	(1) dispersion (2) highest
77. The range for the height distribution below is (1)________ inches.	(1) 7

77. (*Cont.*)

TABLE 8.5

Height	*Frequency*
68	2
67	3
66	2
65	2
64	3
63	2
62	0
61	1

78. Although the (1)________ is an important measure of (2)________, it is not adequate for two reasons.

(1) range
(2) dispersion.

79. First, the range takes into account only the extreme (highest and lowest) scores. For instance, by changing only one height score, below, the range is (1)________ (doubled/tripled) in distribution B.

TABLE 8.6

Distribution A	*Distribution B*
68	75
67	67
66	66
65	65
64	64
63	63
62	62
61	61

(1) doubled

80. Secondly, the (1)________ is not an entirely adequate measure of dispersion because it (2)________ (does/does not) take the intermediate scores into account.

(1) range
(2) does not

81. For instance, while the two distributions below have the same (1)________, the spread or (2)________ of the intermediate scores around the mean is quite different.

(1) range
(2) dispersion

81. (*Cont.*) 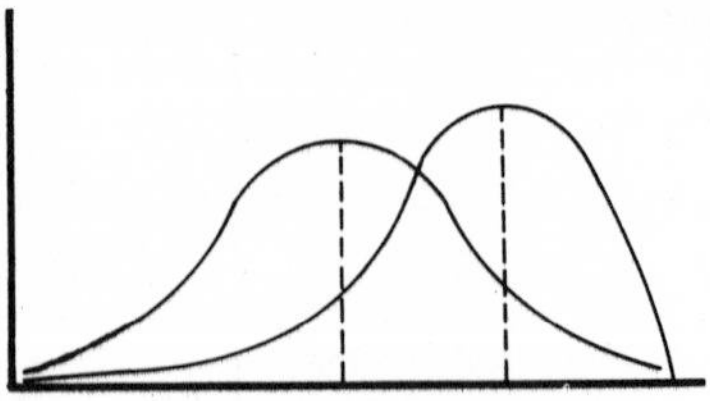 FIGURE 8.19	
82. A more useful measure of (1)________, then, would be one which is based on all the scores in the distribution.	(1) dispersion
83. One such measure, the average deviation, is based on the *deviations* of all the scores from the mean of the distribution. As you might surmise, the greater the number and extent of the (1)________ from the mean, the greater the dispersion.	(1) deviations
84. To illustrate the relationship of (1)________ (deviations/differences) from the mean with dispersion, let us consider two hypothetical distributions.	(1) deviations
85. In the first situation, all of the scores are three: 3, 3, 3, 3, 3. Obviously, the mean is (1)________, there are no deviations from the mean, and there is (2)________ (little/no) dispersion.	(1) 3 (2) no
86. Consider a second hypothetical distribution: 1, 2, 3, 4, 5. There are (1)________ deviations from the mean in this distribution and, accordingly, the degree of dispersion is (2)________(high/low) in comparison with our first example.	(1) 4 (2) high

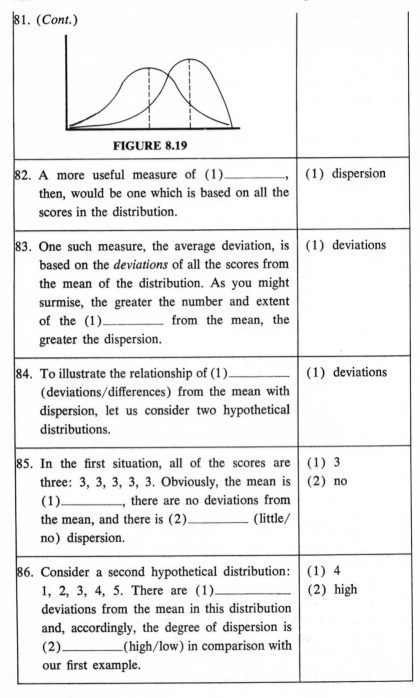

87. One way to measure dispersion is to take an average of all the deviations from the (1) ________. This will give us the (2)________ Deviation or A.D. For example: given the scores 1, 2, 3, 6, 8, the mean is (3)________. 1 deviates 3 points from the mean; 2 deviates 2 points from the mean; 3 deviates 1 point from the mean; 6 deviates 2 points from the mean and 8 deviates 4 points from the mean. There are 5 deviations from the mean and the sum of these deviations is 12. Therefore the *Average* Deviation is (4)________.	(1) mean (2) Average (3) 4 (4) 12/5 or 2.4
88. The Average Deviation (A.D.), though it is easily understood and computed, is seldom used in statistics. It serves the purpose, however, of introducing the most important measure of dispersion, the S.D. or Standard (1) ________.	(1) Deviation
89. The Standard Deviation is based on the squared (1)________ of each score from the mean.	(1) deviation
90. Thus, the (1)________ Deviation is also a measure of the amount of dispersion or deviation of scores from the (2)________.	(1) Standard (2) mean
91. A large (1)________ ________, then would indicate a high degree of dispersion of scores. For example, there is a high degree of (2) ________ in set (3)________ (A/B) below. Set A: 91, 107, 101, 134, 84, 61, 148. Set B: 102, 98, 99, 104, 96, 101, 110.	(1) Standard Deviation (2) dispersion (3) A

92. A small (1)________ ________ indicates that the scores cluster tightly around the mean, as illustrated by curve (2)________ (A/B).	(1) Standard Deviation (2) B

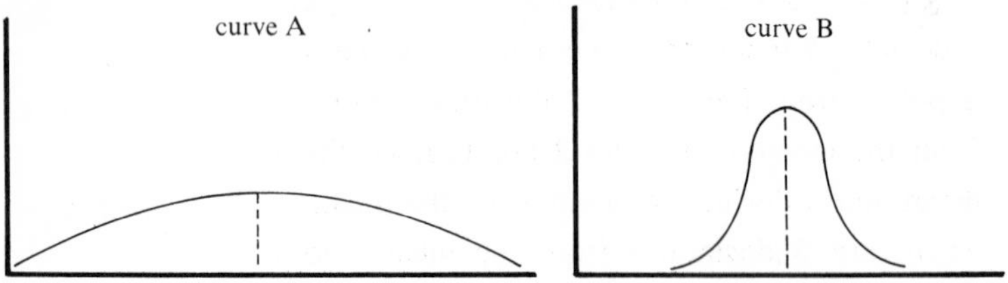

FIGURE 8.20

93. The formula for the (1)________ ________ or S.D. is S.D. $= \sqrt{\frac{\Sigma(X-M)^2}{N}}$ where X = an individual score, M = the mean, Σ = the sum of, N = the number of (2)________. $\sqrt{\ }$ = the square root of.	(1) Standard Deviation (2) scores
94. The quantity $\Sigma(X-M)^2$ or the (1)________ of the (2)________ (squared/cubed) deviations from the mean for the three scores given below is (3)________.	(1) sum (2) squared (3) 2

X	M	$(X-M)$	$(X-M)^2$
1	2	−1	+1
2	2	0	0
3	2	+1	+1
			?

95. It is important to note that the square of the negative or positive number is always positive. Thus, the square of −1 is (1)________ (−1/+1) and the square of −2 is (2) ________.	(1) +1 (2) +4

96. According to the formula, once we have obtained the (1)______________of the squared deviations, we divide it by the (2)________ of scores.

$$S.D. = \sqrt{\frac{\Sigma(X - M)^2}{N}}$$

(1) sum
(2) number

97. Finally, the radical ($\sqrt{}$) indicates that we take the (1)______________ (square/cube) root of $\frac{\Sigma(X - M)^2}{N}$

(1) square

98. Working through the following example should clear up any misconceptions about the calculation of the S.D. the blank in the deviation column should be filled with (1)________. Since all squared numbers are positive, the missing squared deviation would be (2) ________, and $\Sigma(X - M)^2 =$ (3)________.

TABLE 8.7

Calculation of S.D.

X	M	$(X-M)$	$(X-M)^2$
1	3	—	—
2	3	−1	1
3	3	0	0
4	3	1	1
5	3	2	4
		$\Sigma(X - M)^2 =$	?

(1) −2
(2) +4
(3) 10

99. The sum of the squared deviations calculated from Table 8.7 is 10, and N equals (1) ______________, so $\frac{\Sigma(X - M)^2}{N}$ = (2) ______________.

(1) 5
(2) 2

100. Substituting these values into the formula we find that the (1)______________ ______________ is $\sqrt{\frac{10}{5}} = \sqrt{2} = 1.41$.

(1) Standard Deviation

101. The purpose of this section, in brief, has been to acquaint you with measures of (1) ______ such as (2) ______, Average (3) ______, and (4) ______ ______.	(1) dispersion (2) range (3) Deviation (4) Standard Deviation
Section 6: Correlation	
102. Before we can define the term "correlation," it is first necessary to (1) ______ the term "variable."	(1) define
103. The term "variable" may be applied to any characteristic which changes or varies in amount, either within a given individual from time to time, or between individuals, some having more and some having less of the characteristic or (1) ______	(1) variable
104. Height would be an example of a (1) ______ since a person's height (2) ______ over time as he grows older, and different people will vary in their height.	(1) variable (2) changes or varies
105. Because the term (1) ______ implies (2) ______ or variation, it will be used in preference to the term "characteristic."	(1) "variable" (2) change
106. The statistical technique by which we describe relationships between two (1) ______ is known as correlation.	(1) variables
107. Breaking the word "correlate" down, we find that the prefix "co" means "with." Thus, to (1) ______ relate two variables is to relate one (2) ______ with the other.	(1) co (2) variable

108. But how do variables (1)________ with one another? Remember that we defined the word "variable" in terms of characteristics which change or (2)________.	(1) relate or correlate (2) vary
109. Variables are said to be related with one another, or (1)________, if they co-vary or change with one another. For example, height and weight are correlated because our weight and height tend to increase *together* as we grow older, i.e., as height increases, weight (2)________ also.	(1) correlated (2) increases
110. Thus, (1)________ is a measure of the extent to which two variables (2) ________ together or co-(3)________.	(1) correlation (2) change (vary) (3) vary
111. That is, if two variables are (1)________, then when one variable changes, the other variable also (2)________.	(1) correlated (2) changes
112. Likewise, if two variables are (1)________, when one variable changes, the other (2)________ or (3)________.	(1) correlated (2) increases (3) decreases
113. There are two important aspects of correlation: 1. Direction of correlation a. positive b. negative 2. Strength of (1)________.	(1) correlation
114. A correlation is said to be positive in direction if the two variables change in the same direction. For instance, the correlation between height and weight is (1)________ because an increase in height is usually accompanied by an (2)________ in weight.	(1) positive (2) increase

115. The correlation between I.Q. and grades is (1)__________ since students with high I.Q. scores usually receive (2)______ grades and those with low I.Q. scores often make (3)______ grades in school. grades in school.	(1) positive (2) high (3) low
116. On the other hand, when two variables change in opposite directions, the correlation is said to be negative. Test anxiety and test performance usually have a (1)________ correlation since the higher the level of test anxiety, the lower the test score and the lower the anxiety level the (2)________ the test score.	(1) negative (2) higher
117. The "strength" of a correlation refers to the consistency with which the two variables co-(1)__________. If every time one variable changes, the other variable consistently changes in proportion, the two variables are said to be (2)__________ (highly/slightly) correlated.	(1) vary (2) highly
118. Suppose we want to measure the relationship between the two variables height and weight in a group of 10 students. That is, we want to (1)__________ these two (2) __________ or characteristics.	(1) correlate (2) variables
119. Note the consistency with which the two variables co-vary.	

TABLE 8.8

Student	A	B	C	D	E	F	G	H	I	J
Height	58″	60″	62″	64″	68″	70″	72″	74″	76″	78″
Weight	90	102	100	120	140	155	170	180	190	200

119. (*Cont.*) That is, the higher the height score, the (1) ________ the weight score in almost every instance. Height and weight, then, co-vary in the (2)________ (same/opposite) directions, and this trend is obviously very consistent.	(1) higher (2) same
120. Therefore, we would say that there is a very strong or (1)________ (high/low) correlation between height and weight and that the correlation is (2)________ (positive/negative) in direction.	(1) high (2) positive
121. With the knowledge of a student's height, then we (1)________ (could/could not) predict or foretell his weight (and vice-versa) with a fair degree of accuracy.	(1) could
122. Below is an example of another strong or (1)________ (high/low) correlation in a negative direction. Student: 1 2 3 4 5 Grade: A B C D E Absenses: 0 2 5 10 15 In this hypothetical example, the lower the number of absences, the (2)________ the grade in every instance, which indicates a (3)________ (positive/negative) correlation.	(1) high (2) higher (3) negative
123. Again, if we knew a person's score on one variable, we could (1)________ his score on the other. That is, knowing that Student X has a high grade (A), we could (2)________ that he has (3)________ (many/few) absences.	(1) predict (2) predict (3) few

124. Finally, the correlation between height and I.Q. (Table 8.9) gives us an example of a (1)_____ (high/low) correlation.	(1) low

TABLE 8.9

Student	A	B	C	D	E	F	G	H	I	J
Height	58″	60″	62″	64″	66″	68″	70″	72″	74″	76″
I.Q.	115	104	90	100	120	98	110	95	110	105

Note the lack of consistency. A high I.Q. score may be accompanied by a high or (2)_____ score on height.	(2) low

125. Therefore, the knowledge of the student's height (1)_____ (does/does not) help (2)_____ the student's level of intelligence.	(1) does not (2) predict

126. Just as diagrams serve to present a clear picture of frequency distributions, they can also be used to demonstrate the direction and strength of the (1)_____ between two (2)_____.	(1) correlation (2) variables

127. Such a diagram is called a scattergram. The scattergram below (Figure 8.21) shows the correlation between (1)_____ and (2) _____ for the sample.	(1) I.Q. (2) grades

TABLE 8.10

Student	I.Q	Grade
A	90	40
B	110	60
C	120	80

127. (*Cont.*)

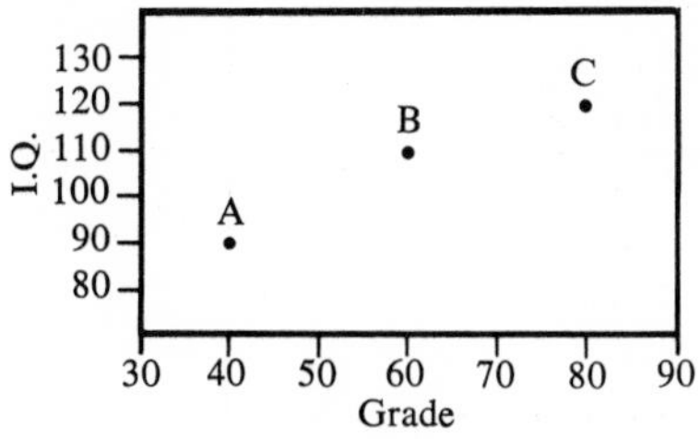

FIGURE 8.21

Note that the numerical grades are scaled along the baseline while the (3)________ scores are scaled along the vertical. | (3) I.Q.

128. Scattergrams are plotted by extending a line from the point at which student A scored on the grade scale, and likewise (1)________ a line from the point at which student A scored on the (2)________ scale. A dot representing student A's I.Q. and grade, is placed where the lines cross. | (1) extending (2) I.Q.

TABLE 8.10

Student	I.Q.	Grade
A	90	40
B	110	60
C	120	80

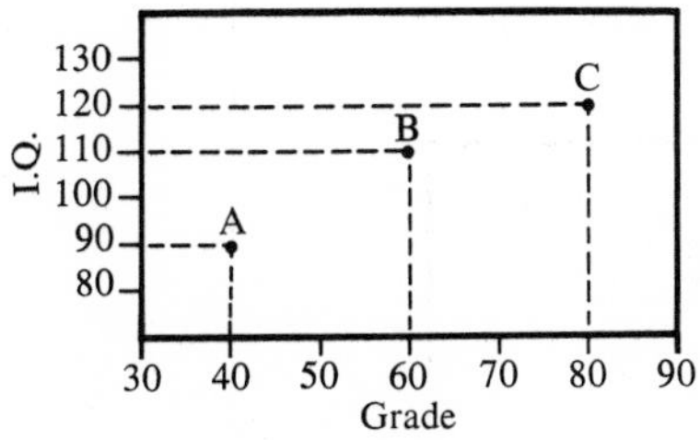

FIGURE 8.22

129.

TABLE 8.10

Student	I.Q.	Grade
A	90	40
B	110	60
C	120	80

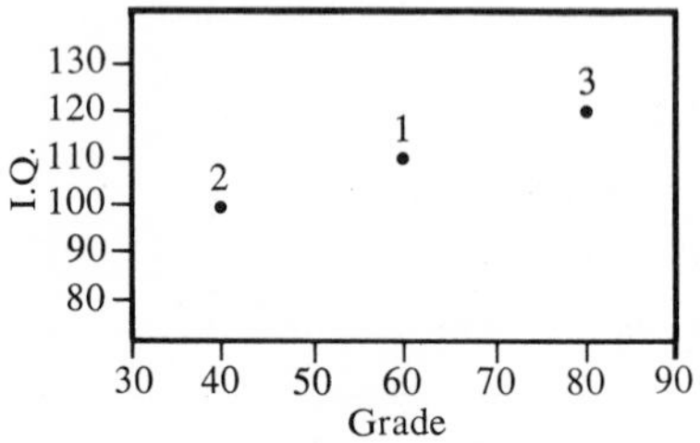

FIGURE 8.23

From the data given in Table 8.10 we can deduce that student A is represented by point (1)________; B is represented by point (2)________; and C is represented by point (3)________.

(1) 2
(2) 1
(3) 3

130.

TABLE 8.10

Student	I.Q.	Grade
A	90	40
B	110	60
C	120	80

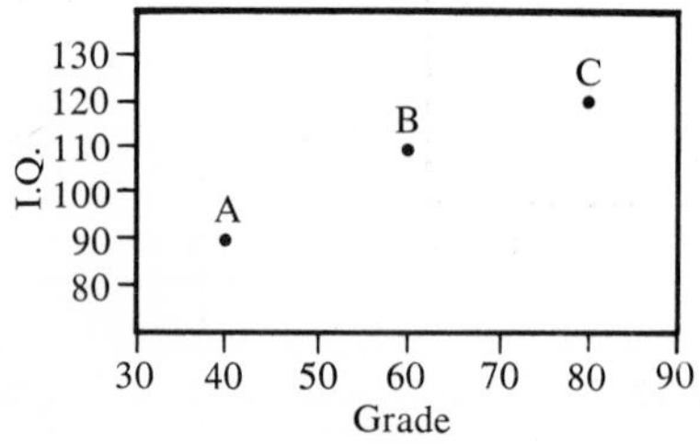

FIGURE 8.24

130. (*Cont.*)
Note that the student who has fairly average scores on both variables (e.g., B) falls near the center of the scattergram. Student C who has high scores on both variables falls in the (1)____________ right corner, and student A who scored low on both variables falls in the lower (2)____________ corner.

(1) upper
(2) left

131. From the three cases given in this example we would suspect that the correlation between I.Q. and grades is (1)____________ (positive/negative). This pattern of a diagonal line rising from left to right is typical of a positive (2)____________ when plotted as a scattergram.

(1) positive
(2) correlation

132. Plot in a scattergram the scores presented in Table 8.11.

TABLE 8.11

Student	I.Q.	Grade
A	85	70
B	95	80
C	105	90
D	115	100

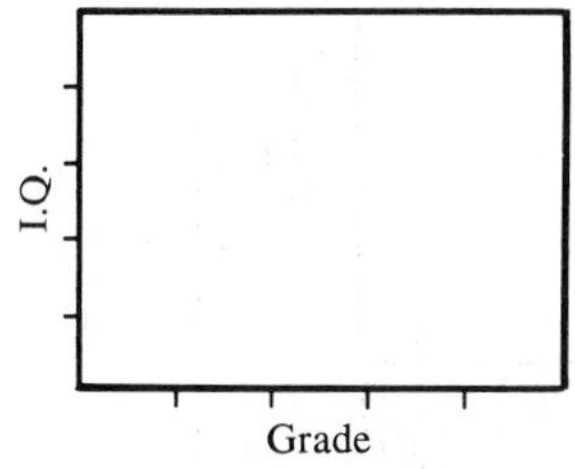

FIGURE 8.25

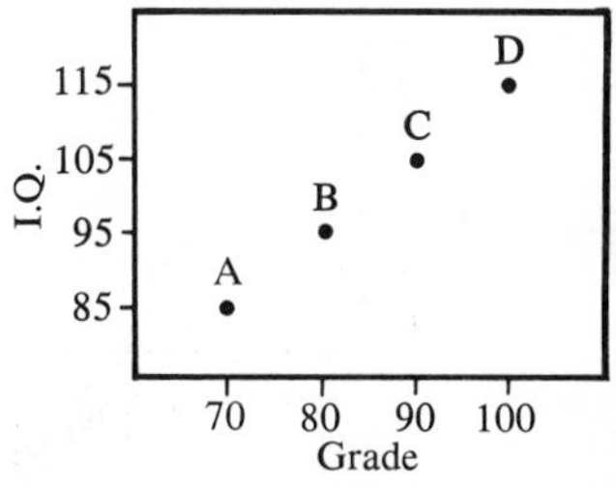

FIGURE 8.25a

133. Now let us look at the (1)__________ for the correlation of grades with number of absences in a small group.	(1) scattergram

TABLE 8.12

Student	Grade	No. of Absences
1	A	0
2	B	2
3	C	4
4	D	8
5	F	12

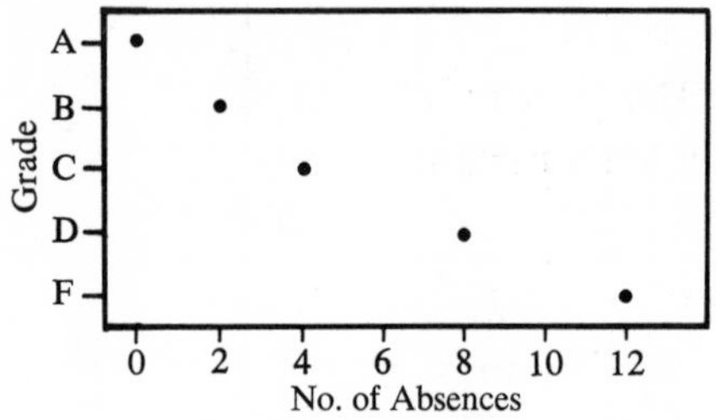

FIGURE 8.26

134. Note that the students with high grades and few absences appear in the (1)__________ __________ corner of the scattergram while those with low grades and many absences appear in the lower right corner.	(1) upper left

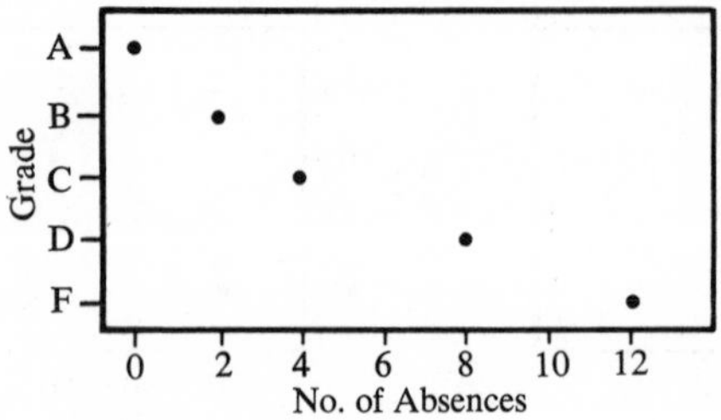

FIGURE 8.27

135. The pattern in Frame 133 is typical of (1) ________ (negative/positive) correlations when plotted as a (2)________.	(1) negative (2) scattergram
136. As you might expect, there is no clearcut direction when a low or zero correlation is (1)________ (plotted/calculated) in a scattergram.	(1) plotted

TABLE 8.13

Student	Height	I.Q.
A	60	115
B	62	90
C	64	100
D	68	120
E	70	110
F	72	95

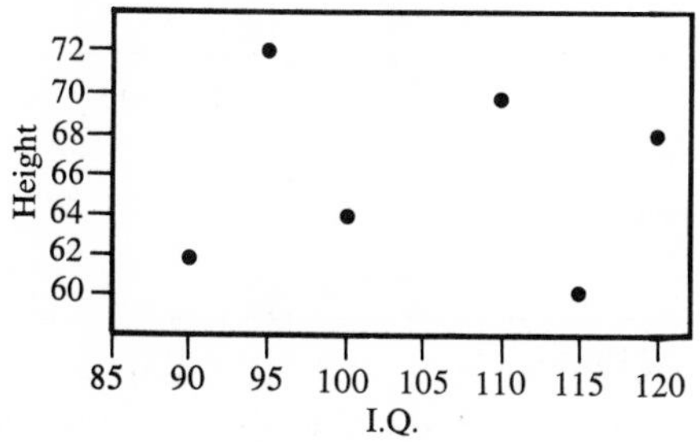

FIGURE 8.28

Section 7: Correlation Coefficients

137. While the (1)________ gives us a rough estimation of the strength and direction of the (2)________, the correlation co- (3)________ is computed for an accurate estimate of the correlation.	(1) scattergram (2) correlation (3) efficient
138. (1)________ coefficients can be defined as numbers which indicate the direction and (2)________ of the relationship between two variables.	(1) correlation (2) strength

139. This coefficient or number is computed in such a way that it ranges from minus one (—1), to plus one (+1). As you might surmise, a correlation (1)__________ of +1 would indicate a perfect (2) __________ (positive/negative) correlation.	(1) coefficient (2) positive
140. A coefficient of —1 would indicate a perfect correlation in a (1)__________ direction.	(1) negative
141. A (1)__________ __________ of zero would indicate that the two variables were not correlated. Thus a (2)__________ __________ near zero (e.g., .16, —.23, .10) indicates (3)__________ (high/low) correlations.	(1) correlation coefficient (2) correlation coefficient (3) low
142. Actually, very few correlation coefficients are as high as plus or minus (1)__________. Most are decimal fractions such as .85, .02, —.26, and so on.	(1) one
143. The symbol for the (1)__________ __________ is the letter "r." A correlation coefficient between height and weight of r = .60 is a (2)__________ (moderate/low) correlation.	(1) correlation coefficient (2) moderate
144. Correlation (1)__________ indicate with what degree of accuracy we can predict one score from the other. For instance, r = .95 for height of identical twins, which is a very high positive (2)__________ __________.	(1) coefficients (2) correlation coefficient
145. This means that, knowing the height of one twin, we can (1)__________ the height of the other twin with (2)__________ (little/great) accuracy.	(1) predict (2) great

146. For height versus I.Q., on the other hand, r = .06. This means that our (1)________ of a person's I.Q. on the basis of his height would be very (2)__________ (accurate/inaccurate).	(1) prediction (2) inaccurate
147. To summarize this section we would first define correlation as a technique for measuring (1)__________ (relationships/differences) between (2)__________.	(1) relationships (2) variables
148. Two variables are said to be correlated if they co- (1)________, or change together, with some degree of (2)__________ (variability/consistency).	(1) vary (2) consistency
149. Correlations can be computed as correlation (1)__________ or plotted on a (2) __________, both of which give us an indication of the direction and (3) __________ of the correlation.	(1) coefficients (2) scattergram (3) strength
150. A correlation coefficient ranges from (1) ________ to (2)________ in strength and direction. If r = + 1, the correlation is (3)________and in a (4)________ direction.	(1) +1 (2) −1 (3) high or perfect (4) positive
151. If r = −1, the correlation is (1)________, but in a (2)__________ direction.	(1) high or perfect (2) negative.

REVIEW TEST

Complete the test and then check your answers with the key provided in the Appendix.

1. Descriptive statistics is a branch of mathematics which deals with numbers which describe____________.
2. The term "sample" is a synonym for____________.
3. A sample is usually described with____________.
4. The term datum refers to how many sets of data____________.
5. The first step toward describing a sample is that of____________.
6. A measure of dispersion which is calculated by: $\sqrt{\frac{\Sigma(X - M)^2}{N}}$ is ____________ ____________.
7. A Frequency____________ is characterized by a line drawn through the midpoint of class intervals.
8. A____________ distribution reveals a mean near the middle of the scale.
9. Draw a positively skewed curve
10. A____________ distribution has two peaks.
11. Discrete attributes are those that can be measured in ____________ intervals.
12. An effective figural description to represent discrete data is a Frequency____________.

(13-15: What are the general terms for each figure?)

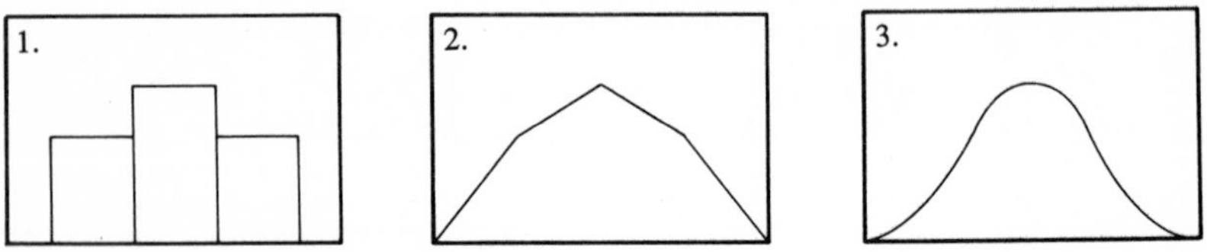

13. (1)____________ ____________
14. (2)____________ ____________
15. (3)____________ ____________

16. The following formula yields the____________ $\frac{(\Sigma X)}{N}$.

17. The most stable measure of dispersion is__________ __________.
18. The simplest measure of dispersion is____________.
19. What does each of the following symbols denote?

a.	f____________	e.	M____________
b.	ΣX____________	f.	r____________
c.	cf____________	g.	N____________
d.	S.D.____________	h.	A.D.____________

20. A synonym for the term "attribute" which implies variation is ____________.

21. The statistical technique by which we describe a relationship between two variables is known as__________ __________.
22. Organize the following data by completing Table I. The data: 97, 93, 88, 87, 83, 82, 78, 77, 75, 74, 73, 71, 69, 65, 63, 62, 56, 52.

TABLE I

Frequency Distribution of Scores on a Test

Score	f	cf
91-100		
51-60		

23. Complete the Histogram below. Use the data summarized in Table I.

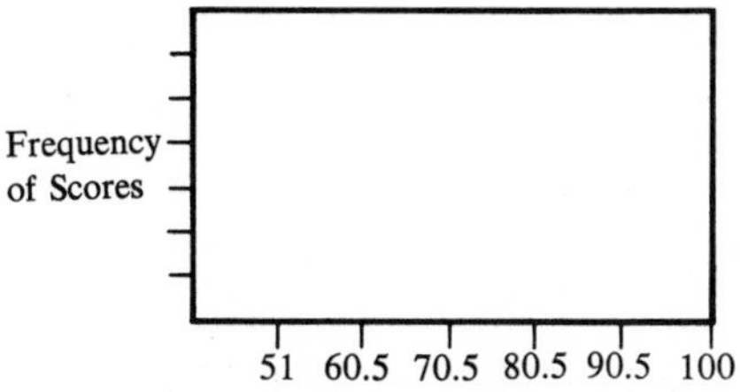

FIGURE 1

Distribution of Grades

24. Compare the following two distributions in a Frequency Polygon:
    Class X: A, B, B, B, B, B, C, C, C, D, F, F
    Class Y: A, A, B, B, C, C, C, D, D, D, D, F

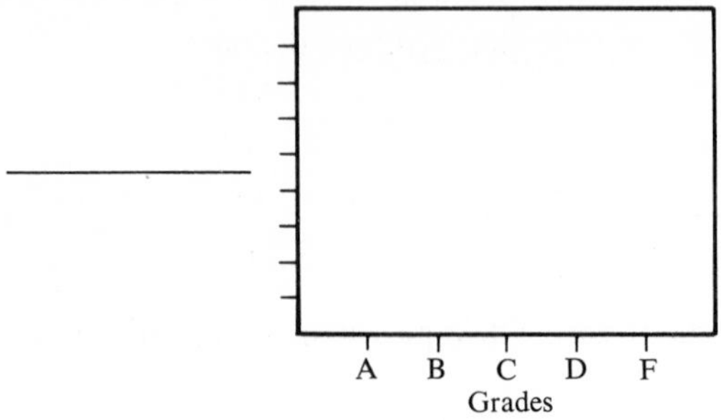

FIGURE 2

Polygon

25. Compute the statistics listed below for the following sample:
    Scores: 1, 1, 2, 2, 2, 2, 3, 3, 5, 5, 7

    a. $M = \frac{\Sigma X}{N} =$ ________ c. Range = ________

    b. Mode = ________ d. $S.D. = \sqrt{\frac{\Sigma(X - M)^2}{N}} = \sqrt{\frac{\quad}{\quad}}$

X	M	$X - M$	$(X - M)^2$
1			
1			
2			
2			
2			
2			
3			
3			
5			
5			
7			

26. Complete the scattergram with the following data:

Student's Code	A	B	C	D	F
Score on Test X	1	2	3	4	5
Score on Test Y	10	8	6	4	2

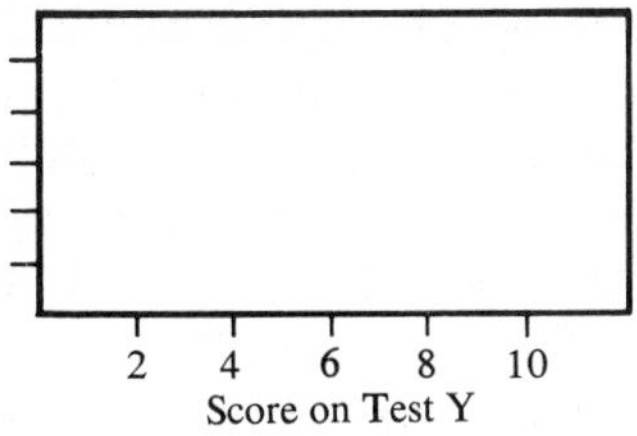

FIGURE 3

Scattergram

ANSWERS FOR THIS TEST ARE GIVEN AT THE END OF THE CHAPTER, PAGES 317-318.

How to Evaluate this Program

You have now completed one "linear type" program. This program has been tested and revised a number of times with educational psychology students. You might wish to locate the "bugs" that remain. First, check your response sheet and count the number of errors you made while responding to the program. Remember, a high error rate is not a student failure — it is a programing error (ours). Check with your fellow students. Have they erred on the same frame? If so, it needs revision. (Can you revise it?) Check frames ones, two, and three. A *rapid* vanishing technique was used (that is by frame three you were required to provide four responses — the terms to be acquired vanished from the frame and no cues or prompts were provided). A high error rate on these (1-3) might indicate additional frames are needed. Second, check your review test. Did you miss many? If so, *we* have failed. Have you and your classmates consistently missed the same question? If you have, can you rewrite that section of the program to eliminate the difficulty?

You were *not* given a pretest; therefore, you cannot calculate a gain score. A pretest, posttest gain is a more appropriate measure because you did not enter the program without some "knowledge" of descriptive statistics. As an exercise you can give the test to a friend who has not been exposed to descriptive statistics. Let the person work the program and then posttest. There are 42 possible points. An index of program effectiveness *G* was constructed by McGuigan and Peters (1965). The *G* is calculated by means of subtracting the pretest score from the number of possible correct responses. Then the gain is calculated by subtracting the pretest score from the posttest score. The *G* is the percent of possible growth realized. For example, there are 42 possible points on the test provided in this chapter. If your friend's pretest was 21 then the possible gain is 21 points (42 − 21 = 21). Now suppose his posttest score was 28. Twenty-eight (posttest) minus 21 (pretest) equals 7. The *G* score would be 7/21 = 33⅓%. He only gained ⅓ of that which he could gain. Theoretically, the best program should result in a *G* of 100%. Unfortunately, we do *not* live in the best world. McGuigan and Peters (1965, p. 29) suggested that programs which yield a *G* of 50% or less should possibly *not* be published without revision.

Evaluation of Linear Programs

Humans learn from programed material and they also learn from books, observation, speech, etc. Research reported on the merits of linear programed material provides an obscure evaluation on all counts but one: they *are* effective. (1) Step size, (2) the need for overt response, (3) the importance of knowledge of results (reinforcement), (4) own pace and (5) ordered sequence are *not* uniformly supported in the literature. Glaser and Taber (1961) suggested that knowledge of results is less important when the probability of error is low. Furthermore, short steps apparently bore the subjects who are working on a *long* program. Schramm (1964) provided a summary of findings which suggested that all the early programing commandments appear to be *less* hard and fast when subjected to investigation. We suspect that "true believers" of the operant view can find inadequacies in the studies which attack their commandments. Until the research air clears, conclusions must be tentative. The authors of this text are struck by two consistent threads apparent in the programed research reviewed: all programs attend to *organization of information* and provide *cues* to highlight important points (either blanks to be filled in or through underlining). Theoretically these devices increase the probability that the individual will *attend* to the relevant information. Indeed, an attention paradigm seems to fit the data better than a reinforcement paradigm.

Branching Programs

McGuigan and Peters (1965) surveyed the reactions of over 1500 students to programed material. When asked to indicate how well they enjoyed the program, 35% reported positive reactions, 41% indicated a 50-50 choice and 14% found programs unenjoyable. Gotkin (1962) indicated that students who are exposed to programed material for an extended period of time become "bored." He suggested that anyone who doubts this statement should try working through Holland and Skinner's (1961) "The Analysis of Behavior." This boredom might be attributed to the fact that self-pacing does not account for *individual* differences. What might be a short step for one person might well be an obvious fact (and trivial) for another. To be sure, Gotkin recognizes that boredom in education is not limited to programed instruction. On the other hand, to expect one program or one text to allow for individual differences was seen by Godkin to be naive.

Branching programs have been on the scene a while, and they attempt to account for individual differences. The branching approach typically provides a test question, and if the student provides the correct answer he is instructed to turn to a particular frame. If he fails, he usually is instructed to another set of frames which are designed to provide information which he needs. Essentially, branching allows the student to skip material he already "knows." Research evidence regarding the effectiveness of branching versus linear programs is mixed. Some "like" branching; others "like" linear. A number of "non-scientific" considerations seem responsible for the indeterminant state of programing. Apparently a clever artistic programer will get "good" results. But, if we are to provide for individual differences, anything *less* than "reaching" all students is *not* "good" results.

In view of the multi-variate approach to human behavior developed within this text, our task is to find which approach is best for each student. Indeed, the more diverse the students' background (reinforcement history), the more modes of individualization are required. A textbook or program written for Eastern Seaboard prep school students most likely would not excite a public school Texan. Gotkin (1962) reported that a number of students "really" appreciated Markle's (1962) humor in a program designed for bright eighth grade students. However, a number of students did not like her "wisecracks."

Can any book, program, or teacher be all things to all students? We think not. There are possibly styles of learning which might be appropriate for many, but not all. Such experiences are often encountered by the "perceptive" student. We have all encountered instructors who are "crashing bores" only to find some classmates have been inspired by this "dud." Apparently, "epistemic curiosity" is initiated via many forms depending upon the receiver of the message.

Ideally, before assigning learning materials to a student we might wish to (1) have a well defined set of behaviors which reflects some hierarchical ordering of the subject matter content, (2) assess the student's level of competency in relation to the hierarchy (level of readiness), (3) have information regarding his interests, tastes, values and goals, and (4) have materials which suit the prescribed level of competency and use a mode which will cause the student to approach the material. Such individualization is a monumental task; nevertheless, if we desire to teach all, that is exactly what we seem to be faced with.

Computer Assisted Instruction

The recent technological explosion seems to have the potential to lead to the individualization just mentioned. Particularly, recent computer facilities have been packaged which can provide for (1) administrative monitoring (recording student behaviors), (2) informational control (selection and presentation of multimedia material) and (3) performing bookkeeping activities (such as testing, evaluation and prescribing).

ILLUSTRATION 1

This picture shows two girls in carrels responding with light pens on the cathode ray tube. The girl on the left is observing the stimulus presented by a slide projector and is asked to point out (with the light pen) the appropriate word. On the right, the girl has responded and is listening to a random access pre-taped audio feedback regarding the appropriateness of the response. (Courtesy of Science Research Associates and International Business Machines.)

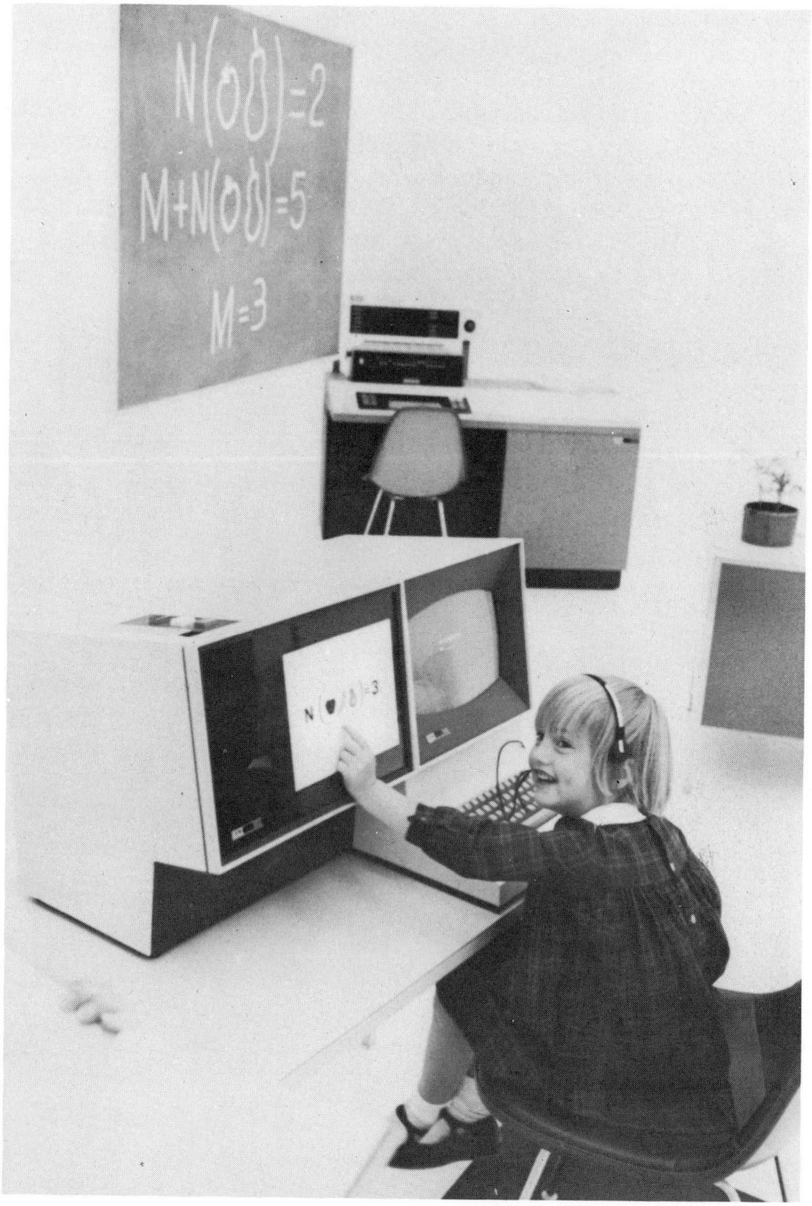

ILLUSTRATION 2

The slide projector screen is presented clearly. Note the girl is responding to Suppes material on set theory (see Chapter 5). (Courtesy of Science Research Associates and International Business Machines.)

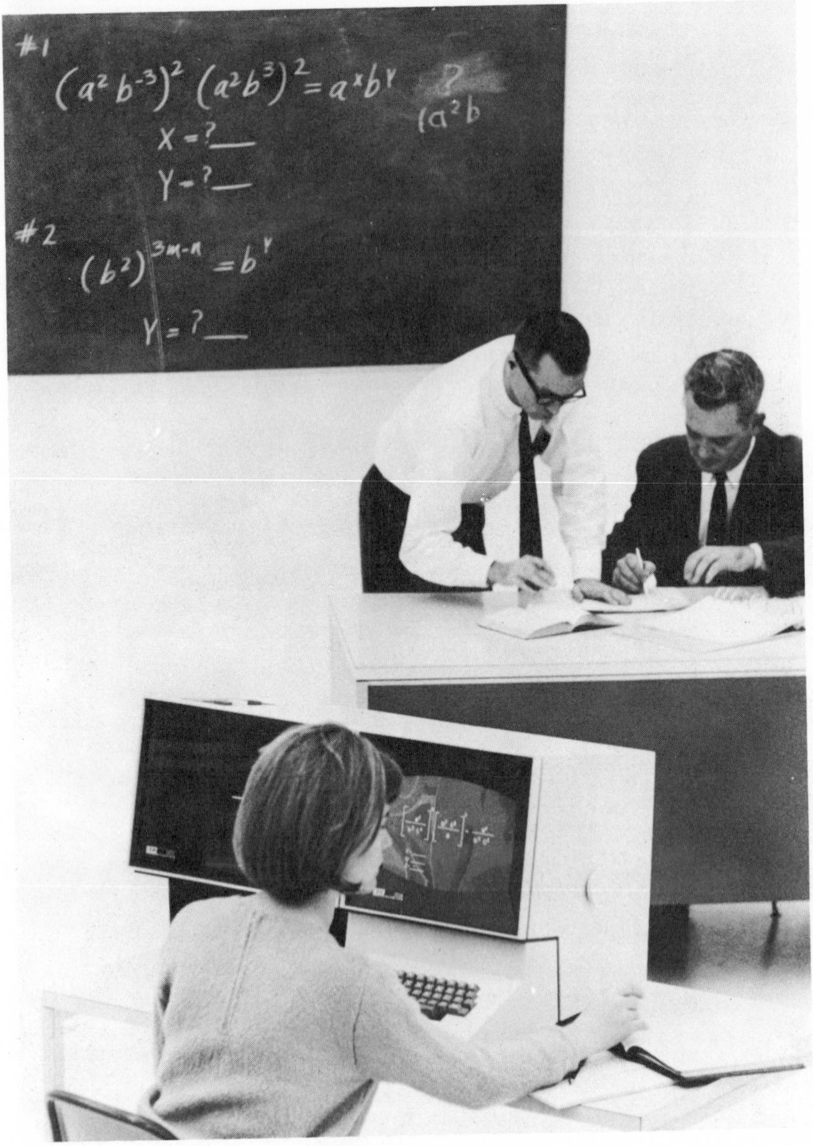

ILLUSTRATION 3

A mathematics problem is presented on the cathode ray tube, and the women responds via the keyboard. The response is evaluated and further instructions may be presented on the basis of the acceptability of the response. (Courtesy of Science Research Associates and International Business Machines.)

Easley (1966) reported preliminary use of the computer for retaining student response to programed instruction which organized the data in a preset sequence that allowed the programer to examine response patterns for possible modification. Programs introduced via student terminals provides electronic storage which is readily available to the programer. Much of the laborious task of correcting, recording, and tabulating response patterns can be eliminated.

Suppes at Stanford University is using an experimental machine (IBM 1500) to introduce elementary mathematics and set theory to five- and six-year-old students. Cathode ray tubes can present problems to students working in carrels, and students can respond to multiple-choice problems using a light pen to designate his response. Random access audio feedback can be presented to the student as well as video prompts to direct the student to the relevant variables. Slide projectors, etc., are available for each terminal. Typewriter "type" keyboards can

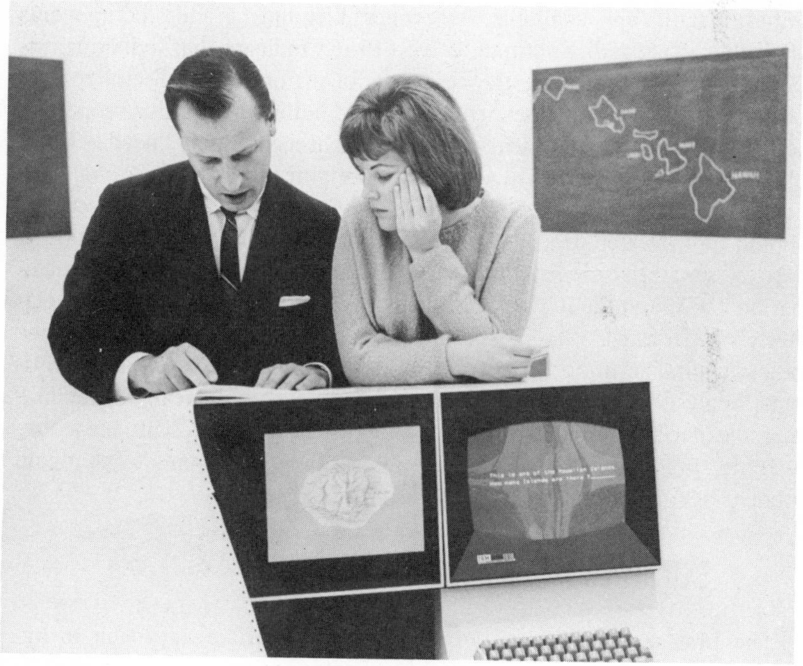

ILLUSTRATION 4

A programer is examining the print-out of response sequences. Such printouts allow rapid checks upon the effectiveness of the program. (Courtesy of Science Research Associates and International Business Machines.)

also be used for communication with the computer and print-out immediate feedback to the student on an individual basis (see Illustrations 1, 2, 3, and 4). Present costs for such a computer with 32 individual student carrels are between $2 and $3 an hour. Surely, costs shall be reduced as production is increased. Fortunately, for the present the IBM 1500 is distributed only for research and development uses.

The "Software" Problem

The jargon designating the electronic equipment is "hardware" and what is programmed into the machine is "software." The promise provided by computer technology is apparently only limited by the "educator's" ability to construct "software" (programed material and programed instructions). Can the individualization discussed within this text be realized? The authors believe all of the ingredients for an initial assault are available; a proper blending of the components is all that is needed. Kaufman, *et al.* (1966) indicate that individualization is possible; however, the resources of a number of disciplines are necessary. First, leading academicians must outline a tentative scope and sequence of significant "ideas" students might legitimately "need." These "ideas" must be specified in some operational terms by *professional educators* with the help of *behavioral scientists. Measurement specialists* should be available to assess the relevant previous learning and learning "styles" (material presentation which might capture the students' "imagination" — the student will approach the task and respond at a "relatively" high rate). Media specialists should be available to help the others capitalize upon the diverse modes of presentation available. Systems analysts must be involved in order to develop a means of facilitating the decision-making process. The system must account for bookkeeping, prescription and resource allocation (i.e., room, teacher and student assignment).

Summary and Implications

The first seven chapters developed a multi-variate approach to human behavior. Apparently a number of intra-individual factors operate in complex relationships within the behaving individual. To admonish the teacher to provide for individual differences within the classroom borders upon the ridiculous for we do *not* "know" how these factors "really" operate within the classroom. Conversely, enough information seems to be available for "dedicated" teams to initiate an assault upon the problem of providing coping responses for all. The possibility (within the next twenty years) of developing curricula which approaches individualization without having a B. F. Skinner as a tutor for each, might well be within the realm of possibility. Lacking the research and development teams, we as educators are doomed to "reach" the 30%-40% of the students whom the exceptional teacher is able to "effectively" teach (a value judgment).

Questions

1. Does the content and the philosophy expressed in this chapter sound ridiculous? Go visit a number of classrooms and observe children. Remember we may be wrong.
2. Is present-day education "really" inefficient? What would be a good measure of efficiency?
3. What results did you obtain upon administration of the Descriptive Statistics Program to your friend? Would you recommend the use of the program? (Remember, do not judge programed instruction on the basis of this one.)

Recommended Readings

Because this chapter presents only a preview to educational technology the student might wish to explore this area more thoroughly. One possible source of information is a book of readings, *Programs, Teachers and Machines,* edited by de Garzia and Sohn. Particularly, articles by Pressey (p. 33), Skinner (p. 43), Markle (p. 145), and Hoth (p. 193) might provide provocative "insights."

Ferster's (1965) "Programmed College Composition" should also be reviewed. This program uses a number of approaches which impressed the present authors.

A relatively up-to-date listing of existing programs is presented in *Programed Instructional Materials, 1964-65,* edited by Komoski, *et al.*

A review of recent articles in *The Journal of Programed Instruction* can suggest the relative status of the "art" of programing.

References

Budloff, M., & Quinland D. M. Auditory and visual learning in primary grade children. *Child Developm.,* (1964) 35, 583-586.

de Garzia, A., & Sohn, D. (Eds.), *Programs, teachers and machines.* New York: Bantam, 1962.

Easley, J. *First annual report for project SIRA*. Urbana: Coordinated Science Laboratory, Univer. of Ill., 1966.

Ferster, M. B. *Programmed college composition.* New York: Appleton-Century-Crofts, 1965.

Glaser, R., & Taber, J. I. *Investigations of the characteristics of programed learning sequences.* Pittsburgh: Programed Learning Lab., Univer. of Pittsburgh, 1961.

Gotkin, L. G. Programed instruction in the schools: individual differences, the teacher, and programing styles. In A. de Garzia & D. Sohn (Eds.), *Programs, teachers, and machines.* New York: Bantam Books, 1962, 159-171.

Holland, J. G., & Skinner, B. F. *The analysis of behavior.* New York: McGraw-Hill, 1961.

Kaufman, B. F., Kelly, F. J., & Robinson, R. R. *Proposal for phase I of a project to create an individualized mathematics curriculum in the spirit of the Cambridge Conference recommendations.* Carbondale, Ill.: S. Ill. Univer. Comprehensive School Math. Proj., 1966.

Komoski, P. K., Bernstein, M., & Pace, D. *Programed instruction materials,* 1964-65. New York: Teachers College, Columbia Univer., 1965.

Markle, M. S. *Words: a programed course in grammar and usage.* Chicago: Science Research, 1962.

McGuigan, F. J., & Peters, R. J. Assessing the effectiveness of programmed texts — methodology and some findings. *J. programmed Instruc.,* 1965, 3, 23-24.

Pressey, S. L. A third and fourth contribution toward the coming "Industrial Revolution" in education, *School and Society,* 1932, 36, 668-672.

Pressey, S. L. Teaching machine (and learning theory) crisis. *J. applied Psychol.,* 1963, 47, 1-6.

Schramm, W. J. *The research on programed instruction: an annotated bibliography.* Washington, D. C.: U. S. Printing Office, 1964.

Skinner, B. F. The science of learning and the art of teaching. *Harvard educ. Rev.*, 1954, 24, 86-97.

APPENDIX

Answers to Test

1. groups
2. group
3. statistics
4. *one*
5. ordering the data
6. Standard Deviation (S.D.)
7. Frequency Polygon
8. normal
9. 
10. bi-modal
11. unit
12. Histogram
13. Frequency Histogram (Bar Graph)
14. Frequency Polygon
15. Frequency Curve (normal curve)
16. mean
17. Standard Deviation
18. the range
19. (a) frequency,
    (b) sum of scores,
    (c) cumulative frequency,
    (d) Standard Deviation,
    (e) mean,
    (f) coefficient of correlation,
    (g) number,
    (h) Average Deviation,
20. variable
21. coefficient of correlation
22.

TABLE I

Frequency Distribution of Scores on a Test

Score	f	cf
91-100	2	2
81-90	4	6
71-80	6	12
61-70	4	16
51-60	2	18

23.

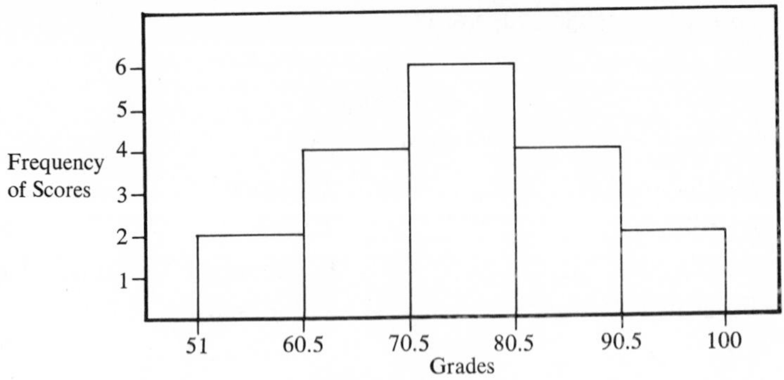

FIGURE 1

Distribution of Grades

24.

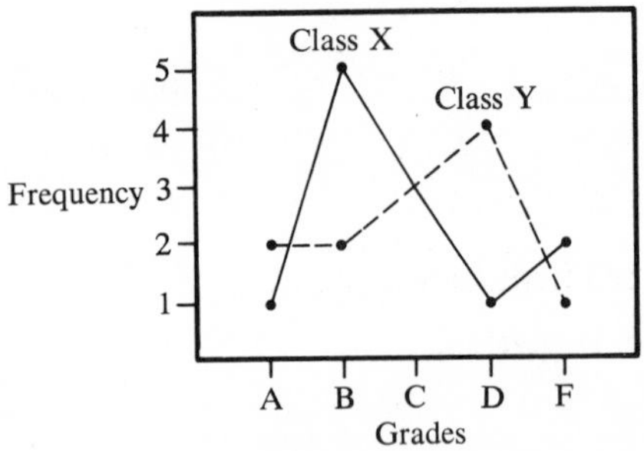

FIGURE 2

Polygon

25. (a) $M = 3$ (b) $\text{Mode} = 2$ (c) $\text{Range} = 6$ (d) $\text{S.D.} = \sqrt{\frac{36}{11}}$

26.

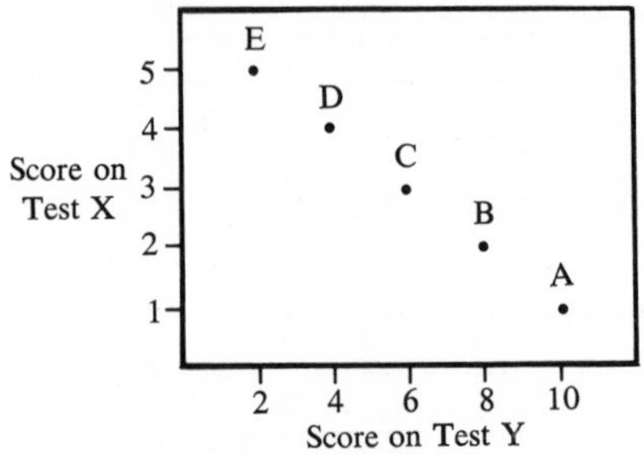

FIGURE 3

Scattergram

Behavioral Science in Education: A Recapitulation

9

Overview

A summary of the major topics discussed in this text is provided here in spite of the risk of sounding redundant. The risk seems small when compared to the advantages of drawing together, in brief form, those notions that were intended to stimulate the reader to think and inquire. Since the tenor of the book has been one which suggested a tentative state of affairs in educational psychology, the concern for inquiry and investigation is held in high regard. Some space is devoted to discussing the important concepts and classroom applications presented in each chapter.

The intent of this chapter is to underscore those notions, recommendations, and implications which seem to hold promise for implementation in the classroom as well as for research purposes. In addition this chapter presents a concluding note that is intended to emphasize the integration of the many ideas that contribute to the subject matter in educational psychology. Perhaps the content of this chapter will encourage readers to scan once more those sections of the text which were most challenging.

Since no new terms are introduced no glossary is presented for this chapter.

Status of Educational Psychology

Educational psychology was presented as a set of theories and hypotheses that are inferences derived from observing behavior, rather than a collection of well-substantiated findings. These theories and hypotheses were presented as summarizing notions which might permit some order to the diverse variables operating within the complex school environment. In the first chapter some space was allocated to setting the limits for the study of human behavior. It seems obvious that little empirical evidence can be found which indicates clearly the contributions of educational psychology to effective teaching or learning.

Prediction and control of behavior were identified as the purposes for studying educational psychology. The major components of behavior which were identified included: physiological, neurological, chemical, language, communication and psychological variables. Selected research reports and theoretical positions were discussed to provide teachers with a repertoire of approaches to employ as summarizing constructs in attempts to control human behavior. Specific concepts of intelligence, arousal, creativity, structure of the intellect, phenomenology, social learning, and technological innovations were discussed also. No attempt was made to completely survey the historical field of educational psychology. To the authors it seemed much more relevant to relate various concepts so that similarities and differences could be analyzed for purposes of examining alternatives in the classroom with a critical eye. Hopefully, such an approach will lead to more "effective teaching"; however, evidence is *not* available to support this hope. Each of the major topics will be summarized briefly and, for emphasis, suggestions for possible application to the classroom setting will be offered when appropriate.

Organismic Development (Chapter 2)

Human behavior was described as the reaction of the organism, with its genetic qualities, to forces which impinge upon it. An $S \rightarrow O \rightarrow R$ model was used to illustrate this proposition.

Physiological Considerations. Donald Hebb's (1958) factors relating to development were employed as a framework for discussion of the physiological and experiential factors which affect behavior. Hebb's

(1958) six factors are: (1) genetic structure; (2) chemical environment, prenatal; (3) chemical environment, postnatal; (4) sensory constants; (5) sensory variables; and (6) trauma. The authors suggested a seventh factor, *sensory* trauma, since the other factors seemed to exclude drastic changes in behavior due to sensory (conceptual) shock.

Conflict over the degree of genetic influence on human behavior can be illustrated by the treatment of intelligence and the nature-nurture issue. It seems clear that heredity has some effect on human behavior; however, genetic development is highly dependent upon and greatly modified by environment. Research regarding the degree of prominence of one factor over the other has little to offer and possibly focuses upon an overly narrow ban. A more fruitful approach might be directed to the question, "How can we jointly manipulate genetic structure and environment to maximize intelligent behavior?"

In order to gain some insight into how genetic factors and environmental factors interact, studies of subhuman animals were cited to provide these insights. Specifically, the studies of McGaugh (1960), Rosenweig and Krech (Rosenweig, 1963), and Melzack and Scott (1957) were discussed. These studies suggest that selective breeding practices and early environmental experience are related to intelligent behavior in subhuman animals.

Psychological Explanations. Concepts of drive, need, and motivation were invented by psychologists to account for the fact that humans move. In addition to these inferred characteristics of human behavior, the observable aspects of stimulus and response were applied to human behavior. While inferred constructs such as drive, need, motivation and arousal are used to tell partly the "why?" of behavior, stimulus and response are terms which define the input and output or the "what?" of human behavior.

Classroom teachers have long been concerned with the innateness of intelligence and the "why" and "what" of human behavior. This introduction to the many variables which affect the human organism should provide teachers with a brief sampling of the complexities of human behaviors called "individual differences." No teaching procedures were presented in Chapter 2. Rather, vocabulary and concepts were introduced. These notions should enhance the possibilities of relating and comparing various approaches to classroom management and instruction.

Mediation and Language (Chapter 3)

Language, its use and interpretation, is one of the most critical areas in classroom instruction. Formal instruction in language arts progresses from kindergarten through the first years of college. Yet, too frequently little thought is "really" directed toward students and the meanings they attach to linguistic signs (words).

Acquisition of Meaning and Distortion. Meaning attached to words was discussed as any other novel response acquisition. Conditioning and environmental possibilities were presented. Research, using the "orienting reflex," by Russian psychologists (Luria and Vinogradova, 1959) was described as a means of indicating some recent trends to investigate semantic relationships. Meaning and distortion apparently are learned in the same manner, and educators should not be shocked that individuals from different backgrounds have acquired peculiar biases in relation to word preferences and meaning. Pairing of linguistic signs (words) such as "vicious" and "communist" have lead to distortions of intended or "real" meaning. Since word pairing is consciously used or experienced in developing socially required concepts it should be recognized in other situations as well. Ramifications of these notions are rampant in the social setting of the school. Of special interest is the apparent disgust held for "vulgar" words which might be excellent vehicles for communicating meaning. Disregarding the utility of "vulgar" words, it was suggested that a teacher who abhors "vulgarity" might wish to extinguish her defensive behavior — especially if she wants to control the class rather than have the class control her.

Apparently distortions of meaning come from (1) over-generalizations from direct experience, (2) the pairing of words without direct experience, and (3) different meanings for the same word.

Syntax. According to Whorf (1956), the linguistic syntax varies among language groups. The English language differentiates the world into things and events (nouns and verbs). Unfortunately this bi-polarity is not consistently interpreted. As a result, learning conflicts arise. In our language structure we tend to generalize after noting similarities and to ignore differences. Consequently, it seems easy to oversimplify the world, and discrimination learning seems handicapped. Problems which accrue in light of these practices were presented, and Korzybski's (1951) extensional devices were cited to illustrate *one* possible solution.

Correlation: A Technique and a Caution. Correlational procedures were discussed in relation to behavior and causes. Implied causation was noted. Curbing enthusiasm for attributing causal relationships is difficult unless an individual is willing to discriminate as well as generalize. Employing statistical techniques while disregarding their legitimate functions might result in many malpractices in education.

Complex Meaning. Research on the Semantic Differential (Osgood 1957) suggested that evaluative meaning structure can be assessed with some degree of accuracy. Three scales (factors) were identified by factor analysis on the Semantic Differential. These expressed factors are: evaluative (good . . . bad), potency (strong . . . weak) and activity (fast . . . slow). Various approaches to research scales similar to the Semantic Differential suggest that meaning can be modified by using set. Staats' and Staats' (1957) and Manson's (1965) studies are representative of these studies.

Language and School Success. Many straw men have been used as "causes" of school failures. Deutsch (1960) pointed out that economic poverty might not be a relevant variable in discussing school success. Instead, he suggested that lack of language stimulation in the home is the most relevant consideration. While investigating language usage of middle-class and lower-class British homes Bernstein (1961; 1962) identified *elaborated* and *restricted* linguistic codes. Among the lower classes little elaboration is common. Usually the lower-class language form stresses short command type phrases (restricted code). Among the middle classes elaboration and restricted codes are used. Bernstein concluded that restricted language codes provide limited differentiation of the world. In addition, the apparent disregard for generalizing results in a lack of basic concepts. These findings coupled with Deutsch's (1960) work seem worthy of review and consideration by teachers. Perhaps children are expected to be aware of language and thinking tasks which are foreign to many in the ordinary classroom. When educators discuss individual differences, starting points might include syntax, meaning, and distortion. Perhaps we tend to ignore the plight of students who do not measure up to supposed levels of verbal competencies.

Central Complexities (Chapter 4).

General intelligence is discussed as a construct invented to account for differential human behaviors. This construct is challenged by several theorists and researchers. Guilford's (1959) model of the structure of intellect with its 120 factors is offered as an alternate view to the concept of general intelligence.

Measurement. The normal distribution accompanied by an explanation of variability is presented to provide a basis for interpreting results of tests, in particular tests of intelligence. Test reliability and validity were defined in conjunction with variability of scores and representativeness of samples. Each of these terms have application in the modern world of measurement. Although intelligence is a frequently misused term, it retains about as much predictive power as any other construct.

Creativity and Other Variables. In the late forties some emphasis was given to creativity. After "Sputnik I" creativity became the battle cry of all those who wished to attack the public schools. But the term "creativity" was defined to suit the speaker or writer. Perhaps the "statistically unique response" approach initiated by Maltzman, *et al.* (1960) represented a simple and refreshing approach to the problem. Argument that creativity and intelligence are not necessarily highly related seems obtainable.

Factors other than creativity and intelligence seem related to intelligent behavior and school achievement. Special abilities, state of psychological fitness (anxiety in particular) for test taking, and classroom performance were explored. Sarason's (1958) work regarding low anxious and high anxious subjects is representative of the kinds of research reported in the literature. As suspicion rose and research findings suggested that many factors were related to behavior, a statistical and design procedure emerged which seemed amenable to investigating multi-variate considerations of complex human behavior.

Multiple Regression Analysis. Multiple regression analysis is a statistical procedure which employs the vector concept with multiple predictors. Utilizing the sum of squares technique and predicting performance levels, this procedure can be employed to analyze many variables as they relate to behavior. Not only can relationships between variables and criterion be established, but identification of those variables (single, or in combination) which contribute most to the prediction criterion can be identified. Whiteside's (1964) study which employed the multiple regression technique with McGuire's (1961) model was presented as an illustration of this means of investigation.

A rationale was developed for testing the results of univariate studies in a complex behavior setting. The interdependency of univariate and multi-variate studies in education was pointed out. McClelland's (1955) report on "Need Achievement" and Adorno's *et al.* (1950) study of authoritarian personality were used as examples to illustrate this point.

With the improvement of research and evaluation techniques classroom teachers should reap benefits. When several variables can be isolated and their relationship to behavior determined, insight into and control of classroom behavior should become a source of practical information for teachers, If, for example, variables were identified which predict school failures, teachers could focus attention on these variables to upset the predictions.

Cognitive Views (Chapter 5)

The process of knowing (cognition), concept formation, concept attainment, operant conditioning, and inquiry training were the major topics discussed. Major emphasis was placed on abstracting from the environment those objects and relationships which go together to form a concept. Bruner's (1957) hypothesis concerning "going beyond the information given" served as a stepping stone for discussing the process of knowing.

Codes. Apparently man classifies events in the universe to enable him to understand his environment, to protect himself and to prepare for the future. In this regard coding has been invented by man to enable him to recall relevant events or occurrences which repeat themselves in his environment. Seemingly, schools attempt to provide students with a repertoire of codes in the form of subject matter. Bruner (1957) indicated four (4) sets of conditions which influence the acquisition of coding systems: (1) set, (2) need state, (3) degree of mastery and (4) diversity of training. For purposes of transfer of learning, coding seems a highly relevant variable.

The Act of Discovery. Hypothetical and expository modes of instruction in the classroom are thought to develop different kinds of achievement behavior. Lecturing and textbook writing are typical examples of the expository mode. On the other hand the hypothetical mode allows students to acquire strategies which seem effective for the individual in the problem solving process. Emphasis was placed on the need to recognize that "learning by discovery" should be a carefully planned experience rather than a hunt and peck fiasco for students. Intrinsic motivation and the concept of competence motive were related to learning by discovery.

Bruner's (1957) ideas and Berlyne's (1960) concept of conceptual conflict were compared. Conceptual conflict was broken into six types: (1) doubt, (2) perplexity, (3) contradiction, (4) conceptual incongruity, (5) confusion, and (6) irrelevance. Although overlap exists between these types they do seem to provide a reasonable means of describing learning behavior.

Inquiry and discovery were discussed as traits of productive scientists. It seemed that attempts to describe and explain the apparent intuitive behavior of productive researchers on the frontiers of "knowledge" were aided greatly by the notions expressed by Bruner (1957) and Berlyne (1960).

Operant Conditioning. B. F. Skinner's emphasis on performance (the observable phenomena) rather than learning (internalized phenomena) seemed to represent a means of combining the technical rigor of operant psychology with the theoretical framework of cognitive psychology. Operant techniques of reinforcement and successive approximation might lend scientific credence to attempts to develop cumulative constructionism in problem solving. Definitions of reinforcement schedules (fixed ratio, variable ratio, fixed interval and variable interval) were presented. Comments relative to positive and negative reinforcement (differs from punishment) in the classroom were inserted. Stimulus discrimination and response differentiation were presented also. The teaching machine as a procedural tool was presented as an application of the operant approach. An attempt was made to insert a note of caution. Otherwise, students might take an "intuitive leap" and assume that all problems could be answered by this approach.

Category Types (Concepts). Bruner, *et al.* (1956) discussed three categories of concepts: conjunctive, relational, and disjunctive. These categories were employed to illustrate the variety of concepts which seem observable in the classroom. In addition, strategies which lead to concept attainment were discussed and related to classroom situations. Focus gambling, negative focusing, conservative focusing, and positive focusing were identified as strategies which might apply to particular kinds of concepts. It was made clear that no single strategy seemed to apply equally well to all categories of concepts.

Creativity. This illusive and many-faceted term was considered in relation to current emphasis in education and as a construct which might be researched. The authors employed a model composed of four dimensions to describe "creative" acts. Creative tasks were depicted as complex, unique, good, and relative to time.

Applications of Cognitive Theory. Despite the complexities of the notions regarding behavior which have been set forth by Bruner and Berlyne, they seem to have many implications for classroom instruction. New mathematics, discovery learning, etc., have already become passwords for the educational jargonist. Some of Davis' (1964) work was reviewed to illustrate the application of cognitive theory to mathematic instruction. In addition Suchman's (1960) work in the area of science was also presented. An attempt was made to relate the concepts postulated by Berlyne, Bruner, and Piaget to the task of classroom instruction. At this time, few definitive conclusions can be presented as a result of evaluating modern approaches to subject matter. However, as students, teachers, academicians, and educational psychologists become more aware of the cooperative ventures required by classroom instruction some progress seems eminent.

Phenomenology in Education (Chapter 6)

In this chapter behavior was discussed in relation to self-concept, conscious awareness and interpersonal "knowing," a departure from the

S → O → R model and observed behavior. The concepts proposed by Carl Rogers (1951, 1956, 1957, 1961 and 1965) were employed to represent the phenomenological viewpoint. Rogers' nineteen propositions were presented and discussed. Similarities and differences between the phenomenological and behavioristic notions of holistic behavior were touched upon. The three conditions for positive therapeutic movement described by Rogers (1961) were identified and examined. These conditions are (1) genuineness, (2) unconditional positive regard, and (3) sensitive, accurate, empathic understanding. These conditions seemed as relevant for classroom learning as they might be for therapeutic treatment.

Educational Implications of Self-Theory. An example of classroom behavior by a teacher (the Miss Shiel example) was employed to illustrate the practical application of phenomenology in the schools. Questions concerned with causes of behavior in Miss Shiel's classroom were raised. No definitive conclusions concerning phenomenology and efficient teaching were isolated.

Indications that curricular change would most likely be required if phenomenological principles were followed in the classroom were noted also. Emphasis was placed on the fact that the school is a social agency. It does not operate in a vacuum. As a result classroom behavior is likely to be affected by forces other than the school environment alone. In general Rogers' theory was discussed as focusing upon conscious experience of the individual and the meaning structure he develops.

Social Learning in Education (Chapter 7)

In this chapter emphasis was changed from variables which affected behavior and those which could be used to predict behavior to concern for social learning. The notion of imitation learning was explored. Bandura's (1965) observation that (1) acquisition of matching responses takes place through contiguity and (2) that performance of the model's behavior depends upon the consequence of the act upon the model. In addition data reported by Lefkowitz, Blake, and Moulon (1955) suggested that the status of the model is related to imitation.

Socialization vs. Maturation as Determinants of Moral Judgments. Piaget (1948) proposed that before age seven children employ objective responsibility in judging the severity of moral deviation. After age seven children seem to employ subjective responsibility. In other words, the socialization process has had an effect upon children by the time they are seven years of age. Bandura and McDonald (1963) tested Piaget's theory and found that older children seem to engage in both kinds of moral judgment rather than exclusively one or the other. Implications of social learning theory were discussed. Special note was made of the varieties of ways of exposing school children to appropriate models.

Soviet Character Training. The collective competition stressed by Soviet character training (Brofenbrenner, 1962) was depicted along with the stress upon individuality in American character training. Similarities between the methodologies employed in these two cultures to affect character training seemed clear.

The American Character. The Lonely Crowd: A Study of the American Character (Reisman, Glazer, and Denny, 1953) was utilized as a reference from which the social organization of America was examined for purposes of identifying variables which might aid prediction. Inner- and other-directedness were considered as propositions which might lead to better understanding of social learning. Relationships between the concepts of other-directedness and teaching middle-class values were noted. Anomie and autonomy were presented and related to the psychological terms superego and adjustment. Blake's (1965) research suggested that at least in the area of science occupations, measures of other- and inner-direction had some relationship to the selection of careers in science by individuals who apparently had few measured interests which were similar to those of successful scientists. It was concluded that concepts such as those postulated by Reisman, Glazer and Denny (1953) might provide interesting and relevant variables for research in education. The mathematical model $B_a = f(P_a, E_{ab}, R_{ba}, rs_{1 \ldots n}) S_a, C_{ab}, X$ was re-introduced and the variables discussed in this chapter were substituted for the letter symbols. In general it seems as though variables associated with social learning theories might help provide order to observed diversities in human behavior.

Technological Considerations (Chapter 8)

Technological developments in education were discussed without concern for relating these instructional innovations to theory. Concern for individual differences in mass education was the rationale presented for the development of technology which is purported to enhance classroom learning. Computer assisted instruction, audio tapes, visual tapes and programed learning were the foci of the discussion. Linear (B. F. Skinner, 1954) programs and branching programs were compared. A linear program in descriptive statistics was presented complete with stated objectives, the program itself, and a self-administered test over the programed material. Guidelines for evaluating the program presented were included also.

In this chapter an effort was made to promote student understanding through experiencing programed instruction. The readers were cautioned that none of these technical advances seemed to solve *all* educational problems. Similarly, it was noted that classroom teachers could not be totally responsible for utilizing adequately each technological innovation. A team approach to meeting the individual differences among students was recommended.

Conclusions

Three notions can be drawn from the study of educational psychology as presented in this text. First, the concept of the "whole child" free from its mask of "jargon" becomes more tenable. *Second,* provision for individual difference in the classroom might allow for greater positive educational outcomes; however, individualization is *not* a simple task. *Third,* the study of human behavior does not result in a collection of facts or "cookbook" rules. Rather it provides the basis for inquiry and experimentation into the educational process.

The Whole Child

If applied research in education is to have any meaning for teaching, then theoretically we must examine the child in the setting of the classroom. Apparently, the "whole child" must be considered if schools are to provide "meaningful" educational "experiences" for students. Such a position need not infer that students cannot be studied unless the entirety of the individual is microscopically scrutinized. The implication is that, through the study of human *behavior,* variables (parts of the whole) which seem most relevant to the child's behavior can be analyzed and the degree to which these variables are "really" important can be tested. Remember these variables might be related to school behavior in complex ways (interacting with each other, etc.). It should be understood that phrases like "students' feelings," "students' total personalities," and "student adjustment" are not applicable to this new look at the "whole child." Instead, specific descriptions of variables which relate to *observable* human *behavior* are the relevant labels applied to inquiry.

Development of digital computers and statistical procedures provide the machines and the system by which many variables and their relation to observed and quantified human behavior can be examined. The multiple regression analytic procedures outlined in Chapter 4 seem ideally suited for examining the new "whole child" concept. In order to "really" understand the opportunities awaiting those who are "truly" interested in education, knowledge concerning human *behavior,* the *specific* social setting of the school, and evaluation and research techniques seem essential.

Attempts to improve learning in the classroom seem thwarted unless educators learn to: (1) observe and record specific behavior, (2) relate theories of behavior to classroom practices, (3) test hypotheses regarding classroom behavior, and (4) develop skills and confidence in taking intuitive leaps from what has been observed to what seems likely to occur. Furthermore, it is naive to expect the teachers to be able to conduct such an inquiry by themselves. Researchers, curriculum specialists, academicians, and administrators need to join forces to realize "effective" classroom learning. The "whole child" concept does not refute the need for continued experimentation with laboratory and univariate techniques. To the contrary, the results of such investigations should blend neatly into the background of information essential for understanding human behavior.

Individual Differences

Whenever psychologists and educators suggest that general factors, which apply to most humans, can be identified and used for purposes of prediction some believe that individual differences are being ignored. Perhaps such claims have some validity. On the other hand, identification of factors which seem to generalize to most humans merely provide general guidelines for examining individual differences. In attempts to predict and control human behavior, variables which do not generalize to most students become important. For those individuals to whom generalized variables do not seem to apply, other variables which at first seem unimportant are brought into focus. Some have the mistaken idea that predictive studies should provide information which will enable the psychologist to "play god." In education, predictive studies are initiated in order to identify variables which can be modified so that prediction can be upset.

If this approach is confusing the following illustration might help. Johnny, a 15-year-old ninth grade student, is among several boys identified as potential dropouts by a prediction study. The challenge for the school is to examine the variables which contributed to this prediction. Then special treatment should be provided which is intended to hold

Johnny in school until he graduates. Typically, school dropouts are characterized as: retarded by at least two years in achievement, a poor school attendance record, environmentally handicapped, older than his classmates and associating with youths who have already left school. Schools might examine these characteristics and determine whether they can attack all of them or select one or two which seem most meaningful to the boy. Special instruction, curricular innovations, involvement in school activities, and consultation with the family are means typically employed by schools to upset prediction. If, then, educators were successful in attending to individual differences, students predicted to leave schools early would instead remain until they graduate. Specifically, this might mean that new curricula would capitalize upon a knowledge of student characteristics, such as stated, measured or otherwise observed interests, values, and abilities. Teachers might help in this management of ΣS presentation and feedback ΣS which is reinforcing for the particular student. To re-emphasize, it is ridiculous to expect the teacher to be the innovator, researcher, and counselor without a *great* deal of help, for individualization is a monumental task.

Inquiry and Experimentation

Careful examination of hypotheses, theories, and research data related to complex human behavior indicate that few (if any) facts can be identified. Theoretical discussions present in definite terms "what is" or "what should be" in relation to human behavior. Results of research applied to classroom situations, on the other hand, do not reinforce such definite statements. When discussing classroom activities and procedures which will result in controlling specified behavior, words such as "perhaps," "maybe," "likely," "might," "seems," "appears," and "may" are about as definite as data will permit. In essence, the study of educational psychology might motivate teachers and potential teachers to join the inquiry process. If education is to really provide for the "whole child" and his idiosyncratic behavior then educators in classrooms must be willing, first, to inquire and experiment and, second, be willing to cooperate with diverse types — researchers, academicians and administrators.

The behavior laboratory of the classroom remains one of the least used research facilities in the realm of the behavioral sciences. As teachers join the effort of scientific inquiry, some definitive knowledge concerning classroom behaviors should result.

A Final Word

Educational psychology is seen by the authors as a joint venture in seeking generalities which apply to behavior in the schools. Sets of gimmicks and procedural rituals are out of place in a scientific approach to studying classroom learning. Currently, the study of behavior should lead to questions which demand answers. Educators seem to lack practice and skill in asking questions in such a manner that data can be gathered to provide empirically verifiable answers. Some might call this position research-oriented. We prefer to call it educational psychology, a behavioral science. Effective and efficient teaching (control of classroom behavior) apparently is the goal of both the teacher and the educational psychologist and collaboration seems necessary.

Index